AN INTRODUCTION TO ASTROPHYSICS

AN INTRODUCTION
TO
ASTROPHYSICS

By

Dr. Ajit Kumar Sharma

M.Sc., Ph.D.

Head

Department of Physics

D.A.V. (P.G.) College, Bulandshahr (U.P.)

(India)

DISCOVERY PUBLISHING HOUSE PVT. LTD.

NEW DELHI-110 002

Published by:
Tilak Wasan

DISCOVERY PUBLISHING HOUSE PVT. LTD.
4383/4B, Ansari Road, Darya Ganj
New Delhi-110 002 (India)
Phone : +91-11-23279245, 23253475, 43596065
E-mail : discoverypublishinghouse@gmail.com
orderdphbooks@gmail.com
web : www.discoverypublishinggroup.com

***First Edition:* 2014**

***Reprinted:* 2025**

ISBN: 978-93-5056-395-3

An Introduction to Astrophysics

Printed at:
Infinity Imaging Systems
Delhi

Contents

Preface (*vii*)

1. **Introduction** 1
   - Astrophysical Experiments
   - A History of Astrophysics
   - Astrophysics—Processes in the Universe
2. **Celestial Mechanics** 29
   - Terms of Celestial Mechanics
   - Historical Background
   - Tidal Development
3. **Celestial Sphere and Time** 77
   - Celestial Sphere
   - Celestial Coordinate Systems
   - The Perceptible Motion of Planets on the Celestial Sphere
   - Timekeeping and the Celestial Sphere
   - Naming the Stars
   - Locating Star Maps and Constellations
   - Celestial Sphere Coordinate System
   - Astronomical Time Keeping
   - Astronomical Calendars
   - The Seasons
   - Precession of the Earth's Rotation Axis
   - Orbit and Phases of the Moon
   - Solar Eclipses
   - Lunar Tides in the Earth Oceans
   - Lunar Eclipses
   - Celestial Measurements
4. **The Nature of Stars, Universe and Planets** 134
   - Motion of Stars
   - Birth of Stars

5. Observational Astronomy **180**
- Introduction
- Regions of the Electromagnetic Spectrum
- Refraction and Diffraction
- Dispersion in Wavelength
- Intensity: The Inverse Square Law
- Geometrical Optics
- Telescopes
- Diffraction

6. Solar Neutrinos **231**
- Introduction
- Neutrinos and the Sun
- BNL and Measurements of Solar Neutrinos
- Organometallic Liquid Scintillator
- The Solar Neutrino Problem
- Solar Neutrino Spectrum

7. Stellar Distances and Magnitudes **253**
- The Parallax Method
- Stellar Magnitudes
- Colour Indices and Surface Temperatures
- Parallax Method
- Stellar Motion
- Space Velocities
- Motion of the Sun
- Secular and Statistical Parallax
- Atmospheric Extinction

8. Instrumentation and Space Technology **284**
- Space Technology
- Multi-wave Length Astronomy
- Infrared Astronomy
- Ultraviolet Astronomy
- Earth's Atmospheric Effects
- Evolution of Earth's Atmosphere
- The Greenhouse Effect
- Atmospheric Effects on Incoming Solar Radiation

Bibliography 341

Index 343

Preface

Astrophysics is a branch of Astronomy that deals with the physics of the universe, physical properties of the celestial objects and their behaviour. Astrophysicists use physics to make clear what astronomers find and observe. The focus of astrophysics in an interesting method without assuming familiarity with practical details of modern astronomical techniques. The opening comprehensive work on the subject to emerge from India and overseas, it includes an extensive spectrum of topics ranging from celestial coordinates to cosmology.

The first astrophysical concept or law to be recognized was the law of gravity. We are all familiar with the force of gravity. Although it is a very weak force compared to the other fundamental forces of nature, it is the dominant factor determining the structure and the fate of the universe. Large structures, such as galaxies, and smaller ones, such as stars and planets, coalesced due to the force of gravity, which acts over vast distances of space. Much of the evolution of our universe is due to gravity's effects. However, scientists generally hold the view that the understanding of atomic processes marks the true beginning of astrophysics. Indeed, even such enormous objects as stars are governed by the interaction and behaviour of atoms. Thus it is often said that astrophysics began in the early decades of the twentieth century, when quantum mechanics and atomic physics were born.

Atmospheric effects can severely hinder the resolution of a telescope. Without some means of correcting for the blurring effect of the shifting atmosphere, telescopes larger than about

15-20 cm in aperture cannot achieve their theoretical resolution at visible wavelengths. As a result, the primary benefit of using very large telescopes has been the improved light-gathering capability, allowing very faint magnitudes to be observed. However the resolution handicap has begun to be overcome by adaptive optics, speckle imaging and interferometric imaging, as well as the use of space telescopes.

Astronomers have a number of observational tools that they can use to make measurements of the heavens. For objects that are relatively close to the Sun and Earth, direct and very precise position measurements can be made against a more distant background. Early observations of this nature were used to develop very precise orbital models of the various planets, and to determine their respective masses and gravitational perturbations. Such measurements led to the discovery of the planets Uranus, Neptune, and Pluto. They also resulted in an erroneous assumption of a fictional planet Vulcan within the orbit of Mercury.

This book conveys a deep and consistent thoughtful of the stellar phenomena and basic astrophysics of stars, galaxies, clusters of galaxies and other heavenly bodies of interest.

— *Author*

Chapter 1

Introduction

The study of Astrophysics—understanding the universe we live in—has been an exciting field of exploration for centuries. How big is the universe? How did it start and what is its fate? What's out there in deep space? What are the stars and galaxies made of? What makes them shine? Are there other planets in the universe and, if so, how many? These basic questions have occupied people's thoughts for generations in challenge to uncover the mysteries of the universe. Remarkable discoveries have been made in Astrophysics in current years ranging from the Big-Bang and the early stage of the universe, to measurement of the structure in the universe, to the existence of Dark Matter and Dark Energy, the discovery of Black Holes, and the discovery of planets around other stars. These discoveries have provided some answers to these fundamental questions. The new discoveries have also produced new fundamental questions: What is the nature of the Dark Matter and the Dark Energy? How do planets form around stars? How does life form on planets (the new field of Astrobiology)? How do massive blackholes form? And more.

Why do the stars shine? How did our galaxy form? Will the universe expand forever? These are the types of questions asked by astrophysicists in an attempt to understand the processes which cause our universe, and everything in it, to behave the way it does. From the low-energy gravitational interactions between planets and stars, to the violent, high energy processes occurring in the centres of galaxies, astrophysical theories are used to explain what we see, and to understand how phenomena are related. For thousands of years, astronomy was purely an observational science—humans could observe phenomena in the sky, but had no physical explanation for what they saw. Early humans could offer only supernatural explanations for what they observed, which seemed drastically different from what they experienced in everyday life. Only in the twentieth century have scientists been able to explain many astronomical phenomena in terms of detailed physical theories, relating them to the same chemistry and physics at work in our everyday lives.

ASTROPHYSICAL EXPERIMENTS

Astrophysical experiments, unlike experiments in many other sciences, cannot be done under controlled conditions or repeated in a laboratory; the energies, distances, and time scales involved are simply too great. As a result, astrophysicists are forced into the role of observer, watching events as they happen without being able to control the parameters of the experiment. For centuries, humans have made such observations and attempted to understand the forces at work. But how did scientists develop our picture of the universe if they could not reproduce what they see in the laboratory? Instead of controlling the experiments, they used what data they were able to obtain in order to develop theories based on extensions of the physical laws which govern our day-to-day experiences on Earth.

Astrophysics often involves the creation of mathematical models as a means of interpreting observations. This theoretical is important not just for explaining what has already been seen, but also for predicting other observable effects. These models are often based on well-established physics, but often must be simplified, because real astronomical phenomena can be enormously complex.

A HISTORY OF ASTROPHYSICS

Even though astronomy is as ancient as recorded history itself, it was long separated from the study of physics. In the Aristotelian worldview, the celestial world tended towards perfection—bodies in the sky seemed to be perfect spheres moving in perfectly circular orbits—while the earthly world seemed destined to imperfection; these two realms were not seen as related.

Anaxagoras of Clazomenae in the fifth century BC was the first of the Pre-Socratic philosophers to live in Athens. He held many controversial theories, including his claim that the stars are fiery stones. He allegedly got this idea when a meteorite fell near Aegospotami. He assumed that it came from the Sun, and since it consisted largely of iron he concluded that the Sun was made of red-hot iron. Not a bad guess for his time, yet he had no way of proving his claims. Neither did Asian or Mesoamerican observers. Some sources indicate that Anaxagoras was charged with impiety, as most Greeks still shared the divine associations with the heavenly bodies, but political considerations may have played a part in this, too.

Since late as in 1835 Auguste Comte (1798-1857), the French philosopher often regarded as the founder of sociology, stated that humans would never be able to understand the composition of stars. He was soon proved wrong by two new techniques—spectroscopy and photography.

The English chemist William Hyde Wollaston (1766-1828) in 1800 formed a partnership with his English colleague Smithson Tennant (1761-1815), whom he had befriended at Cambridge. Tennant discovered the elements iridium and osmium, extracted from platinum ores, in 1803. The platinum group metals—platinum, ruthenium, rhodium, palladium, osmium and iridium—have similar chemical properties. Osmium (Os, atomic number 76) is the heaviest natural element with a density of more than 22.6 kg/dm^3, twice as much as lead at 11.3 kg/dm^3.

Platinum (Pt, atomic number 78) and its dense sister metals are very rare in the Earth's crust. It had been introduced to Europe from South American mines in the 1740s by men such as the Spanish explorer Antonio de Ulloa (1716-1795). Wollaston was the first person to produce pure, malleable platinum and became wealthy from supplying Britain with the precious metal. The Wollaston Medal, granted by the

Geological Society of London, is named after him. The German chemist Martin Klaproth (1743-1817) was born in Wernigerode in Prussian Saxony and worked as an apothecary for years before continuing his career as a professor of chemistry at the newly established University of Berlin.

He discovered uranium as well as zirconium (Zr, 40) in 1789. Uranium (symbol U, atomic number 92) was named for the planet Uranus, which had been found just before this. Wollaston detected the chemical elements palladium in 1803 and rhodium in 1804. He named palladium (Pd, 46) after the asteroid Pallas, which had been discovered a year earlier by the German astronomer Olbers and was initially believed to be a planet, until the full extent of the asteroid belt had been grasped.

Birth of Spectroscopy

The birth of spectroscopy, the systematic learning of the interaction of light with matter, followed shortly after the creation of scientific chemistry in Europe. William Hyde Wollaston in 1802 noted some dark features in the solar spectrum, but he didn't follow this insight up. In 1814, the German physicist Joseph von Fraunhofer (1787-1826) independently discovered these dark features (absorption lines) in the optical spectrum of the Sun, which are now known as Fraunhofer lines. He carefully studied them and noted that they exist in the spectra of Venus and the stars, too, which meant that they had to be a property of the light itself.

In the 1780s a Swiss artisan, *Pierre-Louis Guinand* (1748-1824), began experimenting with the manufacture of flint glass, and in 1805 managed to produce a nearly flawless material. He passed on this secret to Fraunhofer, who worked in the secularized Benedictine monastery of Benediktbeuern. Fraunhofer improved upon Guinand's techniques and began a more systematic study of the mysterious spectral lines. To the stronger ones he assigned the letters A to Z, a system which is also used today. Yet it was left to two other German scholars to prove the full significance of these unique lines, corresponding to specific chemical elements.

Robert Bunsen (1811-1899) is often associated with the Bunsen burner, a device found in many chemistry laboratories around the word, but the truth is that he made a few alterations to it rather than inventing it. He was born in Göttingen, where his father was a professor of languages. He obtained his doctorate in chemistry at the University of Göttingen and spent years travelling through Western Europe. He eventually settled at the scenic university town of Heidelberg in southwest Germany, where he taught from 1852 until his retirement. In the late 1850s, Bunsen began a new and very fruitful collaboration there with the physicist Kirchhoff.

Gustav Kirchhoff (1824-1887), the son of a lawyer, was born and educated in Königsberg, Prussia, on the Baltic Sea, now the Russian city of Kaliningrad. He graduated from Albertus University there in 1847 and relocated to the rapidly growing city of Berlin. After 1850 he became acquainted with Bunsen, who urged him to follow him to Heidelberg. Kirchhoff in 1859 coined the term blackbody to describe a hypothetical perfect radiator that absorbs all incident light and emits all of that light when maintained at a constant temperature. His findings proved instrumental to Max Planck's quantum theory of electromagnetic radiation from 1900.

They demonstrated in 1859 that all pure substances display a characteristic spectrum. Together, Bunsen and Kirchhoff assembled the flame, prism, lenses and viewing tubes necessary to produce the world's first spectrometer. They identified the alkali metals cesium (chemical symbol Cs, atomic number 55) and rubidium (Rb, 37) in 1860-61, showing in each case that these new elements produced line spectra that were unique for them, a chemical 'fingerprint.' The dark lines in the solar spectrum show the selective absorption of light, caused by the transition of an electron between specific energy levels in an atom, in the gases of various elements that exist above the Sun's surface. In the first qualitative chemical analysis of a celestial body, Kirchoff in the 1860s identified 16 different elements from the Sun's spectrum and compared these to laboratory spectra from known elements here on Earth. *The* great physicist George Gabriel Stokes (1819-1903) attended school in Dublin, Ireland, but later moved to England and Cambridge University. He theorized a reasonably correct explanation of the Fraunhofer lines in the solar spectrum, but he did not publish it or develop it further. According to the Molecular Expressions website, "Throughout his career, George Stokes emphasized the importance of experimentation and problem solving, rather than focussing solely on pure mathematics. His practical approach served him well and he made important advances in several fields, most notably hydrodynamics and optics. Stokes coined the term fluorescence, discovered that fluorescence can be induced in certain substances by stimulation with ultraviolet light, and formulated Stokes Law in 1852. Sometimes referred to as Stokes shift, the law holds that the wavelength of fluorescent light is always greater than the wavelength of the exciting light. An advocate of the wave theory of light, Stokes was one of the prominent nineteenth century scientists that believed in the concept of an ether permeating space, which he supposed was necessary for light waves to travel."

Fluorescence microscopy has turn into an important tool in cellular biology. The Polish physicist Alexander Jablonski (1898-1980) at the University of Warsaw was a pioneer in fluorescence spectroscopy. Stokes was a formative influence on subsequent generations of Cambridge men and was one of the great names among nineteenth century mathematical physics, with included Michael Faraday, James Joule, Siméon Poisson, Augustin Cauchy and Joseph Fourier. The English mathematician George Green (1793-1841), known for Green's Theorem, inspired Lord Kelvin and devised an early theory of electricity and magnetism that formed some of the basis for the work of scientists like James Clerk Maxwell.

Scientific Discipline of Astrophysics

Astrophysics as a scientific discipline was born in mid-nineteenth century Europe, and only there; it could not have happened earlier as the crucial combination of chemical and optical knowledge, telescopes and photography did not exist before. In case we forget what a huge step this was, let us recall that in the sixteenth century AD in Mesoamerica, the region usually credited with having the most sophisticated American astronomical traditions, thousands of people had their hearts ripped out every year to please the gods and ensure that the Sun would keep on shining. A little over three centuries later, European scholars could empirically study the composition of the Sun and verify that it was essentially made of the same stuff as the Earth, only much hotter. Within the next few generations, European and Western scholars would proceed to explain how the Sun and the stars generate their energy and why they shine. By any yardstick, this represents one of the greatest triumphs of the human mind in history.

Photography was born in France in the 1820s with Joseph-Nicéphore Niépce, who teamed up with the painter Louis Daguerre. As Eva Weber writes in her book *Pioneers of Photography*, "In March 1839 Daguerre personally demonstrated his process to inventor and painter Samuel Morse (1791-1872) who enthusiastically returned to New York to open a studio with John Draper (1811-1882), a British-born professor and doctor. Draper took the first photograph of the moon in March 1840 (a feat to be repeated by Boston's John Adams Whipple in 1852), as well as the earliest surviving portrait, of his sister Dorothy Catherine Draper."

The American physician Henry Draper (1837-1882), son of John Draper, was a pioneer of astrophotography. In 1857 he visited Lord Rosse, or William Parsons (1800-1867), famous for his construction in Ireland in the 1840s of the most powerful reflecting telescope in the Victorian period, frequently referred to as the Leviathan. It remained the world's largest telescope until the twentieth century. Draper became a passionate amateur astronomer, and after reading about the work on star spectra carried out by William Huggins and Joseph Lockyer he built his own spectrograph. He died at the young age of forty-five, but his widow established the Henry Draper Memorial to support photographic research in astronomy. This funded the Henry Draper Catalogue, a massive photographic stellar spectrum survey. The first winning daguerrotype photography of the Sun was made in 1845 by the French physicists Louis Fizeau and Léon Foucault, who are mainly remembered for their accurate measurements of the speed of light. Warren de la Rue (1815-1889), a British-born astronomer, astrophotographer and chemist educated in Paris, designed a special telescope dubbed the photoheliograph. On an expedition to Spain in 1860 during a total solar eclipse, his images demonstrated clearly that the corona is a phenomenon associated with the Sun.

The technique of spectral analysis caught on after the work of Robert Bunsen and Gustav Kirchhoff. One of those who quickly took it up was the great English chemist William Crookes (1832-1919), who discovered the metal thallium (Tl, atomic number 81) in 1862. The Englishman William Huggins (1824-1910) built a private observatory in South London and tried to apply this method to other stars. Through spectroscopic methods he showed that they are composed of the same elements as the Sun and the Earth. He collaborated with his friend William Allen Miller (1817-1870), a professor of chemistry at King's College, London.

According to his Bruce Medal biography, "Huggins was one of the wealthy British 'amateurs' who contributed so much to 19th century science. At age 30 he sold the family business and built a private observatory at Tulse Hill, five miles outside London. After G.R. Kirchhoff and R. Bunsen's 1859 discovery that spectral emission and absorption lines could reveal the composition of the source, Huggins took chemicals and batteries into the observatory to compare laboratory spectra with those of stars. First visually and then photographically he explored the spectra of stars, nebulae, and comets. He was the first to show that some nebulae, including the great nebula in Orion, have pure emission spectra and thus must be truly gaseous, while others, such as that in Andromeda, yield spectra characteristic of stars. He was also the first to attempt to measure the radial velocity of a star. After 1875 his observations were made jointly with his talented wife, the former Margaret Lindsay Murray."

The Austrian mathematician and physicist Johann Christian Doppler (1803-1853) was born in Salzburg, the son of a stonemason, and studied in Vienna. In 1842 he proposed that observed frequency of light and sound waves is dependent upon how fast the source and observer are moving relative to each other, a phenomenon called the Doppler Effect. For instance, most of us have heard how the sound of a car or a train changes in frequency as it moves towards us and then away from us.

A more correct explanation of the principle involved was published by the French physicist Armand-Hippolyte-Louis Fizeau in 1848. The Doppler Effect has proved to be an invaluable tool for astronomical research. Most notably, the motions of galaxies detected through this manner led to the conclusion that the universe is expanding.

In 1864, probably as a result of discussions with his countryman William Huggins, the astronomer Joseph Norman Lockyer (1836-1920), originally from the town of Rugby in the West Midlands of England, obtained a spectroscope. In 1868 he was able to confirm that bright emission lines from prominences of the Sun could be seen at times other than during total solar eclipses. The same technique had been demonstrated by the French astronomer Pierre Janssen (1824-1907). Janssen was born in Paris, where he studied mathematics and physics, and took part in a long series of solar eclipse-expeditions around the world. Lockyer and Janssen are credited with independently discovering helium (chemical symbol He, atomic number 2) in 1868 through studies of the solar spectrum. *Helium, from the Greek helios for the Sun, remains the only element so far discovered in space before being identified on Earth.* Lockyer was also the founder of the prominent British scientific journal *Nature* in 1869.

Whereas the centre of astronomy was still in Western Europe, Europeans overseas were starting to leave their mark, above all in North America. The U.S. physicist Henry Rowland (1848-1901) did notable work in spectroscopy, and the American astronomer Vesto Slipher (1875-1969) was the first person to measure the enormous radial velocities of spiral nebulae. As the excellent reference book *The Oxford Guide to the History of Physics and Astronomy* states:

"In 1868, however, Huggins found what appeared to be a slight shift for a hydrogen line in the spectrum of the bright star Sirius, and by 1872 he had more conclusive evidence of the motion of Sirius and several other stars. Early in the twentieth century Vesto M. Slipher at the Lowell Observatory in Arizona measured Doppler shifts in spectra of faint spiral nebulae, whose receding motions revealed the expansion of the universe. Instrumental limitations prevented Huggins from extending his spectroscopic investigations to other galaxies. Astronomical entrepreneurship in America's gilded age saw the construction of new and larger instruments and a shift of the centre of astronomical spectroscopic research from England to the United States. Also, a scientific education became necessary for astronomers, as astrophysics predominated and the concerns of professional researchers and amateurs like Huggins diverged. George Ellery Hale, a leader in founding the *Astrophysical Journal* in 1895, the American Astronomical and Astrophysical Society in 1899, the Mount Wilson Observatory in 1904, and the International Astronomical Union in 1919, was a prototype of the high-pressure, heavy-hardware, big-spending, team-organized scientific entrepreneur."

George Ellery Hale (1868-1938), a university-educated solar astronomer born in Chicago, represented the dawn of a new age, not only because he was American and the United States would emerge as a leading centre of astronomical research (although scientifically and technologically speaking a direct extension of the European tradition), but at least as much because he personified the increasing *professionalization* of science and astronomy.

The telescope Galileo used in the early 1600s was a simple refractor. The sheer weight of the glass lens makes a refracting telescope larger than one meter in diameter impractical. The introduction of the reflecting mirror telescope by Newton in 1669 paved the way to virtually all modern telescopes. Hale built the largest telescope in the world four times: Once at Yerkes Observatory, then the 60-and 100-inch reflectors at Mt. Wilson and finally the 200-inch reflector at Mt. Palomar. As an undergraduate student at the Massachusetts Institute of

Technology, Hale co-invented the spectroheliograph, an instrument to photograph outbursts of gas at the edge of the Sun, and discovered that sunspots were regions of relatively low temperatures and high magnetic fields. He hired Harlow Shapley and Edwin Hubble and encouraged research in astrophysics and galactic astronomy.

There is still room for non-professional astronomers; good amateurs can occasionally spot new comets before the professionals do. Yet it is a safe bet to say that never again will we have a situation like in the late eighteenth century when *William Herschel, a musician by profession, was one of the leading astronomers of his age. From a world of a few enlightened and often wealthy gentlemen in the eighteenth century would emerge a world of trained scientists in the twentieth; the nineteenth century was a transitional period. As the example of* William Huggins demonstrates, amateur astronomers were to enjoy a final golden age.

The English entrepreneur William Lassell (1799-1880) had made good money from brewing beer and used some of it to indulge his interest in astronomy, employing very good self-made instruments at his observatory near the city of Liverpool. Liverpool was the fastest-growing port in Europe, and the world's first steam-hauled passenger railway ran from Liverpool to Manchester in 1830. The Industrial Revolution, where Britain played the leading role, was a golden age for the beer-brewing industry. The combination of beer and science is not unique; the seventeenth-century Polish astronomer Hevelius came from a brewing family, and the English scientific brewer James Joule seriously studied heat and the conservation of energy.

In 1846 William Lassell discovered Triton, the largest moon of Neptune, shortly after the planet had itself been mathematically predicted by the French mathematician Urbain Le Verrier and spotted by the German astronomer Johann Gottfried Galle. Lassel later discovered two moons around Uranus, Ariel and Umbriel; a satellite of Saturn, Hyperion, was spotted by him as well as the American father-and-son team William Bond (1789-1859) and George Bond (1825-1865).

William Bond was a clockmaker in Boston who became a passionate amateur astronomer. In 1848, with his son George, he discovered Hyperion. They were among the first in the USA to use Daguerre's photographic process for astrophotography.

The US astronomer Asaph Hall (1829-1907) discovered the two tiny moons of Mars, Deimos and Phobos, in 1877 and calculated their orbits. While only a few kilometers in diameter, the moons could be seen by viewers using smaller telescopes, which means their discovery owed as much to Hall's observational skills as to his equipment. Asaph Hall was the son of a clockmaker and worked for a while with George Bond at the Harvard College Observatory.

In 2010, photos taken by the European Space Agency's Mars Express spacecraft of Phobos, the larger of the two tiny, potato-shaped Martian moons, showed potential landing sites for Russia's unmanned Phobos-Grunt mission, which is designed to bring samples of the Martian moon back to the Earth after 2012. The Russian Space Agency intends to include a Chinese Mars orbiter, Yinghuo-1, together with the mission. It will be China's first interplanetary probe. China in 2003 became only the third nation to achieve human spaceflight, after the Soviet Union/Russia and the United States, and has plans for manned missions to the Moon.

The largely self-taught American astronomer Edward Barnard (1857-1923), originally a poverty-stricken photographer, made his own telescope and after some notable observations joined the initial staff of the Lick Observatory in 1887. He introduced wide-field photographic methods to study the structure of the Milky Way. The faint Barnard's Star, which he discovered in 1916, had the largest proper motion of any known star. At a distance of about six light-years it is the closest neighbouring star to the Sun next to the members of the Alpha Centauri system, around 4.4 light-years away. In 1892 he observed Amalthea, the first moon of Jupiter to be discovered since the four largest ones described by Galileo Galilei in 1610.

The Swiss natural philosopher Pierre Prévost (1751-1839), the son of a clergyman from Geneva, Switzerland, who served as a professor of physics at Berlin, showed in 1791 that all bodies radiate heat, regardless of their temperature.

Early estimates of stellar surface temperatures gave results that were far too high. More accurate values were obtained by using the radiation laws of the Slovenian physicist Joseph Stefan from 1879 and the German physicist Wilhelm Wien from 1896. Stefan calculated the temperature of the Sun's surface to 5400°C, the most sensible value until then. The Stefan-Boltzmann Law, named after Stefan and his Austrian student Ludwig Boltzmann, suggests that the amount of radiation given off by a body is proportional to the fourth power of its temperature as measured in Kelvin units.

The surface temperature is not necessarily needy upon the size of the star (the core temperature is a different matter). You can easily find red supergiants with many times the mass of the Sun, but with a surface temperature of less than 4000 K, compared to the Sun's 5800 or so K. The surface temperature of a bright red star is approximately 3500 K, whereas blue stars can have ones of tens of thousands of degrees. Dark red stars have surface temperatures of about 2500 K. Blue stars are extremely hot and bright and live short lives by astronomical standards. The bright star Rigel in the constellation of Orion is a blue supergiant of an estimated 20 solar masses, shining with tens of thousands of times the Sun's luminosity.

The procedure of combining light elements into heavier ones—nuclear fusion—happens in the central region of stars. In their extremely hot cores, instead of individual atoms you have a mix of nuclei and free electrons, what we call plasma. The term 'plasma' was first applied to ionized gas by Irving Langmuir (1881-1957), a physical chemist from the USA, in 1923. It is the fourth and by far the most common state of matter in the universe in addition to the three we are familiar with from everyday life on Earth: solid, liquid and gas. Extreme temperatures and pressure is needed to overcome the mutual electrostatic repulsion of positively charged atomic nuclei (ions), often called the Coulomb barrier after the French natural philosopher Charles de Coulomb, who formulated the laws of electrostatic attraction and repulsion.

While their work represented a huge conceptual breakthrough, the initial theories of Weizsäcker and Bethe did not explain the creation of elements heavier than helium. Edwin Ernest Salpeter (1924-2008) was anastrophysicist who emigrated from Austria to Australia, studied at the University of Sydney and finally ended up at Cornell University in the USA, where he worked in the fields of quantum electrodynamics and nuclear physics with Hans Bethe. In 1951 he explained how with the 'triple-alpha' reaction, carbon nuclei could be produced from helium nuclei in the nuclear reactions within certain large and hot stars.

The synthesis of hydrogen to helium by the proton-proton chain or CNO cycle requires temperatures in the order of 10 million degrees Celsius or Kelvin. Only at those temperatures will there be enough hydrogen ions in the plasma with high enough velocities to tunnel through the Coulomb barrier at sufficient rates. There are no stable isotopes of any element with atomic masses 5 or 8; beryllium-8 (4 protons and 4 neutrons) is highly unstable and short-lived. Only at extremely high temperatures of around 100 million K can the sequence called the *triple-alpha process* take place. It is so called because the net effect is to combine 3 alpha particles, which means standard helium-4 nuclei of two protons and two neutrons, to form a carbon-12 nucleus (6 protons and 6 neutrons). In main sequence stars, the central temperatures are too low for this process to take place, but not in stars in the red giant phase.

More advances were made by the English astrophysicist Fred Hoyle (1915-2001). He was born in Yorkshire in northern England and educated in mathematics and theoretical physics at the University of Cambridge by some of the leading scientists of his day, among them Arthur Eddington and Paul Dirac. During World War II he contributed to the development of radar. With the German American astronomer Martin Schwarzschild (1912-1997), son of the astrophysicist Karl Schwarzschild and a pioneer in the use of electronic computers and high-altitude balloons to carry scientific instruments, he developed a theory of the evolution of red giant stars. Hoylestayed at Cambridge from 1945 to 1973. In addition to his career in physics he is known for his popular science works and wrote novels, plays and short stories. He attributed life on Earth to an infall of organic matter from space. He remained controversial throughout his life for his support of many highly unorthodox ideas, yet he made indisputable contributions to our understanding of stellar nucleosynthesis and together with a few others convincingly showed how heavy elements are created during supernova explosions.

The English astrophysicist Margaret Burbidge (born 1919) was educated at the University of London. She worked in the USA for a long time, but also served as director of the Royal Greenwich Observatory in her native Britain. She studied spectra of galaxies, determining their masses and chemical composition and married fellow Englishman Geoff Burbidge (1925-2010), who was educated at the University of Bristol and at University College, London, where he earned a Ph.D. in theoretical physics. The American astrophysicist William Alfred Fowler (1911-1995) earned his B.S. in engineering physics at Ohio State University and his Ph.D. in nuclear physics at the California Institute of Technology. He and his colleagues at Caltech measured the rates of nuclear reactions of astrophysical interest. After 1964, Fowler worked on problems involving supernovae and the formation of light elements.

Building on the work of Hans Bethe, Hoyle in 1957 co-authored with Fowler and the husband-and-wife team of Geoffrey and Margaret Burbidge the paper *Synthesis of the Elements in Stars*. They demonstrated how the cosmic abundances of all heavier elements from carbon to uranium could be explained as the result of nuclear reactions in stars. Out of the four, William Fowler alone shared the Nobel Prize in Physics in 1983 with Subrahmanyan Chandrasekhar for work on the evolution of the stars. By then Fred Hoyle was known for, among other things, attributing influenza epidemics to viruses carried in meteor streams.

The Canadian scientist Alastair G. W. Cameron (1925-2005) further aided our understanding of these stellar processes. Astrophysicists spent the 1960s and 70s establishing detailed descriptions of the internal workings of stars. Chushiro Hayashi (1920-2010), educated at the University of Tokyo, together with his students made valuable contributions to stellar models. He found that pre-main-sequence stars follow what are now called 'Hayashi tracks' downward on the Hertzprung-Russell diagram until they reach the main sequence. He was a leader in building astrophysics as a discipline in Japan. The Armenian scientist Victor Ambartsumian (1908-1996) was a pioneer in astrophysics in the Soviet Union, studied stellar evolution and hosted international conferences to search for extraterrestrial civilizations.

The Austrian physicist Wolfgang Pauli in 1930, trusting the principle of energy conservation, proposed that an unknown particle carries off some missing energy. If it existed it had to be electrically neutral, possess virtually zero mass and move at nearly the speed of light. Enrico Fermi named it the neutrino, meaning 'little neutral one' in Italian. Because of their weak interactions with matter, neutrinos are extremely difficult to detect, but their existence was confirmed through experiments with tanks containing hundreds of liters of water by the scientists Frederick Reines (1918-1998) and Clyde Cowan (1919-1974) in the USA in 1956. This achievement was decades later rewarded with a well-deserved Nobel Prize in Physics.

Physicists realised that the nuclear reactions in stars should produce enormous amounts of neutrinos. In 1967, the physicist Raymond Davis, Jr. (1914-2006) installed a large tank of cleaning fluid in a deep gold mine in South Dakota in the United States. In the 1990s, Japanese and American scientists obtained experimental evidence indicating that neutrinos have non-zero mass, yet it is extremely small even compared to electrons. The Kamiokande detector in the Japanese Alps was of pivotal importance. Davis and the Japanese physicist Masatoshi Koshiba (born 1926) shared the 2002 Nobel Prize in Physics for work on neutrinos.

From the 1960s to about 2002, scientists struggled to explain what appeared to be a number of observed neutrinos from the Sun that was less than predicted. The mystery of the "missing solar neutrinos" was finally solved when it was understood that neutrinos can change type, and that certain types are more challenging to detect than others. After these adjustments had been made, the number of observed solar neutrinos closely matched theoretical predictions, which indicates that our understanding of the nuclear processes in stars like the Sun is pretty accurate. As the leading American neutrino physicist John N. Bahcall (1934-2005) writes:

"A 1 per cent error in the [Sun's central] temperature corresponds to about a 30 per cent error in the predicted number of neutrinos; a 3 per cent error in the temperature results in a factor of two error in the neutrinos. The physical reason for this great sensitivity is that the energy of the charged particles that must collide to produce the high-energy neutrinos is small compared to their mutual electrical repulsion. Only a small fraction of the nuclear collisions in the Sun succeed in overcoming this repulsion and causing fusion; this fraction is very sensitive to the temperature. Despite this great sensitivity to temperature, the theoretical model of the Sun is sufficiently accurate to predict correctly the number of neutrinos."

Neutrinos have become an important tool for astrophysicists. 1987 was a landmark year in neutrino astronomy, with the first naked-eye supernova seen since 1604. That event, called SN1987A, took place in our galactic neighbour the Large Magellanic Cloud. The two most sensitive neutrino observatories in the world, one in Japan and another in the USA, detected a 12-second burst of neutrinos roughly three hours before the supernova became optically visible, which, again, seemed to match theoretical predictions for such events pretty well.

In 1911 the American astronomer Edward Pickering differentiated between low-energy novae, often seen in the Milky Way, and novae seen in other nebulae (galaxies) like Andromeda. By 1919, the Swedish astronomer Knut Lundmark (1889-1958) had realised that low-energy novae occur commonly whereas the brighter novae, which are vastly more luminous, occur rarely. The challenge was to explain the difference between them. In 1981, Gustav A. Tammann from Switzerland estimated that three supernovae occur every century in the Milky Way, yet most of them go undetected owing to obscuring interstellar material.

A nova (pl. novae) is a nuclear explosion caused by the accretion of hydrogen from a nearby companion onto the surface of a white dwarf star, which briefly reignites its nuclear fusion process until the hydrogen is gone. From the Earth we will see what appears to be a *nova* ('new' in Latin), but in reality it is an old star undergoing an eruption. It is possible for a star to become a nova repeatedly as this process does not destroy it, unlike a supernova event which obliterates a massive star in a cataclysmic explosion. A supernova explosion can release extraordinary amounts of energy and for a limited period outshine an entire galaxy.

If a white dwarf gains so much more additional mass that it exceeds the Chandrasekhar Limit of about 1.44 solar masses, electron degeneracy pressure can no longer sustain it. The star will then collapse and explode in a so-called Type Ia supernova. Since this limit is constant, this type of supernovas has been used as a kind of standard candles to measure cosmic distances. Observations of Type Ia supernovas were used in 1998 to demonstrate that the expansion of the universe is accelerating. However, some observations indicate that such events can also be triggered by two white dwarves colliding, which might make them slightly less reliable as uniform standard candles as the weight limit could be less constant than once believed.

The neutron was discovered in 1932. Shortly after, the German-born Walter Baade (1893-1960) and the Swiss astronomer Fritz Zwicky (1898-1974), both eventually based in the United States, proposed the existence of neutron stars. Zwicky had a number of brilliant teachers at the ETH in Zürich, including Herman Weyl, Auguste Piccard and Peter Debye, but left Switzerland for the United States and the California Institute of Technology in 1925 to work with Robert Millikan. Another notable Swiss-born astronomer, Robert Trumpler (1886-1956) from Zürich, had immigrated to the USA in 1915.

Trumpler studied galactic open star clusters and clusters of interstellar dust and discovered the interstellar extinction.

Zwicky was not as systematic a thinker as Baade, but he could have excellent intuitive ideas. He was a bold and visionary scientist, but also eccentric and not always easy to work with. He stated that "Astronomers are spherical bastards. No matter how you look at them they are just bastards." His colleagues did not appreciate his often aggressive attitude, but he was friendly towards students and administrative staff. In the words of the English-born physicist Freeman Dyson, "Zwicky's radical ideas and pugnacious personality brought him into frequent conflict with his colleagues at Caltech. They considered him crazy and he considered them stupid."

Educated at Göttingen, Walter Baade worked at the Hamburg Observatory in Germany from 1919 to 1931 and at the Mount Wilson Observatory outside of Los Angeles, California, from 1931 to 1958. During the World War II blackouts, Baade used the large Hooker telescope to resolve stars in the central region of the Andromeda Galaxy for the first time. This led to the realization that there were two kinds of Cepheid variable stars and from there to a doubling of the assumed scale of the universe. The German American astronomer Rudolph Minkowski (1895-1976) joined with him in studying supernovae. He was a nephew of the German Jewish mathematician Hermann Minkowski, who did important work on four-dimensional space-time.

The optician Bernhard Schmidt (1879-1935) was born off the coast of Tallinn, Estonia, in the Baltic Sea, then a part of the Russian Empire. He spoke Swedish and German and spent most of his adult life in Germany. During a journey to Hamburg in 1929 he discussed the possibility of making a special camera for wide angle sky photography with Walter Baade. He then developed the Schmidt camera and telescope in 1930, which permitted wide-angle views with little distortion and opened up new possibilities for astronomical research. Yrjö Väisälä (1891-1971), a meteorologist, astronomer and instrument maker from Finland, had been working on a related design before Schmidt but left the invention unpublished at the time. Zwicky and Baade introduced the term 'supernova' and suggested that these are completely different from ordinary novae. They proposed that after the turbulent collapse of a massive star, the residue of which would be an extremely compact *neutron star*, there would still be a large amount of energy left over. According to the book *Cosmic Horizons*:

"Baade knew of several historical accounts of 'new stars' that had appeared as bright naked eye objects for several months before fading from view. The Danish astronomer Tycho Brahe, for example, had made careful observations of one in 1572. Zwicky and Baade thought that such events must be supernova explosions in our own Galaxy. At a scientific conference in 1933, they advanced three bold new ideas: (1) massive stars end their lives in stupendous explosions which blow them apart, (2) such explosions produce cosmic rays, and (3) they leave behind a collapsed star made of densely-packed neutrons. Zwicky reasoned that the violent collapse and explosion of a massive star would leave a dense ball of neutrons, formed by the crushing together of protons and electrons. Such an object, which he called a 'neutron star,' would be only several kilometers across but as dense as an atomic nucleus. This bizarre idea was met with great skepticism. Neutrons had only been discovered the year before. The notion that an entire star could be made of such an exotic form of matter was startling, to say the least."

Astronomers readily accepted supernovas, but remained doubtful about neutron stars for many years, believing that such strange objects were unlikely to exist in real life. To transform protons and electrons into neutrons, the density would have to approach the incredible density of an atomic nucleus, about 10^{17} kg/m^3. A neutron star of twice the mass of our Sun would have a diameter of only 20 kilometers and would therefore fit inside any major city on Earth. Despite the name, a neutron star is probably not composed solely of neutrons. As Neil F. Comins and William J. Kaufmann III state in their book *Discovering the Universe*: "Its interior has a radius of about 10 km, with a core of superconducting protons and superfluid neutrons. A *superconductor* is a material in which electricity and heat flow without the system losing energy, whereas a *superfluid* has the strange property that it flows without any friction. Both superconductors and superfluids have been created in the laboratory. Surrounding a neutron star's core is a layer of superfluid neutrons. The surface of the neutron star is a solid, brittle crust of dense nuclei and electrons about 9-km thick. The gravitational force of the neutron star is so great at its surface that climbing a bump there just 1-mm high would take more energy than it takes to climb Mount Everest. Neutron stars may also have atmospheres, as indicated by absorption lines in the spectrum of at least one of them."

Neutron stars were first observed in the 1960s with the rapid development of non-optical astronomy. In 1967 the astrophysicist Jocelyn Bell (born 1943) and the radio astronomer Antony Hewish (born 1924) at Cambridge University in England discovered the first pulsar. They were looking for variations in the radio brightness of quasars and discovered a rapidly pulsating radio source. The radiation had to come from a source not larger than a planet. The Austrian-born, USA based Jewish astrophysicist Thomas Gold (1920 2004) identified these objects as rotating neutron stars, pulsars, with extremely powerful magnetic fields that sweep around many times per second as the stars rotate, making them appear as cosmic lighthouses.

Antony Hewish won the Nobel Prize for Physics in 1974, the first one awarded for astronomical research, although his graduate student Bell made the initial discovery. He shared the Prize with the prominent English radio astronomer Martin Ryle (1918-1984), who helped develop radar countermeasures for British defence during World War II and after the war became the first professor of radio astronomy in Britain. Ryle became a leading opponent of the steady state cosmological model proposed by the English astrophysicist Fred Hoyle. The process of converting lower-mass chemical elements into higher-mass ones is called nucleosynthesis. One or more stars can be formed from a large cloud of gas and dust. As it slowly contracts due to gravity, the condensation releases energy which in turn heats up the central region of the cloud. The protostar continues to contract until the core temperature reaches about 10 million K, which constitutes the minimum temperature required for normal hydrogen-to-helium fusion to begin. A main sequence star is then born. When a star exhausts its hydrogen supply the pressure in its core falls and it begins to shrink, releasing energy and heating up further. The next step is core helium-to-carbon fusion, the triple-alpha process, which requires a central temperature of about 100 million K. Helium fusion also produces nuclei of oxygen 16 (8 protons and 8 neutrons) and neon 20 (10 protons and 10 neutrons).

At core temperatures of 600 million K, carbon 12 can fuse to form sodium 23 (11 protons, 12 neutrons) and magnesium 24 (12 protons, 12 neutrons), but not all stars can reach such temperatures. Stars with higher masses fuse more elements than stars with lower masses. High-mass stars have more than 8-9 solar masses; intermediate-mass ones 0.5 to 8 solar masses and low-mass stars 0.1 to 0.5 solar mass. After exhausting its central supply of hydrogen and helium, the core of a high-mass star undergoes a sequence of other thermonuclear reactions at increasingly faster pace, reaching higher and higher temperatures.

When helium fusion ends in the core of a star with more than 8 solar masses, gravitational compression collapses the carbon-oxygen core and drives up the temperature to above 600 million K. Helium fusion continues in a shell outside of the core, and this shell is itself surrounded by a hydrogen-fusing shell. At 1 billion K oxygen nuclei can fuse, producing silicon 28 (14 protons, 14 neutrons), phosphorus 31 (15 protons, 16 neutrons) and sulphur 32 (16 protons, 16 neutrons). Each stage goes faster and faster. At 2.7 billion K, silicon fusion begins. Every stage of fusion adds a new shell of matter outside the core, creating something resembling the layers of a massive onion. The outer layers are pushed further and further out.

Energy production in big stars can continue until the various fusion processes have reached nuclei of iron 56 (26 protons, 30 neutrons), which has one of the lowest existing masses per nucleon (nuclear particle, proton or neutron). The mass of an atomic nucleus is less than the sum of the individual masses of the protons and neutrons which constitute it. The difference is a measure of the nuclear binding energy which holds the nucleus together. Iron has the most tightly bound nuclei next to ^{62}Ni, an isotope of nickel with 28 protons and 34 neutrons, and consequently has no excess binding energy available to release through fusion processes.

No star, regardless of how hot it is, can generate energy by fusing elements heavier than iron; iron nuclei represent a very stable form of matter. Fusion of elements lighter than this or splitting of heavier ones leads to a slight loss in mass and a net release of nuclear binding energy. The latter principle, nuclear fission, is employed in nuclear fission weapons ("atom bombs") by splitting large, massive atomic nuclei such as those of uranium or plutonium, while nuclear fusion of lighter nuclei takes place in hydrogen bombs and in the stars.

When a star much more massive than our Sun has exhausted its fuel supplies it collapses and releases enormous amounts of gravitational energy converted into heat. It then becomes a (Type II) supernova. When the outer layers are thrown back into interstellar space, the material can be incorporated into clouds of gas and dust (nebulae) that form new stars and planets. The remaining core of the exploded star will become a neutron star or a black hole, depending upon how massive it is. It is believed that the heavy elements we find on Earth, for instance gold with atomic number 79, are the result of ancient supernova explosions and were once a part of the Solar Nebula that formed our Solar System almost 4.6 billion years ago.

"Without any nuclear fusion reactions to create the temperatures and pressures needed to support the star, gravity takes over and the star collapses in a matter of seconds. Fowler and colleagues calculated that the energy generated within the collapsing star is so great that it provides the conditions needed to create all the elements heavier than iron. As the outer layers of such a star collapse and fall inwards they are met by a blast wave rebounding from the collapsing core. The meeting of these two intense pulses of energy creates a shock wave that is so extreme that iron nuclei absorb progressive numbers of neutrons, building all the heavier elements from iron to uranium. The blast wave continues to spread outwards, and in its final and perhaps finest flourish it creates a supernova explosion that blows the star apart."

The Ukraine-born astrophysicist Iosif Shklovsky (1916-1985), who became a professor at Moscow University and a leading Soviet authority in radio astronomy and astrophysics, has proposed that cosmic rays from supernovae might have caused mass extinctions on Earth. The hypothesis is difficult to verify even if true, but such explosions are among the most violent events in the universe, and a nearby (in astronomical terms) supernova could theoretically cause such a disaster. Shklovsky made theoretical and radio studies of supernovas.

Since a star that dies passes along its heavier elements, this means that each successive generation contains a higher percentage of heavy elements than the former one. The Sun is a member of a generation of stars known as Population I. An older generation is called Population II. A hypothetical Population III of extremely massive, short-lived stars is thought to have existed in the early universe, but as of 2010 no such stars have been directly observed in distant galaxies. This constitutes an area of active astronomical research. If such objects are not found then we have to adjust our theoretical models. Astrophysicists currently believe that the young universe consisted entirely of hydrogen and helium with trace amounts of lithium and beryllium, all created through Big Bang or primordial nucleosynthesis. All other chemical elements have been created later through stellar nucleosynthesis and supernova explosions.

Even though it took only about a decade for nuclear fission to go from weapons to be used for peaceful purposes in civilian power plants, this transition has been much slower for nuclear fusion. The American physicist Lyman Spitzer Jr., a graduate of the Princeton and Yale Universities, in 1951 founded the

Princeton Plasma Physics Laboratory, a pioneering programme in thermonuclear research to harness nuclear fusion as a clean source of energy. In Britain, the English Nobel laureate George Paget Thomson and his team began researching fusion. In the Soviet Union, similar efforts were led by the Russian physicists Andrei Sakharov and Igor Tamm. In 1968 a team there under the leadership of the Russian Lev Artsimovich (1909-1973) achieved temperatures of ten million degrees in a tokamak magnetic confinement device, which became the preferred device for experiments with controlled nuclear fusion.

Although progress has been made at sites in the USA, Europe and Japan, no fusion reactor has so far managed to generate more energy than has been put into it. ITER (International Thermonuclear Experimental Reactor), an expensive international tokamak fusion research project with European, North American, Russian, Indian, Chinese, Japanese and Korean participation, is scheduled to be completed in France around 2018.

There is substantial disagreement over how close we are to achieving commercially viable energy production based on nuclear fusion. Pessimists say we are still a century away, while optimists point out that promising advances have been made in recent years using high-energy laser systems. At the end of the 19th century, it was discovered that, when decomposing the light from the Sun, a multitude of spectral lines were observed (regions where there was less or no light). Experiments with hot gases showed that the same lines could be observed in the spectra of gases, specific lines corresponding to unique chemical elements.

In this way it was proved that the chemical elements found in the Sun (chiefly hydrogen) were also found on Earth. Indeed, the element helium was first discovered in the spectrum of the Sun and only later on Earth, hence its name. During the 20th century, spectroscopy (the study of these spectral lines) advanced, particularly as a result of the advent of quantum physics that was necessary to understand the astronomical and experimental observations.

ASTROPHYSICS—PROCESSES IN THE UNIVERSE

Even looking close to the Earth, in our own solar system we observe widely varying conditions. The properties of the rocky planet Mercury, very close to the Sun, differ dramatically from those of the gas giant Saturn, with its complex ring structure, and from the cold, icy Pluto. But the range of variations found in our solar system is minuscule when compared to that of the stars, galaxies, and more exotic objects such as quasars. The properties of all of these objects, however, can be measured by observation, and an understanding of how they work can be reached by the extension and application of the same physical laws with which we are familiar.

The first astrophysical concept or law to be recognized was the law of gravity. We are all familiar with the force of gravity. Although it is a very weak force compared to the other fundamental forces of nature, it is the dominant factor determining the structure and the fate of the universe. Large structures, such as galaxies, and smaller ones, such as stars and planets, coalesced due to the force of gravity, which acts over vast distances of space. Much of the evolution of our universe is due to gravity's effects. However, scientists generally hold the view that the understanding of atomic processes marks the true beginning of astrophysics. Indeed, even such enormous objects as stars are governed by the interaction and behaviour of atoms. Thus it is often said that astrophysics began in the early decades of the twentieth century, when quantum mechanics and atomic physics were born.

Theoretical Astrophysics

Theoretical astrophysicists use a wide variety of tools which include analytical models (for example, polytropes to approximate the behaviours of a star) and computational numerical simulations. Each has some advantages. Analytical models of a process are generally better for giving insight into the heart of what is going on. Numerical models can reveal the existence of phenomena and effects that would otherwise not be seen. Theorists in astrophysics endeavour to create theoretical models and figure out the observational consequences of those models. This helps allow observers to look for data that can refute a model or help in choosing between several alternate or conflicting models. Theorists also try to generate or modify models to take into account new data. In the case of an inconsistency, the general tendency is to try to make minimal modifications to the model to fit the data. In some cases, a large amount of inconsistent data over time may lead to total abandonment of a model.

Topics studied by theoretical astrophysicists include: stellar dynamics and evolution; galaxy formation; magnetohydrodynamics; large-scale structure of matter in the Universe; origin of cosmic rays; general relativity and physical cosmology, including string cosmology and astroparticle physics. Astrophysical relativity serves as a tool to gauge the properties of large scale structures for which gravitation plays a significant role in physical phenomena investigated and as the basis for black hole (*astro*) physics and the study of gravitational waves. Some widely accepted and studied theories and models in astrophysics, now included in the Lambda-CDM model are the Big Bang, Cosmic inflation, dark matter, dark energy and fundamental theories of physics. Wormholes are examples of theories which are yet to be proven.

Astrophysics—Importance of Instrumentation

Scientists learn about distant objects by measuring the properties that we can observe directly—by detecting emissions from the objects. The most common measurements are of electromagnetic radiation, extending from radio waves, through visible wavelengths to high energy gamma rays. Each time a class of objects has been studied in a new wavelength region, astrophysicists gain insights into composition, structure, and properties. Emissions from each wavelength region are generated by and affected by different processes, and so provide fresh understanding of the object. For this reason, the development of new instrumentation has been crucial to the development of astrophysics. The development of space instrumentation that can detect photons before they are obscured by the Earth's atmosphere has been critical to our understanding of the universe. Large space-based observatories, such as the Hubble Space Telescope, continually spawn major advances in astrophysics due to their ability to study the universe over specific regions of the electromagnetic spectrum with unprecedented sensitivity. In addition, probes such as the *Voyagers,* which visited most of the outer planets of our solar system, have provided detailed measurements of the physical environment throughout our solar system. The use of spectroscopy, which can determine the chemical composition of distant objects from their wavelength distribution, is a particularly important tool of the astrophysicist.

In addition to the photons of electromagnetic radiation, emitted particles can be detected. These can be protons and electrons, the constituents of ordinary matter on Earth (though often with extremely high energies), or ghostly neutrinos, which only weakly interact with matter on Earth (and are thus extremely difficult to detect), but help us learn about the nuclear reactions which power stars. Astrophysics proceeds through hypothesis, prediction, and test (via observation), its common belief being that laws of physics are consistent throughout the universe. These laws of physics have served us well, and scientists are most skeptical of proposed explanations that violate them.

Chapter 2

Celestial Mechanics

TERMS OF CELESTIAL MECHANICS

Celestial mechanics, in the broadest sense, the application of classical mechanics to the motion of celestial bodies acted on by any of several types of forces.

By far the most important force experienced by these bodies, and much of the time the only important force, is that of their mutual gravitational attraction.

But other forces can be important as well, such as atmospheric drag on artificial satellites, the pressure of radiation on dust particles, and even electromagnetic forces on dust particles if they are electrically charged and moving in a magnetic field.

The term celestial mechanics is sometimes assumed to refer only to the analysis developed for the motion of point mass particles moving under their mutual gravitational attractions, with emphasis on the general orbital motions of solar system bodies.

The term astrodynamics is often used to refer to the celestial mechanics of artificial satellite motion.

Dynamic astronomy is a much broader term, which, in addition to celestial mechanics and astrodynamics, is usually interpreted to include all aspects of celestial body motion (*e.g.*, rotation, tidal evolution, mass and mass distribution determinations for stars and galaxies, fluid motions in nebulas, and so forth).

HISTORICAL BACKGROUND

Early Theories

Celestial mechanics has its beginnings in early astronomy in which the motions of the Sun, the Moon, and the five planets visible to the unaided eye—Mercury, Venus, Mars, Jupiter, and Saturn—were observed and analysed. The word planet is derived from the Greek word for wanderer, and it was natural for some cultures to elevate these objects moving against the fixed background of the sky to the status of gods; this status survives in some sense today in astrology, where the positions of the planets and Sun are thought to somehow influence the lives of individuals on Earth. The divine status of the planets and their supposed influence on human activities may have been the primary motivation for careful, continued observations of planetary motions and for the development of elaborate schemes for predicting their positions in the future.

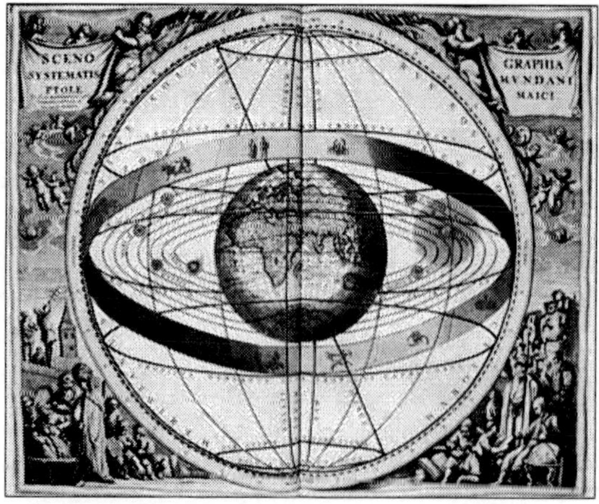

Fig. 2.1 Ptolemaic Diagram of a Geocentric System, from the Star Atlas *Harmonia Macrocosmica* by the Cartographer Andreas Cellarius, 1660

The Greek astronomer Ptolemy (who lived in Alexandria about 140 ce) proposed a system of planetary motion in which Earth was fixed at the centre and all the planets, the Moon, and the Sun orbited around it. As seen by an observer on Earth, the planets move across the sky at a variable rate. They even reverse their direction of motion occasionally but resume the dominant direction of motion after a while. To describe this variable motion, Ptolemy assumed that the planets revolved around small circles called epicycles at a uniform rate while the centre of the epicyclic circle orbited Earth on a large circle called a deferent. Other variations in the motion were accounted for by offsetting the centres of the deferent for each planet from Earth by a short distance. By choosing the combination of speeds and distances appropriately, Ptolemy was able to predict the motions of the planets with considerable accuracy. His scheme was adopted as absolute dogma and survived more than 1,000 years until the time of Copernicus.

Nicolaus Copernicus assumed that Earth was just another planet that orbited the Sun along with the other planets. He showed that this heliocentric (centred on the Sun) model was consistent with all observations and that it was far simpler than Ptolemy's scheme. His belief that planetary motion had to be a combination of uniform circular motions forced him to include a series of epicycles to match the motions in the non-circular orbits. The epicycles were like terms in the Fourier series that are used to represent planetary motions today. (A Fourier series is an infinite sum of periodic terms that oscillate between positive and negative values in a smooth way, where the frequency of oscillation changes from term to term. They represent better and better approximations to other functions as more and more terms are kept.) Copernicus also determined the relative scale of his heliocentric solar system, with results that are remarkably close to the modern determination.

Tycho Brahe (1546–1601), who was born three years after Copernicus' death and three years after the publication of the latter's heliocentric model of the solar system, still embraced a geocentric model, but he had only the Sun and the Moon orbiting Earth and all the other planets orbiting the Sun. Although this model is mathematically equivalent to the heliocentric model of Copernicus, it represents an unnecessary complication and is physically incorrect. Tycho's greatest contribution was the more than 20 years of celestial observations he collected; his measurements of the positions of the planets and stars had an unprecedented accuracy of approximately 2 arc minutes. (An arc minute is $^1/_{60}$ of a degree.)

Kepler's Laws of Planetary Motion

Johannes Kepler (1571-1630) discovered that the planets moved in elliptical orbits, and his three laws permit the calculation of planetary position once the orbit is known. Although correct, the loss of ideal circular motion as a fundamental (though impossible to apply) concept was a disappointment. This was changed into beautiful triumph in 1686 by Isaac Newton (1642-1727), who showed that the observed orbital motion was a consequence of fundamental principles of universal application.

Newton's formulation of mechanics, which involved the new concepts of mass and force, was subjected to intense, but sterile, criticism by Ernst Mach (1838-1916) and others, which did not change its application to the slightest degree, and shed no light on its fundamentals. The ideas of Albert Einstein (1879-1955), on the other hand, modified the fundamentals essentially, especially in the theory of gravity and the kinematics of motion, making the theory able to explain the smallest discrepancies with the earlier predictions. This *theory of relativity* has also been abundantly proved by observation. Except for Newton and Einstein, all the vast amount of work in mechanics has been the elaboration and application of the theory, which has proved in every respect correct. Particularly notable is the work of Joseph Louis Lagrange (1736-1813) in The Beautiful Theory, where forces are replaced by work and energy, and the laws of mechanics can be expressed as problems in maxima and minima. This branch of mechanics is usually called *analytical mechanics,* and mechanics with forces is called *vector mechanics,* from the convenient use of that formalism.

Newton's theory of motion, in its original form, is still the basis of engineering mechanics, and a fundamental part of engineering training. Indeed, it is still used in celestial mechanics. The only aspect needing relativistic corrections so far has been the time effects in the Global Positioning System. In the solar system, velocities are very comfortably less than the speed of light, 3×10^8 m/s, although distances are great. Light requires about 8 minutes to pass from the sun to the earth, and gravity travels at the same speed. However, the sun does not care a great deal about the force exerted on it by the earth, while the earth moves in a static gravitational field, so the effects of the finite speed of gravity are not evident. These effects have, however, recently been measured and verified, so it is known that gravity is not instantaneous.

Kepler empirically determined his famous three laws describing planetary motion: (1) the orbits of the planets are ellipses with the Sun at one focus; (2) the radial line from the Sun to the planet sweeps out equal areas in equal times; and (3) the ratio of the squares of the periods of revolution around the Sun of any two planets equal the ratio of the cubes of the semi-major axes of their respective orbital ellipses.

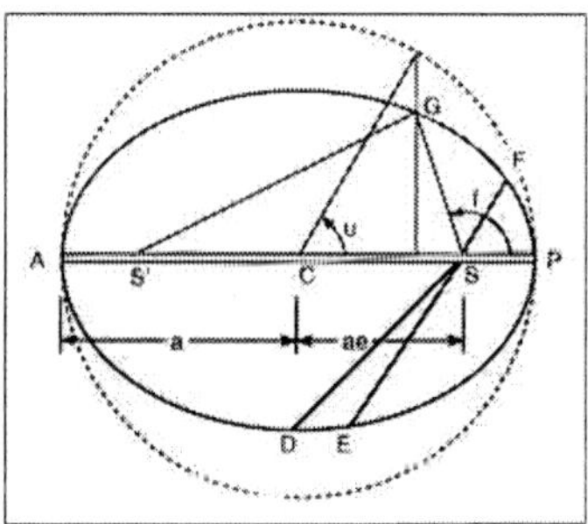

Fig. 2.2 : The Orbital Elements *a* (the Semi-major Axis) and *e* (the Eccentricity) Characterize an Elliptical Orbit; the Angles *f* and *u* Allow Location of the Position of a Planet on the Orbit Relative to the Point *P*; the Shaded Areas Illustrate Kepler's Second Law

An ellipse is a plane curve defined such that the sum of the distances from any point *G* on the ellipse to two fixed points is constant. The two points *S* and *S2* are called foci, and the straight line on which these points lie between the extremes of the ellipse at *A* and *P* is referred to as the major axis of the ellipse. Hence, $GS + GS2 = AP = 2a$, where a is the semi-major axis of the ellipse. A focus is separated from the centre C of the ellipse by the fractional part of the semi-major axis given by the product ae, where $e < 1$ is called the eccentricity. Thus, $e = 0$ corresponds to a circle. If the Sun is at the focus S of the ellipse, the point P at which the planet is closest to the Sun is called the perihelion, and the most distant point in the orbit A is the aphelion. The term helion refers specifically to the Sun as the primary body about which the planet is orbiting. As the points P and A are also called apses, periapse and apoapse are often used to designate the corresponding points in an orbit about any primary body, although more specific terms, such as perigee and apogee for Earth, are often used to indicate the primary body.

If G is the instantaneous location of a planet in its orbit, the angle f, called the true anomaly, locates this point relative to the perihelion P with the Sun (or focus S) as the origin, or vertex, of the angle. The angle u, called the eccentric anomaly, also locates G relative to P but with the centre of the ellipse as the origin rather than the focus S. An angle called the mean anomaly l is also measured from P with S as the origin; it is defined to increase uniformly with time and to equal the true anomaly f at perihelion and aphelion.

Kepler's second law is also illustrate the time required for the planet to move from P to F is the same as that to move from D to E, the areas of the two shaded regions will be equal according to the second law. The validity of the second law means a planet must have a higher than average velocity near perihelion and a lower than average velocity near aphelion. The angular velocity (rate of change of the angle f) must vary around the orbit in a similar way.

The third law can be used to determine the distance of a planet from the Sun if one knows its orbital period, or *vice-versa*. In particular, if time is measured in years and distance in units of the semi-major axis of Earth's orbit (*i.e.*, the mean distance of Earth to the Sun, known as an astronomical unit, or AU), the third law can be written $\tau^2 = a^3$, where τ is the orbital period.

Newton's Laws of Motion

Newton's Laws

Newton's laws of motion are:

- A body under no forces moves uniformly in a straight line;
- The acceleration of a body is equal to the force acting on it divided by its mass; and
- The mutual forces acting between two bodies are equal and opposite.

Newton stated the laws in this form so that these *axioms* would use only common notions and not involve any results following from them, in the spirit of Euclidean geometry. The different words in an attempt at conciseness, but the import is the same. The first law gives an operational method for determining an *inertial system*, a way of describing the position of a mass point in space as a function of time. In the absence of gravitating masses (such as the earth) it is found that a Euclidean space is such a system, in which a uniform time can be approximated by periodic events (such as the oscillations in lasers). Strictly (and uselessly) speaking, the definition is circular, but in practice it is clearly possible to establish inertial systems at least approximately, and the results obtained agree perfectly with observation.

The second law defines force as the cause of a time rate of change of velocity, by $dv/dt = f/m$. Again, the definition is logically faulty, but can be realised with great accuracy in practice. Whatever causes a change in velocity in an inertial system is a force. Masses can be compared dynamically, or more easily by the gravitational forces on them. A consistent array of masses and forces can be assembled, which always gives the observed motion. When the velocity is known, the position can be found from the kinematical relation $dr/dt = v$. Relations not involving force we call *kinematical*, those involving force, *dynamical*.

The third law guarantees that the total linear momentum and total angular momentum will be conserved; that is, that they will remain constant during the motion. These quantities are defined later, and their conservation is the motive for the third law, which cannot be stated in a general form in other than an extremely tedious and unilluminating way. Of course, not all forces obey it (magnetic forces between currents are an example), but nevertheless momenta are conserved. The conservation of momentum is an important fundamental of mechanics; the third law is a way of introducing it in terms of forces. In celestial mechanics, all the forces are central (act along the line joining two interacting masses) and so the simple statement is sufficient.

The path traced by the tip of the velocity vector v as time elapses is called the *hodograph,* and the path traced by the tip of the position vector r is called the *trajectory*. An orbit is a special kind of trajectory, a closed (or almost closed) curve. These curves are useful in describing, visualizing and analysing the motion.

The *momentum* is the product $p = mv$. The second law can be written $dp/dt = f$, so that force is the rate of change of momentum. If two particles m and m′ interact, then $f' = -f$ from the third law, so that $(d/dt)(p + p') = f + f' = 0$, or $dP = 0$, where $P = p + p'$ is the total momentum. The two particles, taken as a whole, constitute an isolated system, on which no net force acts, so the rate of change of momentum is zero, and thus the momentum is constant.

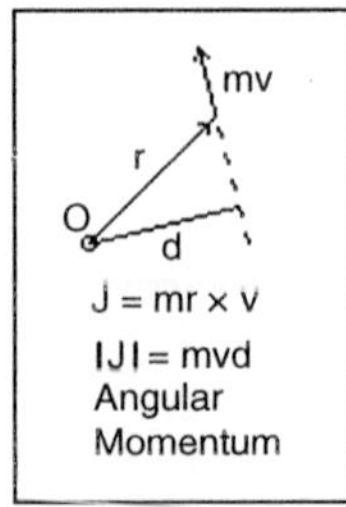

J = mr × v
|J| = mvd
Angular Momentum

The *angular momentum* with respect to a point O is the vector $J = r \times p$, where r is the radius vector from O to any point on the line of action of $p = mv$. If we use $r \times p$ instead of p in the equations of the preceding paragraph, we can prove that the total angular momentum is conserved. The conservation of linear and angular momentum gives us six scalar constants of the motion, useful in analysing and understanding the motion. The existence of these constants is no trivial matter, but a beautiful and fundamental result of the theory.

The second law can be formally integrated to give $p = \int f dt = I$, where I is a vector called the *impulse,* the integral of the force with respect to time. By taking moments about point O, we obtain a similar expression for the angular impulse. Of course, the limits on the integrals must be handled properly.

If the second law is scalar-multiplied by v, we find $mv \cdot (dv/dt) - f \cdot v$, or $(d/dt)(mv^2/2) - f \cdot v = -dW/dt$. This introduces two new scalar quantities, the *kinetic energy* $T = mv^2/2$, and the *work* $-W = \int f \cdot dr$. It simply means that work is being done *on* the particle, while W is conventionally the work done *by* the particle. If W is a function of position, then in vector notation $f = -$ grad W. In one dimension, $f = -dW/dx$, which may be more familiar. What we have shown is that $(d/dt)(T + W) = 0$, or $T + W =$ constant, a new conservation law. If W is a *conservative* quantity (that is, its value is independent of path and depends only on position), it is called the *potential energy* V. Then, the *total energy* $E = T + V$ is conserved in the motion. Energy is a widely used and misused quantity that could be discussed in great detail, but only its bare definition is required here, and the reader is assumed to be familiar with it.

The opening of energy permits the use of *generalized coordinates,* and the derivation of equations of motion by the Lagrange procedure, which uses the Lagrangian function $L = T - V$. This facilitates the solutions of very many problems, since we are liberated from carrying around a basket of vector components. For vector mechanics, it is convenient to have expressions for the velocity and acceleration components in polar coordinates. These are derived in the References, but will be summarized here. $v = (dr/dt)r' + (rd\theta/dt)\theta'$. r' and θ' are unit vectors pointing radially outward, and tangentially in the anticlockwise sense, with respect to the position vector r.

The rectangular unit vectors i and j are also shown. Note that $dr'/d\theta = \theta'$ and $d\theta'/d\theta = -r'$, while the derivatives with respect to r are zero.

$$dv/dt = [d^2r/dt^2 - r(d\theta/dt)^2]r' + (1/r)(d/dt)(r^2 d\theta/dt)\theta'.$$

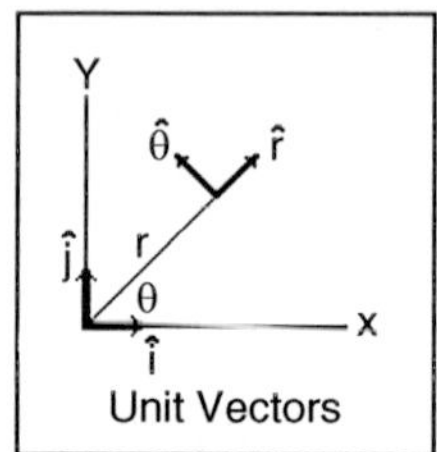

Unit Vectors

The reader should carefully note the distinction between, for example, d^2r/dt^2 and d^2r/dt^2. The first is the second derivative of a scalar quantity, a simple thing. The second is a vector, and since the direction of r can change, the complete expression is somewhat elaborate, as we have just seen. It is essential to distinguish carefully between scalars and vectors, which are arrays of scalars.

These relations are very useful. For example, suppose that the force is central, so that the tangential component of the acceleration is zero. This means that $(d/dt)(r^2 d\theta/dt) = 0$, or $r^2 d\theta/dt$ = constant = h. Now, half of r times $r\ d\theta$ is the area dA swept out by the radius vector in dt, so h is $2dA/dt$. Also, $mrd\theta/dt$ is the component of the momentum perpendicular to the radius vector, so $mr^2 d\theta/dt = mh$ is the angular momentum. We then have that the angular momentum $L = mh$ is a constant. Also, this means that the motion takes place in a plane, and L is perpendicular to this plane. We have found out a lot here with very little effort. The constancy of areal velocity is one of the most useful properties of orbital motion, not just a curiosity. It relates the rate of change of the angle θ to the radius r.

The Estimated Nature of Kepler's Laws

The constraints placed on the force for Kepler's laws to be derivable from Newton's laws were that the force must be directed towards a central fixed point and that the force must decrease as the inverse square of the distance. In actuality, however, the Sun, which serves as the source of the major force, is not fixed but experiences small accelerations because of the planets, in accordance with Newton's second and third laws. Furthermore, the planets attract one another, so that the total force on a planet is not just that due to the Sun; other planets perturb the elliptical motion that would have occurred for a particular planet if that planet had been the only one orbiting an isolated Sun.

Kepler's laws therefore are only approximate. The motion of the Sun itself means that, even when the attractions by other planets are neglected, Kepler's third law must be replaced by $(M + m_i)\tau^2 \propto a^3$, where m_i is one of the planetary masses and M is the Sun's mass. That Kepler's laws are such good approximations to the actual planetary motions results from the fact that all the planetary masses are very small compared to that of the Sun. The perturbations of the elliptic motion are therefore small, and the coefficient $M + m_i \approx M$ for all the planetary masses m_i means that Kepler's third law is very close to being true.

Newton's second law for a particular mass is a second-order differential equation that must be solved for whatever forces may act on the body if its position as a function of time is to be deduced. The exact solution of this equation, which resulted in a derived trajectory that was an ellipse, parabola, or hyperbola, depended on the assumption that there were only two point particles interacting by the inverse square force. Hence, this "gravitational two-body problem" has an exact solution that reproduces Kepler's laws. If one or more additional bodies also interact with the original pair through their mutual gravitational interactions, no exact solution for the differential equations of motion of any of the bodies involved can be obtained.

The motion of a planet is almost elliptical, since all masses involved are small compared to the Sun. It is then convenient to treat the motion of a particular planet as slightly perturbed elliptical motion and to determine the changes in the parameters of the ellipse that result from the small forces as time progresses. It is the elaborate developments of various perturbation theories and their applications to approximate the exact motions of celestial bodies that has occupied celestial mechanicians since Newton's time.

Keplerian Orbits

Kepler's three laws of planetary motion, deduced by prolonged and tedious consideration of the observed position of Mars, are:

- The planets move in ellipses with the sun at one focus;
- The areas swept out by the radius vector in equal time intervals are equal; and
- The cubes of the mean distances (half the major axis of the orbit) are proportional to the squares of the periodic times.

These laws are sufficient to determine the position of a planet at any later time if its position is known at one time, and the dimensions and orientation of the orbit are known.

Meant for a deeper understanding, and the power to attack an arbitrary problem in orbital motion, such as the movement of earth satellites, we should consider the dynamics, on the basis of Newton's theory. The force acting between two spherical, radially symmetric bodies of masses M and m a distance r apart is, by Newtonian gravitation, GMm/r^2 in magnitude, and is directed along the line joining the centres of the two bodies. G is the Newtonian gravitational constant, 6.67259×10^{-11} $m^3/kg\text{-}s$. Since the force is central, the angular momentum is conserved, and the bodies revolve about one another in a plane with the centre of mass (the barycentre) fixed. The motion can be analysed as the rotation of a *reduced mass* $Mm/(M + m)$ about the centre of gravity. The potential energy V is $-GMm/r$, and is negative because the particles attract. For the total energy to be zero, $T = mv^2/2 = GMm/r$, or $v = \sqrt{(2GM/r)}$. This is the *escape velocity* from the particle of mass M at the distance r. At the surface of the earth, the escape velocity is 11, 200 m/s or 25, 200 mph. This is also the velocity of a meteor that comes in from infinity. The escape velocity from the *sun* at the distance of the earth is 42, 000 m/s or about 95,000 mph. It is not easy to get away from the earth; it is even harder to escape from the sun.

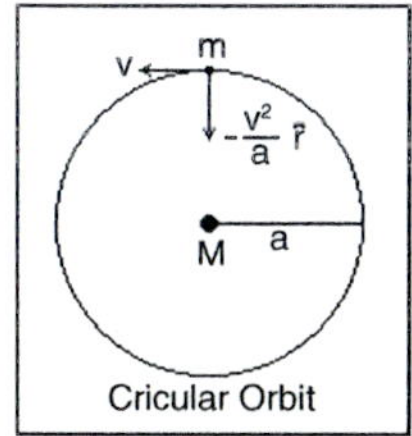

Cricular Orbit

If we consider a circular orbit of radius a, then $GMm/a^2 = [Mm/(M + m)]a(d\theta/dt)^2$, since $v = a(d\theta/dt)$ and the centripetal acceleration is v^2/a. This is the equation of motion for the relative motion, with r the distance between M and m. The centre of gravity of M and m moves with constant velocity, not affected by the relative motion.

Thus, $G(M + m) = a^3(d\theta/dt)^2 = 4\pi^2(a^3/P^2)$, where P is the period of the motion. This is a derivation of Kepler's third law for a special case, but it is a general result when a is the mean distance of any orbit. The quantity $G(M + m)$ is usually called μ, so that $r^3/P^2 = \mu/4\pi^2$. If r is in astronomical units (radius of the earth's orbit, about 150×10^6 km), and the period P is in years, then $G(M + m) = 4\pi^2 = \mu$. The quantity GM is called the Gaussian gravitational constant k^2 if time is in days instead of years, so we get approximately $k^2 = 4\pi^2/(365.25)^2$, and $k = 0.017202$. A more precise value is 0.01720209895. Untangling G from GM means knowing the mass of the sun accurately, which is impossible, so celestial mechanics uses k instead of G. The value should be corrected for the finite mass of the earth, but since the ratio of the sun's to the earth's mass is 332,946 the correction is small.

The polar equation of an ellipse, with the origin in a focus, is $r = p/(1 + e \cos \theta)$. The *eccentricity* of the ellipse is e, and p is a length called the semi-latus-rectum. In connection with orbits, the angle θ is called the *true anomaly*. In an elliptical orbit, $0 \le e < 1$. When $e = 0$, we have a circular orbit $r = p$. The same formula gives a parabola for $e = 1$, and a hyperbola for $e > 1$. In an ellipse, the maximum and minimum radii are $p/(1 - e)$ and $p/(1 + e)$, respectively, and the corresponding points on the orbit are called *aphelion* and *perihelion*, respectively. The distance from perihelion to aphelion is the major axis of the ellipse, twice the mean distance a. Therefore, $2a = p/(1 - e) + p/(1 + e) = 2p/(1 - e^2)$, or $p = a(1 - e^2)$. The perihelion distance is a $(1 - e)$, the aphelion distance $a(1 + e)$. The distance from the centre to a focus is $a - a(1 - e) = ea = c$. This defines the eccentricity as $e = c/a$. Since the ellipse is the locus of points the sum of whose distances to the two foci is a constant, $2a$, the length of the radius from a focus to the end of the minor axis is a. Since this is the hypotenuse of a right triangle, $a^2 = c^2 + b^2$, where b is the semiminor axis. Hence $b = a\sqrt{(1 - e^2)}$. The reader can show that the average value of r over one revolution is a. This is about all we need to know about the geometry of the ellipse for present purposes.

If we recognize the orbit is an ellipse, and the areal velocity is constant, we should be able to prove that the force is central and varies as the inverse square of the distance. On the other hand, if we know that the force is central and inverse-square, then we should be able to prove that the orbit is an ellipse and the areal velocity is constant. Either of these things can be done fairly easily. In the first case, differentiate the expression for r with respect to time, obtaining $dr/dt = (e/p) \sin\theta\, 2A$, where A is the areal velocity. Then differentiate again to find $d^2r/dt^2 = (4A^2e/pr^2) \cos\theta$. The tangential acceleration is zero from the constancy of the areal velocity. The radial acceleration is $a_r = (4A^2e/pr^2) \cos\theta - 4A^2/r^3 = -4A^2/pr^2$, which shows that the force is inverse square, and we have already shown that it is central. In fact, $GM = 4A^2/p$.

In the second container, the equations of motion in the plane of the orbit are ;

$d^2r/dt^2 - r(d\theta/dt)^2 = -GM/r^2$ and $rd^2\theta/dt + 2(dr/dt)(d\theta/dt) = 0$.

Now, $(d/dt)(r^2d\theta/dt) = 2r(dr/dt)(d\theta/dt) + r^2d^2\theta/dt^2 = 0$, so the areal velocity $A = (1/2)r^2(d\theta/dt) =$ constant. Using this result, the radial equation becomes $d^2r/d\theta^2 - (2/r)(dr/d\theta)^2 - r = -r^2GM/4A^2$. Making the substitution $u = 1/r$, this equation can be thrown into the form $d^2u/d\theta^2 + u = GM/4A^2$. This second-order linear equation with constant coefficients is easy to solve. We find $u = 1/r = GM/4A^2 + C\cos\theta$. This is the equation of a conic section. If $p = 4A^2/GM$ and $e = pC$, we have $r = p/(1 + e\cos\theta)$, which is what we wanted to prove.

Now we can find the components of the velocity. The transverse component is $rd\theta/dt = 2A/r = 2A(1 + e\cos\theta)/p$, where A is the areal velocity. The radial component is $dr/dt = 2A(e/p)\sin\theta$.

The square of the velocity is the sum of the squares, or $v^2 = 4A^2[(1 + e^2 + 2e\cos\theta]/p^2] = 4A^2[(1 - e^2)/p^2 + 2/pr] = -4A^2/pa + 4A^2/pr$, from which the kinetic energy per unit mass (*i.e.*, setting $m = 1$ for simplicity) is: $v^2/2 = -GM/2a + GM/r$, since $4A^2/p = GM$. Rearranging, $v^2/2 - GM/r = -GM/2a$, which is to say, $T + V = E$, with $T = v^2/2$, $V = -GM/r$ and $E = -GM/2a$. The total energy is negative (*i.e.*, the orbiting particle is "trapped") and a function of the mean distance a only. The eccentricity is determined by the angular momentum h through $e^2 = 1 - h^2/aGM$. When $h = \sqrt{aGM}$, the orbit is circular.

The quantity a, called the 'mean distance,' is not the average value of the radius vector r. It is the average of the perihelion and aphelion distances, however. The time average value of $1/r$ turns out to be $1/a$, which is its real definition. A proof will not be supplied here until I find a simple one. This means that the time average potential energy is $-GM/a$, and the time average kinetic energy is $-GM/2a + GM/a = +GM/2a$. For a circular orbit, the kinetic and potential energies are constant. The time average value of r is $a(1 + e^2/2)$, and the average of r over the true anomaly is b, the minor axis of the orbit. The average of $1/r$ over the true anomaly is $1/p$.

We obtained the relation between the mean distance a and the orbital period P for the special case of a circular orbit. A more general proof is as follows.

The areal velocity $dA/dt = h/2$ = constant, so integrating from $t = 0$ to $t = P$ we find $A = hP/2 = \pi ab$. We also know that $p = a(1 - e^2) = h^2/GM$. Therefore, $P^2 = 4\pi^2a^2b^2/h^2 = [4\pi^2/GM]a^3$, since $b^2/p = a$. This is the desired general result. If we know the period and mean distance of any orbit, we can calculate the gravitational constant GM, which in the general case is $G(M + m)$.

Coordinates and Orbits

The angular coordinates that are used to describe directions in space. The dihedral angle between these two planes is

ε = 23° 26' 21".412, or thereabouts. The equatorial coordinates are the right ascension α and the declination δ, while the analogous ecliptic coordinates are the longitude λ and the latitude β. The relations between the coordinates are best found by considering the rectangular components of the vector *OP*, considered as of unit length, and then performing the rotation about the x-axis that takes one system into the other. We will not require these relations at the present time.

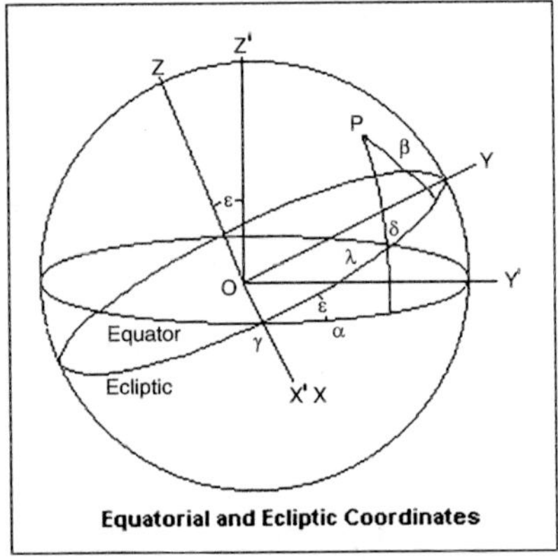

Equatorial and Ecliptic Coordinates

The situation of a body in the solar system can be specified in terms of a gigantic rectangular coordinate system centred on the sun. The x-axis is always taken as pointing to the vernal equinox, a direction specified by the line of intersection of the orbital plane of the earth (the ecliptic plane) with a plane parallel to the equator of the earth, the equatorial plane. Both contain the centre of the sun. This is made interesting by the precession of the normal to the equatorial plane around the pole of the ecliptic. In the diagram, this is the movement of z' (the pole of the equator) around z (the pole of the ecliptic). Fortunately, this is not too rapid, taking about 26,500 years for one revolution. The equatorial plane has to be considered because our earth-based measurements use it as a reference, when directions are given in terms of right ascension and declination. If we know a vector whose components are referred to this plane, we can find the right ascension and declination of its direction. When the earth is located in its orbital plane on the line of intersection of the ecliptic and equatorial planes, the sun is seen in front of the vernal equinox about March 21. At this time, when we look at the sun (careful!) we are looking in the direction of the x-axis of the heliocentric coordinate system.

The *y*-axis of the ecliptic coordinates is in the plane of the ecliptic, at right angles to the x-axis, and in the direction in which the planets move, in which a screw would advance in the direction of the north pole of the earth. The ecliptic *z*-axis is then perpendicular to the *x*- and *y*-axes, and makes a right-handed coordinate system with them. The equatorial rectangular coordinates are defined analogously. If we represent these coordinates by primes, x and x′ are the same, while x', y' is rotated with respect to x, y by the dihedral angle between the planes. The rotation from the z' axis to the z axis is a right-handed rotation about the positive x, x' axis.

Longitudes are measured clockwise (eastwards) on the ecliptic plane from the vernal equinox, from 0° to 360°. The *longitude of perihelion*, ψ, is the angle measured clockwise from the vernal equinox to the radius passing through perihelion. The longitude of perihelion of the earth's orbit is currently about 103°. This locates the major axis of the orbit and the direction from which the true anomaly is measured.

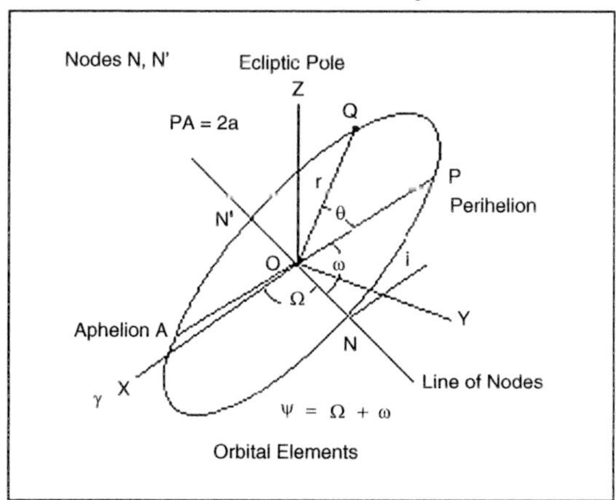

Orbital Elements

Supplementary planets move on orbital planes inclined to the ecliptic by the *inclination*, *i*. They intersect the ecliptic on a line called the *line of nodes*. The *longitude of the ascending node*, Ω, is the angle measured clockwise from the vernal equinox to the line of nodes, on the end where the orbit is climbing above the ecliptic plane, called the *ascending node*. The node 180° away is, not surprisingly, the *descending node*. The traditional symbol for the ascending node is used, which we represent in text by Ω, which looks similar. The symbol for the descending node is inverted, with the two little loops on the top. The longitude of perihelion in this case is the longitude of the ascending node, *plus* the angle ω in the orbital plane from the node to the perihelion. This may be a little odd, but it does locate the perihelion. That is, $\psi = \Omega + \omega$. These quantities are illustrated in the diagram.

At the present that the orbital plane and the direction of the perihelion have been specified by the three orbital elements *i*, Ω and ψ, we proceed to specify the shape of the orbit by its mean distance a and its eccentricity e. The position of the body in its orbit at a specified time is given by a sixth element, the mean longitude at the epoch. The 'epoch' is just the reference time assumed, usually by its Julian date. The mean distance a determines the orbital period *P* through Kepler's third law. Therefore, only one of *a* or *P* need be specified. The *mean daily motion*, 360° divided by the orbital period, is often given in place of *P*. Orbital elements for planets, asteroids and comets can be found online at the Jet Propulsion Laboratory website whose link is given in the References.

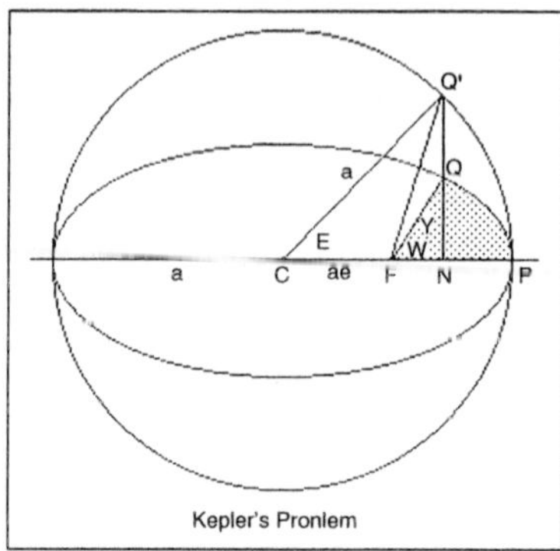

Kepler's Pronlem

The constancy of the areal velocity is used to locate the body in its orbit at a specified time. This is called Kepler's

Problem, which Kepler also solved. The circle of radius a is drawn around the orbital ellipse. Point Q is projected onto the auxilary circle by a perpendicular to the major axis to point Q'. The line CQ' then defines the angle E at the centre of the circle, called the *eccentric anomaly*. We can show that it is related to the radius vector r and the true anomaly θ by $r = a(1 - e\cos E)$ and $\tan(\theta/2) = \sqrt{[(1 + e)/(1 - e)]} \tan E/2$. The shaded sector PFQ is the area swept out by the radius vector, and the area is proportional to the time. The area FPQ' is proportional to the area FPQ, since it is merely magnified vertically in the ratio $a/b = 1/\sqrt{(1 - e^2)}$. Indeed, the total area of the orbit is πab, while the total area of the circle is πa^2. Therefore, this larger area FPQ' increases uniformly with time as well. Since the total area is πa^2, the area swept out is given by $(\pi a^2/P)$t, where t is the time since perihelion passage. This area can also be found in terms of E, since it is the area of the whole sector PCQ' less the area of the triangle $CQ'F$. The area of the sector is $\pi a^2(E/2\pi) = (a^2/2)E$.

The area of the triangle is $(1/2)(a \sin E)(ae) = (a^2/2)e \sin E$. Therefore, we have $E - e \sin E = 2\pi t/P = M$, called Kepler's Equation. M is called the *mean anomaly* and increases proportionally to time after perihelion passage. This is really a beautiful result, allowing us to find the position in orbit in terms of a uniformly increasing quantity.

Kepler's Equation can be easily solved by iteration. If it is written $E = M + e \sin E$, we find the iteration equation $E_{n+1} = M + e \sin E_n$ (e is the eccentricity here, not the base of natural logarithms). Starting with $E_0 = M$, a few interations are enough to get good precision, especially when e is small. The iterations are very easy, and can be performed on a pocket calculator. For $e = 0.1$, six iterations give 8 digits. The Newton-Raphson method can also be used. This method finds the roots of the equation $f(x) = 0$ by improving an initial guess x_0 by the formula $x_{n+1} = x_0 - f(x_n)/f'(x_n)$. A sketch will reveal the reasoning behind this formula. In this case, $f(E) = M - E + e \sin E = 0$ is the function, and $f'(E) = e \cos E - 1$. Fewer iterations are required, but each requires more work, than in the case of simple iteration. In practice, an expansion in powers of e is often used for small e, but the iteration methods are no more trouble, especially for a computer.

Even though the determination of position in orbit may sound complicated, it is really quite straightforward, and after you have done it a few times, it will be easy. Let's find the position of the earth on 2003 April 2. The *Astronomical Almanac for 2003*. On Jan 1, JD 245 2640.5, the mean longitude of the earth was 100.2440°, and the longitude of perihelion was 103.0°. April 2 is 91 days later, so $M = 100.2440 - 103.0 + 91 \times 0.9856 = 86.93° = 1.5172$ radians. A first approximation to E is $M + e \sin M$, and $e = 0.0167$, so the correction is 0.01668 radians, and $E = 1.5339$ radians or 87.89°. There is no need to iterate again. The mean distance can be taken as 1.00000, so $r = 0.9994$ and $\theta = 88.84°$. The earth's longitude is 103.0 + 88.84 = 191.84°. On *p.* C8, the solar ephemeris gives longitude 11.8506° and $r = 0.9994$. The solar longitude is 180° less than the earth's, or 11.84° according to our calculation. In both cases, we are using the mean ecliptic of date, and came quite close using Keplerian orbital elements instead of the more elaborate calculations used to calculate the solar ephemeris. Precise orbits require the consideration of planetary perturbations, and this is a very difficult subject indeed.

The orbit of the moon is an instance, since it is subject to perturbations by the earth's spheroidal shape and the sun that make its orbit vary in a very complicated way. In the case of the earth's orbit, we really calculate the position of the earth-moon barycentre. This point is 4671 km from the centre of the earth, about two-thirds of the way to the surface. The mean distance of the moon is 3.844×10^5 km, and its sidereal period is 27.321661 days, from which $G(M + m)$ can be calculated and used to relate mean distance and period for other earth satellites after correcting for the mass of the moon. The moon's radius is 1738 km, and its mass 7.3483×10^{22} kg. $m/M = 0.0123$, which is not quite negligible. The eccentricity of the moon's orbit is about 0.0549, and its inclination 5.145396°. The plane of the orbit and the position of perigee change rather rapidly. The small eccentricity of the earth's orbit suggests that the earth-moon system did not suffer any external disturbance during its formation, and in particular any collision which created the moon. This was a one-time event, so speculations on what happened can never be proved, since no similar state is known, or is ever likely to become known.

Apart from for the Mercury and Pluto, orbital inclinations are less than 4°, and eccentricities less than 0.0936, the value for Mars. Kepler was fortunate to have picked Mars for study because of its relatively large eccentricity, about twice those of Jupiter and Saturn. Venus's orbit is practically circular, with $e = 0.0067$. Mercury not only has a large inclination, 7.005°, but an eccentric orbit, with $e = 0.2056$. Only Pluto has a greater inclination and eccentricity, but it is probably a special case. Observations of Mercury and Pluto were not available to Kepler, who had to work with Tycho's naked-eye observations.

The angle made by r with the x-axis in our problem was 191.84°, so the coordinates will be $x = 0.9994 \cos 191.84° = -0.97814$, and $y = 0.9994 \; x \; \sin 191.84° = -0.20506$, in astronomical units. In the more general case of a planet in an inclined orbital plane, the radius is first projected on the line of nodes $[a = r \cos(\omega + \theta)]$ and on a perpendicular (dip) line $[b = r \sin(\omega + \theta)]$. Then $z = b \sin i$, $y = b \cos i \cos \Omega + a \sin \Omega$, $x = a \cos \Omega - b \cos i \sin \Omega$. It is just a matter of projecting r on the coordinate axes. There is an expansion for the true anomaly directly in terms of the mean anomaly, without going through the eccentric anomaly. To find the equatorial rectangular components, rotate about the x-axis through an angle of i. This gives $y' = y \cos i - z \sin i$ and $z' = y \sin i + z \cos i$. If x', y' and z' are the components of a vector in equatorial rectangular components, then the right ascension α is given by $\cos \alpha = x'/\sqrt{(x'^2 + y'^2)}$, and the declination δ by $\sin \delta = z'/\sqrt{(x'^2 + y'^2 + z'^2)}$. The proper quadrants have to be determined. In this way, the direction in which a planet is seen from the earth can be found.

Cometary Orbits

Comets can be divided into two classes, the *short-period* comets, like Halley's Comet, with a period of 76 years, and *long-period* comets, like Hale-Bopp, which do not return for thousands of years, if at all. A period of 200 years is the conventional dividing-line. Short-period comets have elliptical orbits like the planets, except that the eccentricity is larger, the inclination can take any value, and the comets can move in a *direct* or *retrograde* direction. Retrograde motion is usually expressed by an inclination greater than 90°. Comets were the first real test for Newton's theory, which finally showed that they were normal members of the solar system, not mysterious atmospheric happenings, as had always been supposed. Positions of short-period comets are calculated in the same way as planetary positions, and the orbital elements are presented the same way.

Long-period comets come from the periphery of the solar system, where they wander in the hypothetical Oort Cloud of cometary debris, normally water and carbon dioxide ice and dust. Their total energy is about zero, so the eccentricity of their orbits when they make an excursion towards the sun is about 1. That is, their orbits are parabolic. Short-period comets are those that have suffered an energy-losing collison with a planet (usually Jupiter) and have dropped into an elliptical orbit. There must also have been comets that have gained energy, entered hyperbolic orbits, and were ejected from the solar system. Few, if any, comets have eccentricities significantly greater than 1, which would indicate that they were encountered by the solar system in its path through space, and are not part of the family. The parabola is a considerably simpler orbit than the ellipse. Its polar formula is $r = p/(1 + \cos\theta) = (p/2)\sec^2(\theta/2)$. The areal velocity $A = \sqrt{(GMp/4)}$. Setting $x = \tan(\theta/2)$, direct integration gives Kepler's Equation as $x + x^3/3 = \sqrt{(GM/2)}(2/p)^{3/2}(t - T)$. The one real root of this equation gives the position in orbit. There are many ways to solve a cubic equation: refer to mathematics handbooks, algebra texts or mathematics programmes. The time to move from perihelion to the end of the latus rectum is $t_1 = (1/2)\sqrt{(p^3/GM)}$. $2t_1$ is a good measure of the time that the comet will spend near the sun.

The orbital elements include the inclination i, longitude of the ascending node Ω, and argument of perihelion ω. The perihelion distance $p/2$ is given, and the JD of perihelion passage. For Hale-Bopp, the perihelion distance was 0.91399384 and the time of perihelion passage was JD 245 0539.60742. The inclination was 89.42064850°, longitude of ascending node 282.47215310°, and argument of perihelion 130.59561740. From these elements, it was possible to find the position of the comet as seen from the earth. Cometary orbital elements are available on the internet soon after the discovery of a comet. The Jet Propulsion Laboratory supplied the elements for Hale-Bopp shortly after it was discovered.

Halley's comet was the first periodic comet to be recognized. Edmund Halley (1656-1742), friend of Newton's and later Astronomer Royal, suspected that the comets of 1531 and 1607 were the same as the comet of 1682, since they had similar orbits. He predicted the return of the comet in 1758, which duly occurred. Halley had published Newton's *Principia* at his own expense in 1678, and made an extensive study of comets using the new theory. Halley's comet is the brightest of the short-period comets; most are quite dim, and can even have orbits of small eccentricity like asteroids.

To demonstrate how to use the orbital elements given by JPL, let's look at them for Halley's comet. The time of perihelion passage, T_p is shown as 19860209.45895, which interpret to mean 1986 February 9, at 0.45895 part of the day, or 11h 0m 53s UT. The Julian Day, which would be unambiguous. The 'epoch' is the date to which the elements apply, which is given as 46480. This is a modified JD. The JD can be obtained by adding 24400000.5, or JD 2446480.5, which is 1986 February 18. The size and shape of the orbit is specified by the perihelion distance q = 0.58710374, in *AU*, and e = 0.96727724. The eccentricity is nearly, but not quite, unity. Near perihelion, the orbit will be indistinguishable from a parabola, so the parabolic formulas can be used for predicting its position while it is near the sun and visible. The orientation of the orbital plane is specified by the longitude of the ascending node, 58.86004°, and the inclination i = 162.24220°. When the numbers are located, look at the symbols used in the website, which may not be the usual ones because of font limitations. Since $i > 90°$, the motion of the comet in its orbit appears to be retrograde, opposite to the direction of motion of the planets, if the inclination is taken to be 180° – 162.24220° = 17.75780°. Finally, the orientation of the orbit in its plane is given by the argument of perihelion, 111.8656°, measured from the ascending node in the direction of movement. It is not easy to comprehend the orbital position from the bare numbers; a drawing, made with some care, will show exactly what is going on.

As the perihelion distance is $q = a(1 - e)$, it is a simple matter to determine a. In fact, $a = q/(1 - e) = 0.58710374/0.03272276 = 17.941755$ *AU*. From this, the orbital period P can be found. Since $P^2/a^3 = 1$ if P is in years (earth = 1) and a is in *AU* (earth = 1), $P = 75.99716$ years, very close to 76.0 years. The aphelion distance is 2(17.941755) – 0.58710374 = 35.296 AU. This is outside the orbit of Neptune (a = 30) but not as far as Pluto (a = 39.5). In accordance with the law of areas, Halley's comet spends most of its time drifting in this dark region, periodically darting in to the sun to have a little more of itself boiled off into space.

Even though orbital elements are given to high precision, the accuracy is not necessarily as high. Especially for comets, they can be changed by planetary perturbations, sometimes by large amounts. The ejection of gases from comets also leads to reaction forces that can affect the orbit. Also, the reference coordinates may change with time, because of precession of the equinoxes and other effects, and this must be taken into account in accurate calculations. These changes are not changes in the orbit, of course.

Determination of Orbits

Pronouncement the orbital elements from observations, and predicting the changes in orbital elements due to perturbations, are two of the most important problems in celestial mechanics, and have received close attention from Newton's time onwards. We cannot give any reasonable account of this work here, but we can show how orbital elements come from observed motions by a graphical analysis that is very instructive, though of little practical use where high precision is required. The reader with drawing supplies is encouraged to follow along.

We suppose recognized the position r of a body *M* from the sun and its velocity *v* relative to the sun. These are six parameters that will serve to determine the six orbial elements. The orbital plane is defined by the plane of *r* and *v*, and can be represented in two views by means of orthographic projection. The line of intersection of the orbital plane with the ecliptic plane can then be found, and the dihedral angle between the two planes. Since the line of intersection will be the line of nodes, we have now found two of the orbital elements, Ω and *i*, which determine the plane of the orbit.

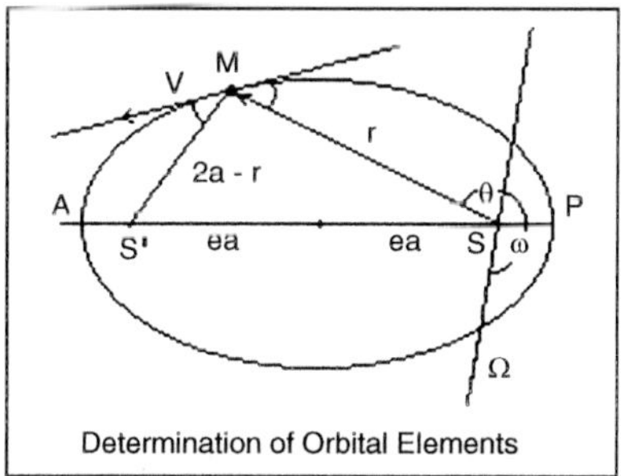

Determination of Orbital Elements

The next step is to calculate the mean distance *a*, using the energy relation $v^2 = GM(1/r - 1/2a)$. From *a* we can find the orbital period by $P^2/a^3 = 4\pi^2/GM$. The radius vector *SM* and the line from *M* to the other focus of the ellipse make equal angles with the tangent to the ellipse at *M*, which is in the direction of *v*. In a view showing the orbital plane in true size, Lay off *SM* and *MQ*, where *MQ* is an arbitrary line in the direction of the empty focus. The empty focus *S'* is located by laying off a distance $2a - r$ along *MQ'*, since the sum of the distances from the foci to *M* is 2*a*. Now we can draw the line *SS'*, find its centre at *O*, and then the locations of perihelion and aphelion. The eccentricity of the orbit is $e = OS/a = OS'/a$. The orbit can now be drawn, and the angle from the line of nodes to the perihelion, the argument of perihelion, ω, can be measured, as well as the true anomaly θ, which is the angle *PSM*. We now have the five elements Ω, *i*, ω, *e*, and *a*.

The remaining element is the time of perihelion passage, which can be found from the true anomaly. First, we find the eccentric anomaly by $tan(E/2) = [(1-e)/(1+e)]^{1/2} \tan(\theta/2)$, and from it the mean anomaly $M = E - e \sin E$. The mean anomaly is $M = 2\pi(t - T)/P$, where T is the time of perihelion passage, and t is the time of observation. That is, the body passed through perihelion at a time $t - T = MP/2\pi$ earlier. We have now determined all six orbital elements from the six components of the initial position and velocity. This was easy because the distance r was one of the given quantities. In general, orbits must be determined by observations of the angular position from earth, not directly in terms of distance and velocity. The position at three different times is sufficient to determine the orbit in this case, but the analysis is more difficult than what we have done.

Orbital elements vary only slowly in the solar system, except when there are near encounters, usually of light bodies with massive planets or satellites, that affect the orbits of the light bodies, but not of the heavier ones. If we know the orbit at one instant, then we can predict the velocity and position at a later time from the orbit. We can also integrate the actual changes in position and velocity at the later time, taking into account forces exerted by bodies other than the sun. The difference will be reflected in the orbital elements, which will slowly change. This is a useful way to take perturbations into account, and is widely used. The maximum errors in using the Keplerian orbits are on the order of 5" to 30" for the inner planets, somewhat more for Jupiter and Saturn. Neptune was discovered in 1846 as a result of its perturbations of the motion of Uranus. This was a remarkable demonstration of the accuracy of Newtonian mechanics.

The earth's mean distance is decreasing by 5×10^{-8} *AU* per century, about 75 m per year. The eccentricity is decreasing by 3.804×10^{-5} per century. The inclination is decreasing by 46.94" per century. These are average rates, and are simply the current values of changes that may be periodic. Nevertheless, they show how gradual any changes are, and allow the calculation of the earth's position with reasonable accuracy for thousands of years either side of the present. The longitude of the node, however, moves at -3.038" per *year* because of the precession of the equinoxes, which moves the reference point. The argument of perihelion is increasing at 11.9828" per year. It is typical for an orbit to show a relatively rapid change in longitude of the node and motion of the perihelion; the moon is an excellent example, and also earth satellites, which are perturbed by the equatorial bulge of the earth and tidal forces exerted by the sun and moon, as well as by atmospheric drag if they are in low orbits.

Earth Satellites

The mass of an earth satellite is infinitesimally small compared to the mass of the earth, so the centre of the earth may be considered as a fixed point. A reference frame fixed to the earth's centre is not an inertial frame, due to revolution about the sun and the moon's motion. The earth-moon barycentre is a 'more inertial' reference point, but in any case the difference from an inertial frame is negligible. There is a change in terminology, as perihelion becomes perigee and aphelion becomes apogee. This useless distinction is regrettable, and can be carried to excess (perijove, etc.). It would be good if there were terms usable in any orbit.

GM for the earth is $3.98600440 \times 10^{14}\ m^3/s^2$. Therefore, $a^3/P^2 = 10097$ if a is in km and P is in seconds. For $P = 86164.0989$ s (sidereal rotation period of the earth), $a = 42{,}164{,}172\ m$, or an altitude above the surface of 22,232 miles. A satellite with this mean distance will return to the same point in the sky each day. If the inclination and the eccentricity are zero, the satellite will appear to hang motionless in the sky. Such an orbit is called *geostationary*, obviously of great value as a communications relay location. An area of very choice space real estate is thereby created, for which there is considerable demand. Satellites occupy fixed stations around the equator. They remain in a constant direction from an observing point on the earth's surface, so an antenna can be permanently pointed at them without having to be continually redirected, which would not be easy nor cheap. Their positions may be adjusted slightly to keep the satellites on station by on-board thrusters during their effective life, and the thrusters are used to remove them from orbit when their fuel runs out, since space is at a premium in the geostationary belt.

Beginning a geostationary orbit, the earth subtends an angle of 17.4°, the same as a 12"-diameter globe at a viewing distance of 40", so it is quite reasonable to take photos of the whole visible hemisphere at once. Examples are available at the Dundee University website in the References. The poles are not visible, since the view extends only to latitude 81.3°.

The first artificial earth satellite was Sputnik I, launched on 4 October 1957 and weighing 83.6 kg. Its orbital period was 96.15 min, so its mean distance was 6953 km. The eccentricity was 0.0517, giving a perigee altitude of 228 km and an apogee altitude of 947 km. The inclination of the orbit was 64.26°, so it could easily be seen in every part of the earth when the sun shone on it. Sputnik remained in orbit until January 1958, making 1350 revolutions. Because of the low perigee, it was considerably affected by atmospheric drag, its final period being near 90 min. The period of a satellite that just grazes the surface of the earth would be 84.48 min, and its velocity 7906 m/s.

The Global Positioning System (GPS) uses satellites that continually radiate very accurate timing information, corrected for relativistic time dilatation due to the satellite's speed, so that their distances from an observer can be found to within a few centimetres from the time differences. The orbits must be known to a similar accuracy, so the effectiveness of this system is evidence of the correctness of the dynamics. Orbit information is broadcast along with timing information. The carrier frequencies are 1.57542 and 1.22760 GHz. The complete GPS system was deployed in 1993, consisting of 21 operational satellites and three spares, on circular orbits inclined at 55° and with a period of one-half a sidereal day (a sidereal day is about 23h 56m), so the satellites are seen to rise and set about 4 minutes earlier each day, and appear twice a day. Four satellites in good postions are intended to be visible from any point at any time, giving a good intersection, and eliminating the necessity for accurate calibration of the receiver clock (the offset of the receiver clock is one of the four unknowns that can be determined). The altitudes, about 20,200 km (a = 26,560 km), are high enough to make atmospheric drag negligible. There are six orbital planes, with four satellites spaced equally in each. The GPS is by no means the only satellite navigation system that has been developed, but it has become the most used, and is replacing the others.

Earth satellites are affected by many small forces in addition to the main inverse-square force directed towards the centre of the earth, and these *perturbations* cause the orbital elements to change slowly with time. In the case of earth satellites, the mean distance *a*, the eccentricity *e* and the inclination i do not change on the average (they may fluctuate slightly over the short term). The longitude of the line of nodes, Ω, the argument of perigee, ω, and the rate of change of mean anomaly change steadily with time. The drag of the atmosphere is negligible for satellites that do not come lower than about 1000 km at perigee, which includes most practical satellites. For lower satellites, atmospheric drag causes a loss of energy at perigee that pulls in the apogee position, making the orbit less eccentric and decreasing the orbital period. Paradoxically, the drag speeds up the satellite! The pulls of the moon and sun, *tidal effects* cause orbital changes. The direct tidal effect is due to the force exerted directly on the satellite, while the indirect tidal effect is due to the changes in mass distribution of the earth caused by tidal motions. Pressure of solar radiation and solar wind is another disturbing effect. The most important perturbing force, however, is that exerted by the equatorial bulge of the earth.

The gravitational potential of the earth can be expressed approximately as $V = GM/r\ [1 - (a_E/r)^2 J_2 P_2(\sin\varphi)]$, where a_E is the equatorial radius of the earth, 6 378 137 m, $J_2 = 0.001082630$, and $P_2(x)$ is the Legendre polynomial of second degree, $(1/2)(3x^2 - 1)$. The argument of this polynomial is usually seen as $\cos\theta$, but here we use the latitude $\varphi = 90° - \theta$. This is the first part of an expansion in spherical harmonics, which can even allow for a lumpy earth that is not symmetric about the polar axis. The correction to the $1/r$ field shown here is a zonal harmonic of order 2, related to the flattening $f = a/(a - b) = 1/298$ of the earth. However, the gravitational potential depends on the distribution of mass in the earth, so it cannot be expressed simply in terms of f. The radial component of the force is $-\partial V/\partial r$, and the tangential part is $(1/r)\partial V/\partial \theta$. The motion of earth satellites has led to a much better knowledge of the earth's gravitational potential.

If a satellite has a mean motion $n = 2\pi/P$, a mean distance a and an inclination i, the movement of the line of nodes is $d\Omega/dt = -(3n/2)(a_E/a)^2[\cos i/(1 - e^2)^2]J_2$, and the change of the argument of perigee is $d\omega/dt = +(3n/4)(a_E/a)^2[(5\cos^2 i - 1)/(1 - e^2)^2]J_2$. The quantities are in MKS units, and the results are in radians per second. For the moon, the line of nodes rotates once in 18.6 years. For a typical GPS satellite, the line of nodes moves about $-0.03°$ per year, the perigee about $0.01°$ per year. All the other perturbations are much smaller in amount, but must be taken into consideration in accurate work. Relativistic perturbing accelerations are inversely proportional to the fourth power of the distance r. Their magnitudes for GPS satellites are about 3×10^{-10} m/s^2, less than other small perturbations, so they have no practical effect, although they have been considered.

The International Space Station (ISS), shown at the right, is a famous earth satellite. The image is from the NASA website. The first two modules, Zarya and Unity, were assembled in orbit in 1998, and now there are 14. It is 73 m across the solar arrays, 44.5 m long and 27.5 m high, with 425 m^3 of habitable space. Power comes mainly from the 892 m^2 of solar arrays. There are thrusters to adjust the orbit when necessary. The total mass is about 179 metric tons. Although this is called 'space travel' by NASA, it is not even outside the earth's atmosphere! Estimated elements of the ISS orbit at 13.49Z, 6 April 2003, are $i = 51.6°$, Ω 19.99°, $e = 0.00083$,

$\omega = 52.91°$, M = 307.29°, and mean motion 15.59579861 rev/day, or 0.0649825°/s. ('Z' is another designation for UT.) Exact orbits, predicted about 10 days in advance, can be found at the NASA link in the References. The period is P = 5539.95 s (1.54 hr), and the mean distance is 6767009 m. This is a low, almost circular orbit at an altitude of about 400 km. Because the orbit is low, the ISS is seldom illuminated by the sun at night, so it is not frequently seen, though a frequent, large and prominent object.

The longitude (RA) of the ascending node changes rapidly, by about -5.00° per day, as does the argument of perihelion, by –3.64° per day. Perturbation by the oblateness of the earth is the reason for most of this change. The inclination, eccentricity and mean distance do not change rapidly. The orbit is just above the maximum ionization in the F layer of the ionosphere, and so is affected by atmospheric drag. The density of the atmosphere at this height is about $\rho = 9 \times 10^{-12}$ kg/m^3. The drag is given by $F = C\rho V^2 A/2$, where C is the drag coefficient, V the satellite velocity, and A the effective projected area. NASA gives $A = 344$ m^2 and $C = 2.36$. $V = 2\pi a/P = 6541$ m/s (assuming a circular orbit), so $F = 0.16$ N, which will produce an acceleration of 8.9×10^{-7} m/s^2. This drag causes the mean distance and period to decrease. NASA notes that the 'decay' is 4.11×10^{-4} rev/day^2. In 100 days, the mean motion will increase by 0.0411 rev/day, or $P = 5527$ s, a decrease of 13 s, or 0.23%. If uncorrected, the satellite would spiral inward at an increasing rate, eventually burning up catastrophically.

It may be interesting to find out where you should look for a satellite in a known orbit. The procedure will be illustrated here without taking all the refinements into account that are necessary for, say, GPS positioning. The idea is to find the rectangular coordinates of the satellite in an approximately inertial system with its origin at the centre of the earth, and then to find the rectangular coordinates of the point of observation in the same system. The differences of the coordinates then give a vector from the point of observation to the satellite. The motion of a satellite as seen from a fixed location on earth may be very complex, because of the interaction of the two motions involved, the revolution of the satellite and the rotation of the earth. Only when these are approximately equal is the situation more or less simple.

Let's suppose the satellite is in a circular orbit with a = 26, 500 000 m and i = 55°, like a GPS satellite. Let the longitude of the ascending node be 40°. Since the orbit is circular, there is no perigee point, so we measure the true anomaly from the line of nodes in the orbital plane. Let the true anomaly at the time we are considering be 70°. The z-axis is taken along the axis of rotation of the earth, and the x-axis in the direction of the vernal equinox. The y-axis then makes a right-handed coordinate system. This is just like the case of planetary motion, except that the role of the ecliptic plane is played by the equatorial plane. The orientation of these axes remains fixed in space as the earth revolves about the sun.

First, resolve the radius vector along and perpendicular to the line of nodes. The components are a cos θ = 9 084 055.0 m and a sin θ = 24 958 236.0. Then, z = a cos θ sin i = 20 444 590.0 m, x = a cos θ cos Ω – a sin θ sin Ω = -9 084 055.0 m, and y = a cos θ sin Ω + a sin θ cos Ω = 24 958 236.0 m. This is the instantaneous position of the satellite in the inertial system, and it could obviously be found for any time equally easily.

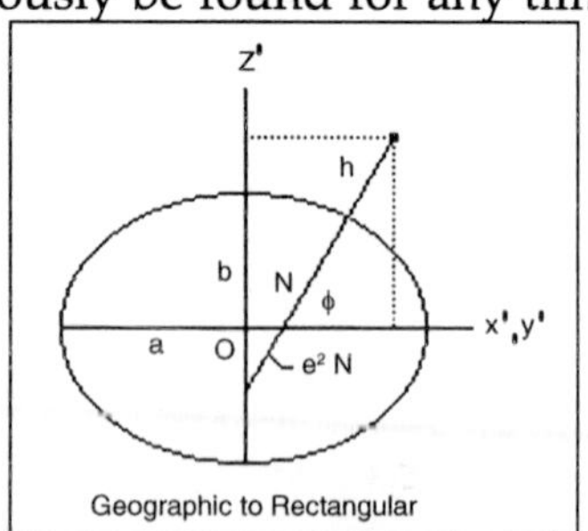

Geographic to Rectangular

Now for the point of observation. Let's use my own location, which is longitude λ = -104.92583°, latitude φ = 39.72694 and height above the ellipsoid (or mean sea level) h = 1633.7 m. Your own coordinates, if you do not know them already, can be found from a USGS topographic map. A meridional section of the earth is shown at the right, where φ is the geographic or spheroidal latitude. The dimensions of the earth are a = 6378136 m and b = 6356752 m. There is a number of reference spheroids, any one of which will work satisfactorily. The eccentricity of the elliptical cross-section of the spheroid can then be found to be e = 0.006694167. The meridional radius of curvature at latitude φ is $N = a[cos^2\varphi + (1 - e^2)sin^2\varphi]^{-1/2}$, or 6 378 194.38 m at my location. The length of N below the equatorial plane is e^2N = 285.8 m.

We now choose an earth-fixed rectangular coordinate system with the z'-axis along the rotational axis of the earth, the x'-axis in the meridian of Greenwich, and the y'-axis making a right-handed system. The rectangular coordinates of my location are then $x' = (N + h)\cos\varphi\cos\lambda$ = –1 263 816.21 m, $y' = (N + h)\cos\varphi\sin\lambda$ = –4 741 167.76 m, $z' = (N + h - e^2N)\sin\varphi$ = 4 077 353.73 m. These coordinates do not change as the earth rotates. The distance from the centre is 6 379 711.32 m.

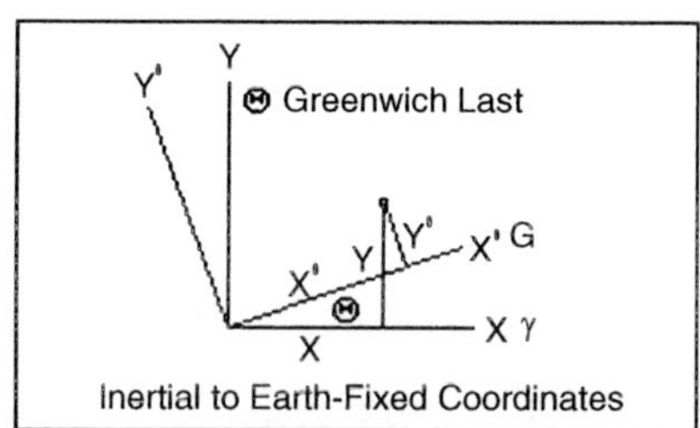

Inertial to Earth-Fixed Coordinates

The relation between the inertial and earth-fixed coordinate systems is shown at the left. The earth-fixed system rotates steadily in the positive direction about the common z and z' axes, and the angle of rotation Θ is the local apparent sidereal time at Greenwich, which is easy to find from the Astronomical Almanac. The rotational period of the earth is 23h 56m 04.09890369732s. When the time is stated to such precision, there are many small corrections to be considered, but we shall ignore them here so the principle is not lost. We shall assume that the inertial and earth-fixed coordinates are related simply by the rotation through an angle Θ, not correcting for polar motion, precession of the equinoxes and nutation. These are simply rotation matrices applied in addition to the one for the main rotation. For accurate work, however, they cannot be ignored. Since sideral time goes from zero to 24 hours in one rotation, we must multiply an ordinary time interval by 24/23.9344719 or 1.00273781195 to find the equivalent sidereal time interval. A sidereal hour is simply equivalent to 15° of angle; it is not an 'hour' in the usual sense of time. The transformation equations are the familiar $x = x' \cos \Theta - y' \sin \Theta$ and $y = x' \sin \Theta + y' \cos \Theta$. All you have to do is check that the signs of the sines are correct. If we put in coordinates in the earth-fixed system (x', y', z') we will get out coordinates in the inertial system (x, y, z) which we can compare with the satellite coordinates. Let's pick 10.00 am MST on 2003 January 1. Since my time zone is +7, the UT is 17.00h January 1. From the Astronomical Almanac, the sidereal time at 0h UT was 6.61651428 hours. The sidereal time elapsed is then 1.00273781195 × 17.00 = 17.04654280 hours. Adding the two, the Greenwich LAST at my 10.00 am will be 23.66305708 hours, or 354.945856°. If it seems easier, this can also be expressed as –5.0541438°. The results are x = –1 676 585.46 m, y = –4 611 395.05, z = 4 077 353.73 m. The square root of the sum of the squares is 6 379 711.32, so the arithmetic checks.

Now we can subtract the coordinates of the observation point from the coordinates of the satellite to find the relative vector (X, Y, Z). *I* find X = –7 407 469.54 m, Y = 29 569 631.05 m, Z = 16 367 236.27 m. The direction of this vector can now be expressed in terms of right ascension and declination, since it is a vector in the inertial system referred to the vernal equinox. The distance from the observer to the satellite is 34 599 423.53 m. The projection on the equatorial plane is 30 483 334.55 m, so that the declination δ = 28.2324° and the right ascension is 75.9363° or 5h 3m 45s. At the date and time specified, this direction is beneath the earth. In fact, the antipodeal point of right ascension 18h and declination –29° is in the southern sky at an altitude of about 20° above the horizon.

Although these calculations are tedious and subject to error, even when done with an electronic calculator, a computer programme can do them with ease, speed and correctness, and even the more precise calculations are not much bother. It would not be difficult to write a programme to determine the visibility of all of the 24 GPS satellites, and the directions in which they are to be seen.

Other Orbit Lore

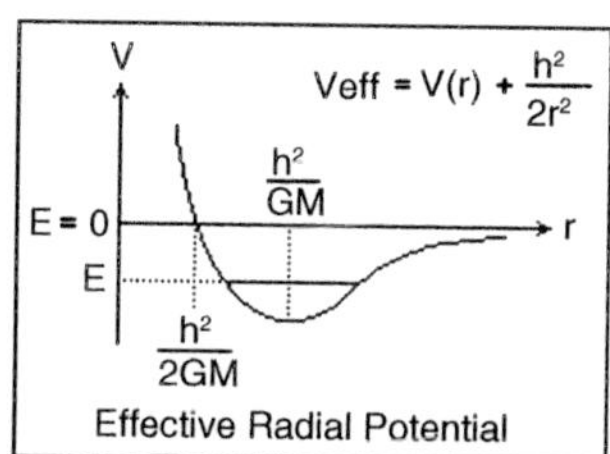

Effective Radial Potential

The total energy E of a body of unit mass moving under the influence of a potential energy per unit mass $V(r)$ is the kinetic energy $T = v^2/2$ plus $V(r)$. In polar coordinates, the components of velocity are dr/dt and $r\, d\theta/dt$, so the total energy becomes $E = (dr/dt)^2/2 + r^2(d\theta/dt)^2/2 + V(r)$. The constancy of angular momentum for a central force gives $r(d\theta/dt)^2 = h$ = constant. Substituting for $d\theta/dt$, we find $E = v^2/2 + h^2/2r^2 + V(r)$. This is the energy equation for a particle of unit mass moving in one dimension with the *effective* potential $h^2/2r^2 + V(r)$. The additional term is called the *centrifugal potential*. In the case of orbital motion under gravity, $V(r) = -GM/r$. The form of the resulting potential. For $E = 0$, a particle coming in from infinity accelerates steadily until $r = h^2/GM$, then is rapidly decelerated, coming to rest at $r = h^2/2GM$, and afterwards retracing its path in reverse. Of course, the particle swings round the centre of force in this motion. For $E = -(GM)^2/2h^2$, r has the constant value that gives the minimum of the curve, and the orbit is circular. For intermediate energies, r oscillates between a minimum and a maximum value, corresponding to perhelion and aphelion.

Consider the vector $B = v \times h + (GM/r)r$. The angular momentum per unit mass, h, is here taken to be a vector perpendicular to the orbital plane. The cross product then lies in the orbital plane, and so then does B. Taking its time derivative, we have $(dv/dt) \times h - (GM/r^3)r(v \cdot r) + (GM/r)v$. Now

$dv/dt = -(GM/r^3)r$, and $h = r \times v$, so the first term becomes $-(GM/r^3)[r(r \cdot v) - r^2 v]$. All the terms cancel, so $dB/dt = 0$, and B is a *constant of the motion*. This is extraordinary, since we already have one constant of the motion, the total energy E, and this is usually the only one that can be found. For an inverse-square force, we have found a second one. It is known that this happens when we have an additional symmetry in the problem—here it happens to be symmetry under rotation in a four-dimensional space, but there is no room to explain this here. We'll just be happy with the result.

Since B is a constant, it can be evaluated at any point of the motion, and it is easiest to choose perihelion. At this point, $v \times h = v_p^2 r_p$, so B is a vector parallel to the line between the focus and perihelion. We will find the same vector if we evaluate B at any point of the motion. Its constancy is a good proof of an exact inverse-square force.

Orbital Resonances

There are constant configurations in the restricted three-body problem that are not stationary in the rotating frame. If, for example, Jupiter and the Sun are the two massive bodies, these stable configurations occur when the mean motions of Jupiter and the small particle—here an asteroid—are near a ratio of small integers. The orbital mean motions are then said to be nearly commensurate, and an asteroid that is trapped near such a mean motion commensurability is said to be in an orbital resonance with Jupiter.

For example, the Trojan asteroids librate (oscillate) around the 1:1 orbital resonance (*i.e.*, the orbital period of Jupiter is in a 1:1 ratio with the orbital period of the Trojan asteroids); the asteroid Thule librates around the 4:3 orbital resonance; and several asteroids in the Hilda group librate around the 3:2 orbital resonance. There are several such stable orbital resonances among the satellites of the major planets and one involving Pluto and the planet Neptune. The analysis based on the restricted three-body problem cannot be used for the satellite resonances, however, except for the 4:3 resonance between Saturn's satellites Titan and Hyperion, since the participants in the satellite resonances usually have comparable masses. Although the asteroid Griqua librates around the 2:1 resonance with Jupiter, and Alinda librates around the 3:1 resonance, the orbital commensurabilities 2:1, 7:3, 5:2, and 3:1 are characterized by an absence of asteroids in an otherwise rather highly populated, uniform distribution spanning all of the commensurabilities. These are the Kirkwood gaps in the distribution of asteroids, and the recent understanding of their creation and maintenance has introduced into celestial mechanics an entirely new concept of irregular, or chaotic, orbits in a system whose equations of motion are entirely deterministic.

Chaotic Orbits

The French astronomer Michel Hénon and the American astronomer Carl Heiles discovered that when a system exhibiting periodic motion, such as a pendulum, is perturbed by an external force that is also periodic, some initial conditions lead to motions where the state of the system becomes essentially unpredictable (within some range of system states) at some time in the future, whereas initial conditions within some other set produce quasi-periodic or predictable behaviour. The unpredictable behaviour is called chaotic, and initial conditions that produce it are said to lie in a chaotic zone. If the chaotic zone is bounded, in the sense that only limited ranges of initial values of the variables describing the motion lead to chaotic behaviour, the uncertainty in the state of the system in the future is limited by the extent of the chaotic zone; that is, values of the variables in the distant future are completely uncertain only within those ranges of values within the chaotic zone. This complete uncertainty within the zone means the system will eventually come arbitrarily close to any set of values of the variables within the zone if given sufficient time. Chaotic orbits were first realised in the asteroid belt.

A periodic term in the expansion of the disturbing function for a typical asteroid orbit becomes more important in influencing the motion of the asteroid if the frequency with which it changes sign is very small and its coefficient is relatively large. For asteroids orbiting near a mean motion commensurability with Jupiter, there are generally several terms in the disturbing function with large coefficients and small frequencies that are close but not identical. These 'resonant' terms often dominate the perturbations of the asteroid motion so much that all the higher-frequency terms can be neglected in determining a first approximation to the perturbed motion. This neglect is equivalent to averaging the higher-frequency terms to zero; the low-frequency terms change only slightly during the averaging. If one of the frequencies vanishes on the average, the periodic term becomes nearly constant, or secular, and the asteroid is locked into an exact orbital resonance near the particular mean motion commensurability. The mean motions are not exactly commensurate in such a resonance, however, since the motion of the asteroid orbital node or perihelion is always involved (except for the 1:1 Trojan resonances).

For instance, for the 3:1 commensurability, the angle $\theta = \lambda_A - 3\lambda_J + \varpi_A$ is the argument of one of the important periodic terms whose variation can vanish (zero frequency). Here $\lambda = \Omega + \omega + l$ is the mean longitude, the subscripts A and J refer to the asteroid and Jupiter, respectively, and $\varpi = \Omega + \omega$ is the longitude of perihelion. Within resonance, the angle θ librates, or oscillates, around a constant value as would a pendulum around its equilibrium position at the bottom of its swing. The larger the amplitude of the equivalent pendulum, the larger its velocity at the bottom of its swing. If the velocity of the pendulum at the bottom of its swing, or, equivalently, the maximum rate of change of the angle θ, is sufficiently high, the pendulum will swing over the top of its support and be in a state of rotation instead of libration. The maximum value of the rate of change of θ for which θ remains an angle of libration (periodically reversing its variation) instead of one of rotation (increasing or decreasing monotonically) is defined as the half-width of the resonance.

One more term with nearly zero frequency when the asteroid is near the 3:1 commensurability has the argument $\theta' = \lambda_A - \lambda_J + 2\varpi_J$. The substitution of the longitude of Jupiter's perihelion for that of the asteroid means that the rates of change of θ and θ2 will be slightly different. As the resonances are not separated much in frequency, there may exist values of the mean motion of the asteroid where both θ and θ′ would be angles of libration if either resonance existed in the absence of the other. The resonances are said to overlap in this case, and the attempt by the system to librate simultaneously about both resonances for some initial conditions leads to chaotic orbital behaviour. The important characteristic of the chaotic zone for asteroid motion near a mean motion commensurability with Jupiter is that it includes a region where the asteroid's orbital eccentricity is large. During the variation of the elements over the entire chaotic zone as time increases, large eccentricities must occasionally be reached. For asteroids near the 3:1 commensurability with Jupiter, the orbit then crosses that of Mars, whose gravitational interaction in a close encounter can remove the asteroid from the 3:1 zone.

By numerically integrating many orbits whose initial conditions spanned the 3:1 Kirkwood gap region in the asteroid belt, Jack Wisdom, an American dynamicist who developed a powerful means of analysing chaotic motions, found that the chaotic zone around this gap precisely matched the physical extent of the gap. There are no observable asteroids with orbits within the chaotic zone, but there are many just outside extremes of the zone. Other Kirkwood gaps can be similarly accounted for. The realization that orbits governed by Newton's laws of motion and gravitation could have chaotic properties and that such properties could solve a long-standing problem in the celestial mechanics of the solar system is a major breakthrough in the subject.

The *n*-body Problem

The universal problem of *n* bodies, where *n* is greater than three, has been attacked vigorously with numerical techniques on powerful computers. Celestial mechanics in the solar system is ultimately an *n*-body problem, but the special configurations and relative smallness of the perturbations have allowed quite accurate descriptions of motions (valid for limited time periods) with various approximations and procedures without any attempt to solve the complete problem of n bodies. Examples are the restricted three-body problem to determine the effect of Jupiter's perturbations of the asteroids and the use of successive approximations of series solutions to sequentially add the effects of smaller and smaller perturbations for the motion of the Moon. In the general n-body problem, all bodies have arbitrary masses, initial velocities, and positions; the bodies interact through Newton's law of gravitation, and one attempts to determine the subsequent motion of all the bodies. Many numerical solutions for the motion of quite large numbers of gravitating particles have been successfully completed where the precise motion of individual particles is usually less important than the statistical behaviour of the group.

Numerical Solutions

Numerical solutions of the exact equations of motion for n bodies can be formulated. Each body is subject to the gravitational attraction of all the others, and it may be subject to other forces as well. It is relatively easy to write the expression for the instantaneous acceleration (equation of motion) of each body if the position of all the other bodies is known, and expressions for all the other forces can be written (as they can for gravitational forces) in terms of the relative positions of the particles and other defining characteristics of the particle and its environment. Each particle is allowed to move under its instantaneous acceleration for a short time step. Its velocity and position are thereby changed, and the new values of the variables are used to calculate the acceleration for the next time step, and so forth. Of course, the real position and velocity of the particle after each time step will differ from the calculated values by errors of two types. One type results from the fact that the acceleration is not really constant over the time step, and the other from the rounding off or truncation of the numbers at every step of the calculation. The first type of error is decreased by taking shorter time steps. But this means more numerical operations must be carried out over a given span of time, and this increases the round-off error for a given precision of the numbers being carried in the calculation. The design of numerical algorithms, as well as the choice of precisions and step sizes that maximize the speed of the calculation while keeping the errors within reasonable bounds, is almost an art form developed by extensive experience and ingenuity. For example, a scheme exists for extrapolating the step size to zero in order to find the change in the variables over a relatively short time span, thereby minimizing the accumulation of error from this source. If the total energy of the system is theoretically conserved, its evaluation for values of the variables at the beginning and end of a calculation is a measure of the errors that have accumulated.

The motion of the planets of the solar system over time scales approaching its 4.6-billion-year age is a classic n-body problem, where $n = 9$ with the Sun included. The question of whether or not the solar system is ultimately stable—whether the current configuration of the planets will be maintained indefinitely under their mutual perturbations, or whether one or another planet will eventually be lost from the system or otherwise have its orbit drastically altered—is a long-standing one that might someday be answered through numerical calculation. The interplay of orbital resonances and chaotic orbits can be investigated numerically, and this interplay may be crucial in determining the stability of the solar system. Already it appears that the parameters defining the orbits of several planets vary over narrow chaotic zones, but whether or not this chaos can lead to instability if given enough time is still uncertain.

If accelerations are determined by summing all the pairwise interactions for the n particles, the computer time per time step increases as n^2. Practical computations for the direct calculation of the interactions between all the particles are thereby limited to $n < 10{,}000$. Therefore, for larger values of n, schemes are used where a particle is assumed to move in the force field of the remaining particles approximated by that due to a continuum mass distribution, or a 'tree structure' is used where the effects of nearby particles are considered individually while larger and larger groups of particles are considered collectively as their distances increase. These later schemes have the capability of calculating the evolution of a very large system of particles using a reasonable amount of computer time with reasonable approximation. Values of n near 100,000 have been used in calculations determining the evolution of galaxies of stars.

Values of n in the billions have been used in calculations of galaxy formation in the early universe. Also, the consequences for distribution of stars when two galaxies closely approach one another or even collide has been determined. Even calculations of the n-body problem where n changes with time have been completed in the study of the accumulation of larger bodies from smaller bodies via collisions in the process of the formation of the planets.

In all n-body calculations, very close approaches of two particles can result in accelerations so large and so rapidly changing that large errors are introduced or the calculation completely diverges. Accuracy can sometimes be maintained in such a close approach, but only at the expense of requiring very short time steps, which drastically slows the calculation. When n is small, as in some solar system calculations where two-body orbits still dominate, close approaches are sometimes handled by a change to a set of variables, usually involving the eccentric anomaly u, that vary much less rapidly during the encounter.

In this process, called regularization, the encounter is traversed in less computer time while preserving reasonable accuracy. This process is impractical when n is large, so accelerations are usually artificially bounded on close approaches to prevent instabilities in the numerical calculation and to prevent slowing the calculation. For example, if several sets of particles were trapped in stable, close binary orbits, the very short time steps required to follow this rapid motion would bring the calculation to a virtual standstill, and such binary motion is not important in the overall evolution of, say, a galaxy of stars.

TIDAL DEVELOPMENT

This conversation has so far treated the celestial mechanics of bodies accelerated by conservative forces (total energy being conserved), including perturbations of elliptic motion by non-spherical mass distributions of finite-size bodies. However, the gravitational field of one body in close orbit about another will tidally distort the shape of the other body. Dissipation of part of the energy stored in these tidal distortions leads to a coupling that causes secular changes (always in the same direction) in the orbit and in the spins of both bodies. Since tidal dissipation accounts for the current spin states of several planets, the spin states of most of the planetary satellites and some of their orbital configurations, and the spins and orbits of close binary stars, it is appropriate that tides and their consequences be included in this discussion.

The twice-daily high and low tides in the ocean are known by all who have lived near a coast. Few are aware, however, that the solid body of Earth also experiences twice-daily tides with a maximum amplitude of about 30 centimetres. George Howard Darwin (1845–1912), the second son of Charles Darwin, the naturalist, was an astronomer-geophysicist who understood quantitatively the generation of the tides in the gravitational fields of tide-raising bodies, which are primarily the Moon and the Sun for Earth; he pointed out that the dissipation of tidal energy resulted in a slowing of Earth's rotation while the Moon's orbit was gradually expanded. That any mass raises a tide on every other mass within its gravitational field follows from the fact that the gravitational force between two masses decreases as the inverse square of the distance between them.

The accelerations due to mass m_s of three mass elements in the spherical mass m_p are proportional to the length of the arrows attached to each element. The element nearest m_s is accelerated more than the element at the centre of m_p and tends to leave the centre element behind; the element at the centre of m_p is accelerated more than the element farthest from m_s, and the latter tends to be left further behind. The point of view of a fictitious observer at the centre of m_p can be realised by subtracting the acceleration of the central mass element from that of each of the other two mass elements. If the mass elements were free, this observer would see the two extreme mass elements being accelerated in opposite directions away from his position at the centre.

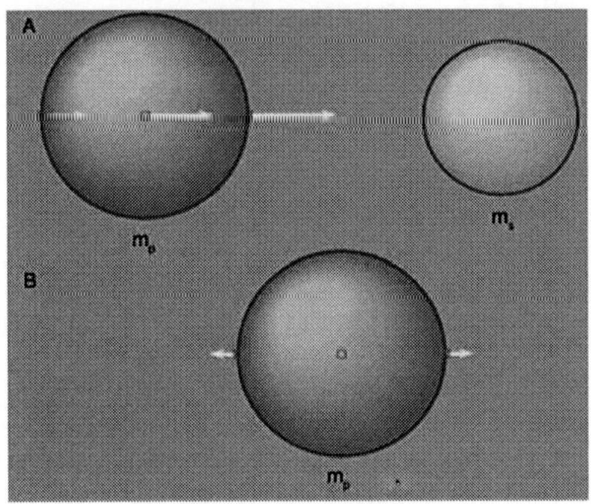

Fig. 2.3 Variation of Gravitational Acceleration Across a Finite-sized Body Leading to Differential Acceleration Relative to its Centre

But the mass elements are not free; they are gravitationally attracted to one another and to the remaining mass in m_p. The gravitational acceleration of the mass elements on the surface of m_p towards the centre of m_p far exceeds the differential acceleration due to the gravitational attraction of m_s, thus the elements do not fly off. If m_p were incompressible and perfectly rigid, the mass elements on the surface would weigh a little less than they would if m_s were not there but would not move relative to the centre of m_p.

If m_p were fluid or otherwise not rigid, it would distort into an oval shape in the presence of m_s. The reason for this distortion is that the mass elements making up m_p that do not lie on the line joining the centres of m_p and m_s also experience a differential acceleration. Such differential accelerations are not perpendicular to the surface, however, and are therefore not compensated by the self-gravity that accelerates mass elements towards the centre of m_p.

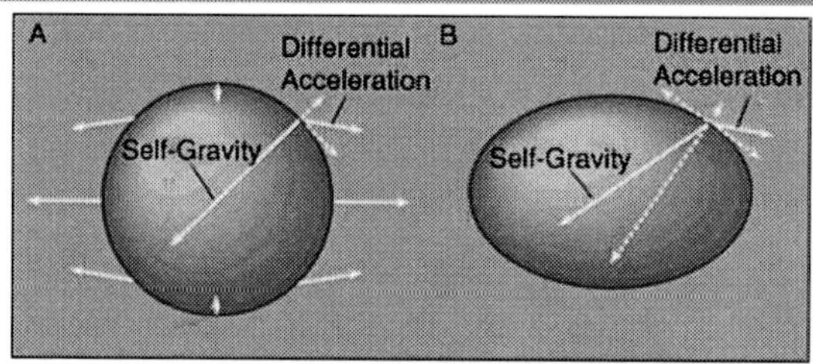

Fig. 2.4 (A) Uncompensated Tangential Accelerations Cause (B) Tidal Distortions in which all the Differential Accelerations are Balanced by the Change in the Self-gravitational Acceleration Resulting from the Distortion and by Internal Stresses

The differential accelerations is resolved into two components (dotted arrows), one perpendicular and one tangential to the surface. The perpendicular component is compensated by the self-gravity; the tangential component is not. If m_p were entirely fluid, the uncompensated tangential components of the differential accelerations due to m_s would cause mass to flow towards the points on m_p that were either closest to m_s or farthest from m_s until m_p would resemble. In this shape the self-gravity is no longer perpendicular to the surface but has a component opposite the tangential component of the differential acceleration. Only in this distorted shape will all the differential accelerations be compensated and the entire body accelerated like the centre. If m_p is not fluid but is rigid like rock or iron, part of the compensating acceleration will be provided by internal stress forces, and the body will distort less. As no material is perfectly rigid, there is always some tidal bulge, and compressibility of the material will farther enhance this bulge. Note that the tidal distortion is independent of the orbital motion and would also occur if m_p and m_s were simply falling towards each other. (There is a similar tide raised on m_s by m_p that will be ignored for the present.)

If m_p rotates relative to m_s, an observer on the surface of m_p would successively rotate through the maxima and minima of the tidal distortion, which would tend to remain aligned with the direction to m_s. The observer would thereby experience two high and two low tides a day, as observed on

Earth. Some of the energy of motion of any fluid parts of m_p and some of the energy stored as distortion of the solid parts as the tides wax and wane is converted into heat, and this dissipation of mechanical energy causes a delay in the response of the body to the tide-raising force. This means that high tide would occur at a given point on m_p as it rotates relative to m_s after m_s passes overhead. (On Earth, the continents alter the motion of the fluid ocean so much that ocean tides at continental coasts do not always lag the passage of the Moon overhead.) If m_p rotates in the same direction as m_s revolves in its orbit, the tidal bulge is carried ahead of m_s, and angle δ.

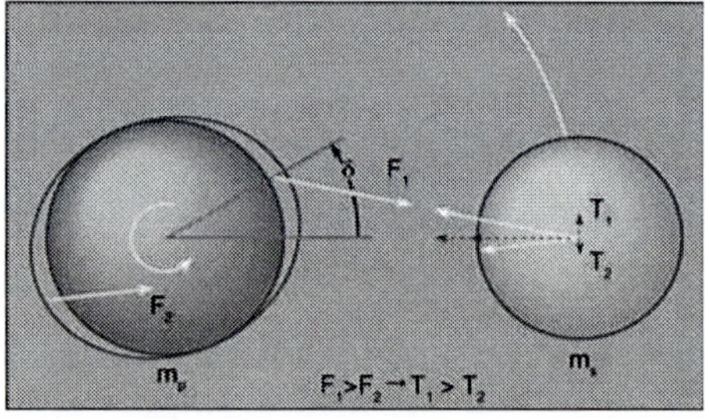

Fig. 2.5 Unequal Forces on Two Tidal Bulges, Leading to Retardation of the Spin of *mp* and an Acceleration of *ms* in its Orbit.

Again, because the gravitational force between two masses varies as the inverse square of their separation, the tidal bulge closest to m_s experiences a greater attraction towards m_s than does the bulge farthest away (F_2). As these two forces are not aligned with the centre of m_p, there is a twisting effect, or torque, on m_p that retards its rate of rotation. This retardation will continue until the rotation is synchronous with the mean orbital motion of m_s. This has happened for the Moon, which keeps the same face towards Earth.

From Newton's third law, there are equal and opposite forces acting on m_s corresponding to F_1 and F_2. These forces are represented as T_1 and T_2, and each has been resolved into two components, one directed towards the centre of m_p and the other perpendicular to this direction. The inequality of these forces causes a net acceleration of m_s in its orbit, which thereby expands, as is observed for the Moon. Both the observed increase in the length of one day of 0.0016 second per century and the observed recession of the Moon of 3 to 4 centimetres per year are understood as consequences of the tides raised on Earth.

It has been assumed that the spin axis of m_p is perpendicular to the plane of the orbit of m_s. If the spin axis is inclined to this plane, the tidal bulge is carried out of the plane as well as ahead of m_s. This means that there is a twist, or torque, that changes the direction of the spin axis, so both the magnitude of spin and the direction of the spin axis experience a tidal evolution. The end point of tidal evolution for the spin state of one body of an isolated pair is rotation synchronous with the mean orbital motion with the spin axis perpendicular to the orbit plane. This simple picture is complicated somewhat if other perturbations cause the orbital plane to process. This precession for the lunar orbit causes its spin axis to be inclined 6°412 to the orbit plane as the end point of tidal evolution.

In addition to those of the Earth-Moon pair, numerous other consequences of tidal dissipation and the resulting evolution can be observed in the solar system and elsewhere in the Milky Way Galaxy. For example, all the major and close planetary satellites but one are observed to be rotating synchronously with their orbital motion. The exception is Saturn's satellite Hyperion. Tidal friction has indeed retarded Hyperion's initial spin rate to a value near that of synchronous rotation, but the combination of Hyperion's unusually asymmetric shape and its high orbital eccentricity leads to gravitational torques that make synchronous rotation unstable. As a result, the tides have brought Hyperion to a state where it tumbles chaotically with large changes in the direction and magnitude of its spin on time scales comparable to its orbital period of about 21 days.

The assembly and maintenance of several orbital resonances among the satellites because of differential tidal expansion of the orbits have also been observed. The orbital resonances among Jupiter's satellites Io, Europa, and Ganymede, where the orbital periods are nearly in the ratio 1:2:4, maintain Io's orbital eccentricity at the value of 0.0041.

This rather modest eccentricity causes sufficient variation in the magnitude and direction of Io's enormous tidal bulge to have melted a significant fraction of the satellite through dissipation of tidal energy in spite of Io's synchronous rotation. As a result, Io is the most volcanically active body in the solar system. The orbital eccentricity would normally be damped to zero by this large dissipation, but the orbital resonances with Europa and Ganymede prevent this from happening.

The remote dwarf planet Pluto and its satellite Charon have almost certainly reached the ultimate end point where further tidal evolution has ceased altogether (the tiny tides raised by the Sun and other planets being neglected). In this state the orbit is circular, with both bodies rotating synchronously with the orbital motion and both spin axes perpendicular to the orbital plane.

Chapter 3

Celestial Sphere and Time

CELESTIAL SPHERE

It is useful in discuss objects in the sky to imagine them to be attached to a sphere surrounding the earth. This fictitious construction is called the *celestial sphere*. At any one time we see no more than half of this sphere, but we will refer loosely to the imaginary half-sphere over our heads as just the celestial sphere.

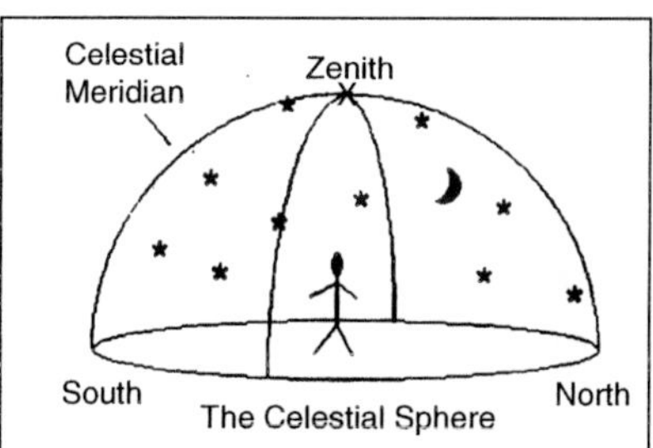

The Celestial Sphere

The point on the celestial sphere that is directly over our heads at a given time is termed the *zenith*. The imaginary circle passing through the North and South points on our horizon and through the zenith is termed the *celestial meridian*. We will introduce additional terminology associated with the celestial sphere later.

Motion in the Sky

It is obvious after only minimal observation that objects change their position in the sky over a period of time. This motion is conveniently separated into two parts:

- The entire sky appears to turn around imaginary points in the northern and southern sky once in 24 hours. This is termed the daily or *diurnal motion* of the celestial sphere, and is in reality a consequence of the daily rotation of the earth on its axis. The diurnal motion affects all objects in the sky and does not change their *relative* positions: the diurnal motion causes the sky to rotate as a whole once every 24 hours.
- Superposed on the overall diurnal motion of the sky is 'intrinsic' motion that causes certain objects on the celestial sphere to change their positions with respect to the other objects on the celestial sphere. These are the 'wanderers' of the ancient astronomers: the planets, the Sun, and the Moon.

CELESTIAL COORDINATE SYSTEMS

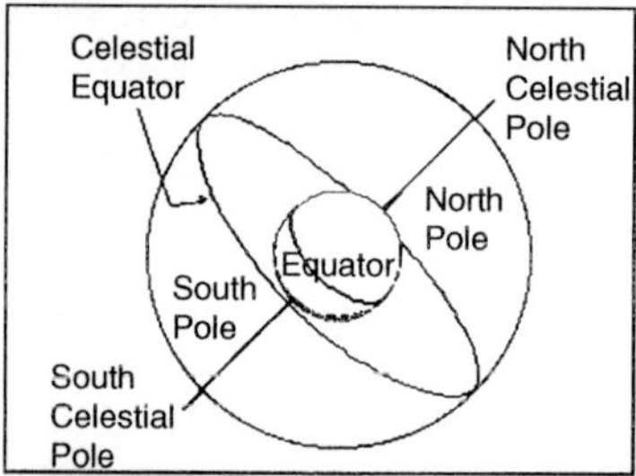

We can describe a useful coordinate system for locating objects on the celestial sphere by projecting onto the sky the latitude-longitude coordinate system that we use on the surface of the earth.

As illustrated in the adjacent figure, this allows us to define 'North and South Celestial Poles' (the imaginary points about which the diurnal motion appears to take place) and a 'Celestial Equator'.

The figure illustrates that these imaginary objects are the exact analogs of the corresponding imaginary objects on the surface of the earth. Thus, we shall be able to specify the precise location of things on the celestial sphere by giving the celestial analog of their latitudes and longtitudes, or something related to those quantities.

The 'Road of the Sun' on the Celestial Sphere

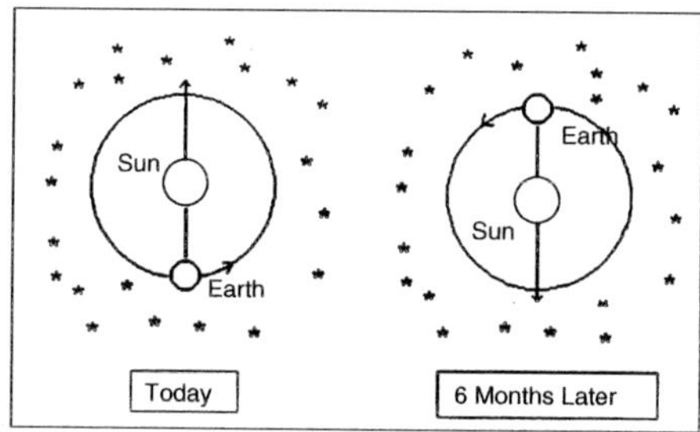

Another important imaginary object on the celestial sphere is the 'ecliptic' or 'Road of the Sun', which is the imaginary path that the Sun follows on the celestial sphere over the course of a year. As the diagram at left indicates, the apparent position of the sun with respect to the background stars (as viewed from Earth) changes continuously as the Earth moves around its orbit, and will return to its starting point when the Earth has made one revolution in its orbit.

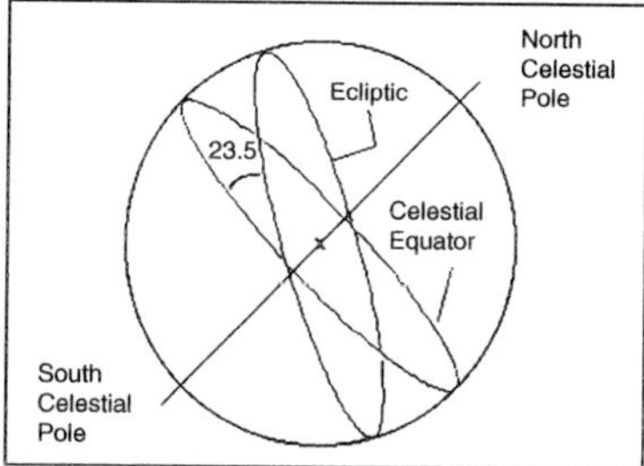

Thus, the Sun traces out a closed path on the celestial sphere once each year. This apparent path of the Sun on the celestial sphere is called the *ecliptic*.

Because the rotation axis of the Earth is tilted by 23.5 degrees with respect to the plane of its orbital motion (which is also called the ecliptic), the path of the Sun on the celestial sphere is a circle tilted by 23.5 degrees with respect to the celestial equator.

The ecliptic is important observationally, because the planets, the Sun (by definition), and the Moon are always found near the ecliptic. This is because all of these objects have orbits that lie nearly in the same spatial plane.

East and West on the Celestial Sphere

It is helpful to define east and west directions on the celestial sphere, as illustrated in the following figure.

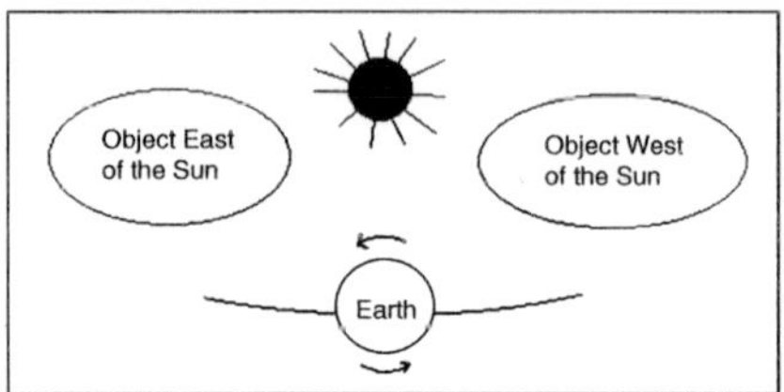

Thus, objects to the west of the Sun on the celestial sphere precede the Sun in the diurnal motion of the celestial sphere (they 'rise' before the Sun and 'set' before the Sun). Likewise, objects to the east of the Sun trail the Sun in the diurnal motion (they 'rise' after the Sun and 'set' after the Sun). Generally, one object is west of another object if it 'rises' before the other object over the eastern horizon as the sky appears to turn, and east of the object if it 'rises' after the other object.

THE PERCEPTIBLE MOTION OF PLANETS ON THE CELESTIAL SPHERE

Two observations about the planets were very difficult to explain for astronomers of the Middle Ages:

- The usual motion of planets as they 'wandered' on the celestial sphere was eastward against the background stars. This is called 'Direct Motion'. However, it was observed that at times the planets moved westward for some period on the celestial sphere; this was termed 'Retrograde Motion'. The episodes of retrograde motion were difficult to explain.

- The planets were observed to be brighter at certain times than others. This varying brightness was also a challenge to explain.

Both retrograde motion and varying brightness are illustrated in the adjacent animation.

A major reason for the difficulty of explaining these features was the dominance of the Greek philosopher Aristotle on mediaeval thought. This philosophy held that the heavens were more perfect than the Earth, and that objects in the heavens were unchanging. As part of this philosophy, it was believed that the only motion permitted objects in the heavens was *uniform circular motion* (motion at constant angular speed on a circle), because such motion brought one back cyclically to the starting point and therefore was (in a sense) unchanging.

This philosophy had no problem with the direct motion of the planets, since that could be explained by uniform circular motion of the planets about the Earth (which, as any fool who looked at the sky could see, was clearly the centre of the Universe). However, neither the varying brightness of the planets, nor the occasional retrograde motion of the planets on the celestial sphere, were easily reconciled with this idea of unchanging objects executing uniform circular motion in the heavens.

The celestial sphere that we introduced previously is a convenient fiction to locate objects in the sky. However, the Greek philosopher Aristotle (many of Aristotles works are available at the Internet Classics Archive) proposed that the heavens were literally composed of 55 concentric, crystalline spheres to which the celestial objects were attached and which rotated at different velocities (but the angular velocity was constant for a given sphere), with the Earth at the centre. The following figure illustrates the ordering of the spheres to which the Sun, Moon, and visible planets were attached.

There were additional 'buffering' spheres that lay between the spheres illustrated. The sphere of the stars lay beyond the ones shown here for the planets; finally, in the Aristotelian conception there was an outermost sphere that was the domain of the 'Prime Mover'. The Prime Mover caused the outermost sphere to rotate at constant angular velocity, and this motion was imparted from sphere to sphere, thus causing the whole thing to rotate.

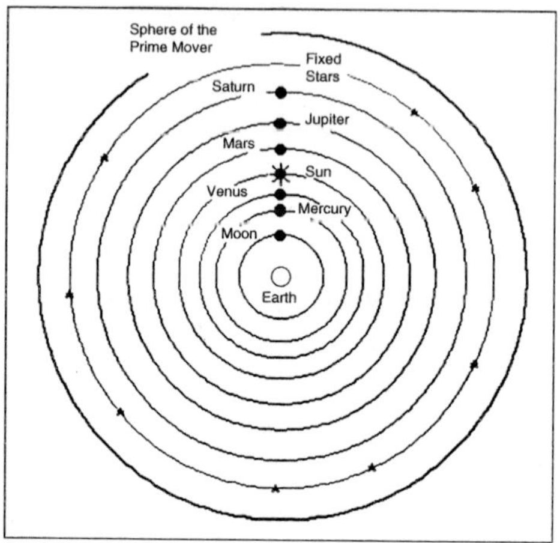

By adjusting the velocities of these concentric spheres, many features of planetary motion could be explained. However, the troubling observations of varying planetary brightness and retrograde motion could not be accommodated: the spheres moved with constant angular velocity, and the objects attached to them were always the same distance from the earth because they moved on spheres with the earth at the centre.

Epicycles and Planetary Motion

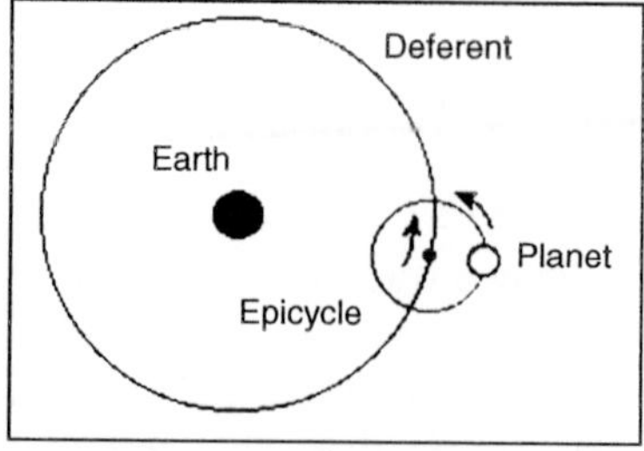

The 'solution' to these problems came in the form of a mad, but clever proposal: planets were attached, not to the concentric spheres themselves, but to circles attached to the concentric spheres, as illustrated in the adjacent diagram. These circles were called 'Epicycles', and the concentric spheres to which they were attached were termed the 'Deferents'. Then, the centres of the epicycles executed uniform circular motion as they went around the deferent at uniform angular velocity, and at the same time the epicyles (to which the planets were attached) executed their own uniform circular motion.

The net effect was as illustrated in the following animation. As the centre of the epicycle moves around the deferent at constant angular velocity, the planet moves around the epicycle, also at constant angular velocity. The apparent position of the planet on the celestial sphere at each time is indicated by the line drawn from the earth through the planet and projected onto the celestial sphere. The resulting apparent path against the background stars is indicated by the line.

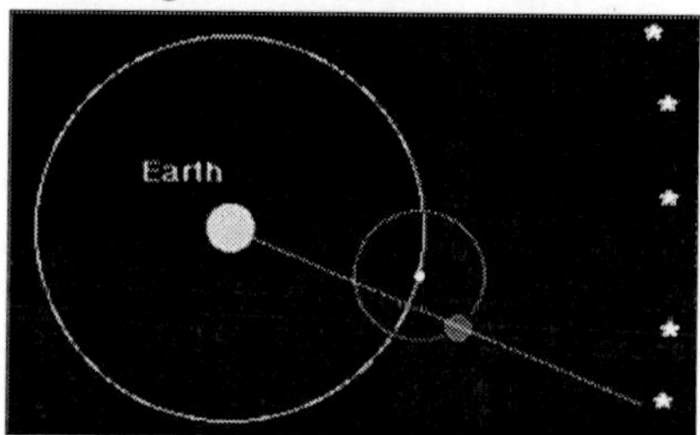

Now, in this tortured model one sees that it is possible to have retrograde motion and varying brightness, since at times as viewed from the earth the planet can appear to move 'backward' on the celestial sphere. Obviously, the distance of the planet from the Earth also varies with time, which leads to variations in brightness. Thus, the idea of uniform circular motion is saved (at least in some sense) by this scheme, and it allows a description of retrograde motion and varying planetary brightness.

Supplementary Sophisticated Epicycles: The Ptolemaic Universe

Though, in practice, even this was not enough to account for the detailed motion of the planets on the celestial sphere!

In more sophisticated epicycle models further 'refinements' were introduced:

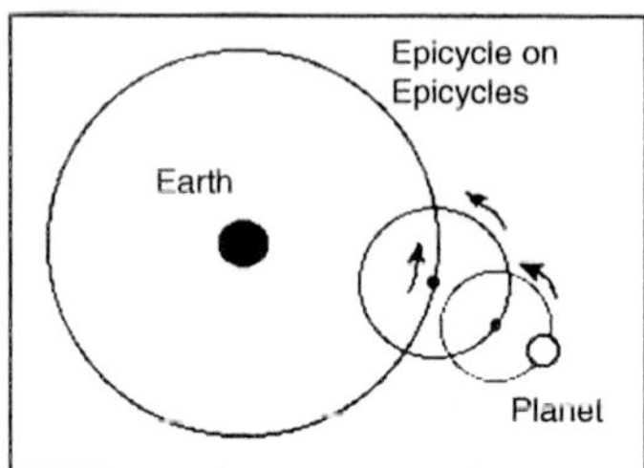

- In some cases, epicycles were themselves placed on epicycles, as illustrated in the adjacent figure.
- In actual models, the centre of the epicycle moved with uniform circular motion, not around the centre of the deferent, but around a point that was displaced by some distance from the centre of the deferent.

That ancient astronomers could convince themselves that this elaborate scheme still corresponded to 'uniform circular motion' is testament to the power of three ideas that we now know to be completely wrong, but that were so ingrained in the astronomers of an earlier age that they were essentially never questioned:

- All motion in the heavens is uniform circular motion;
- The objects in the heavens are made from perfect material, and cannot change their intrinsic properties (*e.g.*, their brightness)'
- The Earth is at the centre of the Universe.

These ideas concerning uniform circular motion and epicycles were catalogued by Ptolemy in 150 A.D. His book was called the 'Almagest' (literally, "The Greatest"), and this picture of the structure of the Solar System has come to be called the 'Ptolemaic Universe'.

Mediaeval Aristotelian Astronomy

By the Middle Ages, such ideas took on a new power as the philosophy of Aristotle (newly rediscovered in Europe) was wedded to Medieval theology in the great synthesis of Christianity and Reason undertaken by philsopher-theologians such as Thomas Aquinas. The Prime Mover of Aristotle's universe became the God of Christian theology, the outermost sphere of the Prime Mover became identified with the Christian Heaven, and the position of the Earth at the centre of it all was understood in terms of the concern that the Christian God had for the affairs of mankind.

Thus, the ideas largely originating with pagan Greek philosophers were baptized into the Catholic church and eventually assumed the power of religious dogma: to challenge this view of the Universe was not merely a scientific issue; it became a theological one as well, and subjected dissenters to the considerable and not always benevolent power of the Church.

TIMEKEEPING AND THE CELESTIAL SPHERE

In this segment we deal with general properties of the celestial sphere: constellations, the naming of stars, and a general coordinate system for the celestial sphere that is analogous to the latitude-longitude system on the surface of the Earth and that allows us to specify precisely a location on the celestial sphere. We shall also consider some general aspects of timekeeping and calendars, because historically, the regular apparent motions of the heavens provided many of the ideas and much of the terminology that we use in timekeeping.

The Constellations

Historically, constellations were groupings of stars that were thought to outline the shape of something, usually with mythological significance. There are 88 recognized constellations, with their names tracing as far back as Mesopotamia, 5000 years ago.

The Historical Constellations

In some cases one can discern easily the purported shape; for example, the constellation Leo shown on the right might actually look like a lion with the dots connected as they are. In other cases the supposed shape is very much in the eye of the beholder, as the example of Canis Minor (The Little Dog) shown on the left indicates. This certainly *could* be a little dog, or a cow, or a submarine.

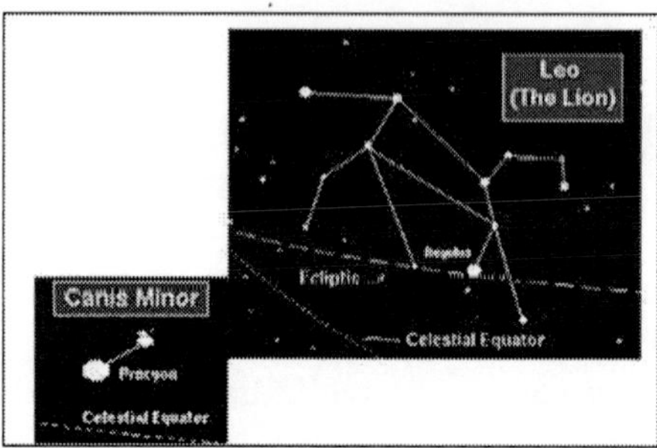

Star Groupings and Asterisms

Some of the more familiar 'constellations' are technically not constellations at all. For example, the grouping of stars known as the Big Dipper is probably familiar to most, but it is not actually a constellation. The Big Dipper is part of a larger grouping of stars called the Big Bear (*Ursa Major*) that *is* a constellation.

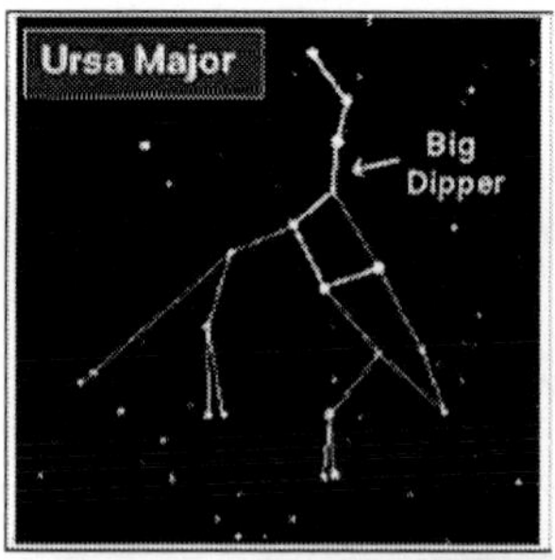

A well-known grouping of stars like the Big Dipper that is not officially recognized as a constellation is called an *asterism*.

Constellations Are Not Physical Groupings

The obvious groupings of stars into constellations that we see on the celestial sphere are not physical groupings. In nearly all cases the stars in constellations and asterisms are each very different distances from us, and only appear to be grouped because they lie in approximately the same direction. This is illustrated in the following figure for the stars of the Big Dipper, where their physical distance from the Earth is drawn to scale (numbers beside each star give the distance from Earth in light years).

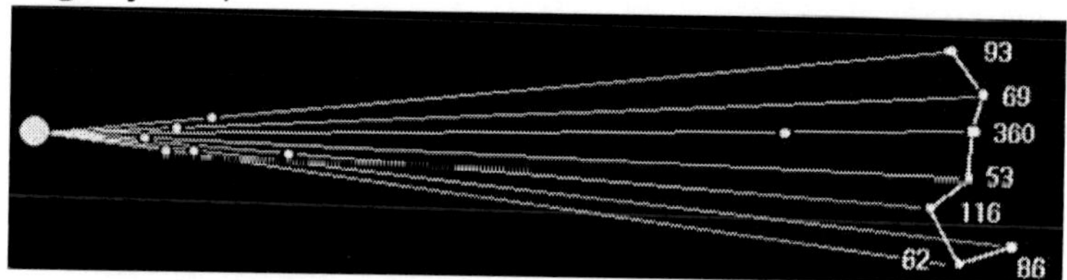

Fig. 3.1 The Relative Distances to Stars in the Big Dipper

It is important to make this distinction because later we shall consider groupings that *are* physical groupings, such as star clusters and binary star systems.

The Constellations of the Zodiac

The *zodiac* is an imaginary band 18 degrees wide and centered on the ecliptic. The constellations that fall in the zodiac are called the *12 constellations of the zodiac*. They were at one time thought to have great mystical and astrological significance.

Astrology is bunk, but the constellations of the zodiac are still of importance because the planets, as well as the Sun and Moon, are all near or on the ecliptic at any given time; thus, they are always found within one of the zodiac constellations.

Constellations in Modern Astronomy

In contemporary astronomy, the significance of constellations is no longer mythological, but practical: constellations define imaginary regions of the sky, just as the individual states each define an imaginary region of the United States. Thus, to say that a planet is in the constellation Leo is to partially locate the planet on the celestial sphere, just as saying that Knoxville is in Tennessee is to partially locate the city on the surface of the Earth. As for states, modern constellations have irregular boundaries that have been agreed upon for various reasons, perhaps not always completely logical.

Drawing the Constellations

Here are two pieces of software that allow you to construct maps of the sky at specified times (now, or in the past or future) that include constellations:

- Starry Night is a $28 shareware programme for the Macintosh that simulates the appearance and motion of the sky from a user chosen vantage point and at a user chosen time.

NAMING THE STARS

The stars on the celestial sphere are named in several different ways. As a result, the brighter stars may have more than one name. We give a brief overview of naming stars here.

Common Names

The majority of the brighter stars in the sky have common names that are of historical and mythological significance. For example, the bright red star in the shoulder region of the constellation Orion (the Hunter) is called Betelgeuse, which comes from Arabic and means (roughly) "the armpit of the mighty one". The brightest star in Orion is a blue-white star called Rigel that is situated at the opposite corner of the constellation from Betelgeuse.

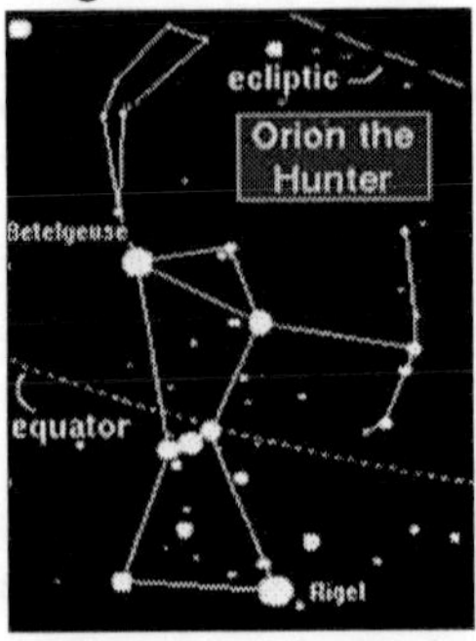

As another example, the brightest star in the constellation Cygnus (the Swan) is situated near the aft portion of the beast and is called Deneb, which is also Arabic in origin and means 'the tail of the hen'.

The Bayer Naming System

Common names are fine for a few bright stars, but we need a more systematic method to name all the stars that we see.

One more systematic method is the Bayer system, which names the brighter stars by assigning a constellation (using the Latin possessive of the name) and a greek letter (Alpha, Beta, Gamma, Delta, Epsilon,...) in an approximate order of decreasing brightness for stars in the constellation. Betelgeuse is also called *Alpha-Orionis* and Rigel is called *Beta Orionis* in the Bayer system.

The ordering of stars by brightness in the classical Bayer system is only approximate. For example, Rigel (Beta Orionis) is actually slightly brighter than Betelgeuse (Alpha Orionis), and Kappa Orionis is considerably brighter than the position of Kappa in the Greek alphabet would suggest.

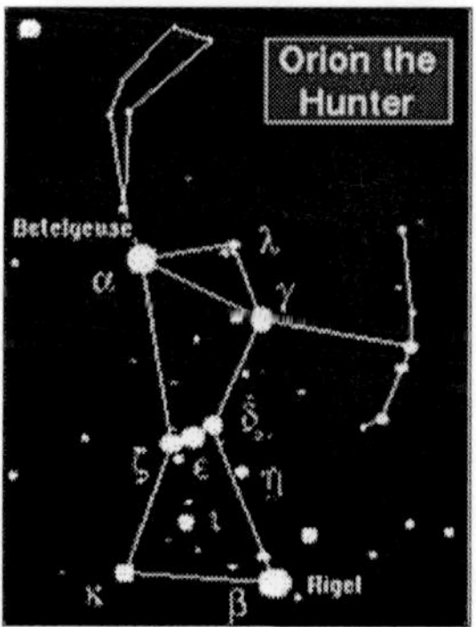

As a final example, the brightest star in the nighttime sky is Sirius, which is in the constellation Canis Major and is termed *Alpha Canis Majoris* in the Bayer naming system. Here is a list of 70 of the brighter stars, including common names, Bayer names, positions on the celestial sphere, and spectral class.

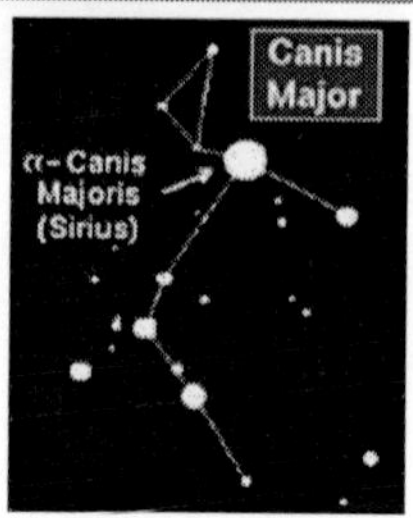

The Flamsteed Naming System

The Bayer system is a little more systematic than a set of common names, but there are only a finite number of letters in the Greek alphabet, so it cannot be used easily to name very many stars. The Flamsteed naming system can in principle be used to name any number of stars. In this system one uses the same Latin possessive of the constellation name as in the Bayer system, but the stars are distinguished, not by their brightness, but by their nearness to the western edge of the constellation by assigning an arabic numeral. Thus, the closest star to the western edge of the constellation Cygnus is called *1-Cygni* in the Flamsteed system and *61-Cygni* denotes the star that is the 61st closest to the western edge.

Star Catalogues

There are various specialized star catalogues in which stars may be given names according to some convention. Such specialized catalogues are of importance in astronomical research, but we won't discuss them further in our introductory course.

LOCATING STAR MAPS AND CONSTELLATIONS

Locating stars and constellations on the celestial sphere is facilitated by a *star map*. The following fig. 3.2 is an example of a star map of the northern hemisphere sky for a winter evening.

This star map was produced by the Star Maps on demand service of Mount Wilson Observatory. Another source of star maps is the Starry Night programme for Windows and Macintosh computers. Here is an online map that shows the position on the celestial sphere of the Sun, Moon, and planets for arbitrary time, date, latitude, and longitude of the observer.

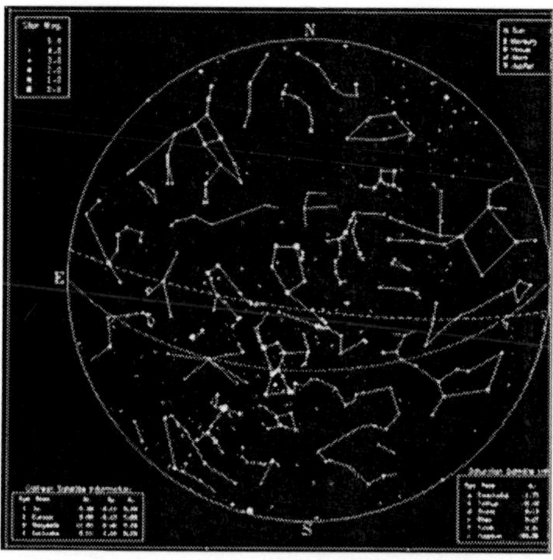

Fig. 3.2 Star Map for Winter Evening in the Northern Hemisphere

To use star maps effectively, you need to know your latitude and longitude on the surface of the Earth, and the offset of your timezone from the Greenwich meridian. Here is a link to the Census Gazeteer, which will return latitude and longitude of locations in U.S. specified by either name or zip code. Likewise, here is a link to information about timekeeping and timezones.

CELESTIAL SPHERE COORDINATE SYSTEM

It is helpful to impose on the celestial sphere a coordinate system that is analogous to the latitude-longitude system employed for the surface of the Earth.

Right Ascension and Declination in Coordinate System

This coordinate system is illustrated in the following figure 3.3.

In the celestial coordinate system the North and South Celestial Poles are determined by projecting the rotation axis of the Earth to intersect the celestial sphere, which in turn defines a Celestial Equator. The celestial equivalent of latitude is called *declination* and is measured in degrees North (positive numbers) or South (negative numbers) of the Celestial Equator.

The celestial equivalent of longitude is called *right ascension*. Right ascension can be measured in degrees, but for historical reasons it is more common to measure it in time (hours, minutes, seconds): the sky turns 360 degrees in 24 hours and therefore it must turn 15 degrees every hour; thus, 1 hour of right ascension is equivalent to 15 degrees of (apparent) sky rotation.

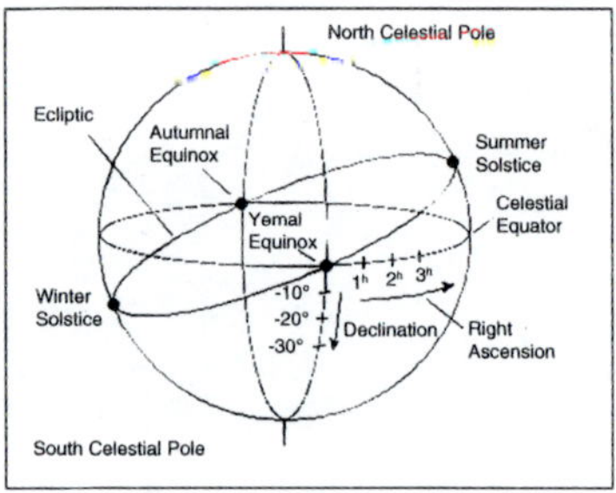

Fig. 3.3 The Celestial Coordinate System

Equinoxes and Solstices

The zero point for celestial longitude (that is, for right ascension) is the *Vernal Equinox*, which is that intersection of the ecliptic and the celestial equator near where the Sun is located in the Northern Hemisphere Spring. The other intersection of the Celestial Equator and the Ecliptic is termed the *Autumnal Equinox*. When the Sun is at one of the equinoxes the lengths of day and night are equivalent (*equinox* derives from a root meaning "equal night"). The time of the Vernal Equinox is typically about March 21 and of the Autumnal Equinox about September 22.

The point on the ecliptic where the Sun is most north of the celestial equator is termed the Summer Solstice and the point where it is most south of the celestial equator is termed the Winter Solstice. In the Northern Hemisphere the hours of daylight are longest when the Sun is near the Summer Solstice (around June 22) and shortest when the Sun is near the Winter Solstice (around December 22). The opposite is true in the Southern Hemisphere. The term *solstice* derives from a root that means to 'stand still'; at the solstices the Sun reaches its most northern or most southern position in the sky and begins to move back towards the celestial equator. Thus, it 'stands still' with respect to its apparent North-South drift on the celestial sphere at that time.

Traditionally, Northern Hemisphere Spring and Fall begin at the times of the corresponding equinoxes, while Northern Hemisphere Winter and Summer begin at the corresponding solstices. In the Southern Hemisphere, the seasons are reversed (*e.g.*, Southern Hemisphere Spring begins at the time of the Autumnal Equinox).

Coordinates on the Celestial Sphere Stipulate

The Right Ascension (R.A.) and Declination (dec) of an object on the celestial sphere specify its position uniquely, just as the latitude and longitude of an object on the Earth's surface define a unique location. Thus, for example, the star Sirius has celestial coordinates 6 hr 45 min R.A. and -16 degrees 43 minutes declination, as illustrated in the following figure 3.4.

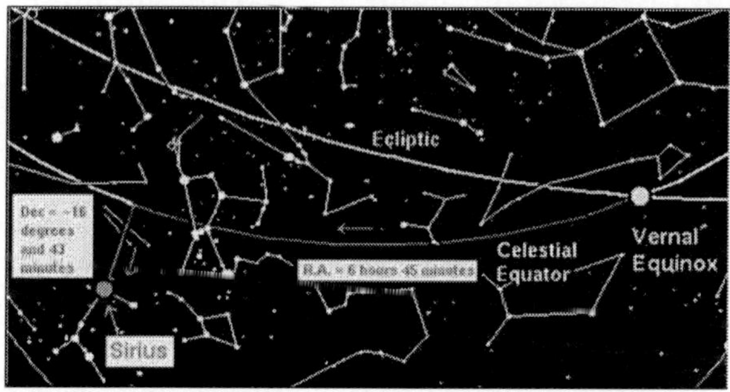

Fig. 3.4 Right Ascension and Declination for Sirius

This tells us that when the vernal equinox is on our celestial meridian, it will be 6 hours and 45 minutes before Sirius crosses our celestial meridian, and also that Sirius is a little more than 16 degrees South of the Celestial Equator.

Keeping your Perspective in Celestial Sphere

Do not turn into confused because the perspectives in the celestial sphere diagram and the sky segment diagram containing Sirius are different. In the celestial sphere diagram one is imagining an *outside view* of the celestial sphere. The position of Sirius in the sky the view is instead the actual sky *as viewed from the Earth.*

Thus, the directions get reversed: moving to the right from the vernal equinox in the first diagram will look like moving to the left as viewed from its centre, which is the perspective of the second diagram (that is, the actual view of the sky from Earth). That direction, by convention, is chosen to be the positive direction for right ascension.

ASTRONOMICAL TIME KEEPING

Timekeeping

In the past, the regular motion of objects in the sky served as the basis for timekeeping. The diurnal motion of the sky caused by the rotation of the Earth on its axis defined the day, the year was defined by the motion of the Earth on its orbit about the Sun, and the month was defined in relation to the revolution of the Moon about the Earth. Although precise modern timekeeping is done electronically, many of the details and the terminology of timekeeping remain rooted in its astronomical heritage.

Siderial Time

The siderial time is deduced from the revolution of the Earth with admiration to the distant stars and can therefore be determined from nightly observations of the starry sky. A siderial day can be defined in a first approximation as the time interval between two successive passages of the same star through the meridian. Here, the meridian of an observational site is the great circle passing through the two celestial poles and the zenith of the site. Expressed in different words, the meridian is the projection of the circle of the site's geographical longitude onto the celestial sphere if projected from the Earth's centre. The passage through the meridian is thus a more accurate determination of the point in time when—in colloquial speech—the star is due south (at least for observers on the northern hemisphere). The duration of a siderial day in units of Universal Time is 23h 56m 04.0905s. To describe more precisely the length of a siderial day and to establish a zero-point for the counting of siderial time, the terms 'hour angle', 'ecliptic', 'celestial equator', and 'vernal equinox' must be introduced. Through any point on the celestial sphere—for example the position of a star—and the two celestial poles passes a uniquely defined great circle that in general does not coincide with the meridian but cuts the meridian at the celestial poles. The cutting angle is called the hour angle of the particular point. This angle isn't usually measured in degrees but in hours, minutes and seconds (hence the name). The full circle of 360 degrees corresponds to exactly 24 hours. Because of Earth's rotation, the hour angle grows by 24 hours within one siderial day.

The celestial equator is the set of all points on the celestial sphere that are 90 degrees away from the celestial poles, or—equivalently—the projection of Earth's equator onto the celestial sphere, if projected from Earth's centre. The ecliptic is the Sun's path on the celestial sphere, among the stars, during the year. The celestial equator and the ecliptic do not coincide (a consequence of the Earth's rotation axis being tilted) but cross each other in two points one of which is called the vernal equinox.

0 o'clock siderial time is defined as the instance when the vernal equinox passes through the meridian. This definition can be generalized to: "Siderial time is the hour angle of the vernal equinox." Of course, the vernal equinox is a fictitious point on the celestial sphere and cannot be observed directly. From the known coordinates of observed stars, however, the location of the vernal equinox can be deduced. A siderial day is the interval between two successive passages of the vernal equinox through the meridian. According to this final definition, a siderial day is shorter by about 9 milliseconds than the approximation given at the beginning. This is a consequence of the fact that due to Earth's precession the vernal equinox is moving with respect to the stars. The local meridian and therefore leads to a siderial time that is

dependent on the place of observation. To define a global standard of siderial time, one refers to the meridian of Greenwich and calls the time scale so derived the "Greenwich Mean Siderial Time" (GMST). To convert between GMST and local siderial time, the geographical longitude of the observation site must be known.

From the siderial time and the celestial coordinates of a star (in particular the right ascension) the hour angle of the star and hence its current apparent position (that is constantly changing because of Earth's rotation) can be computed. Moreover, siderial time is one of the constituents of Universal Time.

Solar Time

Solar time follows the apparent revolution of the Sun around the Earth. A solar day is the interval between two successive passages of the Sun through the meridan, or—colloquially—from noon to noon. Of course, this apparent revolution only reflects the true rotation of the Earth. However, because in the run of one day the Earth also travels a considerable part of its orbit around the Sun, a complete rotation with respect to the Sun lasts longer than a complete rotation with respect to the stars. Consequently, a true solar day is longer by about 4 minutes than a siderial day.

The orientation point of the true solar time again can be expressed as an hour angle. Since the time reading at the Sun's passage through the meridian should be 12 h, though, the true solar time comes out as the hour angle of the anti-sun (which is the fictitious point on the ecliptic opposite to the Sun). A sundial displays the true solar time at its location.

The period of the true solar day varies with the seasons. This is a consequence both of the eccentricity of the Earth's orbit and the obliquity of the ecliptic (the tilt of Earth's rotation axis). Firstly, the Earth moves at different speeds in different parts of its elliptical orbit, according to Kepler's second law, hence the sun seems to move at different speeds among the stars. Secondly, even with a perfectly circular Earth orbit, the Sun would move evenly along the ecliptic but its projection onto the celestial equator would move at varying speeds. In spring and autumn, the Sun is close to the crossing points of ecliptic and celestial equator. Its movement from day to day therefore is slanted to the equator, the projected velocity is thus reduced. During summer and winter, however, the Sun is close to a vertex of the ecliptic and moves parallel to the celestial equator, making the projected velocity large. Both effects result in a variation of the 4 minutes correction to the siderial day, with the obliquity of the ecliptic having the slightly larger influence.

To obtain a more even time scale, one defines a fictitious "Mean Sun". This Mean Sun takes the same time from one vernal equinox to the next as the true Sun, but it is supposed to move with constant velocity along the celestial equator. Mean Solar Time is therefore the hour angle of the mean anti-sun.

The difference between True and Mean Solar Time is called the equation of time. Because two different effects with different time scales overlap (the eccentricity causes a period of one year, the obliquity of the ecliptic one of half a year), the equation of time has two minima and two maxima per year:

~ 11. Feb	~ – 14.5	min
~ 14. Mai	~ + 4	min
~ 26. Jul	~ – 6.4	min
~ 3. Nov	~ + 16.3	min

The equation of time also causes asymmetrical shifts of the rising and setting times of the Sun. The earliest sunset, for instance, does not happen on the winter solstice on Dec. 22 but about 11 days earlier. The latest sunrise on the other hand happens about 10 days after the winter solstice. For the same reason, morning and afternoon have different lengths on the equinoces on Mar 21 and Sep 23.

Universal Time (UT) and Greenwich Time

The Universal Time (UT) was introduced in the year 1926 to replace the Greenwich Mean Time (GMT). At this time, several definitions of GMT were in use, sometimes with considerable differences. The term GMT had thus become useless and was dropped and replaced by a more stringent definition of UT.

For the majority practical purposes, UT is equivalent to the Mean Solar Time for the Greenwich reference meridian. The relation between UT and local Mean Solar Time is the same as between Greenwich Mean Siderial Time and local Siderial Time. Basically, however, UT is not a solar time in the sense that the observed solar position would be used to define this time. The achievable accuracy for a measurement of the Sun's position is far too insufficient for this purpose. Instead, UT is derived from the more precise Siderial Time by means of a mathematical formula. This formula accounts for the known shape of Earth's orbit with which the position of the fictitious Mean Sun can be calculated. Consequently, UT and Siderial Time are not independent time scales but two forms of the same scale, although with units of different length.

Upon closer inspection, the Universal Time has to be differentiated further. The directly observable Siderial Time, converted to the Greenwich reference meridian and subjected to the transformation formula determines the time UT0. Due to the slight movements of the Earth's poles of rotation the difference in geographical longitude between the place of observation and the reference meridian varies. Therefore, the conversion to the reference meridian according to tabulated common longitudes is incorrect. If the pole variation is accounted for, one obtains the time UT1. This timescale is consistent for all places on the Earth but still irregular since the rotational velocity of the Earth is known to be variable. A correction of UT1 for the strongest and most regular variations yields the time UT2. This correction amounts to +/- 30 milliseconds at most. UT2 is the most uniform timescale that can be predicted from Earth's rotation. Because of the availability of time standards that are more precise and easier to obtain (atomic clocks) UT2 has hardly any practical use. The Universal Time commonly adopted in astronomy is therefore the UT1 scale.

UT1 has the benefit of predicting the solar position to sufficient accuracy. Its disadvantage, however, is that the length of a second derived from UT1 varies noticably (caused by the irregularities of Earth's rotation). Therefore, a timescale named Coordinated Universal Time (UTC) was invented in which the SI-second—as implemented by atomic clocks—is the unit of time. In addition, it is required that the absolute value of the difference UTC—UT1 never exceeds 0.9 seconds. UTC therefore offers both a highly constant unit of time as well as agreement with the position of the Sun. For this reason, UTC is the basis for all civil time keeping today. It is distributed publicly by DCF77 radio transmitters and other time services, together with an extrapolation of the current time difference DUT1=UTC—UT1. (This difference has to be extrapolated because UT1 must be determined from observations and cannot be calculated and distributed instantly.)

Since UTC as well as Atomic Time TAI are based on the SI-second, both timescales are basically in step with each other. However, the SI-second does not agree with the UT1-second, therefore UTC drifts with respect to UT1. About UTC-UT1, leap seconds must occasionally be inserted into or dropped from UTC. This happens—if necessary—on Jun 30 or Dec 31 at the end of the last minute of the day. Currently, about two leap seconds must be inserted in an interval of three years. The need for a leap second is determined by the Bureau International de l'Heure (BIH) in Paris, after consultation with several time laboratories.

The require for leap seconds is not caused by the secular slowdown of Earth's rotation (which is less than 2 milliseconds per century) but by irregular variations in this rotation and by the fact that the definition of the SI-second is fixed on the duration of the year 1900 which was shorter than average.

Timezones

The organization of timezones accounts for the fact that for any given instance the Sun is rising on one place on the Earth, is standing high in the south at noon for another place, and is setting for a third place. Considering these astronomical facts, it makes sense to use different civil timescales at different places on the Earth. Ultimately, however, the adoption of a local timescale is a political decision and is therefore handled differently in individual countries.

A timezone is a region of a common civil timescale that is in general oriented along a meridian of constant geographical longitude. The local time of a timezone usually differs by an integer number of hours from Universal Time, although sporadically other differences occur. The differenz 'local time' minus 'Universal Time' is positiv for timezones east of Greenwich and negative for western timezones. Frequently mentioned timezones are:

- West European Time (= Universal Time, difference 0 hours)
- Central European Time (+1 hour)
- in the USA:
  1. Atlantic Standard Time (-4 hours)
  2. Eastern Standard Time (-5 hours, east coast)
  3. Central Standard Time (-6 hours)
  4. Mountain Standard Time (-7 hours)
  5. Pacific Standard Time (-8 hours)
- Moscow Time (+3 hours)
- Tokyo Time (+9 hours) Daylight saving time is decreed for entirely political reasons and has no astronomical basis.

Atomic Time

In the Systeme Internationale of units of measurements the second is defined as the duration of 9, 192, 631, 770 cycles of a particular hyperfine structure transition in the ground state of Cesium-133. This definition was chosen to match as best as possible the length of the ephemeris second that was used before.

The SI-second only defines an abstract atomic time. To obtain a timescale of practical usabilty a device is required that attempts to realise the SI-second. Such a device is called an atomic clock. Real-word atomic clocks do not agree fully with each another. Therefore, the weighted mean of many atomic clocks—distributed over various laboratories on the whole Earth—is used to define the Atomic Time TAI (french Temps

Atomique International). TAI is currently the best realization of a timescale based on the SI-second, with a relative accuracy of +/- 2*10^-14 (as of 1990).

According to the General Relativistic Theory, the time measured depends on the location on Earth (or more precisely, on the altitude) and also on the spatial velocity of the clock. TAI thus refers to a location on sea sevel that rotates with the Earth.

Ephemeris Time, Dynamical Time Scales (TDT, TDB)

Ephemerides are tables that list the positions of Sun, Moon, planets and their respectives moons at different times.

Formerly, the positions were given as a function of Greenwich Mean Time (GMT) which lead to recurring problems, in particular with predictions for the Moon's motion.

Finally (at about 1930), it was realised that Earth's rotation is irregular and that any timescale derived from it must be erratic. However, the application of dynamical laws of motion—like for instance Newton's laws of force—requires a smoothly flowing time as the independent variable.

The Ephemeris Time (ET) was consequently defined as the timescale that together with the laws of motion correctly predicts the positions of celestial bodies, and it is therefore used as the argument in the ephemerides. The current Ephemeris Time is thus determined by comparing the observed positions with the ephemerides.

Formally, ET was defined by Newcomb's theory of the Sun. In 1958, the International Astronomical Union (IAU) at its 10th general assembly stipulated that:

"... Ephemeris time is reckoned from the instant, near the beginning of the calendar year AD 1900, when the geometric mean longitude of the Sun was 279 degrees, 41 minutes 48.04 seconds, at which instant the measure of Ephemeris Time was 1900 January 0, 12 o'clock precisely."

With respect to the unit of time, the IAU and the International Committee for Weights and Measures agreed on the definition;

``The second is the fraction 1/31 556 925.9747 of the tropical year at 1900 January 0, 12 O'clock Ephemeris Time.'' (Translation DH) which was published in 1957. With these definitions, Ephemeris Time is equivalent to the time values in Newcomb's tables of the solar position. For sensible time measurements, however, the quoted definitions are unsuitable because precise determinations of the actual solar position are difficult. Instead, the difference ΔT between ET and UT was deduced from observations and ephemerides of the Moon. Observationally, the Moon is well suited for this purpose because of its fast apparent motion on the celestial sphere. However, the computation of its ephemerides is difficult and requires the knowledge of some physical constants in addition to the gravitational constant. Between the years 1960 and 1984 the Moon theory was repeatedly improved on, each time with consequences for the realization of Ephemeris Time. For precise computations, the applied realization of ET (named as ET0, ET1, and ET2) must therefore be taken into account.

In adding to being dependent on the details of the Moon theory, ET has the further disadvantage of not accounting for effects to be expected according to the theories of Special and General Relativity. When this deficit became important as the accuracy of measurements and the demands on theoretical prediction increased, ET had to be replaced by better timescales. These successors are generally called dynamical timescales because they are based (like ET) on planetary and lunar motions calculated from dynamical laws. In contrast to ET, relativistic equations of motion are used here.

In the context of the theory of relativity, time measurements depend on the reference point. Such reference points with astronomical importance are the Earth's surface and the solar system's centre of mass. The two timescales created for these reference points depend in different ways on the dynamical theory (where we accept the possibility that the theory of relativity does not correctly describe the true dynamics of the system). One is free, however, to define one of these two timescales. In 1977, the general assembly of the IAU in Grenoble, France defined the timescale TDT (Terrestrial

Dynamical Time) of a reference point on Earth's surface through the requirements that the unit of TDT time should be the SI-second and that the instant 1977, January 1, 0 O'clock TAI corresponds to 1977, January 1, 0 hour 0 minutes 32.184 seconds TDT. The difference of 32.184 seconds is in keeping with the difference between TAI and ET at that time and was chosen for continuity in the change from ET to TDT. Despite the reference to the common SI-second, TAI and TDT are basically not identical timescales. TAI is subject to possible systematical errors in the realization of atomic time whereas TDT is an idealized uniformly flowing time. In the foreseeable future, the difference is at best noticeable in the timing of milli-second pulsars.

The IAU also decreed that timescales that refer to the centre of gravity (the barycentre) of the solar system differ from TDT only in periodical terms. Such timescales are called TDB (Barycentric Dynamical Time). In practise, they are calculated from TDT with consideration of the constants, positions, and motions of the Sun, the Moon, Jupiter, Saturn, and the barycentre of the solar system and the assumption of a theory of gravitation. For the latter, the theory of General Relativity is employed nowadays. The TDB so derived differs by at most 10 milliseconds from TDT. This difference is negligible for most applications.

Accompanying timescales with the names Terrestrial Time (TT), Geocentric Coordinate Time (TCG), and Barycentric Coordinate Time (TCB) were introduced by the IAU in the year 1991, in an attempt to clarify the relations between space-time coordinates. All these timescales are proper times in the diction of the General Relativistic Theory. TT refers to the surface of Earth (at sea level) and is identical to TDT. TCG measures the proper time at Earth's centre and differs from TT by a constant scale factor that follows from the different gravitational potentials at the two reference points. TCB is the proper time of the barycentre of the solar system. It deviates from TDB by a constant scale factor, due to some slighty altered astronomical constants and requirements that TDB should differ from TDT only by periodic terms. TDB is therefore tied to the proper time on Earth's surface and because of distinct potentials progresses at a different speed than TCB.

Julian Day Numbers

The Julian day number—or simply the Julian day—is a continuous count of days, starting with the day 0 that began on the 1st of January, 4713, BC at 12 O'clock noon. Consequently, a new Julian day always begins at 12 o'clock noon that originally gave European astronomers the advantage that all observations of any particular night happened at the same Julian day. This property is unimportant today. The Julian day count can easily be extended to a precise measure of time by appending the fraction of the day elapsed since 12 O'clock noon. For instance, JD 2 451 605 signifies the day that will begin on March 1, 2000, 12 O'clock noon whereas JD 2 451 605.25 means the point of time at 18 O'clock of the same day. This extension is called the Julian date in many texts (as for example in the Astronomical Almanac). Other sources propose to restrict this designation to date specifications in the Julian calendar to prevent confusion. This proposal has not carried through, yet.

Julian days were formerly (if nothing else was specified) counted according to Mean Solar Time, today in UT. Alternatively, specifications were given in Ephemeris Time which was indicated by appending the letters JED or JDE. Also today it is sometimes appropriate to specify Julian Days in another timescale than UT. The employed timescale should then be appended to the time specification, for instance JD 2 451 545.0 TDT for Januar 1, 2000, 12 O'clock noon as measured in TDT.

Occasionally, time specifications are given in a Modified Julian Day format (MJD). The most common definition of a MJD follows from

MJD = JD – 2 400 000.5

with a zero point on November 17, 1858 at 0 o'clock (!) UT, However, there exist other definitions as well so one has to be careful when dealing with times in MJD. For this reason, the International Astronomical Union does not approve of MJD and advices against its use. In contemporary astronomy, Julian day numbers are readily employed because they allow compact unambiguous time specifications and the easy computation of time differences, periods etc.

The Julian day number was introduced in 1581 by the French scholar Joseph Justus Scaliger (in his book "Opus novum de emendatione temporum") to define a non-ambiguous time reckoning without negative year numbers. To this end, the beginning of time reckoning had to be sufficiently far back in pre-historic times. Scaliger first construed a Julian Period with a length of 7980 years by combining the following cycles:

- The 28 year-long Sun cycle in which (in the Julian calendar) the calendar dates repeat on the same days of the week (this cycle would be 400 years long in the Gregorian calendar);
- The 19 year-long Metonic cycle in which the phases of the Moon and the Moon eclipsis repeat on almost the same calendar dates; and
- The 15 year-long cycle of indiction that was used in the Roman empire for tax collection and census.

The last year in which all three cycles simultaneously began a new period was 4713 BC. Scaliger started his reckoning of time on Januar 1 of this year. For most people of that time, this date was entirely fictitious as according to their religious belief the world was created a long time after that. Scaliger himself believed Earth was created in the year 3267 BC.

As for the naming of this day count, some contradictory statements can be found in the literature. According to some sources Scaliger named the scale in honour of his father Julius Scaliger. Other sources maintain that Scaliger defended the Julian calendar (against reformatory efforts in the Vatican) and chose the name in this context; the name would then go back to Julius Cesar.

Sidereal Days and Solar Days

The *sidereal day* is defined to be the length of time for the vernal equinox to return to your celestial meridian. The *solar day* is defined to be the length of time for the Sun to return to your celestial meridian.

Because the Earth is in motion on its orbit around the Sun in the course of a day, the Earth must turn about 4 minutes longer each day (3 minutes and 56 seconds, to be exact) to bring the Sun back to the celestial meridian than to bring the vernal equinox back to the celestial meridian.

Thus, the solar day is 3 minutes and 56 seconds longer than the sidereal day. It is this almost 4 minute per day discrepancy that causes the difference in sidereal and solar time, and is responsible for the fact that different constellations are everhead at a given time of day during the Summer than in the Winter.

Time Zones and Universal Time

As a matter of civil convenience, the Earth is divided into various time zones. The time for many astronomical events is given in *Universal Time* (UT), which is (approximately) the local time for Greenwich, England—the *Greenwich Mean Time* or GMT.

ASTRONOMICAL CALENDARS

There are two essential sources for calendars presently in use: the monthly motion of the Moon *(Lunar calendars)* and the yearly motion of the Sun *(Solar Calendars)*. Examples of Lunar calendars still in use are the traditional Jewish and Chinese calendars. The difficulty with Lunar calendars is that the seasons are correlated with the Sun, not the Moon. Thus, Lunar calendars require elaborate adjustments or translations to relate to the seasons. That calendars correlate with seasons is now primarily a matter of convenience, but in more ancient cultures keeping track of the seasons was serious business: it could be a matter of survival to know things like the proper time to plant to ensure a bountiful harvest.

The Roman Lunar Calendar

Our present calendar is a basically solar calendar that grew from what was originally a Lunar calendar used by the

Romans. The original calendar contained 10 months of length 29 or 30 days. This was later modified to a 12 month calendar, but 12 months of average length 29.5 days gives only 354 days in the year, whereas the orbital period of the Earth is 365.242199 days.

Thus, at the end of each year this calendar was 11 days out of step with the seasons and at the end of 3 years it was almost a month out of step. This was initially corrected in an arbitrary way by adding 13th months, but this was used for various political purposes and soon threw the calendar into severe confusion.

The Julian Calendar

The Julian calendar is based on a solar year with originally 365 days.

To account for the fact that the tropical year is longer than 365 days by about a quarter day, a leap day is inserted at the end of month of February in every fourth year. This simple leap year rule was already known in late Egypt. It was in fact an Alexandrian scholar named Sosigenes who advised Julius Cesar during the introduction of the calendar into the Roman empire in the year 46 BC. The calendar is named after Julius Cesar.

Julius Cesar had to start the introduction of his calendar with an anomalous leap year with 445 days for the year 46 BC to compensate for the inaccuracies of the Roman calendar used before.

The following year 45 BC was a normal leap year with 366 days. After Cesar's death the new leap year rules were at first incorrectly applied and too many leap years occurred. This was corrected under the government of Augustus and the Julian calendar was strictly obeyed since the year AD 8. For earlier years date estimates are uncertain by a few days since the sequence of leap years is not exactly known.

In astronomy and for historical purposes the Julian calendar is also applied to epochs earlier than the year 46 BC when this calendar was not yet defined and the people of that time could not know their date in it. To indicate this extension, the term *proleptic Julian calendar* is occasionally used (proleptic= brought forward).

The Gregorian Calendar

Though, the Julian year still differs from the true year of 365.242199 days by 11 minutes and 14 seconds each year, and over a period of 128 years even the Julian Calendar was in error by one day with respect to the seasons. By 1582 this error had accumulated to 10 days and Pope Gregory XIII ordered another reform: 10 days were dropped from the year 1582, so that October 4, 1582, was followed by October 15, 1582. In addition, to guard against further accumulation of error, in the new *Gregorian Calendar* it was decreed that century years not divisible by 400 were not to be considered leap years. Thus, 1600 was a leap year but 1700 was not. This made the average length of the year sufficiently close to the actual year that it would take 3322 years for the error to accumulate to 1 day.

A further modification to the Gregorian Calendar has been suggested: years evenly divisible by 4000 are not leap years. This would reduce the error between the Gregorian Calendar Year and the true year to 1 day in 20,000 years. However, this last proposed change has not been officially adopted; there is plenty of time to consider it, since it would not have an effect until the year 4000.

Adoption of the Gregorian Calendar

An interesting chronological sidelight on the Gregorian Calendar is that not all countries adopted it immediately. In particular, it was adopted uniformly in Catholic countries, but Protestant countries often still used the Julian Calendar. Thus, the date could change by 10 days simply by crossing certain country borders! England and its American colonies did not adopt the Gregorian Calendar until 1752, when 11 days were removed from the calendar, and Russia resisted this change until after the 1917 Revolution. One conseqence of the British adoption of the Gregorian Calendar in 1752 is that George Washington was born on February 11, 1731, according to the calendar in use on his birthday, but we now celebrate his date of birth as February 22, 1731 (actually, even that is no longer true with the advent of Presidents Day).

Easter Date

The Christian Easter feast was derived from the Jewish Passover which begins on the first full moon in spring. This day can obviously fall on a random day of the week. Easter, in contrast, begins on a Sunday by definition. At first, the Easter date was calculated very differently in the diverse Christian parishes. Only at the 1.council in Nicäa in the year AD 325 an agreement was achieved that Easter should begin on the first Sunday—after—the first full moon in spring. The latter is the first full moon that occurs either on or after the day of the spring equinox.

However, with the decree of Nicäa the difficulties were not entirely removed because the precise determination of the first full moon in spring had its own problems. Finally, at the request of Pope John I, the roman abbot Dionysius Exiguus established in AD 525 the rule as previously used in Alexandria. According to this rule:

- Spring is defined to begin at March 21, 0 O'clock; and
- The moon is assumed to move at constant speed on a circular orbit.

Both assumptions are simplifications that lead to deviations from the true astronomical facts. The true beginning of spring happens some time between March 19, 8 O'clock and March 21, 20 O'clock UT. Consideration of the true lunar orbit leads to time differences of up +/- 0.7 days with respect to a circular orbit. Moreover, the Gregorian calendar reform forced the Easter date to fall into the time interval from March 22 to April 25 (both dates included). For these reasons, shifts between the factual Easter date and the date calculated from the astronomically correct spring full moon can occur which are called 'Easters paradoxes'. The last paradox happened in 1974 (Easter was celebrated on April 14 instead of April 7), the next one will be in the year 2000 (April 23 instead of March 26).

The Easter date is nowadays calculated from tables specifically constructed for that purpose or from the Easter formulae of Carl Friedrich Gaub. Both methods are valid for all years since AD 532. Simplified formulae for easier use, that explicitly assume either the Gregorian or the Julian calendar, are given by J.Meuus.

Even today, the various Christian churches differ in the fixation of the Easter feast. The eastern churches, for example, stick to the beginning of spring on March 21 of the Julian calendar and calculate the true astronomical full moon for the meridian of Jerusalem.

Other Calendars

Egypt (historical): Since the fourth millennium before Christ a solar year with a length of 365 days was used. The year was divided into 12 months with 30 days each, plus five additional days. The months were combined into groups of four months each to form the flooding, seeding, and harvesting seasons, referring to the yearly floods of the river Nile. The relation of these seasons to the beginning of the Egyptian calendar year was variable, though, because on average the Nile flood appears at the same time of the tropical year and consequently seeding and harvesting have to follow in step. The start of the seasons was therefore defined by the heliacal rising of the star Sirius (the Egyptian name of which was Sothis). (The heliacal rising is the first rise of a star visible in the pre-dawn after its conjunction with the sun. Strictly speaking, the heliacal rising does not define the length of a tropical, but of a siderical year if the star's proper motion can be ignored. However, the difference was insignificant for Egyptian time keeping.)

The Egyptian calendar made no use of leap days, so in a period of 1460 years the new year's day moved through all seasons. For the Egyptians, however, it appeared as if the heliacal rising of the Sothis (=Sirius) moves with this period through the calendar. It was therefore called the Sothis cycle.

In the year 238 BC Ptolemeus Euergetes tried to establish a sixth additional day in every fourth year (that would have been a leap day). This attempt, however, was largely ignored. Only under the direction of the Roman emperor Augustus since about 26 BC, the new calendar was slowly adopted, although old and new calendars were still used in parallel for many centuries to come. The new calendar was largely similar to the Julian calendar but the leap day was inserted at the end of the Egyptian year which corresponded to August 29 in the Julian calendar.

China (historical): In ancient China a luni-solar year was used. The necessary intercalation of leap months lead—as in other cultures—to the development of the Metonic cycle of 19 years. Years were not counted. Instead, they were designated by a combination of a (non-translatable) symbol from the Chinese philosophy of nature and a zodiacal sign. (These zodiacal signs were specific to ancient China and have nothing to do with the zodiacal signs used in the western astrology.)

There were 10 symbols and 12 zodiacal signs which were used cyclically. In a period of 60 years, each year therefore had a unique designation. The 60-year periods were named according to an important event or a sovereign of that epoch.

Greece (antique): In old Greece a luni-solar year was used, with intercalation rules that were in the beginning primitive and irregular. Since about 500 BC the *octaeteris* gained widespread acceptance, a rule with 8-year cycle in which five ordinary years with 12 months each are combined with three leap years of 13 months each. In the year 432 BC, Meton in Athens found the 19-year cycle named after him (although it was discovered independently in other cultures). Of similar quality, although longer in period and therefore more difficult to use, was the Callipic cycle that equated 76 years with 940 months and 27759 days.

Latin America (historical): The advanced cultures in Latin America used a ritual calendar with a period of 13 times 20 days in combination with a solar year that consisted of 18 months with 20 days each plus five extra days (which were considered calamitous).

This resulted in a 52-year cycle. In general, there was no continuous count of the years. Only the Maja counted the years, starting from September 6, 4113 BC in units of 'kin' (1 day), 'vinal' (20 days), 'tun' (360 days = 18 vinals), 'katun' (7200 days = 20 tuns) and 'baktun' (144000 days = 20 katuns).

Calendar of the French revolution: This calendar was designed by S. Marechal in 1787 and established in post-revolutionary France on October 5, 1793. Its first year began (nominally) on September 22, 1792, and new years started on the astronomically determined autumn equinox. The year was divided into 12 months with 30 days each, to which were added five or six extra days (the 'sansculotides'). Each month consisted of three decades of 10 days length, the day was divided into 10 hours, the hour into 10 parts and so on. The Gregorian calendar was re-established on January 1, 1806.

India: The historical Indian time keeping is characterized by a vast multitude of calendar systems. A reformed Indian calendar was established on March 22, 1957. Its year length and its leap year rule are the same as in the Gregorian calendar, but the new year's day and the year count differ. For instance, March 22, 1957 corresponded to the beginning of the year 1879 in the historical Saka year reckoning, and in leap years the new year's day falls on March 21 of the Gregorian calendar. Even today many traditional calendars are in use for religious purposes. For the year count alone more than 20 variants exist. Characteristic for Indian time keeping is also the division of the day into 60 parts with a constant length of 24 minutes. The division into 60 equal parts is repeated three times, so the smallest time unit has a length of a little under seven milliseconds.

Jewish calendar: The year reckoning of the modern Jewish calendar begins with the year 3761 BC when according to the Jewish creed the world was formed. This reckoning was established in about the 10th century AD, the calendar itself found its final form already in the 4th century AD. The calendar is based on a luni-solar year with a complicated set of intercalation rules. The particular complexity is the consequence of an attempt to avoid certain feasts to fall on week days considered improper. Therefore, one distinguishes 'defective', 'normal', and 'complete' ordinary years with 353, 354, and 355 days, respectively, and corresponding leap years with 383, 384, and 385 days. The day commences at 18 o'clock in the Jewish calendar. This is a common characteristic of lunar calendars since the moon's slim crescent after the new moon is visible shortly after sunset. With it begins a new month and thusly also a new day.

Islamic calendar: The year reckoning of the islamic calendar begins with Mohammed's emigration to Medina (the hidjra) on July 15 or 16, 622 AD in the Julian calendar. (Which of the two days is correct is controversial.) Year numbers in this reckoning are often characterized by the suffix 'Anno Hegirae' (A.H. for short).

For profane purposes a tabulated lunar calendar is used with an ordinary year with 354 days and 12 months that have alternating lengths of 29 and 30 days. In a cycle of 30 years, 11 leap years with 355 days appear in which the twelfth month has 30 instead of 29 days. There are, however, two different structures of the 30-year cycle in use which cause differences in the date by one day during 348 of the 360 months. In either case the new year's day of the fixed islamic calendar moves through all seasons within 33 years.

For religious purposes, the start of a new month is not determined by the tables of the fixed calendar but through actual observation of the young moon's crescent. Accordingly, in this calendar the day begins with the sunset on the evening preceding the same day according to the profane calendar.

Civilian Calendar of the Federal Republic of Germany: With typical German thoroughness, this calendar is standardized in the norm DIN 1355. It defines the length(s) of the year, the leap year rules, the names of months and week days, the suffixes *vor Christus* and *nach Christus* (for BC and AD, respectively), and the reckoning of years and weeks. These specifications are in general agreement with the Gregorian calendar and add only items unspecified by the Gregorian calendar.

THE SEASONS

There is a accepted misconception that the seasons on the Earth are caused by varying distances of the Earth from the

Sun on its elliptical orbit. This is not correct. One way to see that this reasoning may be in error is to note that the seasons are out of phase in the Northern and Southern hemispheres: when it is Summer in the North it is Winter in the South.

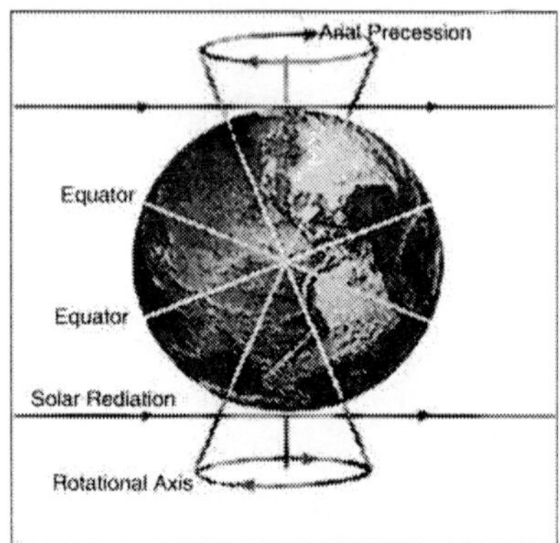

Seasons in the Northern Hemisphere

The main reason of the seasons is the 23.5 degree of the Earth's rotation axis with respect to the plane of the ecliptic, as illustrated in the adjacent image. This means that as the Earth goes around its orbit the Northern hemisphere is at various times oriented more towards and more away from the Sun, and likewise for the Southern hemisphere, as illustrated in the following figure 3.5.

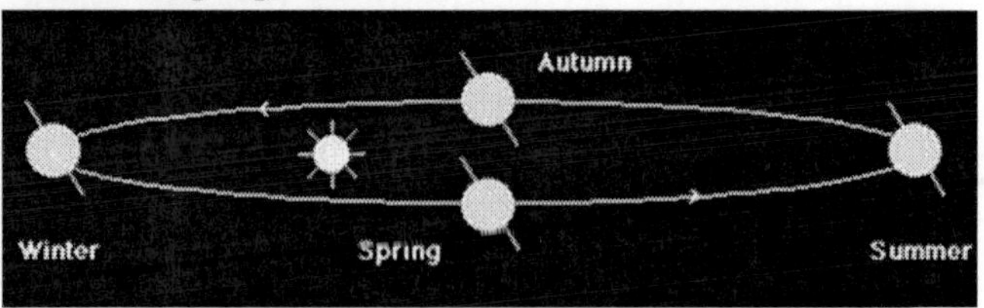

Fig. 3.5 The Seasons in the Northern Hemisphere

Thus, we knowledge Summer in the Northern Hemisphere when the Earth is on that part of its orbit where the N. Hemisphere is oriented more towards the Sun and therefore the Sun rises higher in the sky and is above the horizon longer, and the rays of the Sun strike the ground more directly. Likewise, in the N. Hemisphere Winter the hemisphere is oriented away from the Sun, the Sun only rises low in the sky, is above the horizon for a shorter period, and the rays of the Sun strike the ground more obliquely.

In fact, as the diagram indicates, the Earth is actually *closer* to the Sun in the N. Hemisphere Winter than in the Summer. The Earth is at its closest approach to the Sun (perihelion) on about January 4 of each year, which is the dead of the N. Hemisphere Winter. (The time for perihelion, aphelion, and the solstices for any year 1992-2000 is available in this compilation.)

Another Fallacy to Avoid

Incidentally, one should be precise in terminology. A common student answer for the cause of the seasons is that "the Earth tips towards the Sun in the Summer,...". This conveys the impression that the Earth moves around its orbit and at certain times of the year the rotation axis suddenly tips one way or another and thus we have seasons. As the preceding diagram makes clear, the rotation axis of the Earth remains pointed in the *same direction* (except for small effects from precession) as it moves around its orbit. It is the relative location of the Sun with respect to this constant tilt angle that causes the seasons, not some elaborate square dance of the Earth bowing to its partner as it moves around its orbit!

Determine of Southern Hemisphere Seasons

As is clear from the preceding diagram, the seasons in the Southern Hemisphere are determined from the same reasoning, except that they are out of phase with the N. Hemisphere seasons because when the N. Hemisphere is oriented towards the Sun the S. Hemisphere is oriented away, and *vice-versa:*

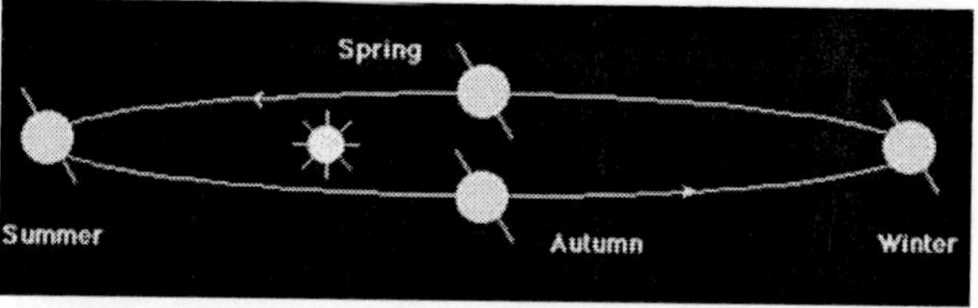

Fig. 3.6 The Seasons in the Southern Hemisphere

The Lag of the Seasons

The preceding reasoning for the causes of the seasons is idealized. In reality, we know that the seasons 'lag': for example, the hottest temperatures in the Summer usually occur a month or so after the time of *maximum insolation* (the time when maximum solar energy is deposited during a day at a point on the surface of the Earth). This is because the Earth and its atmosphere store heat (the oceans are particularly effective heat sinks). Thus, a detailed description of the seasons is quite complicated since it must take into account complex local variations in the storage of solar energy.

Simulating the Apparent Motion of the Sun

One can use the Starry Night programme for Windows and the Macintosh to simulate the appearance of the sky at any time, from any chosen vantage point in the Solar System. Thus, by choosing different points on the surface of the Earth at different times of the year, this programme can be used to show the motion of the Sun through the sky and illustrate clearly the preceding points about the causes for the seasons. Here is an extreme example:

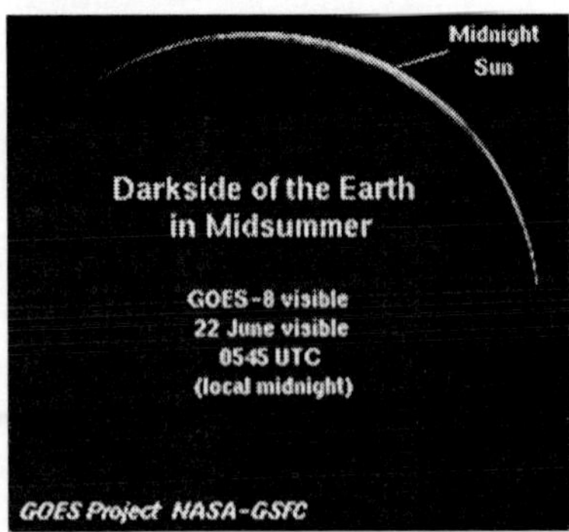

In the N. Hemisphere Summer at latitudes above the Arctic Circle (23.5 degrees away from the N. Pole) the Sun stays above the horizon for the entire day (*midnight sun*). The adjacent image illustrates the midnight sun. This GOES-8 weather satellite visible light image is taken from a vantage point high above the western hemisphere, with the North at the top. Even though the local time for the longitude line under the satellite is near midnight, the Northernmost portion of the globe is illuminated by sunlight.

This imitation of the midnight sun was made using the Starry Night programme with a 'fisheye lens' perspective to show a wide (180 degree) region of the sky from a vantage point at the North Pole on July 4, 1996. As the movie illustrates, the Sun moves more or less parallel to the horizon and never it during the course of a day at these latitudes at this time of the year. Conversely, in the N. Hemisphere Winter the Sun never comes *above* the horizon for the entire day at this latitude. This is an extreme example of the difference in insolation in Winter and Summer for the N. Hemisphere that is responsible for the seasons.

PRECESSION OF THE EARTH'S ROTATION AXIS

The Earth's rotation axis is not fixed in space. Like a rotating toy top, the direction of the rotation axis executes a slow precession with a period of 26,000 years.

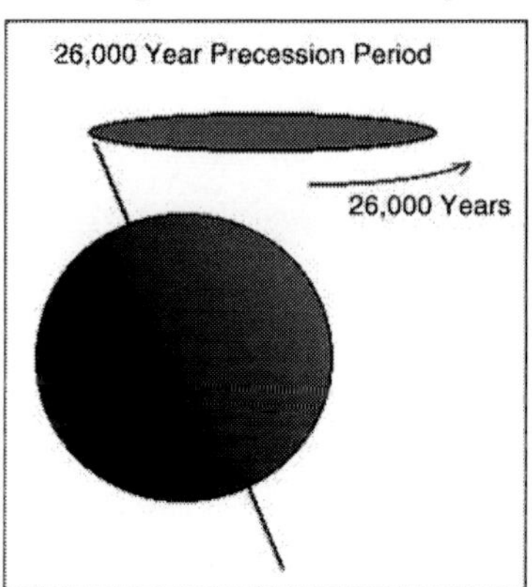

Pole Stars are Transient

Thus, Polaris will not always be the Pole Star or North Star. The Earth's turning round axis happens to be pointing almost exactly at Polaris now, but in 13,000 years the precession of the rotation axis will mean that the bright star Vega in the constellation Lyra will be approximately at the

North Celestial Pole, while in 26,000 more years Polaris will once again be the Pole Star.

Precession of the Equinoxes

While the rotation axis is precessing in space, the orientation of the Celestial Equator also precesses with the same period. This means that the position of the equinoxes is changing slowly with respect to the background stars. This *precession of the equinoxes* means that the right ascension and declination of objects changes very slowly over a 26,000 year period. This effect is negligibly small for casual observing, but is an important correction for precise observations.

The Dawning of the Age of Aquarius (Almost)

Since of the precession of the equinoxes, the vernal equinox moves through all the constellations of the Zodiac over the 26,000 year precession period. Presently the vernal equinox is in the constellation Pisces and is slowly approaching Aquarius.

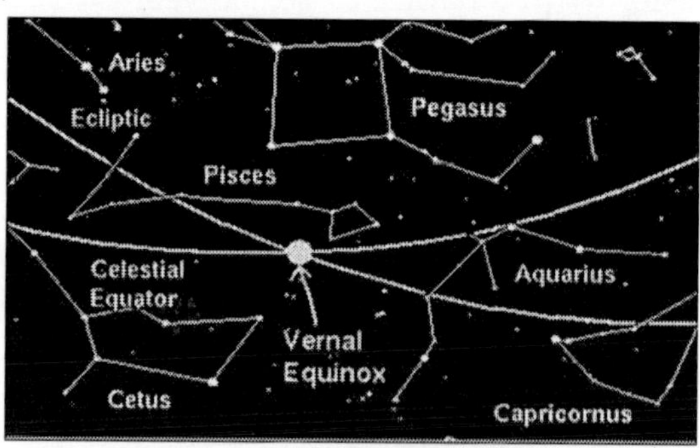

Fig. 3.7 The Vernal Equinox

This is the origin of the 'Age of Aquarius' celebrated in the musical *Hair*: a period when according to astrological mysticism and related hokum there will be unusual harmony and understanding in the world. We could certainly use a dose of harmony and understanding in this old world; unfortunately, it is unlikely to come because of something as irrelevant as the position of the vernal equinox with respect to the constellations of the Zodiac.

ORBIT AND PHASES OF THE MOON

The orbit of the Moon is very nearly circular (eccentricity ~ 0.05) with a mean separation from the Earth of about 384,000 km, which is about 60 Earth radii. The plane of the orbit is tilted about 5 degrees with respect to the ecliptic plane.

Revolution in Orbit

The Moon appears to move completely around the celestial sphere once in about 27.3 days as observed from the Earth. This is called a *sidereal month,* and reflects the corresponding orbital period of 27.3 days The moon takes 29.5 days to return to the same point on the celestial sphere as referenced to the Sun because of the motion of the Earth around the Sun; this is called a *synodic month* (Lunar phases as observed from the Earth are correlated with the synodic month).

There are effects that cause small fluctuations around this value that we will not discuss. Since the Moon must move Eastward among the constellations enough to go completely around the sky (360 degrees) in 27.3 days, it must move Eastward by 13.2 degrees each day (in contrast, remember that the Sun only appears to move Eastward by about 1 degree per day). Thus, with respect to the background constellations the Moon will be about 13.2 degrees further East each day. Since the celestial sphere appears to turn 1 degree about every 4 minutes, the Moon crosses our celestial meridian about $13.2 \times 4 = 52.8$ minutes later each day.

Lunar Phases in Moon Appears

The Moon appears to go through a complete set of phases as viewed from the Earth because of its motion around the Earth, as illustrated in the following figure. In this shape, the various positions of the Moon on its orbit are shown (the motion of the Moon on its orbit is assumed to be counter-clockwise). The outer set of figure 3.8 shows the corresponding phase *as viewed from Earth,* and the common names for the phases.

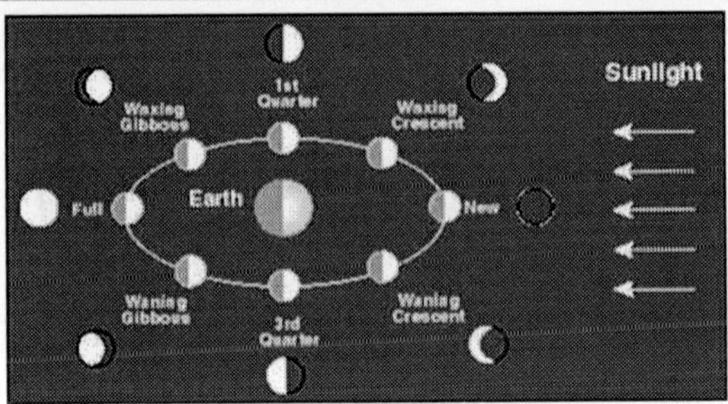

Fig. 3.8 Phases of the Moon

Here is an animation of actual lunar phases, and here is a Java applet illustrating the orbit of the moon around the Earth and the corresponding phases of the Moon as viewed from Earth. Notice that you can set this applet to a top view, an Earth view, or both on a split screen, and that you can start and stop the animation with a button.

Perigee and Apogee

The largest separation between the Earth and Moon on its orbit is called *apogee* and the smallest separation is called *perigee*. Here is an online *Lunar Perigee and Apogee Calculator* that will allow you to determine the date, time, and distance of lunar perigees and apogees for a given year.

Rotational Period and Tidal Locking

The Moon has a rotational period of 27.3 days that (except for small fluctuations) exactly coincides with its (sidereal) period for revolution about the Earth. This is no coincidence; it is a consequence of *tidal coupling* between the Earth and Moon. Because of this tidal locking of the periods for revolution and rotation, the Moon always keeps essentially the same face turned towards the Earth.

SOLAR ECLIPSES

One consequence of the Moon's orbit about the Earth is that the Moon can shadow the Sun's light as viewed from the Earth, or the Moon can pass through the shadow cast by the Earth. The former is called a *solar eclipse* and the later is called a *lunar eclipse*. The small tilt of the Moon's orbit with respect to the plane of the ecliptic and the small eccentricity of the lunar orbit make such eclipses much less common than they would be otherwise, but partial or total eclipses are actually rather frequent.

Frequency of Eclipses

For example there will be 18 solar eclipses from 1996-2020 for which the eclipse will be total on some part of the Earth's surface. The common perception that eclipses are infrequent is because the observation of a *total eclipse from a given point on the surface of the Earth* is not a common occurrence. For example, it will be two decades before the next total solar eclipse visible in North America occurs. The next total solar eclipse will be on August 11, 1999, with the path of totality crossing the North Atlantic, Europe, the Middle East, and India. In this section we consider solar eclipses and in the next we discuss lunar eclipses.

Geometry of Solar Eclipses

The geometry associated with solar eclipses is illustrated in the following figure 3.9.

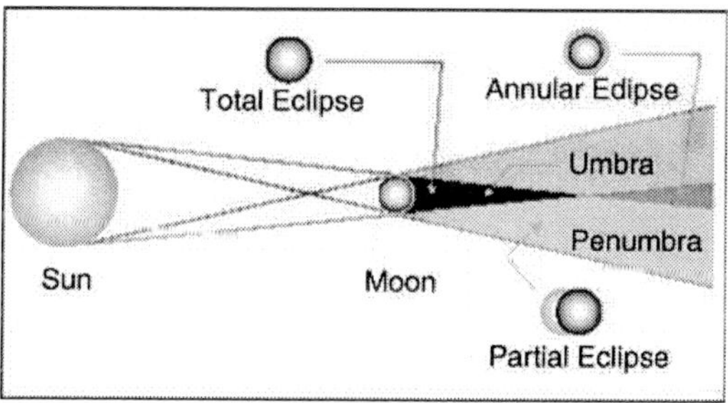

Fig. 3.9 Geometry of Solar Eclipses

The shadow cast by the Moon can be divided by geometry into the completely shadowed *umbra* and the partially shadowed *penumbra*.

Types of Solar Eclipses

The universal classes of solar eclipses (as observed from any particular point on the Earth) to be defined:

- *Total Solar Eclipses* occur when the umbra of the Moon's shadow touches a region on the surface of the Earth.
- *Partial Solar Eclipses* occur when the penumbra of the Moon's shadow passes over a region on the Earth's surface.
- *Annular Solar Eclipses* occur when a region on the Earth's surface is in line with the umbra, but the distances are such that the tip of the umbra does not reach the Earth's surface.

A total eclipse the surface of the Sun is completely blocked by the Moon, in a partial eclipse it is only partially blocked, and in an annular eclipse the eclipse is partial, but such that the apparent diameter of the Moon can be seen completely against the (larger) apparent diameter of the Sun.

For example, in the *path of totality* (the track of the umbra on the Earth's surface) the eclipse will be total, in a band on either side of the path of totality the shadow cast by the penumbra leads to a partial eclipse, and in some eclipses the path of totality extends into a path associated with an annular eclipse because for that part of the path the umbra does not reach the Earth's surface.

Total Solar Eclipses

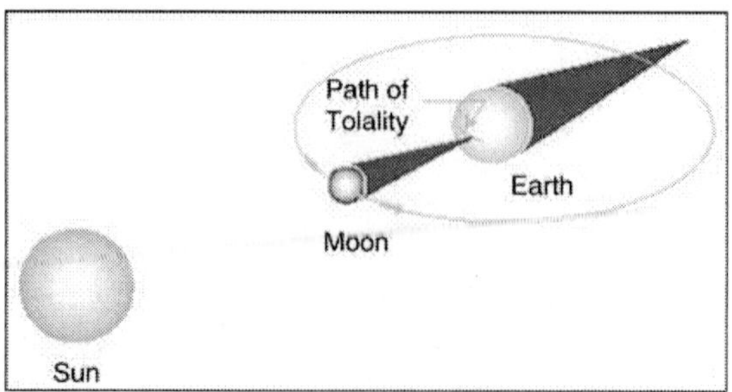

Fig. 3.10 Solar Eclipse (Not to Scale)

A total solar eclipse requires the umbra of the Moon's shadow to touch the surface of the Earth. Because of the relative sizes of the Moon and Sun and their relative distances from Earth, the path of totality is usually very narrow (hundreds of kilometers across). The above figure 3.10 illustrates the path of totality produced by the umbra of the Moon's shadow.

The true relative sizes of the Sun and Earth and Moon, and their distances.

Animations of Solar Eclipses

The first demonstrates generally the case of a total solar eclipse; the next two are simulated views of two recent solar eclipses from unusual vantage points, one from the Moon and one from the Sun (these last two were constructed using the programme Starry Night).

- Solar Eclipse Animation.
- 1994 Solar Eclipse (simulated view from the Sun: 445 kB streaming animation)
- 1995 Solar Eclipse (simulated view from the Moon: 291 kB streaming animation).

In these last two simulations, the shadow cast on the Earth is the penumbra, which can cover a region thousands of kilometers in diameter. If the eclipse is total, the path of totality traced out by the umbra is much narrower.

Appearance of a Total Solar Eclipse

The path of totality the eclipse begins with a partial phase in which the Moon gradually covers more and more of the Sun. This typically lasts for about an hour until the Moon completely covers the Sun and the total eclipse begins. The duration of totality can be as short as a few seconds, or as long as about 8 minutes, depending on the details.

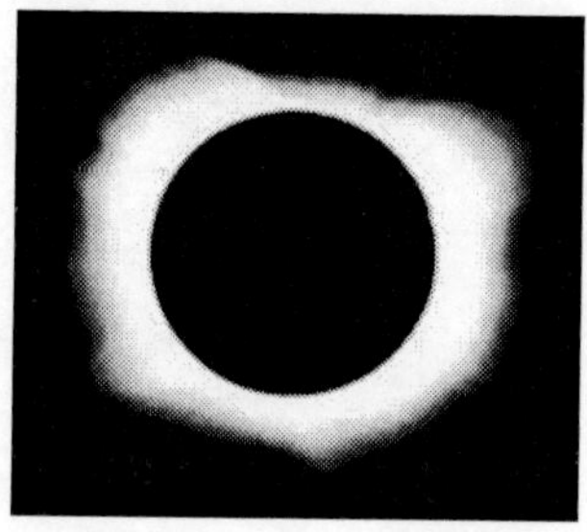

As totality approaches the sky becomes dark and a twilight that can only be described as eerie begins to descend. Just before totality waves of shadow rushing rapidly from horizon to horizon may be visible. In the final instants before totality light shining through valleys in the Moon's surface gives the impression of beads on the periphery of the Moon (a phenomenon called *Bailey's Beads*). The last flash of light from the surface of the Sun as it disappears from view behind the Moon gives the appearance of a diamond ring and is called, appropriately, the *diamond ring effect*.

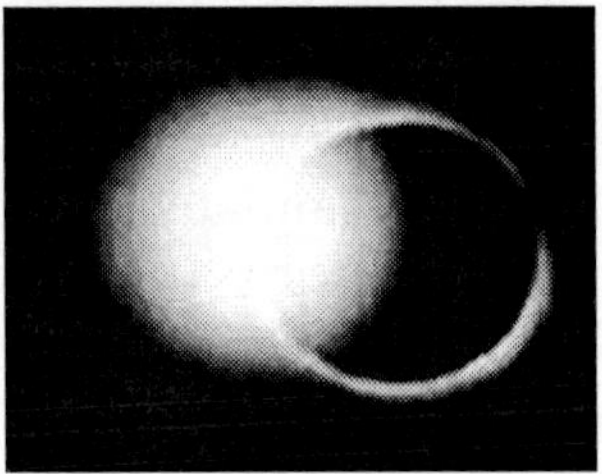

As totality begins, the solar corona (extended outer atmosphere of the Sun) blazes into view. The corona is a million times fainter than the surface of the Sun; thus only when the eclipse is total can it be seen; if even a tiny fraction of the solar surface is still visible it drowns out the light of the corona. At this point the sky is sufficiently dark that planets and brighter stars are visible, and if the Sun is active one can typically see solar prominences and flares around the limb of the Moon, even without a telescope.

The period of totality ends when the motion of the Moon begins to uncover the surface of the Sun, and the eclipse proceeds through partial phases for approximately an hour until the Sun is once again completely uncovered. There is a movie of the 1994 total solar eclipse.

A partial solar eclipse is interesting; a total solar eclipse is awe-inspiring in the literal meaning of the phrase. If you have an opportunity to observe a total solar eclipse, don't miss it! It is an experience that you will never forget.

Patterns of Eclipses

Since solar eclipses are the result of periodic motion of the Moon about the Earth, there are regularities in the timing of eclipses that give cycles of related eclipses. These cycles were known and used to predict eclipses long before there was a detailed scientific understanding of what causes eclipses. For example, the ancient Babylonians understood one such set of cycles called the *Saros*, and were able to predict eclipses based on this knowledge. Here is a link to a discussion of such cycles and regularities in eclipse patterns.

LUNAR TIDES IN THE EARTH OCEANS

The tides at a given place in the Earth's oceans occur about an hour later each day. Since the Moon passes overhead about an hour later each day, it was long suspected that the Moon was associated with tides. Newton's Law of Gravitation provided a quantitative understanding of that association.

Differential Forces

Consider a water molecule in the ocean. It is attracted gravitationally by the Earth, but it also experiences a much smaller gravitational attraction from the Moon (much smaller because the Moon is much further away and much less massive than the Earth). But this gravitational attraction of the Moon is not limited to the water molecules; in fact, the Moon exerts a gravitational force on every object on and in the Earth. Tides occur because the Earth is a body of finite extent and these forces are not uniform: some parts of the Earth are closer to the Moon than other parts, and since the gravitational force drops off as the inverse square distance, those parts experience a larger gravitational tug from the Moon than parts that are further away.

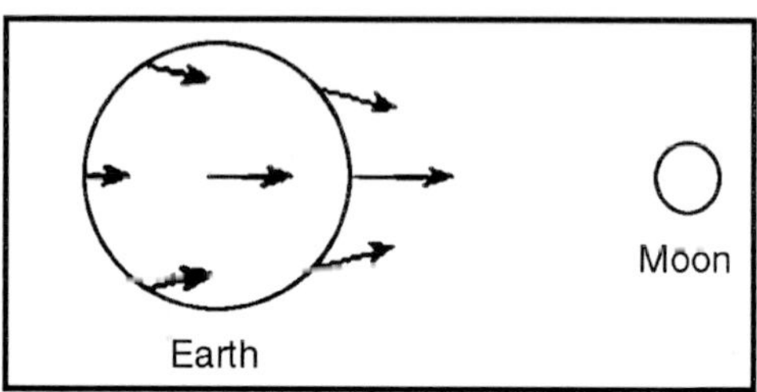

In this situation, which is illustrated schematically in the adjacent figure, we say that *differential forces* act on the body. The effect of differential forces on a body is to distort the body. The body of the Earth is rather rigid, so such distortion effects are small (but finite). However, the fluid in the Earth's oceans is much more easily deformed and this leads to significant tidal effects.

A Simple Tidal Model

We may illustrate the basic thought with a simple model of a planet completely covered by an ocean of uniform depth, with negligible friction between the ocean and the underlying planet. The gravitational attraction of the Moon produces two tidal bulges on opposite sides of the Earth.

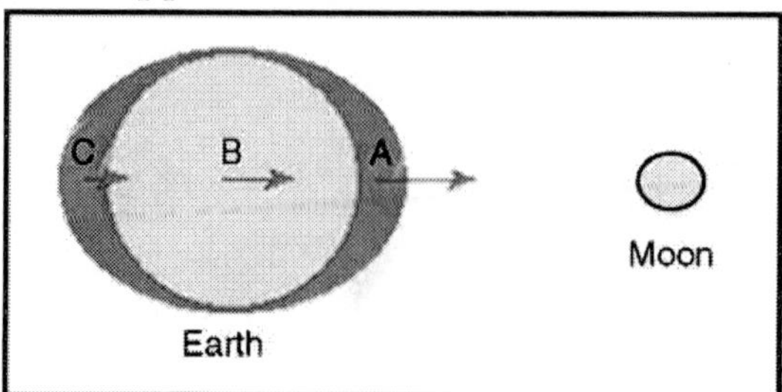

Without getting too much into the technical details, there are two bulges because of the differential gravitational forces. The liquid at point *A* is closer to the Moon and experiences a larger gravitational force than the Earth at point *B* or the ocean at point *C*. Because it experiences a larger attraction, it is pulled away from the Earth, towards the Moon, thus producing the bulge on the right side. Loosely, we may think of the bulge on the left side as arising because the Earth is pulled away from the water on that side because the gravitational force exerted by the Moon at point *B* is larger than that exerted at point *C*. Then, as our idealized Earth rotates under these bulges, a given point on the surface will experience two high and two low tides for each rotation of the planet.

Supplementary Realistic Tidal Models

The realistic situation is considerably more complicated:

- The Earth and Moon are not static, as depicted in the preceding diagram, but instead are in orbit around the common centre of mass for the system.
- The Earth is not covered with oceans, the oceans have varying depths, and there is substantial friction between the oceans and the Earth.

These make a more realistic description much more complicated, but the essential ideas remains as illustrated in the preceding diagram. Here are realtime links to the present tidal conditions in San Francisco Bay and Houston-Galveston and here is a link to a set of graphs for the tidal levels over current 24-hour periods for various tidal stations. Notice in comparing these graphs the differences in the detailed tidal fluctuations for different locations.

Spring Tides and Neap Tides

One more complication of a realistic model is that not only the Moon, but other objects in the Solar System, influence the Earth's tides. For most their tidal forces are negligible on Earth, but the differential gravitational force of the Sun does influence our tides to some degree.

For instance, particularly large tides are experienced in the Earth's oceans when the Sun and the Moon are lined up with the Earth at new and full phases of the Moon. These are called *spring tides* (the name is not associated with the season of Spring). The amount of enhancement in Earth's tides is about the same whether the Sun and Moon are lined up on opposite sides of the Earth (full Lunar phase) or on the same side (new Lunar phase). Conversely, when the Moon is at first quarter or last quarter phase (meaning that it is located at right angles to the Earth-Sun line), the Sun and Moon interfere with each other in producing tidal bulges and tides are generally weaker; these are called *neap tides*.

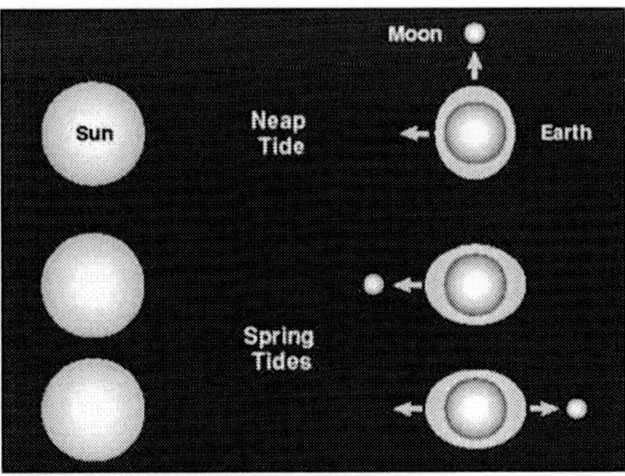

Fig. 3.11 Competition between the Sun and Moon in Producing Tides

Tidal Coupling and Gravitational Locking

We have introduced tides in terms of the effect of the Moon on the Earth's oceans, but the effect is much more general, and has a number of important consequences. For example, as a consequence of tidal interactions with the Moon, the Earth is slowly decreasing its rotational period and eventually the Earth and Moon will have exactly the same rotational period, and these will also exactly equal the orbital period. Thus, billions of years from now the Earth will always keep the same face turned towards the Moon, just as the Moon already always keeps the same face turned towards the Earth.

LUNAR ECLIPSES

The Earth casts a shadow that the Moon can pass through. When this happens we say that a *lunar eclipse* occurs. Just as for solar eclipses, lunar eclipses can be partial or total, depending on whether the light of the Sun is partially or completely blocked from reaching the Moon. A total lunar eclipse with the Moon lying in the umbra of the Earth's shadow.

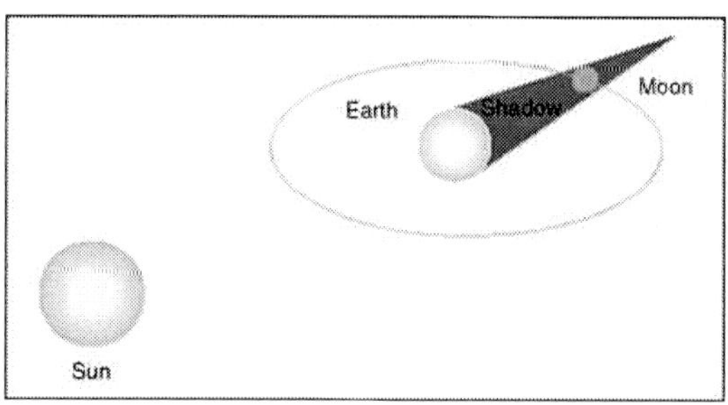

Fig. 3.12 A Lunar Eclipse

During a total lunar eclipse the Moon takes on a dark red colour because it is being lighted slightly by sunlight passing through the Earth's atmosphere and this light has the blue component preferentially scattered out (this is also why the sky appears blue from the surface of the Earth), leaving faint reddish light to illuminate the Moon during the eclipse.

CELESTIAL MEASUREMENTS

Right Ascension and Declination

Although we distinguish that the objects we see in the sky are of different sizes and at different distances from us, it is convenient to visualize all the objects as being attached to an imaginary sphere surrounding the Earth. From our vantage point, the sky certainly looks like a dome. The celestial sphere is mapped in Right Ascension (RA) and Declination (Dec). Declination is the celestial equivalent of latitude, and is simply the Earth's latitude lines projected onto the celestial sphere. A star that can be directly overhead as seen from the Earth's Equator (0° latitude) is said to be on the Celestial Equator, and has a declination of 0°. The North Star, Polaris, is very nearly overhead as seen from the North Pole (90° North latitude). The point directly over the North Pole on the celestial sphere is called the North Celestial Pole, and has a declination of +90°. Northern declinations are given positive signs, and southern declinations are given negative signs. So, the South Celestial Pole has a declination of -90°.

Right Ascension is the equivalent of longitude, but since the Earth rotates with respect to the celestial sphere we cannot simply use the Greenwich Meridian as 0° RA.

Instead, we set the zero point as the place on the celestial sphere where the Sun crosses the Celestial Equator (0° Dec) at the vernal (spring) equinox. The arc of the celestial sphere from the North Celestial Pole through this point to the South Celestial Pole is designated as Zero hours RA.

Right Ascension increases eastward, and the sky is divided up into 24 hours. This designation is convenient because it represents the sidereal day, the time it takes for the Earth to make one rotation relative to the celestial sphere. If you pointed a telescope (with no motor drive) at the coordinates (RA=0h, Dec=0°), and came back one hour later, the telescope would then be pointing at (RA=1h, Dec=0°). Because the Earth's revolution around the Sun also contributes to the apparent motion of the stars, the day we keep time by (the solar day) is about four minutes longer than the sidereal day.

So, if you pointed a telescope at (RA=0h, Dec=0°) and came back 24 hours later, the telescope would now be pointing at (RA=0h 4m, Dec=0°). A consequence is that the fixed stars appear to rise about four minutes earlier each day.

Increments of Measurement

Both RA and Dec can be divided into minutes and seconds. One minute of RA is equal to 1/60 of an hour, and 1 second of RA is equal to 1/60 of a minute. At the Celestial Equator, Right Ascension can be measured in degrees equal to those of Declination (since the Celestial Equator is a great circle. With 360° in a circle, each of the 24 hours of RA is equal to an angle of 15°. This angle decreases until it becomes zero at the poles (just as the meridians of longitude meet at the poles on Earth).

The angular distance between any two points on the celestial sphere can be expressed in degrees, minutes, and seconds of arc by placing the two points on an imaginary great circle of the celestial sphere. The Full Moon's diameter, for example, is about 30 arcminutes, or 30', or 0.5°. A close double star might have a separation of 5 arcseconds (5").

Determining Angular Sizes

For rough estimation with the naked eye, it is possible to 'eyeball' angles in the sky. For example, one index finger tip at arm's length subtends an angle of a little more than 1° in the sky. A fist (with the thumb flat against the end) at arm's length subtends about 10°. This can be useful if you know an object (like a planet in bright twilight) should be 20° above the western horizon or 5° south of a brighter object.

In a telescope, we often want to know the field of view with a given eyepiece.

So, we point the 'scope at a star near 0° Dec and put the star on the eastern edge of the field. Because of the Earth's rotation, the star will appear to drift westward. The time in minutes it takes the star to cross the entire field is equal to the telescope-eyepiece combination's field of view in minutes of RA (at the celestial equator only).

Because each hour of RA at the equator is equal to 15 degrees of arc, and each minute of RA is 1/60 of an hour, one minute of RA at the equator is equal to (15/60 = 1/4°). So, if the field of view is 2 minutes of RA, the field of view in degrees is 2/4=0.5°. Distances between stars or objects can then be measured in fields of view and converted to degrees of arc. If a new eyepiece is used, the field of view for that eyepiece will need to be determined.

True Distances and Diameters

If we identify the actual distance to an object, and measure its angular diameter in the sky, we can determine its actual diameter by solving a right triangle.

Always remember to convert the angular size (theta) to degrees of arc before taking the tangent. In other words, if theta is given in minutes it must be divided by 60. If theta is given in seconds, it must be divided by 3600.

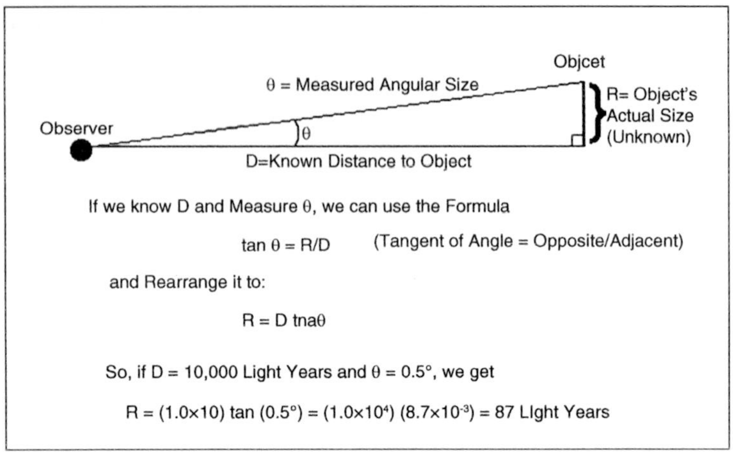

Loose Ends Points on the Celestial Sphere

Points on the celestial sphere remain fixed with respect to the stars, except for small changes due to precession of the Earth and independent proper motions of the stars. To an Earthbound observer, there are a couple of dynamic points and circles that are useful for describing the appearance of the sky. The point directly overhead is known as the zenith. The declination at the zenith is equal to the site's latitude; therefore, the zenith for an observer at 45°N will be +45°. The Right Ascension at the zenith is not fixed, and varies as the Earth rotates and revolves. If we draw an arc from the North Celestial Pole (in the Northern Hemisphere) through the zenith down to the southern horizon, we describe what is known as the meridian. Objects rise in the East, reach their greatest altitude at the meridian, and set in the West.

The Right Ascension of the meridian is known as the sidereal time. A clock adjusted to gain four minutes each day will keep rough sidereal time. It is important to know the time an object crosses the meridian, or culminates, since the object will be highest in the sky and most easily visible at that time. The edge of the visible portion of the celestial sphere is, of course, the horizon. An object will never be visible from a given latitude if it is below the horizon when it is on the meridian. The declination of the horizon at the meridian is equal to the site's latitude minus 90° (Southern Hemisphere observers will have to treat their latitude as negative and add 90° to get their meridional horizon). Certain objects near the visible celestial pole will not rise or set. These are known as circumpolar objects. Any star with a positive (negative for the Southern Hemisphere) declination greater than a site's latitude will be circumpolar from that site. An object's altitude when on the meridian (Am) can be determined by the formula $Am = 90° - |L - Dec|$, where L is the site's latitude and Dec is the object's declination. Note the absolute value notation. From 45° North latitude, an object at -30° Dec would attain an altitude of 15°. An object at +30° Dec would reach 75°, and one at +75° Dec would reach 60° altitude. An object at +45° Dec would, of course, reach the zenith at 90° altitude.

Chapter 4

The Nature of Stars, Universe and Planets

MOTION OF STARS

Everyone knows that the Sun rises from the east and sets in the west. Less well known is that almost everything on the sky, including the Moon, planets and most of the stars, also rises from the east and sets in the west. This is the major movement of objects on the sky and it is due to the rotation of the Earth.

We might envision that the Earth is at the centre of a large sphere, called the celestial sphere; and the Sun, stars, etc. are located on the sphere. Because the Earth is rotating from the west to the east, everything on the celestial sphere will apparently move from the east to the west. This is why the Sun rises from the east.

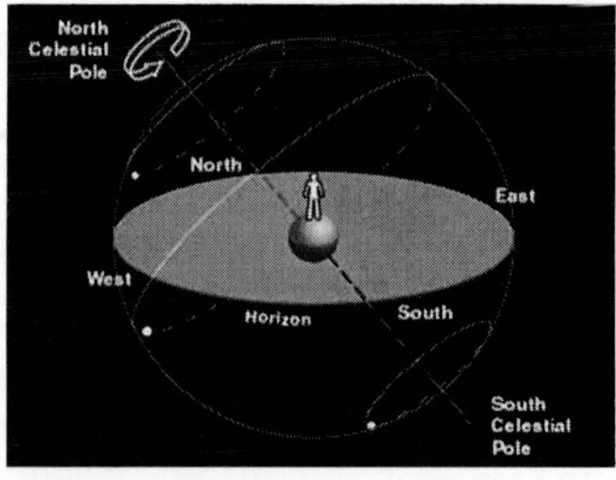

The circumpolar star, called Polaris, is special because it is very near the north celestial pole. Thus, it appears to be stationary. The position of Polaris relative to the ground depends on the latitude of the observer. For example, for people in Hong Kong, Polaris will be about 22.4° above the ground due north.

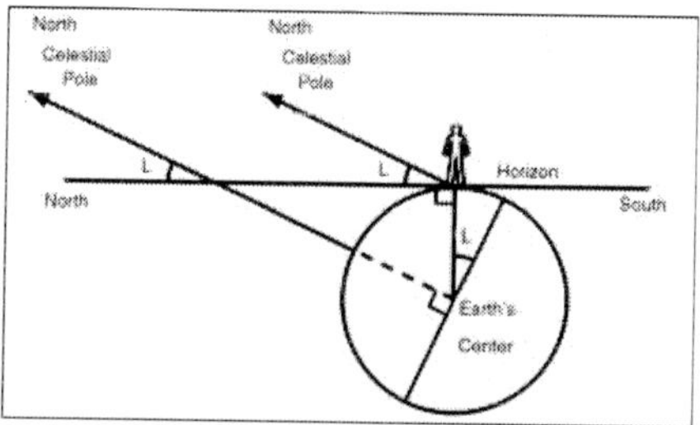

Also, some stars never rise. People in the northern hemisphere can never see stars near the south celestial pole, and people on the southern hemisphere can never see Polaris. Poor southerners, there is no bright star near the south celestial pole. There are three simulations of what can be seen in the northern hemisphere. The first one is pointing to the north. The second and the third show the motions of other stars at south and the east respectively.

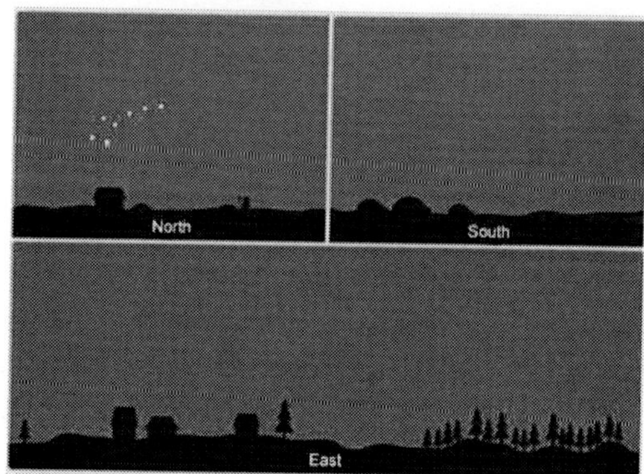

Motion of the Sun in the Celestial Sphere

Stars do not move on the celestial sphere. They are fixed. Thus, if we throw away the rotation of the Earth, stars are stationary. There is one significant exception however. The Sun is also a star, but the Sun does move on the celestial sphere because the Earth revolves around it. It moves from west to east, and completes a full circle in a year. The path that the Sun traces out on the celestial sphere is called the ecliptic and the twelve constellations that the Sun goes through are the zodiac. These are the origin of zodiac in astrology. Contrary to common belief, the Sun does *not* spend equal time on each ecliptic constellation.

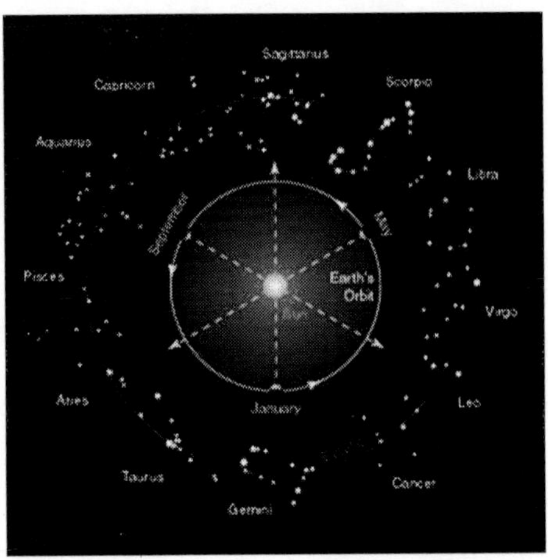

What is a Day?

Most people will define a day as the time the Sun comes back to the same position relative to the ground, for example, from one midday to another. This is exactly how the sundial works. This defines the solar day. There is another less common definition. We call it a day if other stars come back to the same positions. This is the sidereal day. Due to the revolution of the Earth, a solar day is longer than a sidereal day. Approximately, a year has 365 solar days but 366 sidereal days. Do you know why?

We say 'approximately' because a year has 365.2422 solar days. To compensate the extra 0.2422 days, some years will have 365 days while some years, called leap years, will have 366 days. One extra day is added to the end of February every four years. By doing this, we are adding too much. Hence, this extra day will not be added every hundred years, and it will be added again every four hundred years. For example, we have February 29 in the years 1988, 1992, 1996, 2000, 2400, 2800, etc., but there will be no February 29 in the years 1997, 1998, 1999 and 1800, 1900, 2100, 2200, etc. This is called the Gregorian calendar. Using Gregorian calendar, the error accumulated in the next 3000 years will not be more than 1 solar day.

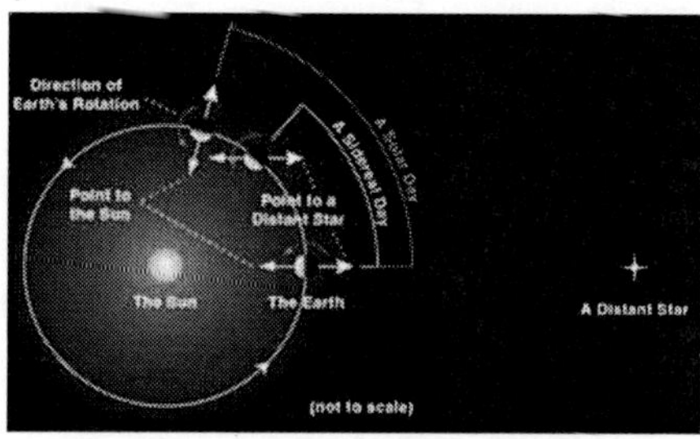

The obvious motion of the Moon is similar. The time between successive full Moons is the synodic month, it is 29.5 days long. Note that the Chinese calendar is based on both the motions of the Moon and the Sun, not just the Moon.

We have not done with the Sun yet. Since the rotational axis of the Earth is tilted from the revolution axis by 23.5°, the Sun, for example, rises at different directions at different times during the year.

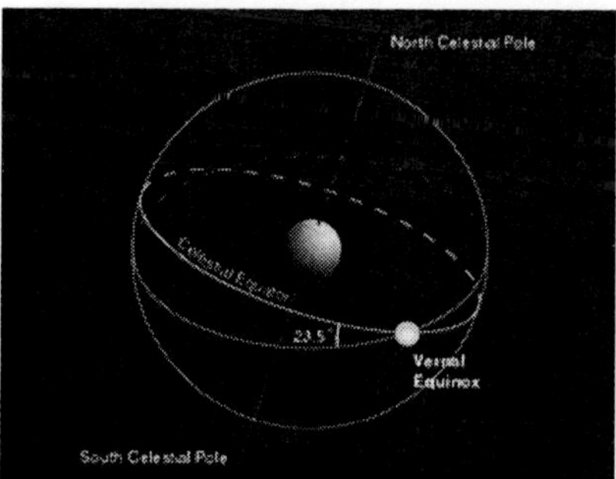

Comparable to the equator on Earth, we have the celestial equator on the celestial sphere. The ecliptic will intersect the equator with an angle 23.5°. The two intersection points are the vernal equinox and autumnal equinox. The two points on the ecliptic which are farthest away from the equator are the summer solstice and winter solstice. Usually, the Sun passes through vernal equinox, summer solstice, autumnal equinox and winter solstice on March 20, June 21, September 23 and December 22 respectively. When the Sun is at the summer solstice, it shines above the northern hemisphere. The northern hemisphere will receive more sunlight and become hotter, hence the summer for the northern hemisphere. Note that in southern hemisphere, it is winter when the Sun is at summer solstice.

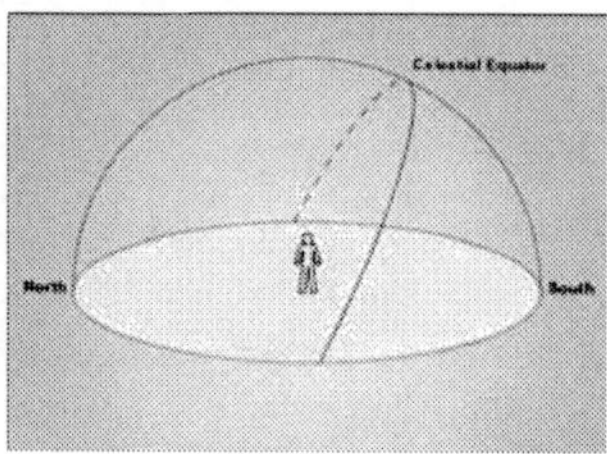

When the Sun is at the summer solstice, it rises at the northern most point and when it is at the winter solstice, it rises at the southern most point. That's why we have long daylight and short shadow in summer while the opposite in winter.

Motions of Planets

To ancient people, planets were 'stars' that moved on the celestial sphere. Actually, they move because they also orbit around the Sun. There are eight major planets: Mercury, Venus, Earth, Mars, Jupiter, Saturn, Uranus and Neptune, and many dwarf planets and minor planets.

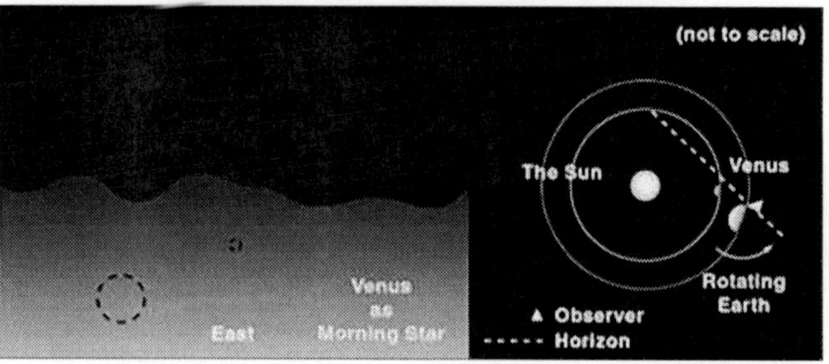

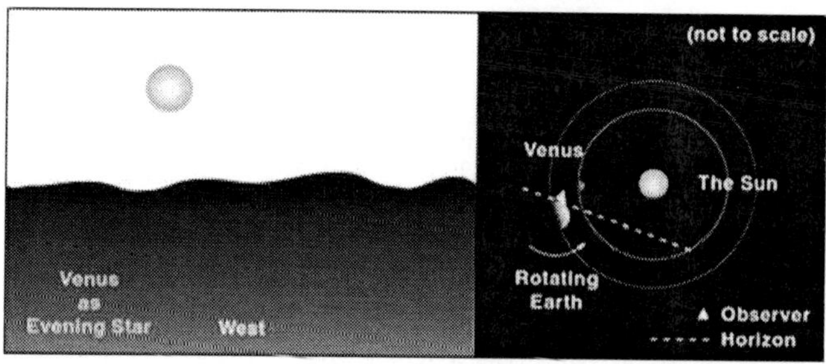

Mercury and Venus are inferior planets because their orbits are inside the orbit of the Earth.

Thus, when watching from the Earth, they are never too far away from the Sun. They just swing from the east of the Sun to the west and back, and we can only see them just before sunrise or just after sunset. During the period that we can see them before sunrise, we call them the 'morning stars.' It lasts for many days. When we can see them after sunset, we call them the 'evening stars.'

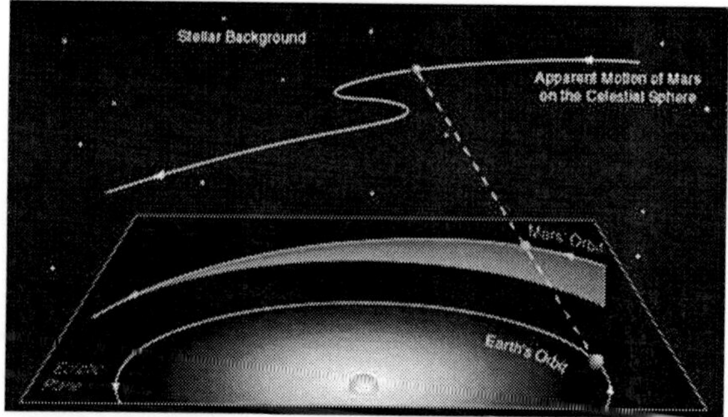

The others (Mars, Jupiter, Saturn, Uranus and Neptune) are called the superior planets. Due to their own revolutions, they move from west to east most of the time. We call it the prograde motion.

Because the orbital speed of the Earth is larger, it sometimes "catches up" the superior planets. Apparently, they will move in the opposite direction, from east to west. We call it the retrograde motion. (Inferior planets also have both prograde and retrograde motions.) Normally, the retrograde motion of one superior planet will last from weeks to months. So, you cannot see it in a single night.

BIRTH OF STARS

Since the average life span of human is relatively short compared to that of stars, we have to study a large number of stars in order to deduce the time scales of different evolutionary stages of stars. The Hertzsprung-Russell (H-R) diagram serves this purpose. It is a plot of absolute magnitude against surface temperature (*i.e.*, spectral type) of stars. The H-R diagram illustrates that most stars spend about 90 per cent of their life-time along the main sequence.

Formation of Stars

There are interstellar clouds in the universe. They are complete up of gas and dust, which are small particles. If the cloud is visible, we call it a nebula.

Fig. 4.1 Anglo-Australian Observatory and Photograph by David Malin

Fig. 4.2 Courtesy STScI

Interstellar clouds might be extremely large and massive, up to thousand of light years in diameter and from 10 to 1000 solar masses. (One solar mass is defined to be the mass of our Sun, which is about $2x10^{30}$kg. It is a convenient mass unit for stars.) As we have discussed in the last chapter, the density of a nebula is very low. And it contains mostly hydrogen.

If undisturbed, the interstellar clouds will not have qualitative changes at all. However, disturbance does occur. Such disturbance may be caused by the collisions of galaxies, the density wave of the hosting galaxy, the shock wave of a supernova, or even the birth of a new star nearby.

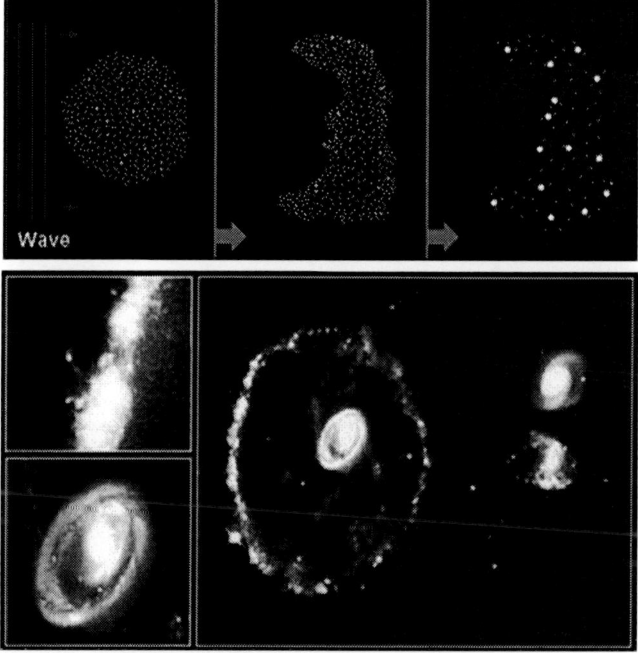

The slight alter in density will trigger the contraction of the cloud by its own gravity. A "sphere" known as protostar is then formed. Since there is no nuclear reaction inside the protostar, a protostar is not a star yet. The clouds that will evolve to stars with a mass of 10 to 30 solar masses contract to approximately the size of our solar system in only 10,000 years or so and become O and B stars. Less massive ones form T

Tauri type stars, which will eventually form stars of spectral types G, K or M. T Tauri stars are surrounded by a huge cloud and they are very young, with low surface temperature. They emit most of their light in the infrared region and they appear red. (A general principle is, a violent reaction will give out short wavelength waves, like gamma rays or X-rays; while a gentle process will radiate long wavelength waves, like radio or infrared.)

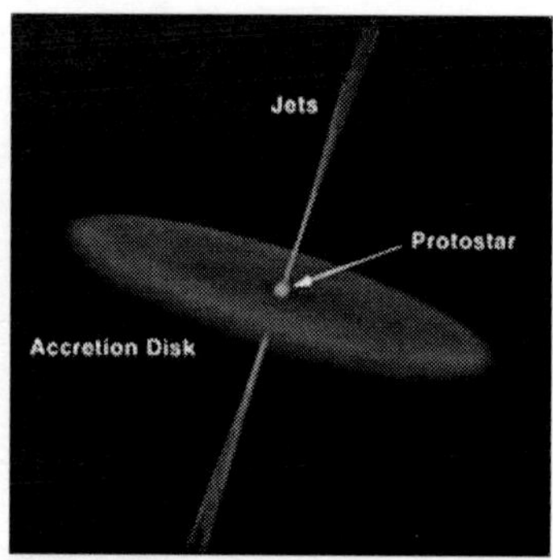

Models of protostar also show that they will have accretion disks and jets. The jets are not long-lived and last only about 100,000 years. If the gas and dust still cover the young star, we may not be able to see the star but we might see the two clouds produced by the jets.

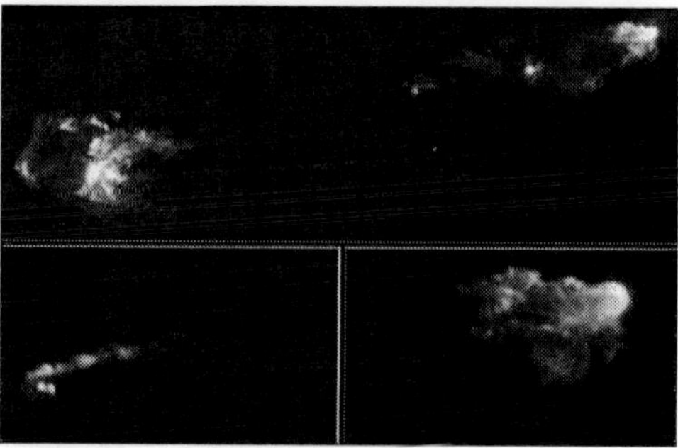

If the protostar is slightly more massive than a planet, but not massive enough to burn its nuclear fuels, it becomes a brown dwarf, which is very dim and hence very difficult to find. If it is massive enough (though model dependent, the lower mass limit is about 0.1 solar mass), the gas in the protostar continues to heat up until the central portion becomes hot and dense enough for, say, the hydrogen nuclei to overcome their mutual electrical repulsion. Nuclear fusion will then take place and a star is finally born. The light and heat generated by the star will push out the surrounding gas and dust.

The accretion disk remains and becomes the protoplanetary disk, where the planets are formed later on. Direct observation of these protoplanetary disks were made only a few years ago.

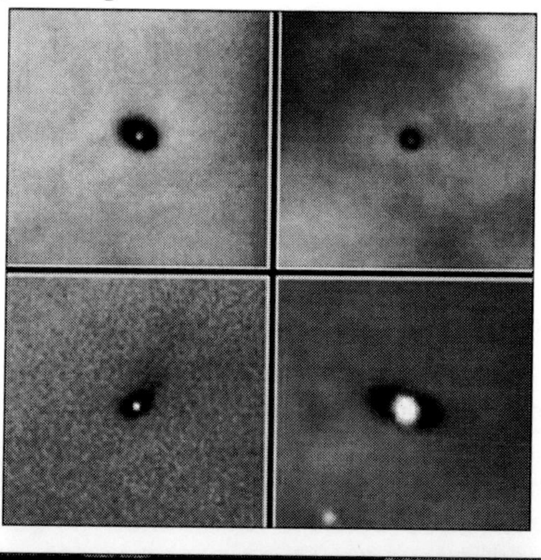

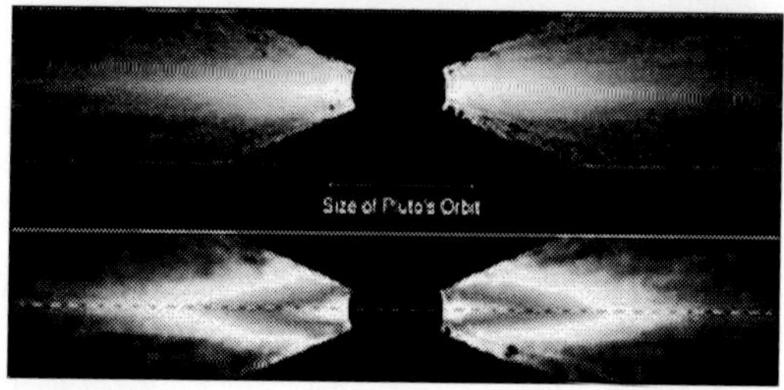

Particles in the star move around rapidly due to high temperature creating a high gas pressure. Together with the radiation pressure generated by the photons, they exert pressure pushing outward to balance gravity's inward pull. Then, a star becomes stable and now enters the main sequence phase.

The H-R Diagram and the Main Sequence Segment

We could represent the process of formation of a star in the H-R diagram by an evolutionary track. And we will see that the mass is the most important factor that determines the fate of a star.

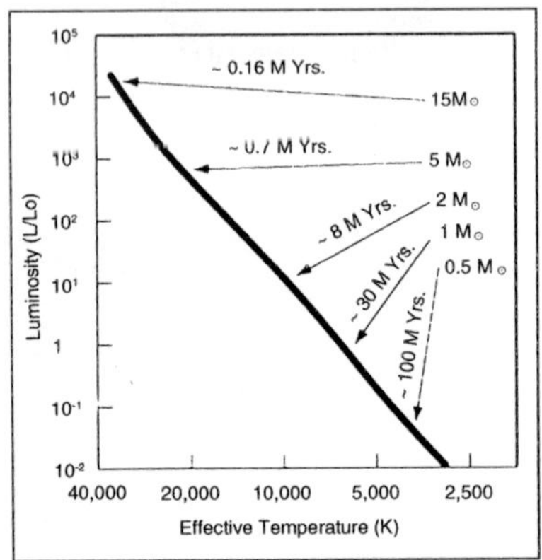

Before the interstellar cloud contracts, it was very cold and dim. Thus, the cloud is represented by a point at the right in the H-R diagram. Upon contraction under its own gravity, the interstellar cloud heats up, and thus moving to the left in the diagram. The luminosity per surface area will increase because the temperature increases. But if a star is not very massive, its luminosity will drop because the size of the star/protostar decreases much faster. It takes about 0.1 to 100 million years for the cloud to become a main sequence star. After it reaches the main sequence, the star will stay there for millions to billions of years.

Most of the energy generated in the protostar stage comes from the gravitational energy of the cloud, just like a ball will drop with increasing speed from your hand if you release it. After the star enters the main sequence stage, energy comes from nuclear fusion, the combination of several small nuclei into a large nucleus. In contrast, the nuclear plants on Earth generate energy by nuclear fission, the splitting of a large nucleus to several smaller ones. If the mass of the star is less than about 1.1 solar masses, the temperature of the core will be less than 15 million K, the main fusion reaction is the p-p chain, which turns four hydrogen nuclei to a helium nucleus. The star will have a convective shell and a radiative core just like our own Sun.

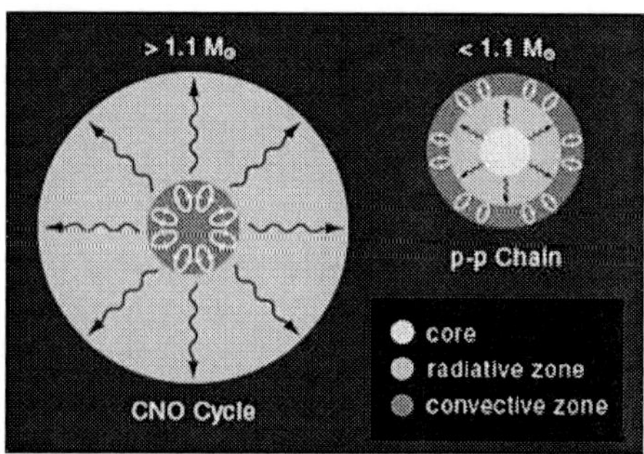

On the other hand, if the mass of the star is greater than about 1.1 solar masses, the dominate reaction will be the carbon-nitrogen-oxygen cycle (CNO cycle). The net effect of the CNO cycle is the same as the p-p chain. But carbon is used as a catalyst. Since a carbon nucleus is six times more positively charged than a hydrogen nucleus, the CNO cycle can only operate at the higher temperature and density provided by the more massive stars.

The CNO cycle is faster and more energy is produced per second. In order to effectively transport the heat energy out from the star, its core has to be convective. The outer part of the star is still quite hot that gas is not too opaque. Therefore, radiation transport is efficient enough to bring the energy almost all the way to the stellar surface. Hence the star will have a radiative shell and a convective core.

The major sequence stage lasts for a long time in the life of a star. For the most massive stars, because the reaction rate is much faster, they will use up their fuel in the core in about one million years. For less massive stars, their lives could be up to tens of billion years.

Death of Less Massive Stars

A star will spend about 90 per cent of its life in the major sequence phase, in which hydrogen nuclei fuse to helium nuclei in the core. A common misconception is that a more massive star has more 'fuel', and will have a longer life-time. But in fact, because the core of a massive star is hotter and denser, it burns much faster and has a shorter life.

One way to see more massive stars have shorter lives is to study the star clusters. The stars in clusters were born at the same time. Hence, they have the same age, but their masses are different. We expect stars with short life span are already dead. When we plot the stars of a cluster in the H-R diagram, we see the more massive stars, which are stars in the upper left, have already evolved off the main sequence. And stars at the turnoff point are just about to die. From the two H-R diagrams below, we can also tell which cluster is older and which is younger.

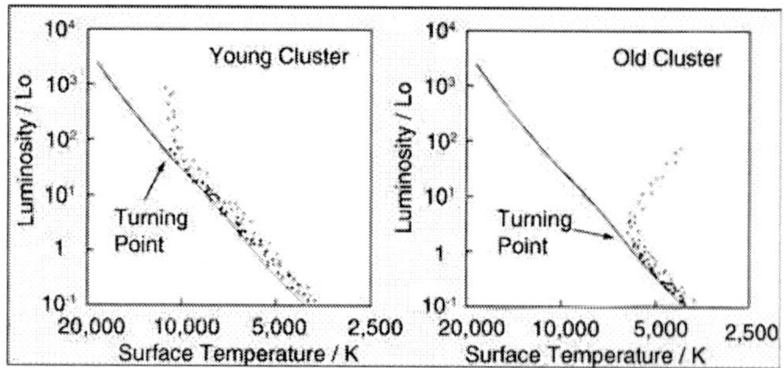

Main sequence stars have stable luminosities and sizes. To be honest, they are quite "boring" compare to their deaths. We have already seen that how long a star lives depends exclusively on its mass. How important the mass of a star in determining its death.

Death of Solar Mass Stars

At what time no hydrogen is left in the core, p-p chain reaction stops. The helium core of the star starts to collapse. This gravitational contraction will heat up the hydrogen envelope surrounding the core. Fusion therefore begins in the envelope and the star expands. The star becomes very big and the surface temperature decreases, although the core temperature is still very high and the total luminosity is also high. Since the average luminosity is low, the star appears red. This big red star is a red giant.

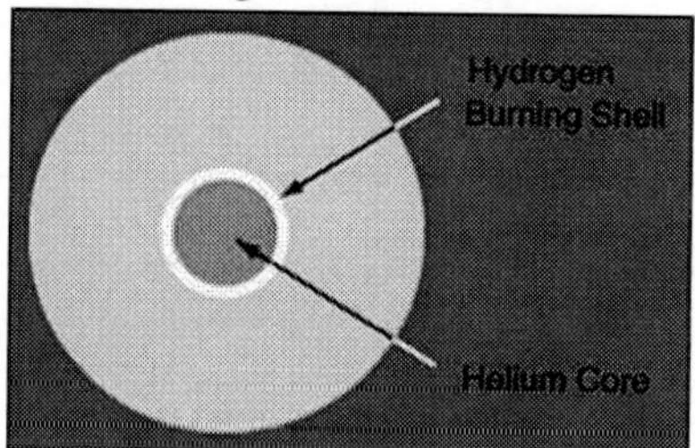

When our Sun becomes a red giant, its size can be as large as the Earth's orbit. The relative sizes of the Earth (the white dot), the Sun now and a typical red giant.

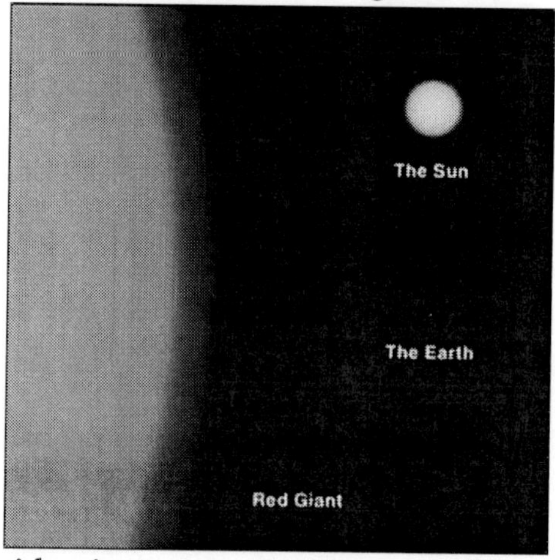

All left side giants are variable stars. The core keeps on contracting and heating up until it is hot enough for the triple-alpha process (also known as helium flash) to take place. In this reaction, three helium nuclei will fuse together to form a carbon nucleus. Since the hydrogen-burning shell and helium-burning core do not produce energy in a stable and steady manner, the star will pulsate and generate strong stellar wind. Eventually, the entire outer shell will be ejected. The gas ejected will form a thin shell around the star. It is a planetary nebula. Here is the Ring nebula, M57, easily visible through a small telescope. Some others were taken by the Hubble Space Telescope.

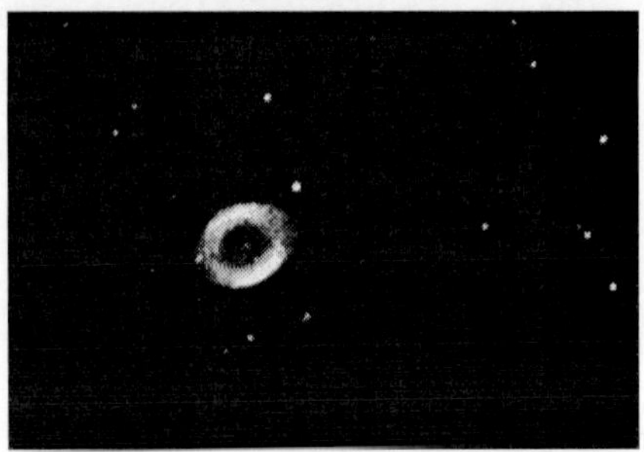

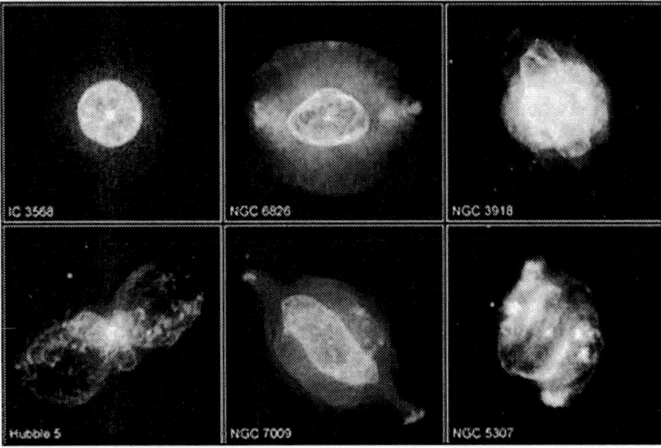

Fig. 4.3 Courtesy STScI

For the core, it does not heat up sufficiently for carbon-burning. When there's no more nuclear burning, it shrinks. It grows fainter as well as hotter and becomes a white dwarf. Then, electron degenerate pressure stops it from further contracting. The electron degenerate pressure does not come from the burning of any nuclear fuel and can therefore support the star from further gravitational contraction forever.

A characteristic white dwarf is slightly smaller than the Earth, but with about the same mass as our Sun. Its density is about 300,000 times of a rock. After it has radiated away all its residue energy, it becomes a black dwarf. However, the time taken is much larger than the age of the universe. So, we believe there is no black dwarf yet. The following picture schematically summarizes the evolution of a solar mass star.

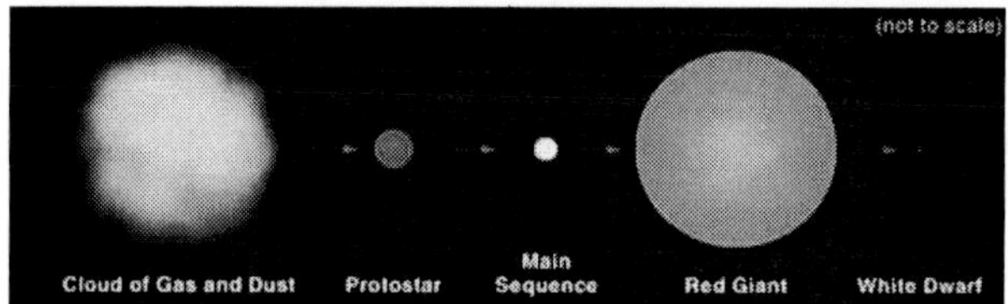

Five billion years later, it will evolve along the curve to become a red giant. It will be unstable and eject the shell forming a planetary nebula, then move quickly along the curve to become white dwarf at the lower left.

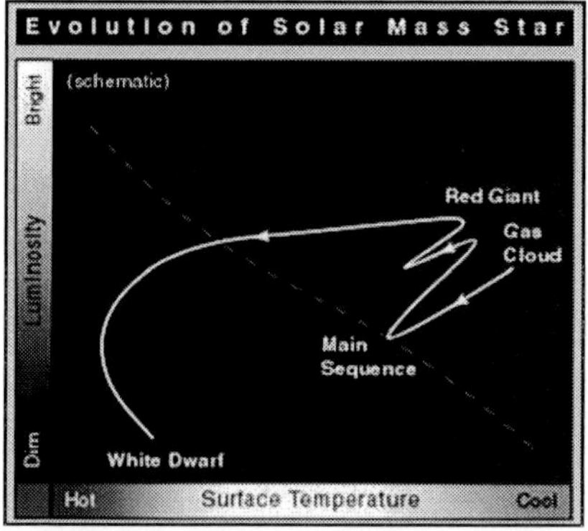

Death of Low Mass Stars

If a star is less enormous than about 0.4 solar mass, its life will be quite uneventful. It will quietly and steadily burn the hydrogen to helium and become a white dwarf.

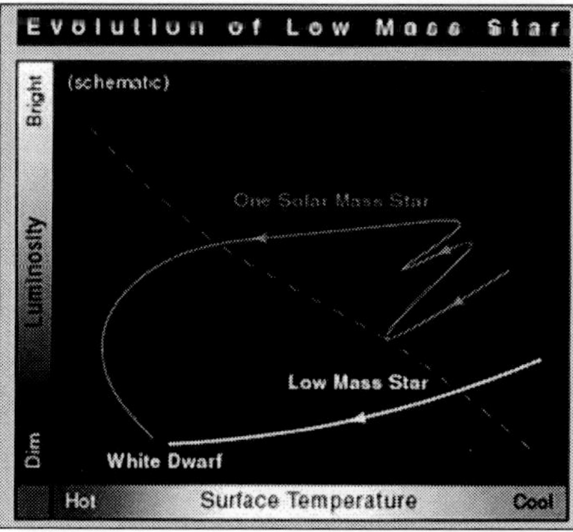

Nova

In a binary system, situations may become additional complicated. For example, it could happen that one has evolved to a white dwarf and the other is becoming a red giant. The two could be very closed to each other, maybe only about the Earth-Moon distance. Matter will be transferred from the red giant to the white dwarf when the gravity of the red giant at its surface is weaker than that of the white dwarf. When sufficient matter is accreted onto the surface of the white dwarf, nuclear reactions will start and sustain for a short period on the white dwarf surface. Enormous energy is produced. The star system could brighten up 100,000 times. We call this brighten star system a nova. This explosion usually will not disturb the white dwarf and the accretion can resume again and again.

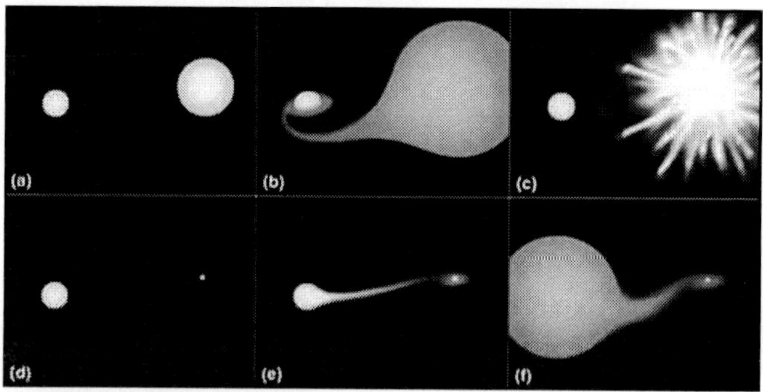

Death of Massive Stars

The death of a star with a mass about or less than that of our Sun. A more massive star will die and one possible form of its corpse, the neutron star.

Red Supergiants and Supernovae

Main sequence star with a mass over about 8 solar masses. Because of its great mass, both the core temperature and density are higher than that of a solar mass star. The nuclear reaction rate is also higher and it produces more energy per second. The star is of spectral type O, B or A.

Similar to other main sequence stars, hydrogen nuclei will be fused to helium nuclei in the core. However, the massive star will have a shorter life span, for example, a 15 solar mass star can only survive for about 10 million years. Because of the large mass, after the hydrogen burning, the temperature and pressure of the core is high enough to trigger helium burning to carbon, and a hydrogen burning shell is developed around the core. The helium will burn steadily and the higher energy production rate will heat up the star. The star will swell to a size even larger than a red giant and we have a red supergiant. A typical red supergiant could be about 100 times larger than the red giant. Its surface temperature is low while the total luminosity remains high, with absolute magnitude up to -10 (comparing to 4.8 of our Sun).

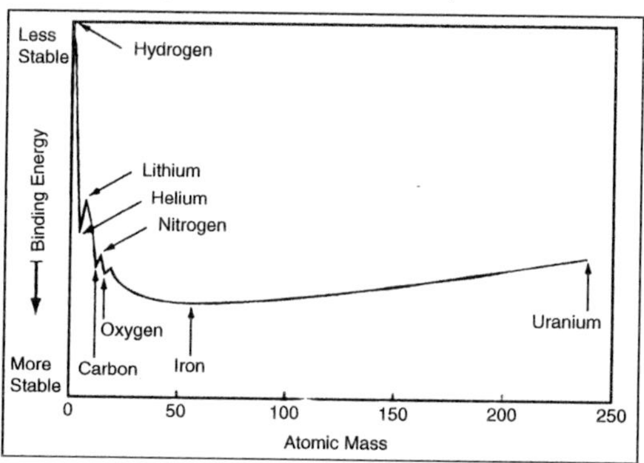

Similar to the helium burning, the strong gravitational force of the star ignites and controls the carbon burning in the core; light nuclei fuse into heavier and heavier elements, until iron. We believe the heavy elements, like oxygen, nitrogen and silicon, found on Earth were made in a star somewhere long time ago by this mechanism.

Elements heavier than iron cannot be made in this way. Iron is, in fact, the dead end of nuclear reaction. When hydrogen is fused to helium, energy is produced. However, we have to supply energy to fuse iron to even heavier elements. This is why we can split a heavy nucleus, like uranium, into several smaller ones to produce energy. Iron burning cannot happen since it takes energy to do so. Therefore, as more and more iron is formed in the core, the pressure there decreases rapidly. After enough iron in the core is accumulated, within one hundredth second, the inner core collapses and heats up dramatically. All fuel, if not burnt up yet, will fuse to iron and nickel.

The outer core will also collapse with the inner core. Electrons will react with protons to form neutrons and neutrinos. Most of the energy generated by the collapse is carried away by neutrinos.

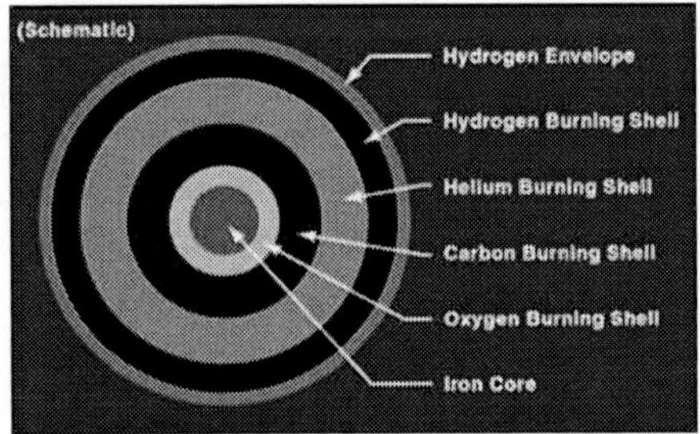

Because of the upper limit of the nuclear compactness, which prevents the core to compress too far, the collapsing inner core will bounce back outwards. This out-going inner core will collide with the incoming outer core, which is collapsing rapidly.

This collision will send off shock waves and create heavy elements, like uranium. Also, the outer layers of the star will be thrown off to space. This is a Type II supernova explosion.

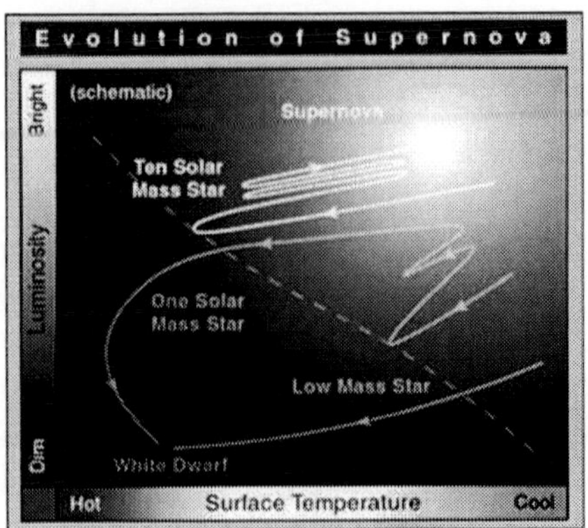

Supernova explosion is extremely violent. The brightness of the star will increase by up to 15 magnitudes. This will be a spectacular astronomical event.

The most recent supernova visible by naked eyes was the SN1987A, which is located in a small nearby galaxy, the Large Magellanic Cloud. Unfortunately, the Large Magellanic Cloud is near the south celestial pole and is not visible in Hong Kong.

Another famous supernova was recorded in 1054 A.D. by Chinese astronomers in the Sung dynasty. They discovered a 'guest star' in where we now call the Taurus region. That star was visible in daytime and remained visible for two months.

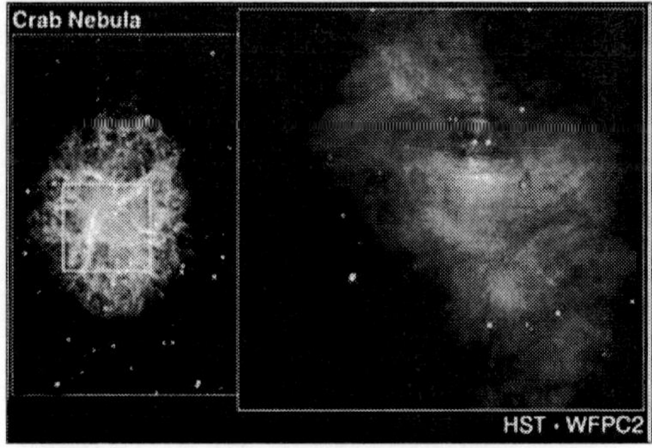

Fig. 4.4 Courtesy STScI

Hundreds of supernovae are discovered each year. However, they are not in our galaxy and usually very dim. Here is one in M51 in 1994.

Fig. 4.5 Courtesy STScI

What will happen to the remains of the supernova explosion? It depends on the mass of the core left. After the explosion, if the mass left is less than 1.4 solar masses, a white dwarf will form. If it is between 1.4 to about 3 solar masses, a neutron star will form. If it is more massive, a black hole will be there. The following table schematically shows the path of the death of a star.

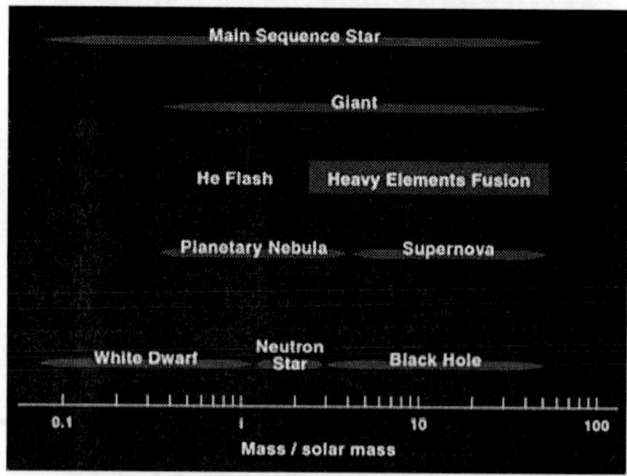

Neutron Stars and Pulsars

The mass of the core after a supernova detonation is more than 1.4 but less than about 3 solar masses, then electron degenerate pressure is not strong enough to support the star. The star will contract to a size even smaller than the white dwarf. The electrons are squeezed into the nuclei and are combined with the protons to form neutrons. The neutron degenerate pressure can stop the star from further collapsing. A neutron star is formed.

A neutron star composes mostly of neutrons, about 95-99 per cent. Yet there is a trace amount of electrons and protons. Its typical size is about 8 to 16 km in radius, which is roughly the size of Hong Kong Island. Since the gravitational field on the surface is very strong, no hills or mountains can be formed on a neutron star. We believe there is a solid crust of heavy nuclei, which is about 1 km thick. There may be a solid core, but we are not sure.

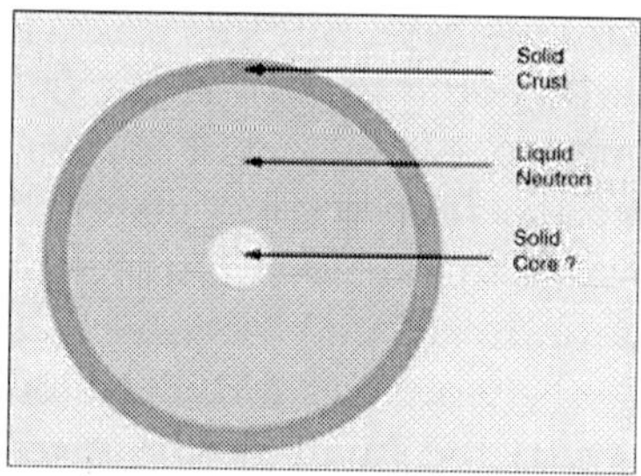

Another very important property of neutron star is its strong magnetic field. It ranges from 10^8 to 10^{15} times the magnetic field on the surface of the Earth. When electrons move in spirals around magnetic lines of force, radio waves are produced and radiated out along the two magnetic poles of the star.

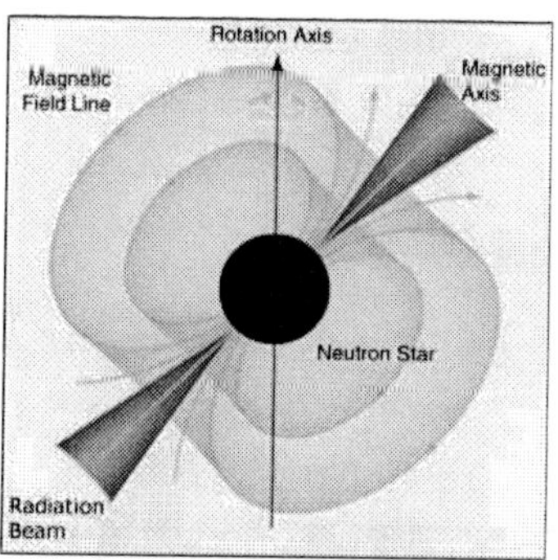

Usually, the rotational axis of the neutron star does not align with the magnetic axis. The radiation beams will sweep around and create the light house effect. What we observe on

Earth will be pulses of radio wave with very stable period. This is a pulsar — one can be found at the centre of the Crab Nebula.

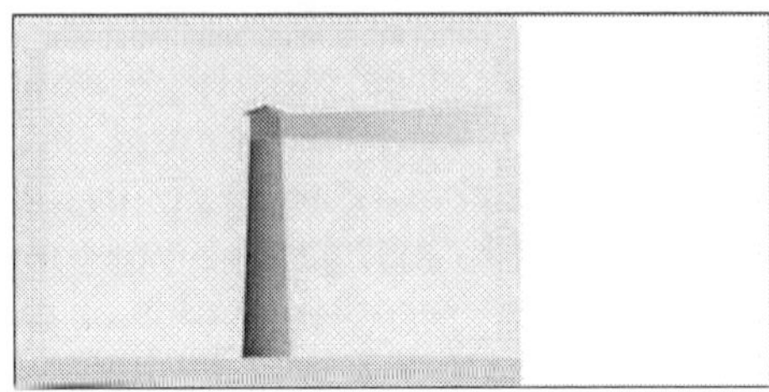

When signals from pulsars were discovered in 1960s, we thought they came from some other civilizations. Later on, we knew that this is not the case. But this raises another question: The rotational period could be as fast as 0.001s, which we call the millisecond pulsars. What kind of objects can rotate so fast without flying apart? The strong gravitational field of a neutron star provides the answer. Due to their large masses, their rotational periods are very regular. We can specify the periods of some pulsars up to more than ten decimal places. This allows us to study the small disturbances around the star. For example, if there is a planet orbiting around the neutron star, it will wobble a little and the pulses will come a little early or late. We can then deduce the mass and the radius of the orbit of the planet from the arrival time of the pulses. This is how the first extrasolar planet is discovered.

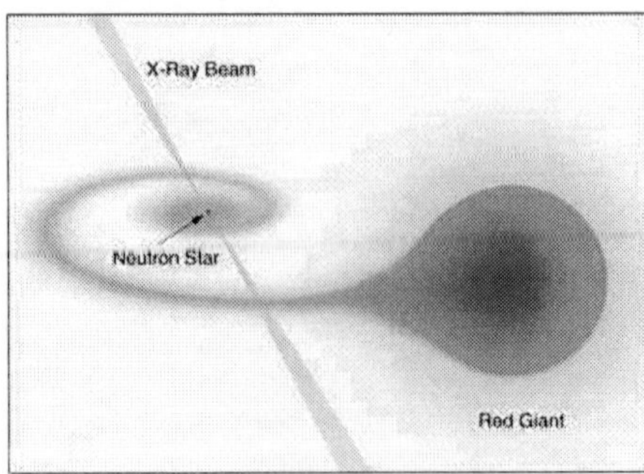

The over conversation concentrates on the single star system. There are many interesting phenomena in a neutron star binary system. We will just mention one. If the companion of the neutron star is a giant, material will be transferred from the giant to the neutron star. X-rays will be emitted and a X-ray pulsar is formed.

Defining a Star

A star is a body that at some occasion in its life generates its light and heat by nuclear reactions, specifically by the fusion of hydrogen into helium under conditions of enormous temperature and density. When hydrogen atoms merge to create the next heavier element, helium, mass is lost, the mass (M) converted to energy (E) through Einstein's famous equation E = mc squared, where 'c' is the speed of light. The Sun is powered by hydrogen fusion, as are many of the other stars you see at night. The fusion does not take place throughout the star, but only in its deep interior, in its core, where it is hot enough. The temperature at the centre of the Sun is 15.6 million degrees Kelvin (K = centigrade degrees above absolute zero, –273 C), and the density is 14 times that of lead. About 40 per cent of the mass of the Sun, occupying about 30 per cent of the radius, is capable of fusing hydrogen. Even under these extreme conditions, the Sun (as well as all other stars) is still a gas throughout. That said, things get more complicated, as nature creates 'substars' called 'brown dwarfs' that do not have enough mass and therefore internal heat to run full fusion. Even though they do not abide by the formal definition of a 'star,' they are still referred to as 'stars' even if their masses are not much greater than those of planets.

Brightness and Distance

In the subsequent century BC, the Greek astronomer Hipparchus divided the stars into six brightness groups called *magnitudes* (now *apparent visual magnitudes* (m or V), first magnitude the brightest, sixth the faintest. The system is still used today, though with a mathematical definition (a star of one magnitude is 2.512... times brighter than the next fainter) that takes the very brightest stars and planets through magnitude zero and into negative numbers. Through the telescope we see much fainter, to near 30th magnitude (4 billion times fainter than the human eye can see alone). Though stars bear some resemblance to the Sun, they appear as points in the sky because they are so far away, the nearest, Alpha Centauri, four light years away. The *light year* is the distance a ray of light will travel in a year at 300,000 kilometres (186,000 miles) per second, so one light year is about 10 trillion kilometres (63,000 *Astronomical Units*, where the AU is the average distance between the Earth and the Sun). The stars are so far that distances were not measured until 1846, by means of *parallax* (viewing the star from opposite sides of the Earth's orbit). The most distant stars the unaided eye can see are over 1000 light years away, which is about the practical limit of parallax measures. The apparent visual magnitude of a star depends on true visual luminosity (in watts) and distance. To compare true visual luminosities, astronomers calculate the *absolute visual magnitude* (M), the apparent magnitude the star would have were it at a distance of 32.6 light years (10 *parsecs*, where the parsec is the professional unit of distance, equal to 3.26 light years). The absolute visual magnitude of the Sun is +4.83. Absolute visual magnitudes range from around –10 (a million times more luminous than the Sun) to below +20 (a million times fainter).

The Galaxy

We need to set the stars in context. All those you see at night are part of our local collection of stars, all part of our *Galaxy*. Trillions of other galaxies flock the Universe, ours one of the larger ones. The principal part of our Galaxy (our own with a capitol 'G') is in the shape of a flat disk about 100,000 light years across that contains some 200 billion stars. Our Sun is towards the edge, about 25,000 light years from the centre, the whole structure at the Sun's distance rotating with a period of 200 million years. A large portion of the disk's stars are set within pinwheel-like spiral arms that over millions of years come and go, the stars moving in and out of them as they orbit the Galaxy's centre. The combined light of its billions of stars around our head as the famed 'Milky Way,' the centre of the Galaxy (which contains a supermassive black hole of three million solar masses) located behind the thick star clouds of

Sagittarius. The age of the disk is about 10 billion years. Surrounding the disk is a thinly populated rather spherical halo that seems to date to 12 to 13 billion years of age.

The Compositions of the Stars

Stars are made of the same chemical elements as found in the Earth, though not in the same proportions, the chemical compositions found from the stars' spectra. Most stars are made almost entirely of hydrogen (about 90% by number of atoms) and helium (about 10%), elements that are relatively rare on our planet. About a tenth of a percent is left over, that tenth containing all the other elements found in nature. Of these, oxygen usually dominates, followed by carbon, neon, and nitrogen. Of the metals, iron usually dominates. Nevertheless, there is only one atom of oxygen in the Sun for every 1200 hydrogen atoms and only one of iron for every 32 oxygen atoms. However, within this tenth of a per cent, the proportions of the numbers of atoms in the Sun is rather similar to what we find here, in the Earth's crust. Other stars can deviate considerably, depending on their states of aging or upon where they are in the Galaxy.

Masses of Stars

To generate the conditions for such 'thermonuclear fusion,' stars must be massive. The Sun has the mass of 333,000 Earths. Stars can range up to about 100 times the mass of the Sun (at which point nature stops making them) down to around 7.5 per cent that of the Sun, at which point the internal temperature is not high enough to run the full range of nuclear reactions (which requires at least 7 million degrees Kelvin). 'Substars' below the 7.5 per cent limit, called 'brown dwarfs,' do exist in significant numbers however, and down to around 1/80 the solar mass (13 Jupiter-masses) can fuse their natural deuterium (heavy hydrogen, with an extra neutron). The lower limit to brown dwarf (substellar) masses is not known. Masses are measured from double stars and can be calculated from luminosity and temperature using the theories of stellar structure.

Hydrogen Fusion of Stars : Proton-Proton Chain

Stars are supported, kept from shrinking under their own gravity, by energy generated by internal fusion of light atoms into heavier ones. Fusion of hydrogen into helium can take place only under the extreme conditions of temperature and density found in a star's deep core. The 'proton-proton chain' operates in ordinary stars (those that have not yet begun the death process) with masses more or less like that of the Sun and under (while higher mass stars do it by the carbon cycle. It begins when two protons (bare hydrogen atoms) ram together strongly enough to overcome the mutual repulsion caused by their positive electric charges and get close enough to stick together under the 'strong force' (which operates only over a very short range). One of the protons ejects its positive charge in the form of a 'positron,' a positive electron that hits a normal electron to generate energy in the form of gamma rays. The conversion creates a deuterium (heavy hydrogen) nucleus as well as a tiny particle called a 'neutrino.' Detection of neutrinos on Earth allow us to 'see' directly into the solar centre. The fusion of the deuterium with another proton produces a light form of helium (with two protons and one neutron), while the fusion of two light helium atoms into a normal helium atom with two protons and two neutrons (with the ejection of two protons) completes the process, each reaction generating heat and light as a result of a slight loss of mass.

Hydrogen Fusion: Carbon Cycle

Higher mass stars (with masses greater than about 1.5 times that of the Sun) fuse hydrogen into helium via the 'carbon cycle,' which works only under high-temperature conditions, but is then more efficient than the proton-proton chain. It begins when a normal carbon atom (C-12, with 6 protons and 6 neutrons) picks up a proton to make radioactive nitrogen-13, one of whose protons ejects a positron (positive electron) to make stable carbon-13 (with the additional ejection of a neutrino). Carbon- 13 plus a proton makes normal nitrogen-14, while an additional proton collision makes oxygen-15, which (like N-13) decays into nitrogen-15. The

N-15 collects another proton, and then falls apart into the original carbon-12 and a helium nucleus. Each event produces some energy either itself or through the collisions of positrons and electrons.

Brown Dwarfs

For decades, astronomers predicted the existence of substars we now call 'brown dwarfs,' stars too small and light (of insufficient mass, less than 0.073 solar masses) to run the full nuclear fusion process (from ordinary hydrogen to helium). After all, the star formation process should 'know' nothing of the conditions under which nuclear reactions should turn on. Brown dwarfs (which are still called 'stars') turned out to be so cool that only new infrared technologies could find them. We now know they are very common, so common that new classes, L and T (cooler than M) had to be made for them. Between 0.073 solar masses (78 Jupiter-masses) and 13 Jupiter-masses, brown dwarfs do fuse their natural deuterium (heavy hydrogen, with an extra neutron) to helium. The lower end of brown dwarf masses is not known. They quite likely overlap the masses of planets. Planets are by current definition made from the 'bottom up,' accumulated from dust in disks surrounding new stars, while stars (including brown dwarfs) are made from the 'top down,' by direct condensation from interstellar gases. But here even the definitions become confused and might overlap as well.

The Birth of Stars

The space between the stars is filled with dusty gas. Thick dust clouds can even be seen with the naked eye within the Milky Way blocking the light of distant stars and providing much of the Milky Way's structure. Interstellar matter is compressed by the Galaxy's winding spiral arms. The clouds can be further compressed through collisions or by blast waves from exploding high-mass stars (supernovae). Lumps of matter therefore form within the interstellar clouds. If their gravity is great enough, they can condense into one or more stars. Contraction causes more rapid spin, which creates a disk around the birthing star, from which it can draw matter. Further condensation within the disk can create planets (or even stellar companions). The contraction of forming stars raises the internal temperature, finally to the point of ignition of hydrogen fusion. Gravity would like to make the star as small as possible, but the fusion reactions stabilize it and keep it from contracting any further. The whole life story of a star from here on out is told by the battle between gravity and nuclear fusion, first one, then the other getting the upper hand. New high mass stars commonly light up their surroundings to produce diffuse nebulae like the Orion Nebula.

Planets

As a fresh star condenses from a gaseous lump in interstellar space, it spins faster, the outer parts of the contracting cloud spinning out into a dusty disk. The dust particles, in orbit about the new star, accumulate, building themselves into planets. Here at home, the planets that formed close to the Sun (Mercury through Mars) were in an environment too hot to incorporate much water or light atoms like hydrogen, so they are made of heavy stuff like iron, silicon, and oxygen. In the outer System, the planets contain huge amounts of hydrogen and helium and could grow large, their satellites made largely of water ice. Other stars should grow planets too, planets that could be quite different from our own and that are now being discovered.

Main Sequence (Dwarf) Stars and Stellar Classes

There are numerous kinds and classes of stars. Those that are actively fusing hydrogen into helium in the middle, that is, in their cores (either through the proton-proton chain or the carbon cycle), are called 'main sequence' stars. The main sequence is the first stage following birth. In general, main sequence stars have chemical compositions similar to that of the Sun. The higher the mass of the main sequence star, the greater its diameter and the higher its surface temperature. Dimensions range from about 10% the size of the Sun (which is 1.5 million kilometres—109 Earths—across) to just over ten times solar, and surface temperatures from under 2000 degrees Kelvin to about 49,000 K (the Sun's surface is at 5780 K). Around the beginning of the 20th century, astronomers divided the stars into seven basic lettered groups that they later learned were related to surface temperature, which for the main sequence are: O (above 31,500 K), B (10,000– 31,500 K), A (7500 –10,000 K), F(6000–7500 K), G(5300–6000 K), K(3800–5300 K), and M (2100–3800 K). A century later, two more classes were added to account for faint red stars turned up by new technologies: class L (1200–2100 K) and T (below 1200 K), the whole set now OBAFGKMLT. Perhaps half of the class L stars and all the class T stars are brown dwarf substars. The Sun is a G star. The system is decimalized, making the Sun class G2. Examples of main sequence stars are Acrux, Vega, Sirius, Porrima, Chara, Alpha Centauri A and B, and Proxima Centauri. The classes are actually derived from the stars' spectra. The stellar astronomer's greatest tool is the HR diagram, a plot of absolute visual magnitude against spectral class, in which we can see nearly all of the stages of stellar life and death. On it, the main sequence is a band that runs from the highest-mass hydrogen-fusing stars at the upper left to the lowest masses at the lower right.

Giant Stars

Begin with stars more or less like the Sun, those with masses from about 0.8 times that of the Sun to about 10 times the solar mass. When the fuel in a solar type star's core runs out, the helium core contracts under the effect of gravity and heats up. Hydrogen fusion then expands into a shell around the old burnt-out core, and so much energy is produced that the star temporarily brightens and expands by many times over, the expansion cooling the surface, turning the star into a class M "red giant." When the temperature hits around 100 million degrees Kelvin, the helium is hot enough to fuse into carbon (through the near-simultanous collision of three helium atoms) and even a bit further, into oxygen. This new power source stops the core's contraction and the star stabilizes for a time, dimming and heating somewhat at the surface. We commonly see these helium-fusing stars as yellow-orange type K giants. On the HR diagram, the giants run roughly from the middle towards upper right (higher luminosity). Among classes G and K, temperatures are up to a few hundred degrees cooler than they are for main sequence dwarfs. Good examples are Aldebaran and Arcturus. Such stars have diameters tens of times that of the Sun. The giant and subsequent stages up to the actual death of the star (the end of nuclear fusion) takes roughly 10 per cent of the main sequence lifetime.

Star Colours

Because the colour of a heated body depends on temperature, the different classes take on different, though subtle, colours, from slightly reddish for class M to orange for K, through yellow-white to bluish for classes B and O. Star colours can be noted rather easily even with the unaided eye, especially when those close together contrast against each other. Stars of classes L and T, none of which are visible to the naked eye, range from red through deep red to 'infrared' (these optically invisible under *any* circumstances).

Lifetimes of Stars

Main sequence (dwarf) stars have only a certain amount of internal fuel available within their hot cores. When the hydrogen fuel has all turned to helium, the stars begin to die and to produce a number of other different kinds, the whole process commonly known as *stellar evolution*. Because higher mass stars use their hydrogen fuel much more quickly than lower mass stars, those of higher mass live shorter lives. The Sun has a 10 billion year main sequence lifetime (of which half is gone).

The most massive stars live only a couple million years, the least massive for trillions, so long that no star with a mass less than about 0.8 solar masses has ever died in the history of the Galaxy. From theory, we calculate that such a 0.8 solar mass star should live for about 13 billion years. The Galaxy should be about as old as its oldest stars, and is thus about 13 billion years old.

Cepheid Variable Stars

When more massive stars (2 to 8 times that of the Sun) pass through mid-temperatures either on their way to fusing helium or during various stages of helium fusion, they can become unstable and pulsate in size, temperature, and luminosity. The first of these discovered, Delta Cephei, gave the name 'Cepheid' variable to the group. Cepheids, usually classed as F and G supergiants (though not as massive as true supergiants), vary by a couple to a few magnitudes over periods of one to 100 days. A strict relation between absolute magnitude and pulsation period allows us to determine their distances (period gives absolute brightness, and comparison to apparent brightness yields distance.) Cepheids are the major keys to learning distances to other galaxies. The brightest Cepheid in the sky is Polaris, though the variations are too small to be seen by eye. Cepheids occupy the upper range of the HR diagram's, 'instability strip.'

Bigger Red Giants and Miras

When the helium in the core has turned to carbon and oxygen, the core shrinks again, and the helium begins to fuse to carbon and oxygen in a shell around the old core, this shell surrounded by another one fusing hydrogen into helium, the two turning on and off in sequence. The star now brightens again, expands even more, and becomes cooler and even redder than before. As the star brightens it becomes unstable and begins to pulsate, the pulsations making it vary, or change in brightness. The star become so huge, near or greater than the orbit of the Earth, that the pulsations can take a year or more.

The first of these found, Mira in Cetus, changes from second or third magnitude to tenth, becoming quite invisible to the naked eye. Such stars are now called 'long-period variables' (LPVs) or 'Mira variables.' Thousands, all cool class M giants, are known. On the HR diagram, such advanced giants are at the cool end of the 'giant branch,' the Miras occupying the coolest and brightest portion. In astronomical jargon, such stars are called *asymptotic giant branch* stars (or *AGB* stars) because of the appearance of their distribution on the HR diagram.

Planetary Nebulae

As a giant star loses almost all of its remaining outer hydrogen envelope, it comes close to revealing its intensely hot core. A fast wind from the core first compresses the inner edge of the old expanding wind. High-energy radiation from the hot core then lights up this inner compressed portion, which is now many times the size of the whole Solar System. These illuminated clouds, which can be quite beautiful, were discovered by William Herschel around 1790, who termed them 'planetary nebulae' for their disk-like appearances (they have nothing else to do with planets).

The best known is the Ring Nebula in Lyra. Their complex appearances depend to a degree on how matter is lost from the giant stars that make them. Expanding at rates of tens of kilometers per second, they last no more than a few tens of thousands of years. From their emission spectra we can analyse their chemical compositions, and find that many are enriched in the by-products of prior nuclear fusion in the parent advanced giant stars.

Creation of Elements

The gases of red giants can circulate upward to the tops of the stars, carrying the by-products of nuclear fusion with them. Oxygen is normally more abundant than carbon. If conditions are right, the surfaces of some stars can change their chemical compositions, some becoming very rich in the carbon that was made below by helium fusion, resulting in the reversal of the normal ratio. Mira variables and other old red giants thus divide into oxygen-rich stars and 'carbon stars.' Raised up along with the carbon are elements such as zirconium and many others that have been made in a huge variety of nuclear reactions that go on at the same time as helium fusion. Other stars' surfaces are enriched in helium and nitrogen.

Winds and Mass Loss

Such huge giant stars have low gravities and lose mass through powerful winds that blow from their surfaces. Some of the gas condenses into molecules and dust. There may be so much that the star can be buried in it and become invisible to the eye, the glow of the heated dust seen only by its infrared (heat) radiation. Oxygen-rich giant stars make silicate dust, while carbon stars make carbon-dust similar to graphite and soot. Most of the dust that inhabits interstellar space began this way, though since inception it has been highly modified in the freezer of interstellar space. These stars therefore play a powerful role in later star formation. The winds are so strong during the giant stage of a star's life that it can lose half or more of its mass back into space, whittling itself down to little more than the parts that underwent nuclear fusion.

White Dwarfs

As the planetary nebula dissipates into the gases of interstellar space, it leaves behind the spent, old core (that now includes the dead nuclear fusing shells). These stars, compressed under their gravity, have shrunk to only about the size of Earth. The first ones found (Sirius-B, Procyon-B, and 40 Eridani B) were fairly hot and white, so the class acquired the name "white dwarf" to discriminate it from the main sequence of stars (which were originally called "ordinary dwarfs" to distinguish them from the giants). Though small, white dwarfs still contain near the mass of the Sun, giving them astonishing average densities of a metric ton per cubic centimeter. The tremendous outward pressure provided by tightly packed 'degenerate electrons' (which behave like waves that keep them from getting closer) prevents gravity from shrinking white dwarfs any further. White dwarfs are therefore also called *degenerate stars*. These small stars, the remains of stars that began their lives between 0.8 and 10 solar masses, no longer have any source of energy generation and are destined only to cool. The cooling time is so long, however, that all white dwarfs ever created are still visible, though the oldest are becoming cool, dim, and reddish. (There is no such thing as an invisible, cold "black dwarf.") The age of the Galaxy calculated (with the aid of theory) from the oldest white dwarfs roughly agrees with that derived from the coolest (lowest mass) evolved main sequence star. On the HR diagram, they fall in a line rather parallel to, but far fainter than, the main sequence dwarfs.

High Mass Stars and Supergiants

As they start to die, higher mass stars (those with masses over about 10 times that of the Sun) initially develop the same way as giants, but then their course of evolution becomes very different. High mass stars are already large and luminous. As their dead helium cores contract, heating and firing to fuse the helium to carbon and oxygen, the stars expand to approach the sizes of the orbits of the outer planets, becoming distended red 'supergiants.' Excellent examples are first magnitude Betelgeuse in Orion and Antares in Scorpius. Supergiants are so massive, in spite of great mass loss through huge winds, that nuclear fusion can proceed farther than it can in ordinary giants. When the helium runs out, the carbon and oxygen mixture compresses and heats, causing it to fuse to a mixture of neon, magnesium and oxygen. Hydrogen and helium fusion had already moved outward into nested shells around the core. When carbon fusion dies out in the core, leaving a mix of neon, magnesium, and oxygen, it too moves outward into a shell. The neon-magnesium-oxygen mixture now in the core then heats and fuses into a mix of silicon and sulphur, each fusion stage taking a shorter period of time. During the course of their evolution, red supergiants can also contract some and heat to make blue supergiants. The great mass-loss suffered by supergiants can strip some of them of their outer envelopes to the point that we see huge surface enrichments of helium, nitrogen, and carbon that have been made by nuclear fusion. Look for them scattered across the top of the HR diagram.

Supernovae

To conclude, the silicon and sulphur fuse to iron, an element that is incapable of energy-generating fusion reactions.

Gravity now wins the war that has been going on for the star's lifetime, and since the iron refuses to support itself, the core catastrophically collapses.

The iron breaks down into its component particles, protons, neutrons, and electrons (the constituents of atoms), and the whole mass gets compressed into a tight ball of neutrons only a few tens of kilometers across. The collapse produces a shocking blast wave that rips through the surrounding nuclear fusing shells and the remaining outer envelope, and rips the rest of the star apart. On Earth we see the star explode in a grand 'supernova,' an event so powerful it is easily visible even in another galaxy a huge distance away. The part of the star that is exploded outward is so hot that nuclear reactions produce all the chemical elements, including a tenth of a solar mass of iron, which then blend with the gasses of interstellar space, out of which new stars are formed.

Frequency and Candidates

There are ways of making supernovae other than through core collapse. Nevertheless, supernovae are still rare, taking place in our Galaxy only two or three times a century. Most are hidden from us by the vast clouds of dust that birth the stars. On Earth we observe about five supernovae per millennium, and have not seen one since Kepler's Star of 1604 (probably created in the collapse of a white dwarf, as described later). The great supernovae of 1006, 1054 (the 'Chinese Guest Star'), and 1572 (Tycho's Star) were visible in daylight.

Our knowledge of supernovae comes almost entirely from observing them in other galaxies, the best of these exploding in 1987 (SN 1987a) in the Large Magellanic Cloud, a companion to our Galaxy some 165,000 light years away. But keep your eye on Betelgeuse or Antares, which are quite good candidates for core collapse. An even better candidate is the southern hemisphere's Eta Carinae, which underwent a huge eruption in the 19th century and produced a surrounding nebula, a vast cloud of dusty gas. The star should go off within the next million years or so. At their current distances, the explosions of such stars would rival the brightness of a crescent Moon.

The blast is so powerful that it if occurred within 30 or so light years, it would probably damage the Earth. Fortunately, no candidate is nearly that close (though such nearby events have almost certainly happened in the past).

Supernova Remnants

As the debris of a supernova clears, we see a gaseous expanding shell approximately the old star, the 'supernova remnant,' which consists of the debris of the explosion that is rich in the by- products of myriad nuclear reactions mixed in with local interstellar matter that is compressed by the mighty blast. Supernova remnats are readily identifiable by their X-rays and radio radiation. We believe all the iron in the Universe has come from such (and related) explosions. Indeed, between ordinary giants, planetary nebulae, and supernovae, all the elements other than hydrogen and helium (and some lithium) were created in or by stars. The most famous supernova remnant is the Crab Nebula in Taurus, the remains of the great supernova of 1054, which was well observed by Chinese astronomers. Tens of thousands of years after a supernova event, we may still see the blast waves sweeping through the gases of interstellar space, compressing and heating them and perhaps making new stars.

Neutron Stars and Pulsars

At the centre of the expanding cloud is a lone neutron star spinning many times per second, with a mass greater than the Sun, a diameter the size of a small town, and an amazing density of 100 million tons per cubic centimeter. As white dwarfs are supported by 'degenerate electrons,' neutron stars are supported by degenerate neutrons. The magnetic fields of such collapsed stars are magnified along with the density to strengths millions of millions of times that of Earth. The magnetism is so strong that radiation is beamed out the magnetic axis. The axis is tilted relative to the rotation axis (like that of the Earth), and wobbles around as the little star spins, the beamed energy spraying into space. From a distance, the star looks like a lighthouse: if the Earth is in the way, we get a blast of radiation, and from here see the neutron star as a "pulsar. Young pulsars emit from low-energy radio waves through high-energy X-rays and gamma rays. As the pulsar ages, it slows, and finally emits only radio waves, which is the case for most of the 600 or so pulsars known. When the rotation period is about 4 seconds there is insufficient energy for the pulsar to be seen at all, and it disappears from view. Not fusing anything, the neutron star is held up forever against gravity by pressure exerted its own extreme density.

Black Holes

The collapsing star of a supernova will turn into a neutron star only if its mass is less than about two or three times that of the Sun. If the mass is greater, then even the star's huge density cannot hold gravity back, and instead of a neutron star the supernova creates a 'star' that nothing can support against gravity, and the body contracts forever. At a small enough radius, the gravitational force becomes so great that light can not escape, and the star disappears forever into a collapsing 'black hole.' What we refer to as the black hole is actually a kind of 'surface' at which the velocity required for escape equals light-speed. What goes on inside is unknown. The centre of our Galaxy, 26,000 light years away, contains a supermassive black hole called Sagittarius A that carries some three million solar masses.

Masses from Double Stars

Double stars are vitally significant in the measure of stellar masses, which are derived from Kepler's Laws as generalized by Isaac Newton. Pretend a lesser star goes around a stationary more massive one, as seen for example for Alpha Centauri, Castor, or Algieba. The first law states that the orbit must be a conic section (circle, ellipse, parabola, or hyperbola), here specifically an ellipse with the more massive member at one focus, the second law that the orbiting star speeds up in a known way as it gets closer to its mate, slows down as it gets farther away. The crucial third law states that the square of the orbital period in years equals the cube of the average distance between the stars divided by the sum of the masses (in solar masses), which can then be found. In reality, the two stars orbit a common centre that lies on a line between them positioned from each in inverse proportion to the mass ratio. The sum of masses along with the location of the centre of mass (and thus the mass ratio) then gives the individual masses, which can be used to test theory. The mass of the Sun is found using the orbit of the Earth (whose mass is inconsequential).

Double Stars

Most of stars you observe at night have companions, with a great many obviously double ("binary") even through a modest telescope. The components of some double stars are nearly equal in mass and brightness. More commonly, one dominates the other, sometimes to the point where a little companion is not really visible at all, and detectable only with the most sophisticated techniques. At the lowest end, we have stars with low-mass brown dwarfs for companions. The stars of some doubles are so far apart that they take thousands of years to orbit; others are so close that they revolve around each other in only days or even hours. Gravitational theory allows us to measure the masses of the stars from the orbits' characters; indeed such measurements are the only way in which we can find stellar masses.

Multiple Stars

Stars can also bond into more complicated multiples. There are two kinds, stable 'hierarchical' systems and unstable 'trapezium' systems. In the first, a distant star orbits an inner double (which it senses gravitationally as one) to make a triple (as in the Zeta Cancri system), or two doubles may orbit each other as a quadruple, of which Epsilon Lyrae (*THE* famed 'Double- Double') is the prime example. In more complex systems, a star or even another double can orbit an inner triple or double-double to make a quintuple or sextuple system (like Mizar-Alcor or Castor). The structures of the orbits will depend on relative masses. In the second kind of multiple, named after the Trapezium (Theta-1 Orionis) in Orion's Sword, the member stars are all rather mixed together, which allows close encounters to eject stars until some kind of stability is achieved. Trapezium systems must all therefore be young.

Formation of Double Stars

Formation is still contended. The oldest idea involves simple fission. When a new star condenses from the interstellar gases, it spins faster. If the contracting blob is spinning rapidly enough, it can separate or otherwise develop into a pair or stars rather than a single star. Each of these contracting components can further separate into a double, producing a 'double-double' star, the most famous of which is fourth magnitude Epsilon Lyrae. This idea is now widely discounted. More likely scenarios involve capture within a dense stellar environment, fragmentation of the collapsing birthcloud, and condensation of a companion from a the circumstellar disk that surrounds a new-born star. Formation of multiples is even less understood, especially of stars with distant fragilely-bound members of the sort we find in the Alpha Centauri system.

Eclipsing Double Stars

If the two stars of a pair are fairly close together, and if the plane of the orbit is close to the line of sight, each star can get in the way of the other every orbital turn, and we see a pair of eclipses, one of which is usually of much greater visibility than the other. Eclipsing systems are very important in stellar astronomy, and are used to help determine masses, to find the stars' diameters, temperatures, and even to assess shapes in the cases that the stars' mutual gravities distort each other. Eclipsing doubles are quite common, the most famous second magnitude Algol in Perseus.

Development of Wide Double Stars

In a double star system in which the two have significantly different masses (by far the most common), the higher mass star will use its internal hydrogen fuel the fastest and become a giant first. We then see a red giant, or maybe a helium-fusing, orange class K giant coupled with a main sequence star, also very common. Eventually, the giant produces its planetary nebula and dies as a white dwarf. Good examples of such systems are Sirius and Procyon, each of which are orbited by the tiny dead stars. For each of these systems, and for many others, the white dwarf is by far the LESS massive of the pair, proving that stars really do lose a great deal of their mass back into interstellar space.

Development of Close Double Stars

If the two stars of a double are close together, they can interact. When the more massive becomes a giant, its surface significantly approaches that of the other star. The lower-mass main sequence star can then raise tides in the giant, distorting it. If the two are close enough, matter can flow from the giant to the main sequence star. Good examples that display such behaviour are Algol and Sheliak. In more extreme cases, the lost matter can encompass both stars, creating a 'common envelope.' Friction will then bring the stars even closer together, making the process go yet faster. The stirring of the lost mass can create unusually distorted planetary nebulae. At the end, the white dwarf created from the giant finds itself very close to the remaining main sequence star. In high mass double stars, the higher-mass component can explode and produce a nearby neutron star or even a black hole companion.

Contamination

Some giant stars have the masses and internal constructions that allow them to bring by-products of deep nuclear fusion to the stars' surfaces, in the most extreme examples creating carbon stars. Mass lost from one of these enriched giants to a close companion can contaminate the companion with the giant's newly- formed chemical elements. When the giant becomes a white dwarf we are left with a seemingly single star (main sequence or evolved giant) with an odd chemical composition. Only with determined observation can we tell that a dim white dwarf is present. Among the most prominent examples are 'barium stars' (Alphard an example), giants that have very strong absorptions—and great overabundances—of the heavy element barium among several others. All seem to be companions of what were once mightier stars that had become carbon stars and that are now reduced to white dwarfs.

Novae

If the white dwarf and main sequence remnant of a close double are close enough, the white dwarf can raise tides in the main sequence star, and mass will flow the other way, from the main sequence star to the white dwarf. Theory and observation both show that the flowing matter first enters a disk around the white dwarf from which it falls onto the white dwarf's surface. Instabilities in the disk can make such a star 'flicker' over periods of days and weeks, even producing sudden outbursts of light. The star that became the white dwarf had lost almost all of its hydrogen envelope during its own evolution. When enough fresh hydrogen from the main sequence star has fallen onto the white dwarf, it can, in the nuclear sense, ignite, fusing suddenly and explosively to helium. The surface of the white dwarf blasts into space, the star becoming temporarily vastly brighter. On Earth we see a 'new' star or 'nova' (meaning 'new in Latin) erupt into the nighttime sky, not a new star at all but an old one undergoing eruption. Novae are common, 25 or so going off in the Galaxy every year, once a generation one close enough to reach first magnitude. Nova Cygni in 1975 rivalled Deneb, giving the celestial Swan two tails.

X-rays, Neutron Stars, and Black Holes

In a massive double star system, the more massive of the pair may develop an iron core and explode as a supernova, becoming either a neutron star or a black hole. Either of these stellar remains in turn may raise tides in the more-normal companion, causing matter to flow into a disk around the collapsed body, from which it falls into an immense gravitational field. Matter in the disk is so hot it can radiate X-rays. From the motion of the normal star, we can calculate information on the mass of the collapsed one. If the mass of the dark orbiting companion is below a two-to-three solar mass limit, as in X Persei, it is a neutron star. But if the mass is great enough, we can infer the existence of an orbiting black hole, the best actual proof we have. Fresh hydrogen falling from the disk onto a neutron star can produce great variability, become compressed and fuse to helium, and then explode violently as the helium fuses to carbon. The result is an X-ray burst similar in nature to a nova.

White Dwarf Supernovae

The term 'supernova' is derived from 'nova' in that the supernova is vastly brighter, no matter that the mechanism of the core collapse of a supergiant is completely different from the mechanism of nova production. White dwarfs, however, can also produce supernovae. No white dwarf can exceed a mass of 1.4 times that of the Sun, a limit discovered in the 1930s by Subramanyan Chandrasekhar when he applied relativity theory to the gases in white dwarfs. If the limit is exceeded, even the white dwarf's enormous pressure cannot hold gravity back and the white dwarf must collapse into a neutron star or a black hole or perhaps even annihilate itself. There are two alternative theories for such an event. A massive white dwarf may accept enough mass from a close main sequence companion and be pushed over the edge before a nova eruption can take place. The white dwarf then collapses, creating a supernova that is grander even than one produced by the collapse of a supergiant's iron core. The main sequence star of a double that contains a white dwarf can also evolve through the giant stage to become a white dwarf, creating a DOUBLE white dwarf system. If the two have been drawn close enough together by interaction during a common envelope phase, they can spiral together by the radiation of gravitational waves predicted by relativity theory. The white dwarfs then merge, again producing a spectacular supernova. In either case, the collapse and resulting explosion makes nuclear reactions that again create all the chemical elements and even more iron than in the type of supernova produced by the collapse of the iron core of a massive star. Kepler's supernova of 1604, the last seen in this Galaxy, was probably of this kind.

Open Clusters

Stars have a strong tendency to be born in groups, in whole clusters. If they are bound together tightly enough by their own gravity, they can survive for millions, even billions, of years, even for the lifetime of the Galaxy. There are two kinds, *open clusters* and *globular clusters*. Open clusters, the sparser but by far the more numerous of the two, are found in the disk of the Galaxy, and therefore lie largely in the plane of the Milky Way. Many of the closer ones, such as the Pleiades and Hyades, are easily visible to the naked eye. Some are angularly so large that they make constellations of their own, or at least significant parts of them. Thousands of open clusters dot the Galaxy's disk. Though their sizes vary greatly, they typically contain a few hundred loosely arranged stars packed within a diameter 10 or so light years across. And though bound together by their own gravity, most open clusters gradually break up as a result of random encounters among stars that speed members to the escape velocity, and because of stretching by tides raised by the Galaxy. Open clusters thus tend to be young, under a billion years of age (indeed, some are just born), though in the far reaches of the outer Galaxy they can survive for far more than a billion years.

Associations

Somewhat related to open clusters, stellar *associations* (commonly called *OB associations*) are large, loosely organized, stellar groupings that lie within the Milky Way and are defined by their young, blue O and B stars. Gravitationally unbound, OB associations are expanding systems, their stars moving away from individual common centres that may have core open clusters. Though they contain stars with a full range of masses, associations are best recognized through their most massive, luminous, and hottest members, which cannot get far away from their birthplaces before they expire, rendering ageing associations essentially invisible. OB associations are mostly named for their constellations of residence, for example *Orion OB1, Perseus OB2, Upper Scorpius,* and so on. Several constellations, in particular Orion and Scorpius, owe their prominence and sparkle to being made largely of OB associations. Having massive stars, associations are prime sources of supernovae.

Globular Clusters

While there are thousands of open clusters in the Galaxy, there are but 150 or so known globular clusters. Distinct from open clusters, their home is a huge spheroidal *halo* that surrounds the Galaxy's disk. And while open clusters are sparse, loose, and comparatively young, globulars are compact, closely spherical, and can contain over a million stars packed into a volume only a hundred or so light years across. Their compactness gives them (at least those that have survived) long lifetimes. With ages of 11 to 12 billion years, formed when the metal content of the Galaxy was much less than it is today (the increase the result of stellar evolution), they are among the oldest things known and among the first things to be created after the Big Bang, the event that formed our Universe.

Cluster Development and Blue Stragglers

Clusters of both kinds are profoundly important in establishing the distance scale in astronomy and in testing and guiding the theories of stellar evolution—the ageing process. Clusters are born with an intact array of stars that occupy the entire main sequence (dwarf sequence) of the HR diagram, in which the higher the mass, the greater the luminosity. Since high mass stars die first, a cluster evolves by losing its dwarf sequence from the top down. Application of evolutionary theory can then tell us the age of any given cluster by the most luminous and hottest dwarfs still left. The Double Cluster's hot class O stars tell that it is young. The most luminous stars of the somewhat older Pleiades are of class B, while the still older Hyades has lost even these. Open clusters range in age from just born to nearly 10 billion years, which gives the age of the Galaxy's disk. By contrast, globular clusters have lost the entire upper main sequence (dwarf) population down to stars somewhat below a solar mass, which gives them ages 11 to 12 billion years or so, nearly the age of the Galaxy itself. In most dense globular clusters, and even in some open clusters, some stars with masses higher than the main sequence cutoff linger, refusing to evolve. Since these stars are also bluer in colour than the majority of evolving dwarfs, they are called *blue stragglers*. Blue stragglers are believed to be caused by stellar mergers within the dense cluster environments, either by direct collision or by the mergers of close double stars, which increases their masses beyond the cutoff and thus seems to hold back their evolution.

Stars and Space Recycling

Stars can range in size, depending on mass and age, from only a few kilometres across to the diameter of the orbit of perhaps Saturn. They can range in temperature from near 'cold' at only 2000 K for an extreme red giant through far over 100,000 K for the star inside a planetary nebula to over a million K for a neutron star. All the stars you see in the sky will eventually expire, some soon, some not for aeons. Lower mass stars create planetary nebulae and white dwarfs, while higher mass stars make supernovae that result in neutron stars or black holes. Double stars add spice to the product, making novae and a different kind of supernova. All these endings send newly made chemical elements into the interstellar stew, out of which new stars are made. As a result, the heavy element content of the Galaxy increases with time. Ancient main sequence stars, the 'subdwarfs,' and their giant star progeny have a low abundance of metals, whereas younger stars like the Sun have higher metal contents, allowing us to track the oldest and youngest stars and to determine the age of the Galaxy. New stars therefore contain the by-products of the old, our Earth a distillate of earlier generations. Our Sun will someday make its own contribution, however modest it may be, to generations of stars and planets yet unborn.

Chapter 5

Observational Astronomy

INTRODUCTION

Observational astronomy deals with the study of Astronomical instruments, it also consists of doing practical observations of astronomical objects like moon, sun, binary stars, comets etc.

The great thing about observational astronomy is that even amateur astronomers can make great contribution to the field (quite contradictory to other sciences). Observational astronomy is a division of the astronomical science that is concerned with getting data, in contrast with theoretical astrophysics, which is mainly concerned with finding out the measurable implications of physical models. It is the practice of observing celestial objects by using telescopes and other astronomical apparatus.

As a science, astronomy is somewhat hindered in that direct experiments with the properties of the distant universe are not possible. However, this is partly compensated by the fact that astronomers have a vast number of visible examples of stellar phenomena that can be examined. This allows for observational data to be plotted on graphs, and general trends recorded.

Nearby examples of specific phenomena, such as variable stars, can then be used to infer the behaviour of more distant representatives. Those distant yardsticks can then be employed to measure other phenomena in that neighbourhood, including the distance to a galaxy.

Optical Telescopes

For much of the history of observational astronomy, almost all observation was performed in the visual spectrum with optical telescopes. While the Earth's atmosphere is relatively transparent in this portion of the electromagnetic spectrum, most telescope work is still dependent on seeing conditions and air transparency, and is generally restricted to the night time. The seeing conditions depend on the turbulence and thermal variations in the air. Locations that are frequently cloudy or suffer from atmospheric turbulence limit the resolution of observations. Likewise the presence of the full Moon can brighten up the sky with scattered light, hindering observation of faint objects.

For observation purposes, the optimal position for an optical telescope is undoubtedly in outer space. There the telescope can make observations without being affected by the atmosphere. However, at present it remains costly to lift telescopes into orbit. Thus the next best locations are certain mountain peaks that have a high number of cloudless days and generally possess good atmospheric conditions (with good seeing conditions). The peaks of the islands of Mauna Kea, Hawaii and La Palma possess these properties, as to a lesser extent do inland sites such as Llano de Chajnantor, Paranal, Cerro Tololo and La Silla in Chile. These observatory locations have attracted an assemblage of powerful telescopes, totalling many billion US dollars of investment.

The darkness of the night sky is an important factor in optical astronomy. With the size of cities and human populated areas ever expanding, the amount of artificial light at night has also increased. These artificial lights produce a diffuse background illumination that makes observation of faint astronomical features very difficult without special filters. In a few locations such as the state of Arizona and in the United Kingdom, this has led to campaigns for the reduction of light pollution. The use of hoods around street lights not only improves the amount of light directed towards the ground, but also helps reduce the light directed towards the sky.

Atmospheric effects (astronomical seeing) can severely hinder the resolution of a telescope. Without some means of correcting for the blurring effect of the shifting atmosphere, telescopes larger than about 15-20 cm in aperture cannot achieve their theoretical resolution at visible wavelengths. As a result, the primary benefit of using very large telescopes has been the improved light-gathering capability, allowing very faint magnitudes to be observed. However the resolution handicap has begun to be overcome by adaptive optics, speckle imaging and interferometric imaging, as well as the use of space telescopes.

Astronomers have a number of observational tools that they can use to make measurements of the heavens. For objects that are relatively close to the Sun and Earth, direct and very precise position measurements can be made against a more distant (and thereby nearly stationary) background. Early observations of this nature were used to develop very precise orbital models of the various planets, and to determine their respective masses and gravitational perturbations. Such measurements led to the discovery of the planets Uranus, Neptune, and (indirectly) Pluto. They also resulted in an erroneous assumption of a fictional planet Vulcan within the orbit of Mercury (but the explanation of the precession of Mercury's orbit by Einstein is considered one of the triumphs of his general relativity theory).

Other Instruments

In addition to assessment of the universe in the optical spectrum, astronomers have increasingly been able to acquire information in other portions of the electromagnetic spectrum. The earliest such non-optical measurements were made of the thermal properties of the Sun. Instruments employed during a solar eclipse could be used to measure the radiation from the corona.

With the discovery of radio waves, radio astronomy began to emerge as a new discipline in astronomy. The long wavelengths of radio waves required much larger collecting dishes in order to make images with good resolution, and later led to the development of the multi-dish interferometer for making high-resolution aperture synthesis radio images (or 'radio maps'). The development of the microwave horn receiver led to the discovery of the microwave background radiation associated with the big bang.

Radio astronomy has continued to expand its capabilities, even using radio astronomy satellites to produce interferometres with baselines much larger than the size of the Earth. However, the ever-expanding use of the radio spectrum for other uses is gradually drowning out the faint radio signals from the stars. For this reason, in the future radio astronomy might be performed from shielded locations, such as the far side of the Moon.

The last part of the twentieth century saw rapid technological advances in astronomical instrumentation. Optical telescopes were growing ever larger, and employing adaptive optics to partly negate atmospheric blurring. New telescopes were launched into space, and began observing the universe in the infrared, ultraviolet, x-ray, and gamma ray parts of the electromagnetic spectrum, as well as observing cosmic rays. Interferometer arrays produced the first extremely high-resolution images using aperture synthesis at radio, infrared and optical wavelengths. Orbiting instruments such as the Hubble Space Telescope produced rapid advances in astronomical knowledge, acting as the workhorse for visible-light observations of faint objects. New space instruments under development are expected to directly observe planets around other stars, perhaps even some Earth-like worlds.

In addition to telescopes, astronomers have begun using other instruments to make observations. Neutrino astronomy is the branch of astronomy that observes astronomical objects with neutrino detectors in special observatories, usually huge underground tanks. Nuclear reactions in stars and supernova explosions produce very large numbers of neutrinos, a very few of which may be detected by a neutrino telescope. Neutrino astronomy is motivated by the possibility of observing processes that are inaccessible to optical telescopes, such as the Sun's core.

Gravitational wave detectors are being designed that may capture events such as collisions of massive objects such as neutron stars.

Robotic spacecraft are also being increasingly used to make highly detailed observations of planets within the solar system, so that the field of planetary science now has significant cross-over with the disciplines of geology and meteorology.

The *electromagnetic spectrum* is the distribution of electromagnetic radiation according to energy.

REGIONS OF THE ELECTROMAGNETIC SPECTRUM

The following table gives approximate wavelengths, frequencies, and energies for selected regions of the electromagnetic spectrum.

Table 5.1 Spectrum of Electromagnetic Radiation

Region	*Wavelength (Angstroms)*	*Wavelength (centimeters)*	*Frequency (Hz)*	*Energy eV)*
Radio	$> 10^9$	> 10	$< 3\times10^9$	$< 10^{-5}$
Microwave	10^9–10^6	10–0.01	3×10^9–3×10^{12}	10^{-5}–0.01
Infrared	10^6–7000	0.01–7×10^{-5}	3×10^{12}–4.3×10^{14}	0.01–2
Visible	7000–4000	7×10^{-5}–4×10^{-5}	4.3×10^{14} –7.5×10^{14}	2–3
Ultraviolet	4000–10	4×10^{-5}–10^{-7}	7.5×10^{14}–3×10^{17}	3–10^3
X-Rays	10–0.1	10^{27}–10^{-9}	3×10^{17}–3×10^{19}	10^3–10^5
Gamma Rays	< 0.1	$< 10^{-9}$	$> 3\times10^{19}$	$> 10^5$

The notation 'eV' stands for electron-volts, a common unit of energy measure in atomic physics. A graphical representation of the electromagnetic spectrum.

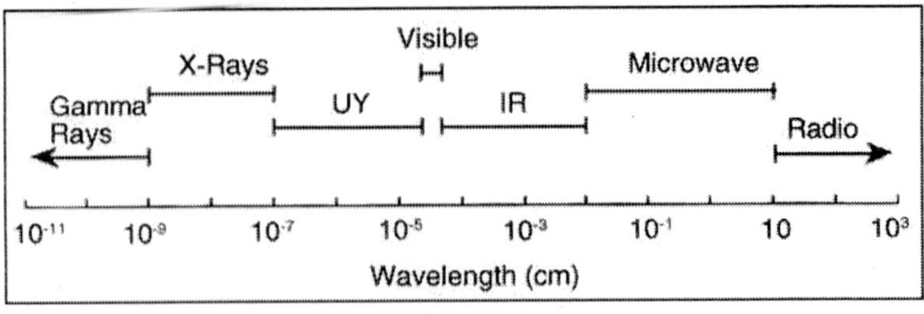

Fig. 5.1 The Electromagnetic Spectrum

Thus we see that visible light and gamma rays and microwaves are really the same things. They are all electromagnetic radiation; they just differ in their wavelengths.

The Spectrum of Visible Light

The visible part of the spectrum may be further subdivided according to colour, with red at the long wavelength end and violet at the short wavelength end.

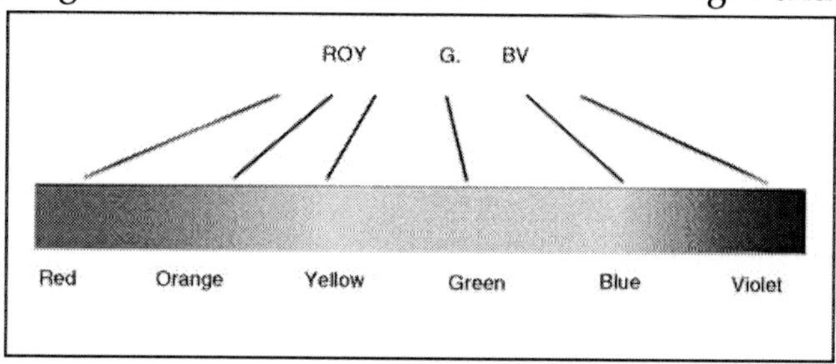

Fig. 5.2 The Visible Spectrum

How Roy G. Bv Lost a Vowel

The sequence of colours red, orange, yellow, green, blue, and violet may be remembered by memorizing the name of that fine fellow 'ROY G. BV'. This was originally 'ROY G. BIV', because it used to be common to call the region between blue and violet 'indigo'. In modern usage, indigo is not usually distinguished as a separate colour in the visible spectrum; thus Roy no longer has any vowels in his last name.

REFRACTION AND DIFFRACTION

The wave nature of light leads to two very important properties: *refraction,* where the direction of light propagation is altered at the boundary between media of different densities, and *diffraction,* which has among its consequences that light can 'bend around corners'.

Refraction of Light

The direction of light propagation can be changed at the boundary of two media having different densities. This property is called *refraction,* and is illustrated in the following figure 5.3 for the boundary between air and water.

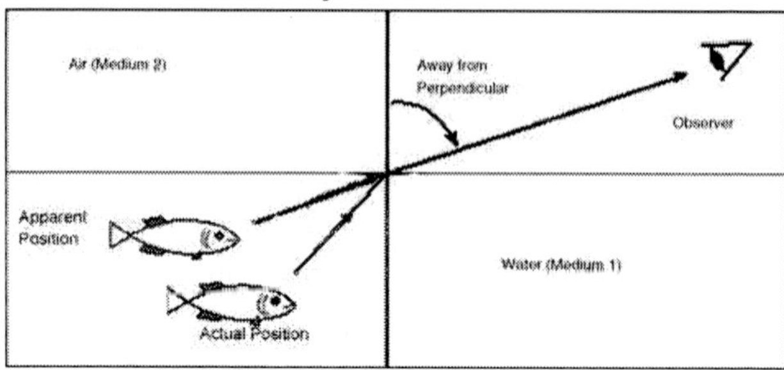

Fig. 5.3 Refraction of Light

The apparent and actual positions of the fish differ because the direction of light propagation has been changed as light passes from the more dense water into the less dense air.

If we adopt the convention that the light passes from medium 1 into medium 2, the general rule is that the refraction is

- *Away from the perpendicular* if medium 2 is less dense than medium 1
- *Towards the perpendicular* if medium 2 is more dense than medium 1

The refraction is away from the perpendicular because air is less dense than water. Such effects form the basis of the refracting telescope, and of optical devices using lenses in general.

Diffraction of Light

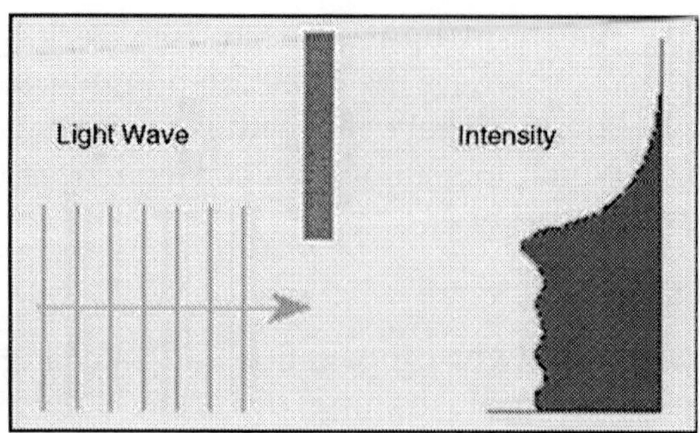

Because light is a wave, it has the capability to 'bend around corners'. This is called *diffraction,* and is illustrated in the adjacent image. The intensity of light behind the barrier is not zero in the shadow region. diffractive effects occur generally when a part of a light wave is cut off by an obstruction. Here is a Java applet illustrating diffraction of light by a single slit, and here is an interactive demonstration of refraction and diffraction for ocean waves.

Diffraction has a number of consequences for astronomy. Two of the more important are that this property is the basis for the *diffraction grating* that can be used to separate light into its constituent colours, and that diffractive effects set an absolute limit on the quality of an image observed through an optical instrument such as a telescope. This *diffractive limit* occurs because the lenses of such objects are of finite size and diffract light because they cut off part of the light wave.

DISPERSION IN WAVELENGTH

In the preceding section we showed that light is refracted at the boundary between two media differing in density. Let us now examine more carefully the factors upon which this refraction depends.

Factors Governing Refraction

The amount of refraction of light at a boundary between two media depends on three things:

- The nature of the media (embodied in a characteristic quantity called the *index of refraction* for a medium).
- The angle of indigence for the light ray on the boundary.
- The wavelength of light.

The dependence of refraction on the wavelength of light is called *dispersion*. This dependence has both positive and negative implications for astronomy. On the positive side, it is the basis for the prism and its ability to separate light according to wavelength; on the negative side, it is the source of *chromatic aberration* in optical devices (the failure of different wavelengths to focus at the same point).

Dispersion and the Prism

Dispersion is the basis for the prism and its ability to spatially separate light according to wavelength. Light separated into its frequency components is called a *spectrum* of light. Visible light, also known as white light, consists of a collection of component colours. These colours are often observed as light passes through a triangular prism. Upon passage through the prism, the white light is separated into its component colours - red, orange, yellow, green, blue and violet. The separation of visible light into its different colours is known as dispersion. It was mentioned in the Light and Colour unit that each colour is characteristic of a distinct wave frequency; and different frequencies of light waves will bend varying amounts upon passage through a prism.

Spectrographs Instrument

A *spectrograph* is a refined instrument that produces a spectrum. Although a prism can disperse light according to colour, in modern spectrographs it is more common to accomplish the same task by using a diffraction grating. The diffraction grating works on a completely different principle (diffraction rather than refraction) but it also can separate light spatially according to wavelength. In subsequent sections that the spectrograph is a central tool of modern astronomy.

INTENSITY: THE INVERSE SQUARE LAW

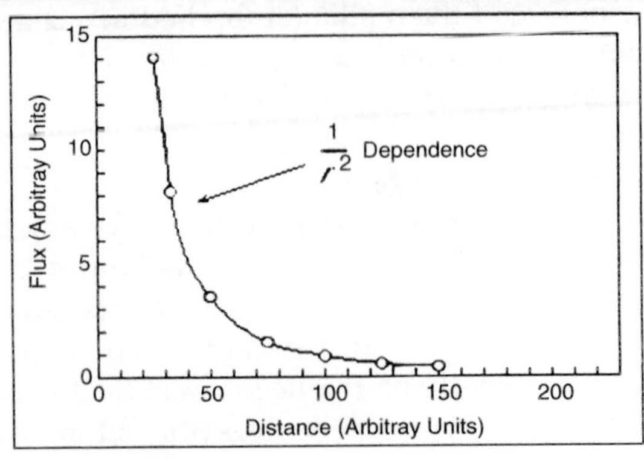

Fig. 5.4 The Inverse Square Law for Intensity

The intensity of light observed from a source of constant intrinsic luminosity falls off as the square of the distance from the object. This is known as the *inverse square law* for light intensity.

Thus, if I double the distance to a light source the observed intensity is decreased to $(1/2)^2 = 1/4$ of its original value. Generally, the ratio of intensities at distances d_1 and d_2 are

$$\frac{I_1}{I_2} = \frac{d_2^2}{d_1^2}$$

Here is a Java virtual experiment illustrating the inverse square law.

Range of the Spectrum

Electromagnetic waves are typically described by any of the following three physical properties: the frequency *f*, wavelength λ, or photon energy *E*. Frequencies range from 2.4×10^{23} Hz (1 GeV gamma rays) down to the local plasma frequency of the ionized interstellar medium (~1 kHz). Wavelength is inversely proportional to the wave frequency, so gamma rays have very short wavelengths that are fractions of the size of atoms, whereas wavelengths can be as long as the universe. Photon energy is directly proportional to the wave frequency, so gamma rays have the highest energy (around a billion electron volts) and radio waves have very low energy (around a femtoelectronvolt). These relations are illustrated by the following equations:

$$f = \frac{c}{\lambda}, \quad \text{or} \quad f = \frac{E}{h}, \quad \text{or} \quad E = \frac{hc}{\lambda},$$

where:

- $c = 299{,}792{,}458$ m/s is the speed of light in vacuum and
- $h = 6.62606896(33) \times 10^{-34}$ J s $= 4.13566733(10) \times 10^{-15}$ eV s is Planck's constant.

Whenever electromagnetic waves exist in a medium with matter, their wavelength is decreased. Wavelengths of electromagnetic radiation, no matter what medium they are traveling through, are usually quoted in terms of the *vacuum wavelength,* although this is not always explicitly stated.

Generally, electromagnetic radiation is classified by wavelength into radio wave, microwave, terahertz (or sub-millimeter) radiation, infrared, the visible region we perceive as light, ultraviolet, X-rays and gamma rays. The behaviour of EM radiation depends on its wavelength. When EM radiation interacts with single atoms and molecules, its behaviour also depends on the amount of energy per quantum (photon) it carries.

Spectroscopy can detect a much wider region of the EM spectrum than the visible range of 400 nm to 700 nm. A common laboratory spectroscope can detect wavelengths from 2 nm to 2500 nm. Detailed information about the physical properties of objects, gases, or even stars can be obtained from this type of device. Spectroscopes are widely used in astrophysics. For example, many hydrogen atoms emit a radio wave photon that has a wavelength of 21.12 cm. Also, frequencies of 30 Hz and below can be produced by and are important in the study of certain stellar nebulae and frequencies as high as 2.9×10^{27} Hz have been detected from astrophysical sources.

Types of Radiation

The types of electromagnetic radiation are broadly classified into the following classes:

- Gamma radiation
- X-ray radiation
- Ultraviolet radiation
- Visible radiation
- Infrared radiation
- Microwave radiation
- Radio waves.

This classification goes in the growing order of wavelength, which is characteristic of the type of radiation. While, in general, the classification scheme is accurate, in reality there is often some overlap between neighbouring types of electromagnetic energy. For example, SLF radio waves at

60 Hz may be received and studied by astronomers, or may be ducted along wires as electric power, although the latter is, in the strict sense, not electromagnetic radiation at all. The distinction between X-rays and gamma rays is based on sources: gamma rays are the photons generated from nuclear decay or other nuclear and subnuclear/particle process, whereas X-rays are generated by electronic transitions involving highly energetic inner atomic electrons. In general, nuclear transitions are much more energetic than electronic transitions, so gamma-rays are more energetic than X-rays, but exceptions exist. By analogy to electronic transitions, muonic atom transitions are also said to produce X-rays, even though their energy may exceed 6 megaelectronvolts (0.96 pJ), whereas there are many (77 known to be less than 10 keV (1.6 fJ)) low-energy nuclear transitions (*e.g.*, the 7.6 eV (1.22 aJ) nuclear transition of thorium-229), and, despite being one million-fold less energetic than some muonic X-rays, the emitted photons are still called gamma rays due to their nuclear origin.

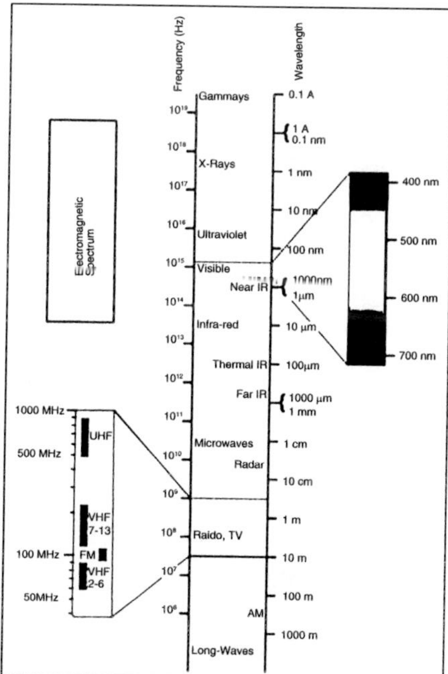

Fig. 5.5 The Electromagnetic Spectrum

Also, the district of the spectrum of the particular electromagnetic radiation is reference frame-dependent (on account of the Doppler shift for light), so EM radiation that one observer would say is in one region of the spectrum could appear to an observer moving at a substantial fraction of the speed of light with respect to the first to be in another part of the spectrum. For example, consider the cosmic microwave background. It was produced, when matter and radiation decoupled, by the de-excitation of hydrogen atoms to the ground state. These photons were from Lyman series transitions, putting them in the ultraviolet (UV) part of the electromagnetic spectrum. Now this radiation has undergone enough cosmological red shift to put it into the microwave region of the spectrum for observers moving slowly (compared to the speed of light) with respect to the cosmos. However, for particles moving near the speed of light, this radiation will be blue-shifted in their rest frame. The highest-energy cosmic ray protons are moving such that, in their rest frame, this radiation is blueshifted to high-energy gamma rays, which interact with the proton to produce bound quark-antiquark pairs (pions). This is the source of the GZK limit.

Radio Frequency Waves

Radio waves generally are utilized by antennas of appropriate size (according to the principle of resonance), with wavelengths ranging from hundreds of meters to about one millimeter. They are used for transmission of data, via modulation. Television, mobile phones, wireless networking, and amateur radio all use radio waves. The use of the radio spectrum is regulated by many governments through frequency allocation.

Radio waves can be made to carry information by varying a combination of the amplitude, frequency, and phase of the wave within a frequency band. When EM radiation impinges upon a conductor, it couples to the conductor, travels along it, and induces an electric current on the surface of that conductor by exciting the electrons of the conducting material. This effect (the skin effect) is used in antennas.

Microwaves Waves

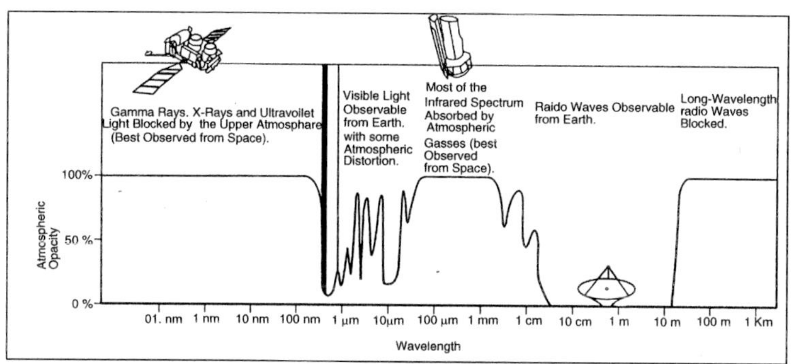

Fig. 5.6 Plot of Earth's Atmospheric Transmittance (or Opacity) to Various Wavelengths of Electromagnetic Radiation

The super-high frequency (SHF) and extremely high frequency (EHF) of microwaves come after radio waves. Microwaves are waves that are typically short enough to employ tubular metal waveguides of reasonable diameter. Microwave energy is produced with klystron and magnetron tubes, and with solid state diodes such as Gunn and IMPATT devices. Microwaves are absorbed by molecules that have a dipole moment in liquids. In a microwave oven, this effect is used to heat food. Low-intensity microwave radiation is used in Wi-Fi, although this is at intensity levels unable to cause thermal heating.

Volumetric heating, as used by microwave ovens, transfers energy through the material electromagnetically, not as a thermal heat flux. The benefit of this is a more uniform heating and reduced heating time; microwaves can heat material in less than 1 per cent of the time of conventional heating methods.

When active, the average microwave oven is powerful enough to cause interference at close range with poorly shielded electromagnetic fields such as those found in mobile medical devices and cheap consumer electronics.

Terahertz Radiation

Terahertz radiation is a region of the spectrum between far infrared and microwaves. Until recently, the range was rarely studied and few sources existed for microwave energy at the high end of the band (sub-millimetre waves or so-called terahertz waves), but applications such as imaging and communications are now appearing.

Scientists are also looking to apply terahertz technology in the armed forces, where high-frequency waves might be directed at enemy troops to incapacitate their electronic equipment.

Infrared Radiation

The infrared part of the electromagnetic spectrum covers the range from roughly 300 GHz (1 mm) to 400 THz (750 nm). It can be divided into three parts:

- Far-infrared, from 300 GHz (1 mm) to 30 THz (10 μm). The lower part of this range may also be called microwaves. This radiation is typically absorbed by so-called rotational modes in gas-phase molecules, by molecular motions in liquids, and by phonons in solids. The water in Earth's atmosphere absorbs so strongly in this range that it renders the atmosphere in effect opaque. However, there are certain wavelength ranges ('windows') within the opaque range that allow partial transmission, and can be used for astronomy. The wavelength range from approximately 200 μm up to a few mm is often referred to as 'sub-millimetre' in astronomy, reserving far infrared for wavelengths below 200 μm.
- Mid-infrared, from 30 to 120 THz (10 to 2.5 μm). Hot objects (black-body radiators) can radiate strongly in this range. It is absorbed by molecular vibrations, where the different atoms in a molecule vibrate around their equilibrium positions. This range is sometimes called the *fingerprint region,* since the mid-infrared absorption spectrum of a compound is very specific for that compound.
- Near-infrared, from 120 to 400 THz (2,500 to 750 nm). Physical processes that are relevant for this range are similar to those for visible light.

Visible Radiation (Light)

Above infrared in frequency comes visible light. This is the variety in which the sun and other stars emit most of their radiation and the spectrum that the human eye is the most sensitive to. Visible light (and near-infrared light) is typically absorbed and emitted by electrons in molecules and atoms that move from one energy level to another. The light we see with our eyes is really a very small portion of the electromagnetic spectrum. A rainbow shows the optical (visible) part of the electromagnetic spectrum; infrared (if you could see it) would be located just beyond the red side of the rainbow with ultraviolet appearing just beyond the violet end.

Electromagnetic radiation with a wavelength between 380 nm and 760 nm (790–400 terahertz) is detected by the human eye and perceived as visible light. Other wavelengths, especially near infrared (longer than 760 nm) and ultraviolet (shorter than 380 nm) are also sometimes referred to as light, especially when the visibility to humans is not relevant. White light is a combination of lights of different wavelengths in the visible spectrum. Passing white light through a prism splits it up in to the several colours of light observed in the visible spectrum between 400 nm and 780 nm.

If radiation having a frequency in the visible region of the EM spectrum reflects off an object, say, a bowl of fruit, and then strikes our eyes, this results in our visual perception of the scene. Our brain's visual system processes the multitude of reflected frequencies into different shades and hues, and through this insufficiently-understood psychophysical phenomenon, most people perceive a bowl of fruit.

At most wavelengths, however, the information carried by electromagnetic radiation is not directly detected by human senses. Natural sources produce EM radiation across the spectrum, and our technology can also manipulate a broad range of wavelengths. Optical fibre transmits light that, although not necessarily in the visible part of the spectrum, can carry information. The modulation is similar to that used with radio waves.

Ultraviolet Light

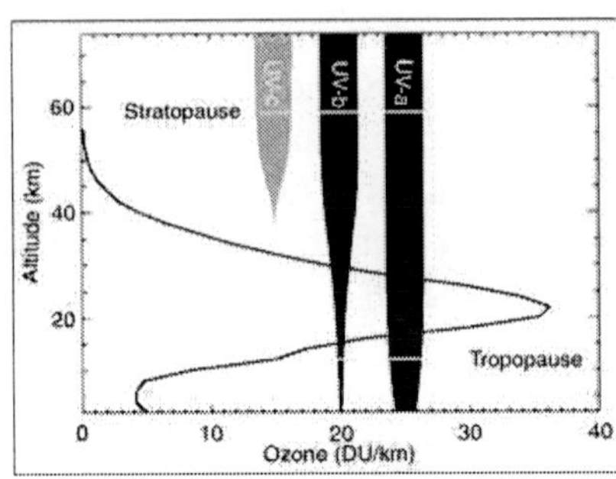

Fig. 5.7 The Amount of Penetration of UV Relative to Altitude in Earth's Ozone

Next in frequency comes ultraviolet (UV). The wavelength of UV rays is shorter than the violet end of the visible spectrum but longer than the X-ray. UV in the very shortest range (next to X-rays) is capable even of ionizing atoms, greatly changing their physical behaviour. At the middle range of UV, UV rays cannot ionize but can break chemical bonds, making molecules to be unusually reactive. Sunburn, for example, is caused by the disruptive effects of middle range UV radiation on skin cells, which is the main cause of skin cancer. UV rays in the middle range can irreparably damage the complex DNA molecules in the cells producing thymine dimers making it a very potent mutagen.

The sun emits a large amount of UV radiation, which could potentially turn Earth's land surface into a barren desert (although ocean water would provide some protection for life there). However, most of the Sun's most-damaging UV wavelengths are absorbed by the atmosphere's nitrogen, oxygen, and ozone layer before they reach the surface. The higher ranges of UV (vacuum UV) are absorbed by nitrogen and, at longer wavelengths, by simple diatomic oxygen in the air. Most of the UV in this mid-range is blocked by the ozone layer, which absorbs strongly in the important 200–315 nm range, the lower part of which is too long to be absorbed by ordinary oxygen in air. The range between 315 nm and visible light (called UV-A) is not blocked well by the atmosphere, but does not cause sunburn and does less biological damage. However, it is not harmless and does cause oxygen radicals, mutation and skin damage.

X-rays

After UV come X-rays, which, like the upper ranges of UV are also ionizing. However, due to their higher energies, X-rays can also interact with matter by means of the Compton effect. Hard X-rays have shorter wavelengths than soft X-rays. As they can pass through most substances, X-rays can be used to 'see through' objects, the most notable use being diagnostic X-ray images in medicine (a process known as radiography), as well as for high-energy physics and astronomy. Neutron stars and accretion disks around black holes emit X-rays, which enable us to study them. X-rays are given off by stars and are strongly emitted by some types of nebulae.

Gamma Rays

After hard X-rays come gamma rays, which were discovered by Paul Villard in 1900. These are the most energetic photons, having no defined lower limit to their wavelength. They are useful to astronomers in the study of high-energy objects or regions, and find a use with physicists thanks to their penetrative ability and their production from radioisotopes. Gamma rays are also used for the irradiation of food and seed for sterilization, and in medicine they are used in radiation cancer therapy and some kinds of diagnostic imaging such as PET scans. The wavelength of gamma rays can be measured with high accuracy by means of Compton scattering. Note that there are no precisely defined boundaries between the bands of the electromagnetic spectrum. Radiation of some types have a mixture of the properties of those in two regions of the spectrum. For example, red light resembles infrared radiation in that it can resonate some chemical bonds.

GEOMETRICAL OPTICS

This SparkNote will apply what we have learned about scattering to the familiar concept of reflection and the perhaps less familiar concept of refraction, the bending of light upon transmission into a dielectric medium. The macroscopic laws of reflection and refraction (Snell's Law) are a result of the interaction of many atomic and sub-microscopic scatterers. In both cases, the laws can be derived directly from the boundary conditions implied by Maxwell's equations. When considering refraction we will study the related phenomenon of dispersion, exploring cases in which the amount of bending of a light ray is dependent upon its frequency (or its wavelength). It is this effect which causes the splitting of white light into a spectrum of colours (different wavelengths) by a prism. The notion of total internal reflection (TIR), responsible for the transmission of light through optic fibres, will also be explored. Finally, from Maxwell's equations we will deduce the so-called *Fresnel Equations,* which allow the relative amplitude of reflected and refracted rays to be computed as a function of the angle from the normal to the interface.

Definitions for Lenses

One extremely useful submission of the properties of light propagation through materials is the formation of an image of an object through the reflection or refraction of light. We form the following definitions:

Object: Anything from which light rays emanate. The object can be *luminous* in which case it is the source of light or can be reflective of light from some other source. Objects can be :

Point Objects: Having no physical extent.

Extended Objects: Having a length, width, and breadth.

Image: A reproduction of an object formed from light. Images can be.

Real Images: Formed on a surface such as a screen.

Virtual Images: Exist only within the brain but are *perceived* to be at a particular location.

A obvious material, *e.g.* glass, which reflects or refracts light can, for particular curve shapes, cause parallel rays of light to converge at a point. Reflecting surfaces, curved or not, are referred to as mirrors in optics. Mirrors have one focal point to go with their one curved surface. A refracting material with two curved surfaces is called a lens. Since a lens has two curved surfaces, it has two focal points. If the curved surfaces are close enough together that we can neglect the distance between the surfaces, we refer to it as a thin lens. A lens can be one of two types:

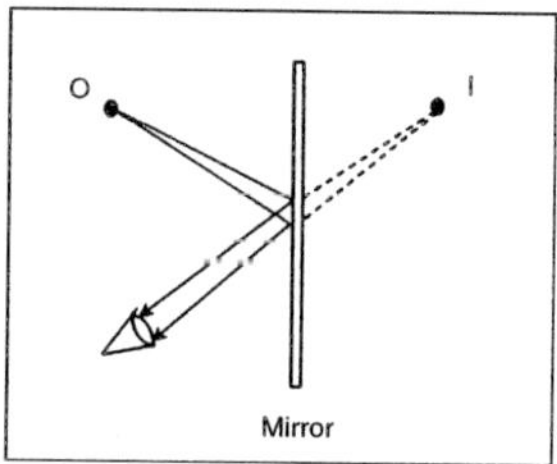

Fig. 5.8 Appearance of a Virtual Image behind a Mirror

Converging: A lens in which parallel rays of light passing through the lens are brought together at the focal point. Rays of light which come from a point object placed at one of the focal points and which pass through the lens are converted into parallel rays.

Diverging: A lens in which parallel rays of light diverge after passing through the lens. The focal length of a diverging lens is defined as a *negative* quantity.

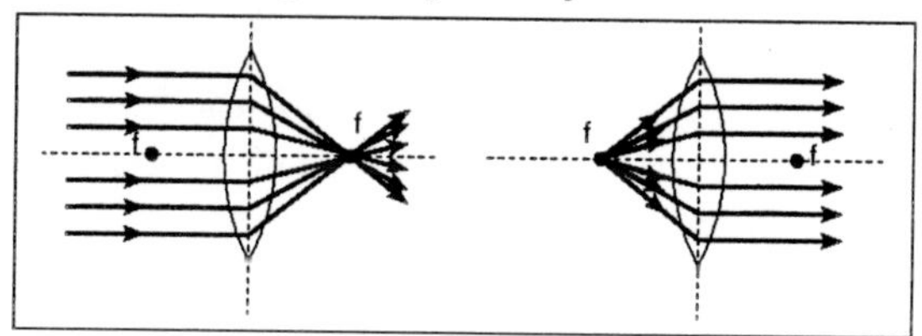

Fig. 5.9 First and Second Focal Points of a Converging thin Lens

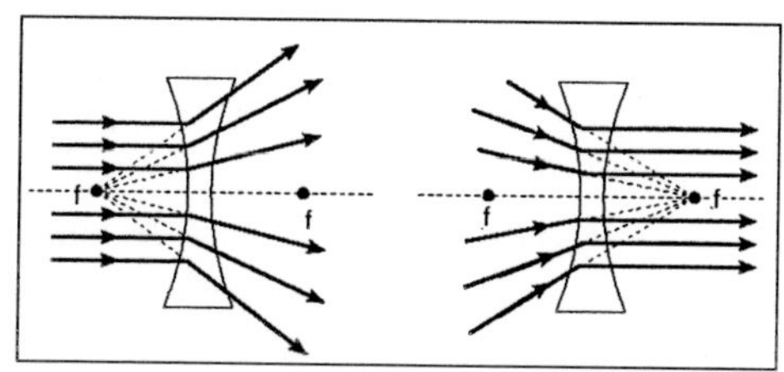

Fig. 5.10 First and Second Focal Points of a Diverging Thin Lens and the Negative Focal Length

We can use a lens to image an object. In the container of a thin lens, we define the object distance, s, as the distance of the object from the centre of the thin lens. The image distance, s¢, is the distance of the image formed from the centre of the thin lens, and we usually term the focal distance, f, as the distance of the focal point from the centre of the thin lens.

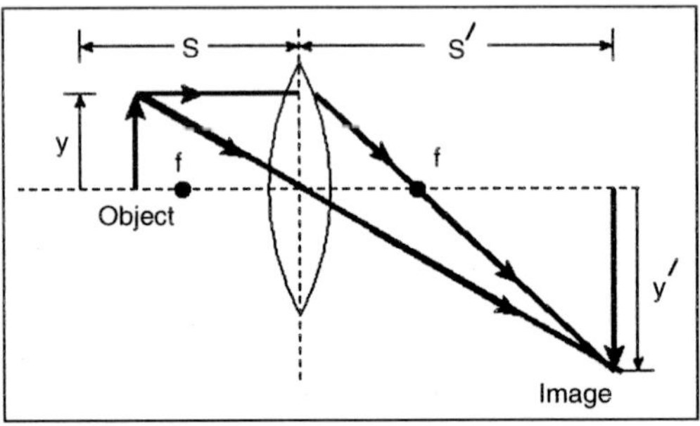

Fig. 5.11 Definition of Image, Object, and Focal Lengths for a Thin Lens

The object, image, and focal lengths are related by the formula

$$\frac{1}{s}+\frac{1}{s'}=\frac{1}{f}$$

Furthermore, the size of the image in the plane of the image, object, and lens, which we depict as y¢, is related to the size of the object (call it y) by the magnification. The magnification is

$$m=\frac{y'}{y}=-\frac{s'}{s}$$

We define images which are on the same side of a converging lens as the object as *virtual*. Note that in such cases s¢ < 0 and the magnification is *positive*. For *real* images, the image is inverted compared to the object, *i.e.* *y*¢ and *y* have opposite signs. Hence a positive magnification corresponds to an erect, virtual image while a negative magnification corresponds to an inverted, real image.

The Law of Reflection in the Light System

The majority visible objects are seen by reflected light. There are few natural sources of light, such as the sun, stars, and a flame; other sources are man-made, such as electric lights. For an object to be visible, light from a source is reflected off the object into our eyes (except in the special case of phosphors). The light is coming from the sun, parallel due to the distance of the source. The light reflects off the object and travels in straight lines to the viewer. Through experience, the viewer has learned to extend the reflected rays entering the eye back to locate the object.

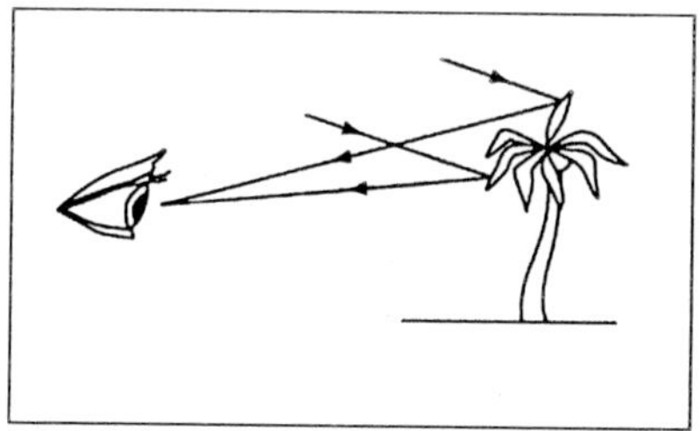

Fig. 5.12 Vision is the Result of Light Reflected from the Object

The original ray is called the incident ray, and after reflection, it is called the reflected ray. The angles of the incident and reflected rays are always measured from the normal. The normal is a line perpendicular to the surface at the point where the incident ray reflects.

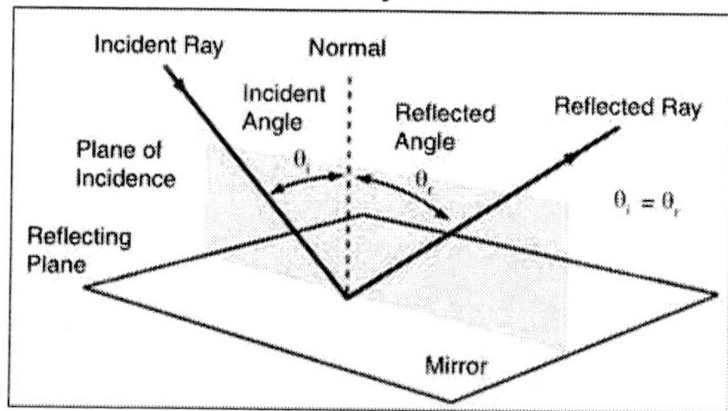

Fig. 5.13 The Law of Reflection.

The incident ray, reflected ray, and normal all lie in the same plane perpendicular to the reflecting surface, known as the plane of incidence. The angle measured from the incoming ray to the normal is termed the incident angle. The angle measured from the outgoing ray to the normal is called the reflected angle. The law of reflection states that the angle of incidence equals the angle of reflection. This law applies to all reflecting surfaces.

Light undergoes either diffuse or regular reflection.

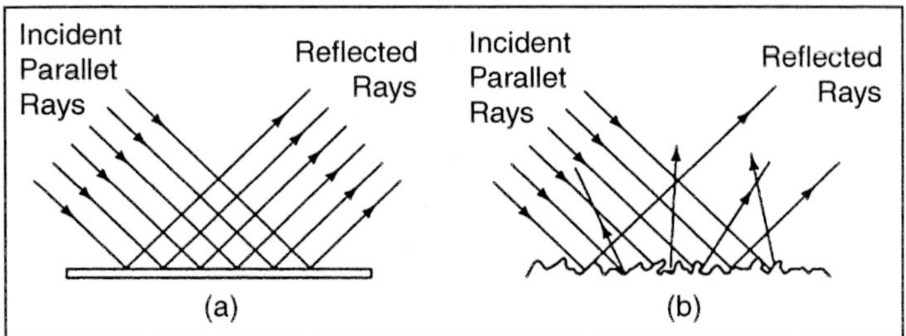

Fig. 5.14 (a) Regular Reflection. (b) Diffuse Reflection

Diffuse reflection occurs when light reflects from a rough surface. Regular reflection is reflection from a smooth surface, such as a mirror. The reflected rays are scattered in diffuse reflection. This scattering is because the local direction of the normal to the surface is different for the different rays. By contrast, in regular reflection, the reflected light rays are orderly because each local region of the surface has a normal in the same direction.

Plane Mirrors

The formation of an image by a plane mirror. Light rays are coming from a source and reflecting off each point of the object (*AB*) in all directions. For simplicity, only a few of the rays are drawn. The rays spread upon leaving the object, and then each ray reflects from the mirror according to the law of reflection. The eye extends back the diverging reflected rays to see an image behind the mirror. An image formed in this manner by extending back the reflected diverging rays is called a virtual image. A virtual image cannot be projected on a screen. The light does *not* physically come together, but rather, the eye (or camera) interprets the diverging rays as originating from an image behind the mirror. Due to the law of reflection, the image formed by a plane mirror is the same distance behind the mirror as the object is in front of the mirror.

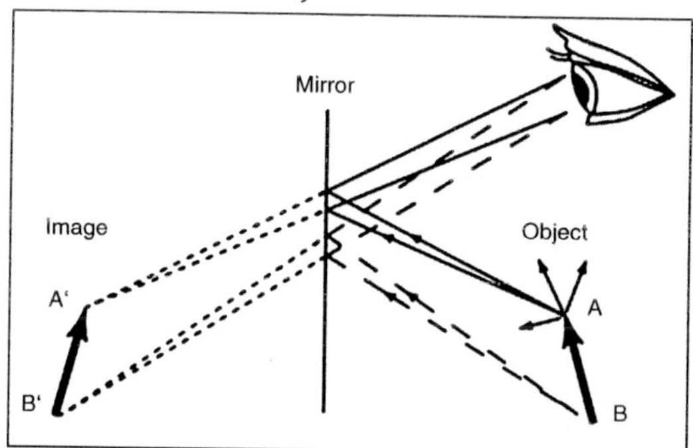

Fig. 5.15 Construction of an Image Reflected in a Mirror

How tall does a mirror need to be so you can see your entire height? Assume the top of the mirror is in line with the top of your head. Does it matter where you stand? From the law of reflection and basic geometry, it can be proven that the marked angles are all equal; therefore, the necessary height of the mirror is approximately half your height. A different distance to show that the distance from the person to the mirror does not change the result.

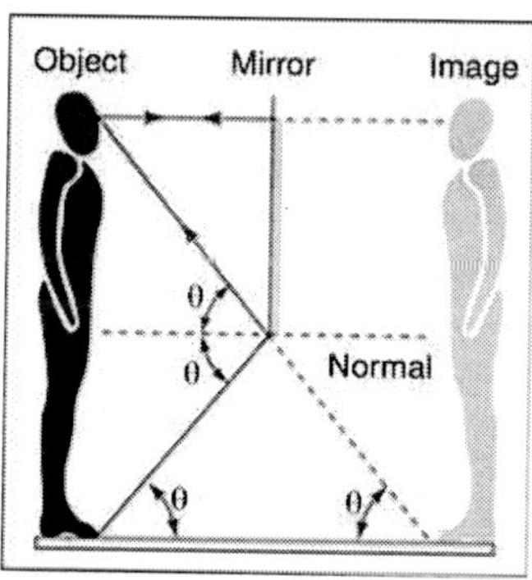

Fig. 5.16 Seeing your own Feet in a Mirror

Concave Mirrors

Customary reflection occurs not only for plane (flat) mirrors but also for curved mirrors. Picture a series of plane mirrors arranged in a semicircle. The incoming light is from a distant source and, therefore, is nearly parallel. After reflection, the light converges on a region. As the number of mirrors increases—the converging region of the light beams decreases.

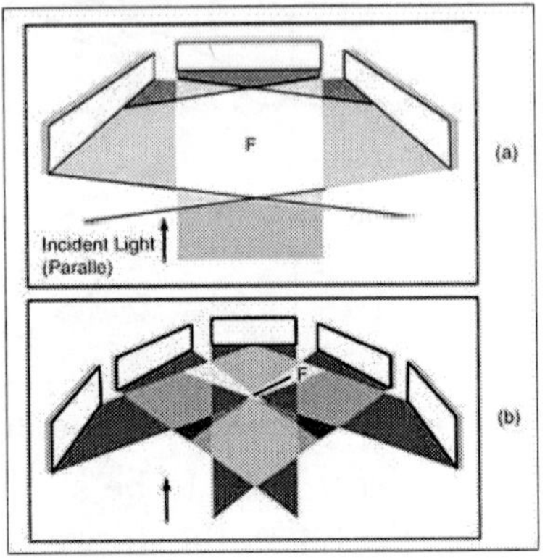

Fig. 5.17 A Semicircular Arrangement of Mirrors Focuses Light in the Region *F*

A concave mirror reflects its light from the inner curved surface. The mirror can be a portion of a sphere, a cylinder, or shaped as a rotated parabolic curve. The light rays intersect after reflection at a common focus called the focal point (F). The focal point is on the optical axis, the symmetry axis of the mirror. The distance f from focal point to the mirror is called the focal length. For a spherical mirror, the focal length is one-half the radius of the sphere that defines the mirror. This distance c is called the radius of curvature, and the centre of the sphere is denoted as $C(c = 2f)$.

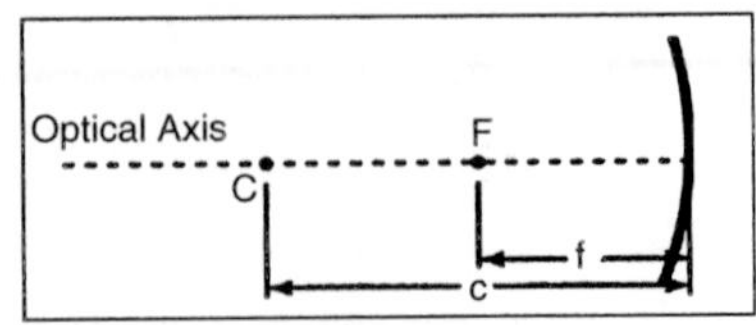

Fig. 5.18 A Concave Mirror with Radius *c* and Focal Length *f*

It is obliging to have a geometric system for locating an image formed by rays reflected from a curved mirror. Any reflected ray follows the law of reflection; however, certain rays have easily defined paths so that measuring angles and finding the normals are not necessary. Four of these rays are:

- The ray directed parallel to the optical axis will reflect through *F*;
- The ray directed through *F* will reflect parallel to the optical axis;
- The ray directed to the centre of the mirror will reflect at the same angle to the optical axis;
- The ray directed along the radius of the sphere will reflect back on itself.

Light rays are drawn for four different positions. It is only necessary to find the intersection of two reflected rays from a point on the object to define the corresponding point on the image. A third one can be used as a check. Sometimes one or another of the rays may be difficult to draw, and so choices can be made.

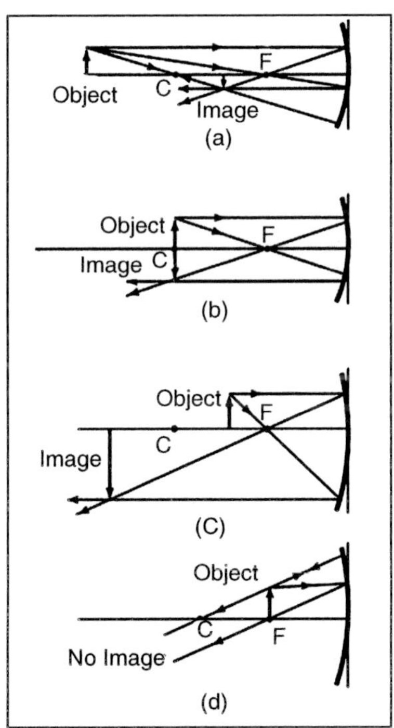

Fig. 5.19 Images from a Concave Mirror

Notice that imagery are formed for the first three cases but not for the last one. No image is formed when the object is at the focal point or, alternatively, the image is formed at infinity and cannot be seen. The three images are all real images. The light physically comes together at a point in space. Note that real images are formed by light that converges after reflection. Also, real images are always inverted—upside down—with regard to the original object. The light rays from the bottom of the object are not drawn. Light travelling along the optical axis will reflect back along the axis, and so if a point of the object is on the optical axis, the corresponding image point will also be on the optical axis.

The images formed can be characterized by size and placement. Let the distance from the object to the mirror be given by *O*. Then the image characteristics can be summarized as follows:

- If $O > 2F$, the image is inverted, smaller, and located between *F* and 2 *F*;
- If $O = 2F$ (at C), the image is inverted, the same size as the object, and located at 2 *F*; that is, the distances of both the object and image to the mirror are equal;
- If $2F < O < F$, the image is inverted, larger than the object, and located >2 *F*. Light paths are reversible. If the object is placed in the position of its former image, the image will then be located where the object was originally; that is, the two will exchange positions.

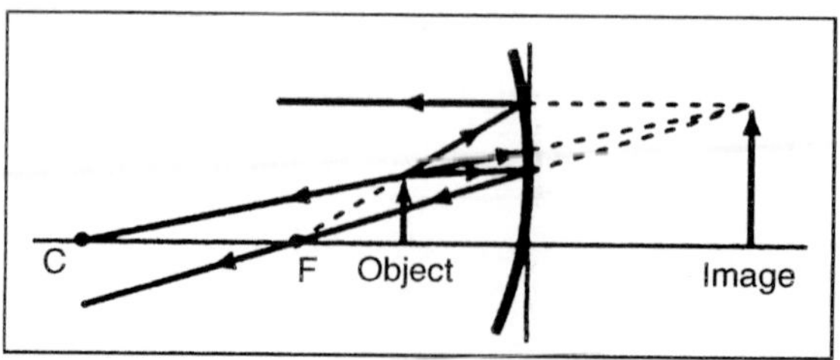

Fig. 5.20 Formation of a Virtual Image in a Concave Mirror.

The diagram for the container when the object is between the focal point (*F*) and the mirror. In this case, a virtual image is formed because the reflected rays diverge from the surface of the mirror.

The virtual image is upright, enlarged, and behind the mirror. Virtual images are *never* inverted.

The following estimated mirror equation relates the distances from the object to the mirror (*O*), the distance from the image to the mirror (*I*), and the focal length (*f*):

$$\frac{1}{O}+\frac{1}{I}=\frac{1}{f}$$

The sign of *f* is positive if it is on the same side as the mirror (a concave mirror) and negative otherwise (convex mirror). Both *O* and *I* are positive in sign if they lie on the same side of the mirror as the incident light and negative if they lie on the opposite side.

The magnification is defined as the ratio of the image size to the object size. This ratio is the same as the ratio of the distances:

$$magnification=\frac{I}{O}$$

Thus, a magnification of 10 × means the image seen is 10 times the size of the object when viewed without a magnifying device.

Convex Mirrors

The graphical method for locating the image of a convex mirror. For convex mirrors, the image on the opposite side of the mirror is virtual, and the images on the same side of the mirror are real.

A virtual, upright, and smaller image. In comparison to the virtual image of the concave mirror, the virtual image of the convex mirror is still upright, but it is diminished (smaller) instead of enlarged and on the opposite side of the mirror instead of the same side.

Again, the virtual image is formed by extending back the reflected diverging rays.

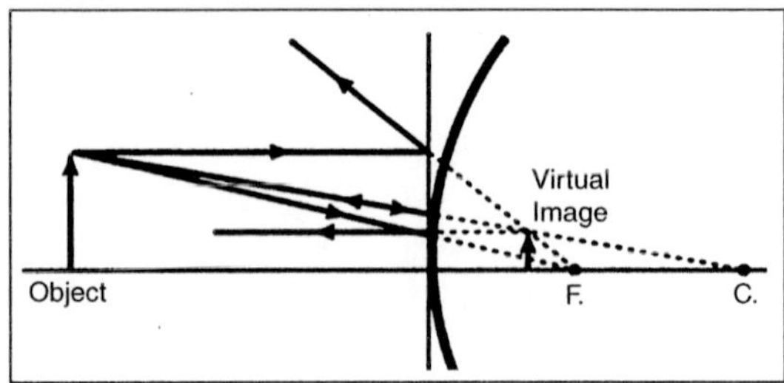

Fig. 5.21 Formation of a Virtual Image in a Concave Mirror

The Law of Refraction

Refraction is the bending of light when the beam passes from one transparent medium into another. A transparent object allows the transmission of light, in contrast to an opaque object, which does not. Some of the light will also be reflected. The incident ray, reflected ray, normal, and refracted ray.

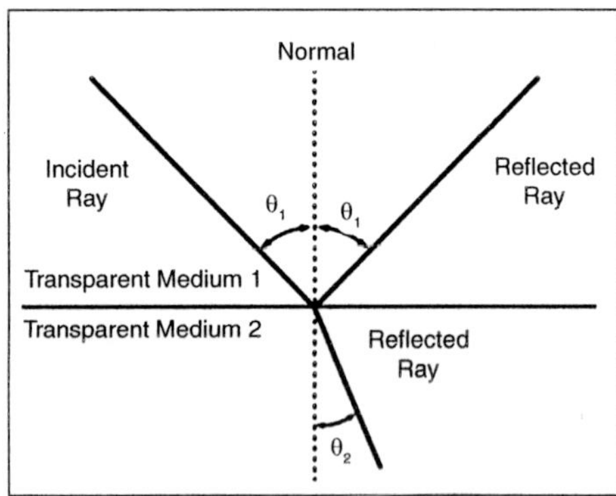

Fig. 5.22 The Law of Refraction

When Willebrod Snell (1580–1626) observed light travelling from air into another transparent material, he found a constant ratio of the sines of the angles measured from the normal to the light ray in the material:

$$n = \frac{\sin\theta_{air}}{\sin\theta_{material}}$$

The constant (n) is called the index of refraction and depends only upon the optical properties of the material. The index of refraction gives a measure of the amount of bending occurring when light travels from air into the material. It is a dimensionless number and can be located in tables of properties of materials. For example, the index of refraction of water is 1.33, and the index of refraction of crown glass varies from 1.50 to 1.62, depending upon the composition of the glass.

For the more general case of light traveling from medium 1 to medium 2, Snell's law can be written $n_1 \sin \theta_1 = n_2 \sin \theta_2$, where the subscripts 1 and 2 refer respectively to the angles and indices of the refraction for material 1 and material 2 respectively. A light ray travelling along the normal, with an incident angle of zero, will not be bent.

The index of refraction is also the ratio of the speed of light in a vacuum (c) and the speed of light in that medium (v); thus,

$$n = \frac{c}{v}$$

Consider the subsequent problem involving both reflection and refraction. Imagine light entering an aquarium and reflecting off a mirror at the bottom. First, what will be the angle of refraction in the water if the angle in air is 30 degrees? Second, at what angle will the beam leave the water?

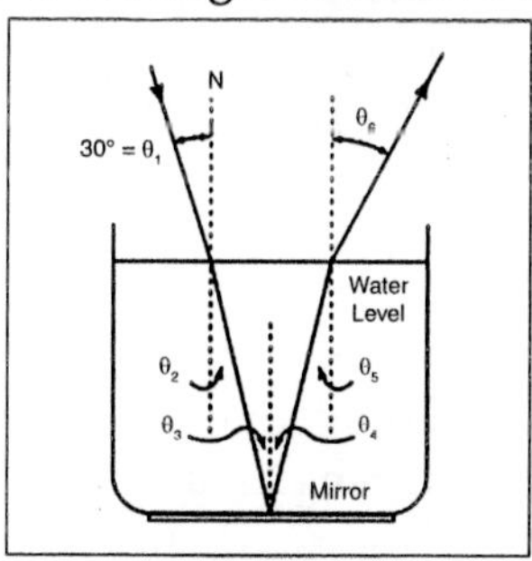

Fig. 5.23 A Problem Combining Refraction and Reflection

Angle θ_2 is determined from θ_1, using Snell's law of refraction. Angle $\theta_2 = \theta_2$ by geometry, $\theta_3 = \theta_4$ by law of reflection, and $\theta_4 = \theta_5$ by geometry. θ_6 is related to θ_5 by Snell's law of refraction, in the same ration as θ_1 to θ_2. Therefore, θ_6—the angle of the ray leaving the water—must be 30 degrees. The problem is symmetrical.

A light ray passing through a rectangular block of transparent material will simply be displaced from its original path. For example, in passing from air to glass, the ray will bend towards the normal. Upon leaving the glass block, the ray will bend away from the normal so that the measured angles in the air on each side of the block are the same.

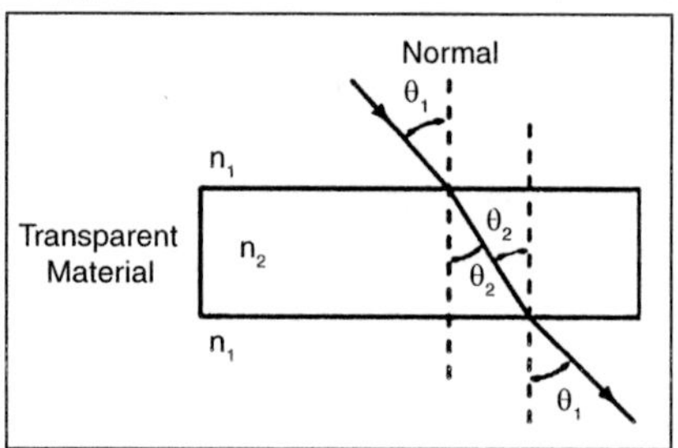

Fig. 5.24 A Light Ray is Displaced after Passing Through a Refracting Medium

Brewster's Angle

Light reflected from the outside of a material is partially polarized. A ray incident on a transparent surface at a certain angle will be partly refracted and partly reflected in a plane polarized ray. This angle of maximum plane polarization is called Brewster's angle, named for Sir David Brewster (1781-1868). The equation is $\tan \theta = n$, where n is the index of refraction of the reflecting surface.

Total Internal Reflection

When light travels from a material with a higher n to one with a lower n, at certain angles all of the light is reflected. This effect is called total internal reflection.

The ray 1 along the normal (no bending), rays 2 and 3 are refracted, and rays 5 and 6 are reflected. Ray 4 is intermediate between reflection and refraction with an angle of refraction of 90 degrees. The incident angle for this case is called the critical angle (θ). If the angle of incidence is less than θ, the light will refract, and if it is greater, the light will reflect.

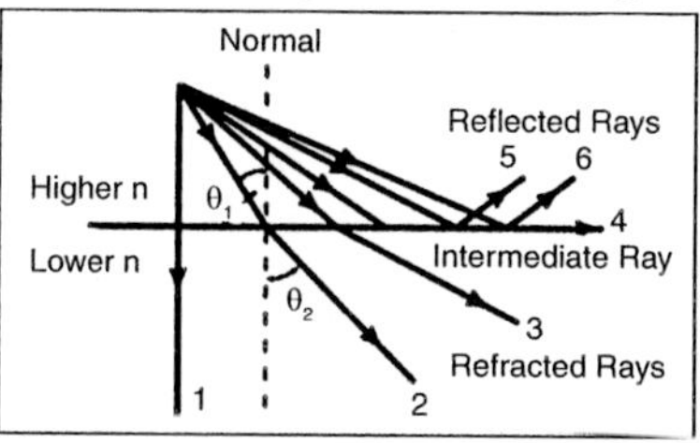

Fig. 5.25 Total Internal Reflection at the Interface of Two Different Media

The equation is

$$\sin\theta_c = \frac{n_2}{n}$$

where $n_1 > n_2$. Find the critical angle from glass to air.

$$\theta_c = \sin^{-1}\left(\frac{n_2}{n_1}\right) = \sin^{-1}\left(\frac{1.00}{1.52}\right)$$

$$\theta_c = 41.1°$$

Therefore, if the incident ray on a glass to air interface is greater than 42 degrees, total internal reflection will occur. The light rays entering and leaving a 45-45-90 glass prism. This phenomenon has broad applications where a mirror is needed, but a silvered surface might corrode after a period of time.

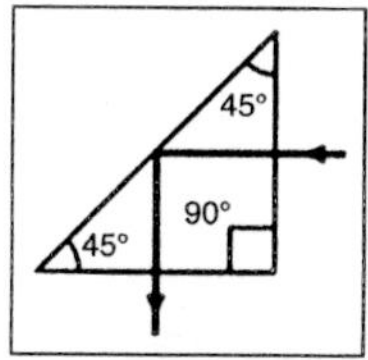

Fig. 5.26 Total Internal Reflection in a Glass Prism

Optical Lenses Function

An optical lens functions by refracting light at its interfaces. In these examples, the lens will be assumed to be thin, in which case the thickness of the lens is negligible compared with it focal length. Lenses are basically of two types. A converging lens causes parallel rays to converge, and a diverging lens causes parallel rays to diverge. The paths of the rays through the lens and the focal point for each case. The definitions for optical axis, focal point, and focal length given for curved mirrors hold true for lenses, with the addition that lenses have focal points on each side of the lens.

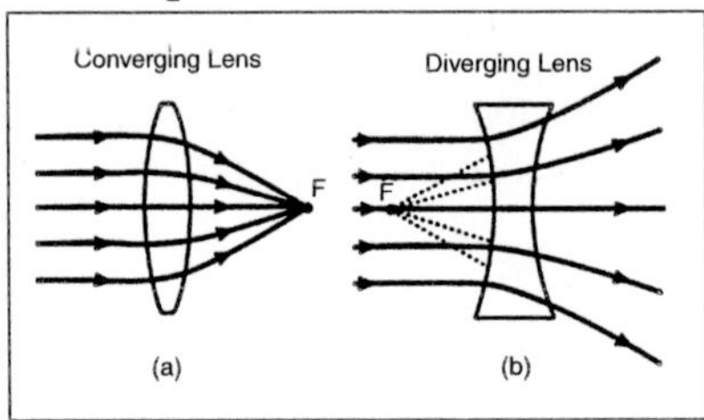

Fig. 5.27 Thin Lenses Function by Refracting Light

Ray diagrams can be made for lenses similar to those drawn for curved mirrors. These three rays can be drawn to locate the image formed by the lens:

- The ray directed parallel to the optical axis refracts through *F* on the far side;
- The ray directed to the near *F* refracts parallel to the optical axis;
- The ray directed to the centre of the lens is undeviated (in the thin lens approximation).

The ray diagrams for two cases of a converging lens.

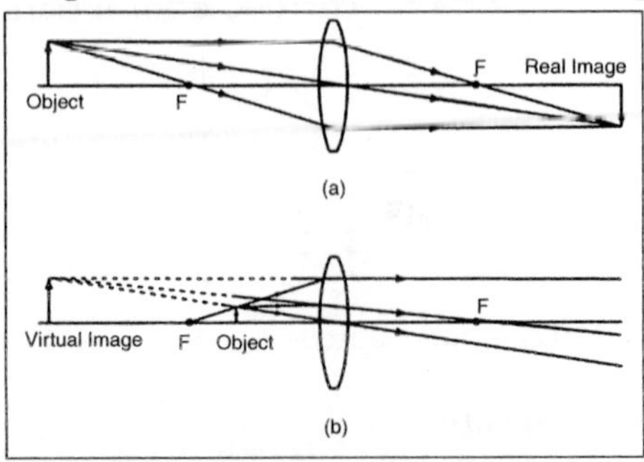

Fig. 5.28 Ray Diagrams for a Converging Lens, Showing the Formation of (*a*) A Real Image or (*b*) A Virtual Image.

In Figure 5.28 (a), a real image is formed, and in Figure 5.28 (b), a virtual image is formed. The lens setup in Figure (b) is called a simple magnifier. With lenses as with mirrors, virtual images are right side up, and real images are inverted. The lens equation is the same relationship used for curved mirrors:

$$\frac{1}{O}+\frac{1}{I}=\frac{1}{f}$$

as is the equation for magnification:

$$magnification=\frac{I}{O}$$

The focal length is optimistic for a converging lens and negative for a diverging lens. The object and image distances are positive if they are on opposite sides of the lens and negative if they are on the same side. The relative sizes and positions of the object and image for a converging lens are similar to the four cases reviewed for the concave mirror.

- If $O > 2\ F$, the image is inverted, smaller, and located between F and $2\ F$, on the opposite side.
- If $O = 2\ F$, the image is inverted, the same size as the object, and located at $2\ F$; that is, the distances of both the object and image to the lens are equal but on opposite sides of the lens.
- If $2\ F < O < F$, the image is inverted, larger than the object, and located $> 2\ F$.
- If $O < F$, the image is virtual, enlarged, and located on the same side of the lens where $I > F$.

The ray diagram for a diverging lens. The image formed by this lens is always virtual, upright, and diminished.

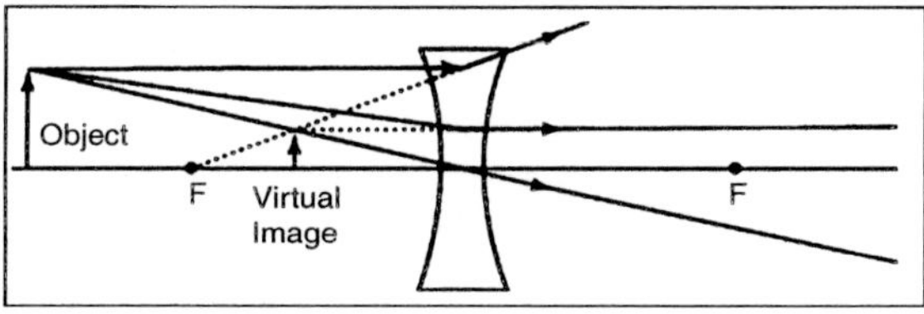

Fig. 5.29 Ray Diagram for a Diverging Lens

The Compound Microscope

When lenses are second-hand in combinations, the image given by one lens becomes the object for a second lens. The compound microscope is an example of the use of several lenses to magnify an object. An objective lens near the object forms an enlarged image. This image is then further magnified by the second lens, called the eyepiece. Both are converging lenses.

The object (*AB*) is placed just below the focal point of the objective lens. The objective lens forms an enlarged, real, and inverted image at a distance greater than 2 *F* from the first lens. This image (*A*2 *B*2) falls inside the focal point of the eyepiece lens; therefore, an enlarged, virtual image is formed by the eyepiece (*A*3 *B*3). The total magnification is the product of the magnifications of each lens.

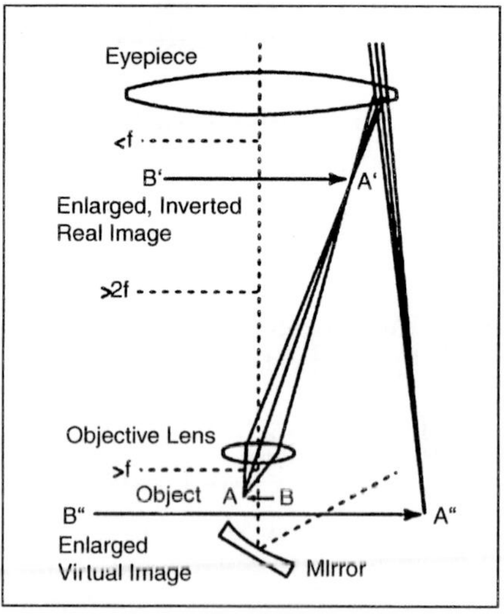

Fig. 5.30 A Compound Microscope

Dispersion and Prisms

An important property of the index of refraction is that it is slightly dependent upon wavelength. For a given material—for example, glass— *n* decreases with increasing wavelength; thus, blue light bends more than red light. This effect is called dispersion. Light is refracted twice as it enters and leaves the prism.

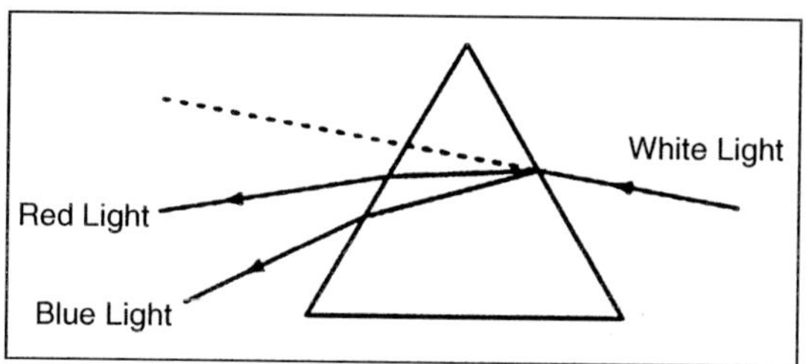

Fig. 5.31 Dispersion of White Light in a Prism

A specified ray is bent from its original direction of travel by an angle (δ), called the angle of deviation. The angle of deviation for the red light is less than that for the blue light; therefore, the prism spreads the light into the colours of the spectrum. These colours are commonly called red, orange, yellow, green, blue, indigo, and violet (often abbreviated with the mnemonic Roy G Biv).

Rainbows are formed by dispersion and total internal reflection of sunlight in raindrops. The critical angle for water to air is approximately 40 degrees. The sunlight enters the drop and is reflected off the side of the drop away from the viewer. Due to dispersion, the violet ray emerges above the red ray. The refraction of sunlight on one idealized raindrop.

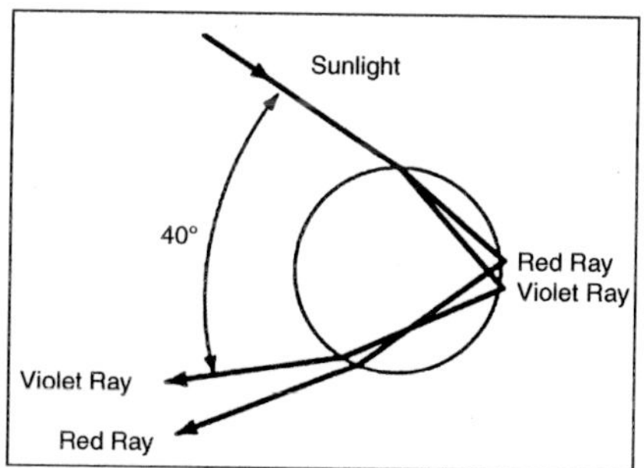

Fig. 5.32 Dispersion and Internal Reflection of Light Passing Through a Raindrop

The rainbow is in the shape of an arc because the circle of drops at the angle of about 40 degrees is in existence only above the ground. It is possible to see a circular rainbow from an airplane in the correct position relative to the sunlight and raindrops.

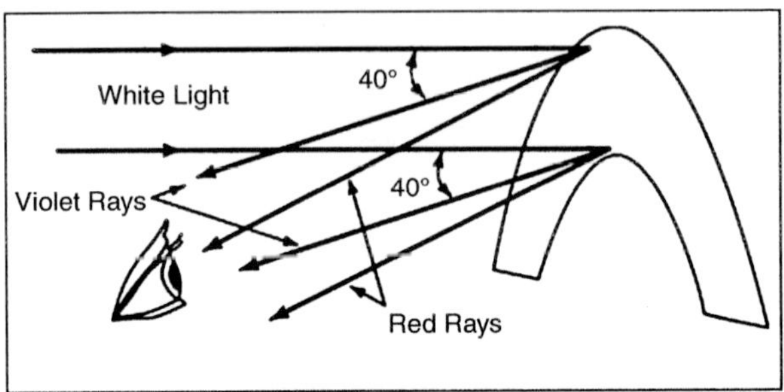

TELESCOPES

Telescopes are one of the major ways that astronomers (both professional and amateur) explore the universe. They come in all shapes and sizes depending on their function. Generally, bigger telescopes are better if you want to see faint, far-away things, because they can gather more light and have better resolution. Resolution is the ability of a telescope to discern objects close together; for example, the ability to clearly separate two stars that are very close together or the ability to see smaller craters on the Moon.

Visible Light Telescopes

The telescopes that most people are familiar with are visible-light (optical) telescopes. There are two main kinds of optical telescope, refractors and reflectors. Refractors use lenses to collect and focus light. However, large pieces of finely ground glass are expensive and heavy, so it's not practical to make large refractors. Yerkes Observatory in Wisconsin is the largest refractor ever made and has lenses that are 40 inches in diameter. Reflecting telescopes use mirrors to focus light, and since they are cheaper they can be made much larger. All major astronomical telescopes built now are reflectors. The largest optical telescopes are currently the Keck telescopes that have 10 metre mirrors and the brand new Gemini telescopes that have 8 metre mirrors.

Seeing the Universe at Different Wavelengths

Although optical telescopes are the type most commonly used for stargazing and amateur astronomy, lots of astronomical research is done on telescopes that look at other wavelengths of light. Each of these wavelength ranges shows us something unique about the universe and allows us to view events and objects that can't be seen with human eyes. Radio telescopes, like the Very Large Array and Arecibo Observatory, look at very long wavelength light. Radio waves are so large that they don't notice small imperfections in the telescope surface, so unlike optical telescope mirrors, radio telescopes often have dishes with lots of holes to reduce the weight. You can see many diverse things with radio telescopes; for example, you can investigate how hydrogen gas is distributed in our galaxy and other galaxies, and you can time the rotation period of pulsars. Telescopes operating at very short wavelengths, like X-Rays and Gamma Rays, have to be located in space since our atmosphere blocks radiation at these wavelengths. At short wavelengths, you see regions where high energy radiation is being created. Some of these places include stellar explosions, galactic centres, and regions near pulsars and black holes. The Chandra X-Ray Observatory is one telescope that looks at these objects.

Infra-red Telescopes

Objects that are cooler than stars don't give off visible light, but they often give off infra-red waves (sometimes called heat waves). Planets, clouds of cosmic dust, and the chair in which you are sitting reading this web page all give off infra-red waves. One of the biggest problems with trying to detect faint infra-red waves from space is that everything on Earth (including everything around the astronomer, and the astronomer for that mater) is giving off infra-red waves. So infra-red telescopes need to be isolated and cooled to very low temperatures so their own infra-red waves don't interfere with the waves coming from objects in space.

The Basics of Telescopes

Telescopes come in three basic designs; Refractor, Reflector, and Catadioptric.

Refractor

A refractor uses two lenses. At one end (the end farther away from the viewer), is the larger lens, called the objective lens or object glass. On the other end is the lens you look through. It is called the ocular or eyepiece.

The objective collects light and focuses it as a sharp image. This image is magnified and seen through the ocular. The eyepiece is adjusted by sliding it in and out of the telescope body to focus the image.

Reflector

A reflector works a bit differently. Light is gathered at the bottom of the scope by a concave mirror, called the Primary. The primary has a parabolic shape. There are several ways the primary can focus the light, and how it is done determines the type of reflecting telescope.

Many observatory Telescopes use a photographic plate to focus the image. Called the Prime Focus Position, the plate is located near the top of the scope. Other scopes use a secondary mirror, placed in a similar position as the photographic plate, to reflect the image back down the body of the scope, where it is viewed through a hole in the primary mirror. This is known as a Cassegrain focus.

Newtonian

Then, there's the Newtonian, a kind of reflector. So named because Sir Isaac Newton created the basic design. In a Newtonian, a flat mirror is placed at an angle in the same position as the secondary mirror in a Cassegrain. This secondary mirror focuses the image into an eyepiece located in the side of the tube, near the top of the scope.

Catadioptric

Finally, there are catadioptric telescopes, which combine elements of refractors and reflectors in their design.

The first such telescope was created by German astronomer Bernhard Schmidt in 1930. It used a primary mirror at the back of the telescope with a glass corrector plate in the front of the telescope, which was designed to remove spherical aberration. In the original telescope, photographic film was placed at the prime focus. There were no secondary mirror or eyepieces. The descendant of that original design, called the Schmidt-Cassegrain design, is the most popular type of telescope. Invented in the 1960s, it has a secondary mirror that bounces light through a hole in the primary mirror to an eyepiece.

Our second style of catadioptric telescope was invented by a Russian astronomer, D. Maksutov. In the Maksutov telescope, a more spherical corrector lens than in the Schmidt is utilized. Otherwise, the designs are quite similar. Today's models are known as Maksutov–Cassegrain.

Refractor Telescope Advantages and Disadvantages

After initial alignment, refractor optics are more resistant to misalignment. The glass surfaces are sealed inside the tube and rarely need cleaning. The sealing also minimizes affects from air currents, providing steadier sharper images. Disadvantages include a number of possible aberrations of the lenses. Also, since lenses need edge supported, this limits the size of any refractor.

Reflector Telescope Advantages and Disadvantages

Reflectors do not suffer from chromatic aberration. Mirrors are easier to build without defects than lenses, since only one side of a mirror is used. Also, because the support for a mirror is from the back, very large mirrors can be built, making larger scopes. The disadvantages include easiness of misalignment, need for frequent cleaning, and possible spherical aberration.

DIFFRACTION

Diffraction refers to various phenomena which occur when a wave encounters an obstacle. Italian scientist Francesco Maria Grimaldi coined the word 'diffraction' and was the first to record accurate observations of the phenomenon in 1665.

In classical physics, the diffraction phenomenon is described as the apparent bending of waves around small obstacles and the spreading out of waves past small openings. Similar effects occur when light waves travel through a medium with a varying refractive index or a sound wave through one with varying acoustic impedance. Diffraction occurs with all waves, including sound waves, water waves, and electromagnetic waves such as visible light, X-rays and radio waves. As physical objects have wave-like properties (at the atomic level), diffraction also occurs with matter and can be studied according to the principles of quantum mechanics.

Richard Feynman said that:

"No-one has ever been able to define the difference between interference and diffraction satisfactorily. It is just a question of usage, and there is no specific, important physical difference between them."

He suggested that when there are only a few sources, say two, we call it interference, as in Young's slits, but with a large number of sources, the process be labelled diffraction.

While diffraction occurs whenever propagating waves encounter such changes, its effects are generally most pronounced for waves where the wavelength is roughly similar to the dimensions of the diffracting objects. If the obstructing object provides multiple, closely spaced openings, a complex pattern of varying intensity can result. This is due to the superposition, or interference, of different parts of a wave that travelled to the observer by different paths.

The formalism of diffraction can also describe the way in which waves of finite extent propagate in free space. For example, the expanding profile of a laser beam, the beam shape of a radar antenna and the field of view of an ultrasonic transducer can all be analysed using diffraction equations.

Diffraction of Light : Light Bending Around an Object

Diffraction is the slight bending of light as it passes around the edge of an object. The amount of bending depends on the relative size of the wavelength of light to the size of the opening. If the opening is much larger than the light's wavelength, the bending will be almost unnoticeable. However, if the two are closer in size or equal, the amount of bending is considerable, and easily seen with the naked eye.

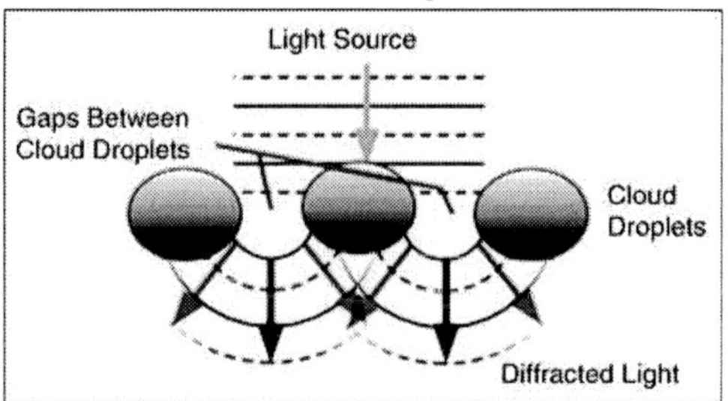

In the atmosphere, diffracted light is in fact bent around atmospheric particles—most commonly, the atmospheric particles are tiny water droplets found in clouds. Diffracted light can produce fringes of light, dark or coloured bands. An optical effect that results from the diffraction of light is the silver lining sometimes found around the edges of clouds or coronas surrounding the sun or moon.

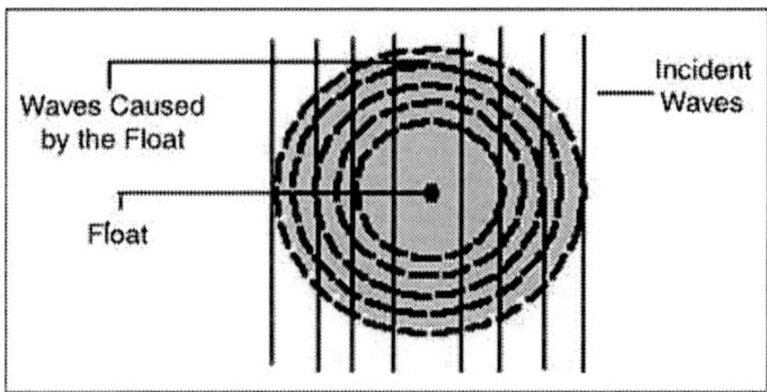

Optical effects resulting from diffraction are shaped through the interference of light waves. To visualize this, imagine light waves as water waves. If water waves were incident upon a float residing on the water surface, the float would bounce up and down in response to the incident waves, producing waves of its own. As these waves spread outward in all directions from the float, they interact with other water waves. If the crests of two waves combine, an amplified wave is produced (constructive interference). However, if a crest of one wave and a trough of another wave combine, they cancel each other out to produce no vertical displacement (destructive interference).

This concept also applies to light waves. When sunlight (or moonlight) encounters a cloud droplet, light waves are altered and interact with one another in a similar manner as the water waves. If there is constructive interference, (the crests of two light waves combining), the light will appear brighter. If there is destructive interference, (the trough of one light wave meeting the crest of another), the light will either appear darker or disappear entirely.

Single-slit diffraction

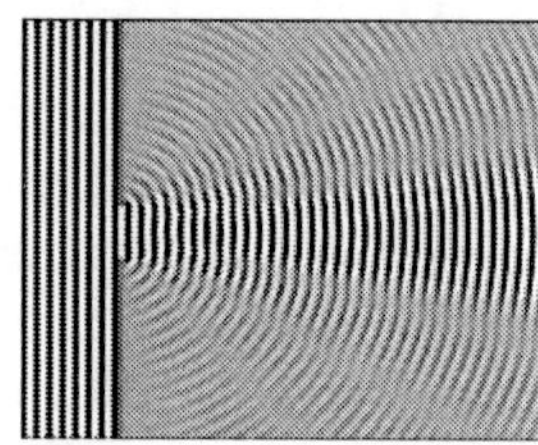

Fig. 5.33 Numerical Approximation of Diffraction Pattern from a Slit of Width Equal to Wavelength of an Incident Plane Wave in 3D Spectrum Visualization

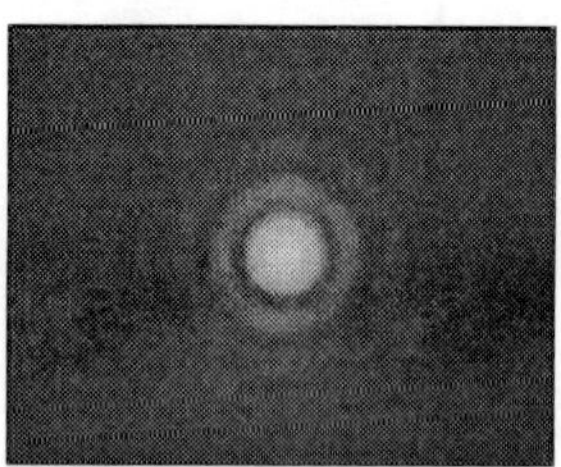

Fig. 5.34 Diffraction of Laser Beam on the Hole

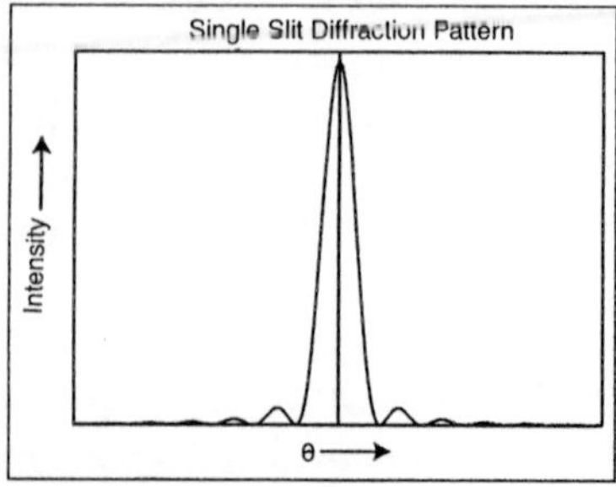

Fig. 5.35 Graph and Image of Single-slit Diffraction

A long slit of infinitesimal width which is illuminated by light diffracts the light into a series of circular waves and the wavefront which emerges from the slit is a cylindrical wave of uniform intensity.

A slit which is wider than a wavelength produces interference effects in the space downstream of the slit. These can be explained by assuming that the slit behaves as though it has a large number of point sources spaced evenly across the width of the slit. The analysis of this system is simplified if we consider light of a single wavelength. If the incident light is monochromatic, these sources all have the same phase. Light incident at a given point in the space downstream of the slit is made up of contributions from each of these point sources and if the relative phases of these contributions vary by 2π or more, we may expect to find minima and maxima in the diffracted light. Such phase differences are caused by differences in the path lengths over which contributing rays reach the point from the slit.

We can find the angle at which a first minimum is obtained in the diffracted light by the following reasoning. The light from a source located at the top edge of the slit interferes destructively with a source located at the middle of the slit, when the path difference between them is equal to $\lambda/2$. Similarly, the source just below the top of the slit will interfere destructively with the source located just below the middle of the slit at the same angle. We can continue this reasoning along the entire height of the slit to conclude that the condition for destructive interference for the entire slit is the same as the condition for destructive interference between two narrow slits a distance apart that is half the width of the slit. The path difference is given by $\frac{d\sin(\theta)}{2}$ so that the minimum intensity occurs at an angle θ_{min} given by

$$d\sin\theta_{\text{min}} = \lambda$$

where

- d is the width of the slit;

- θ_{min} is the angle of incidence at which the minimum intensity occurs; and
- λ is the wavelength of the light

A similar argument can be used to show that if we imagine the slit to be divided into four, six, eight parts, etc., minima are obtained at angles θ_n given by

$$d\sin\theta_n = n\lambda$$

where

- n is an integer other than zero.

There is no such simple argument to enable us to find the maxima of the diffraction pattern. The intensity profile can be calculated using the Fraunhofer diffraction equation as

$$I(\theta) = I_0 \operatorname{sinc}^2(\frac{d}{\lambda}\sin\theta)$$

where

- $I(\theta)$ is the intensity at a given angle;
- I_0 is the original intensity; and
- the sinc function is given by $\operatorname{sinc}(x) = \sin(\pi x)/(\pi x)$ if $x \neq 0$, and $\operatorname{sinc}(0) = 1$.

This analysis applies only to the far field, that is, at a distance much larger than the width of the slit.

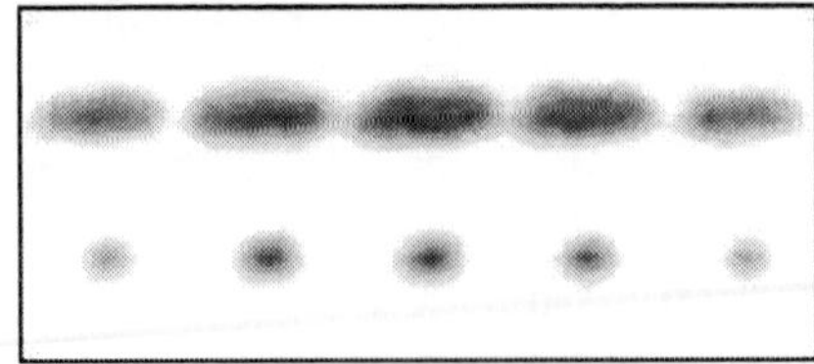

Fig. 5.36 2-slit (top) and 5-slit Diffraction of Laser Light

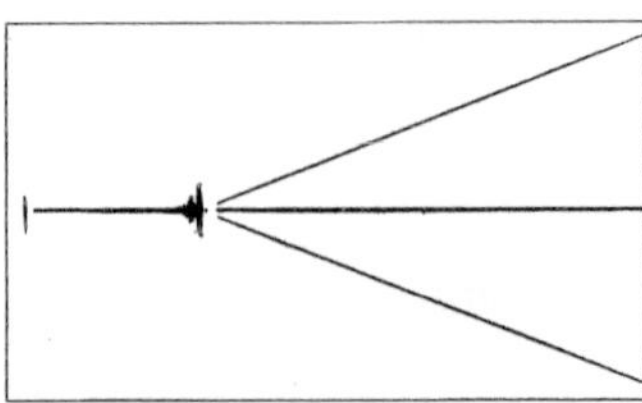

Fig. 5.37 Diffraction of a laser using a Diffraction Grating

Diffraction Grating

A diffraction grating is an optical constituent with a regular pattern. The form of the light diffracted by a grating depends on the structure of the elements and the number of elements present, but all gratings have intensity maxima at angles θ_m which are given by the grating equation

$$d\left(\sin\theta_m + \sin\theta_i\right) = m\lambda.$$

where

- θ_i is the angle at which the light is incident;
- *d* is the separation of grating elements; and
- *m* is an integer which can be positive or negative.

The light diffracted by a grating is found by summing the light diffracted from each of the elements, and is essentially a convolution of diffraction and interference patterns.

The figure 5.36 shows the light diffracted by 2-element and 5-element gratings where the grating spacings are the same; it can be seen that the maxima are in the same position, but the detailed structures of the intensities are different.

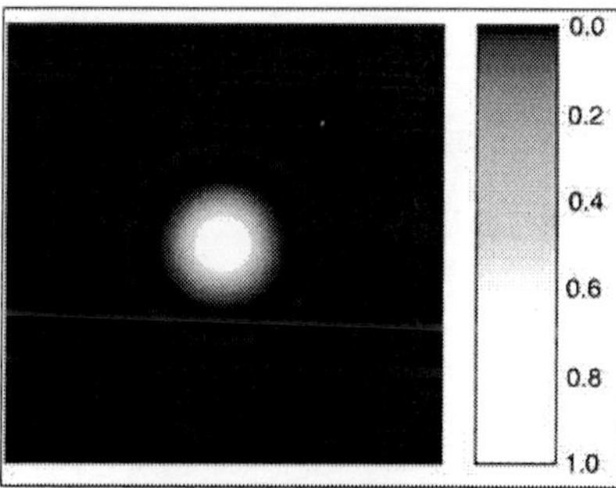

A computer-generated image of an Airy disk

Computer generated light diffraction pattern from a circular aperture of diameter 0.5 micrometre at a wavelength of 0.6 micrometre (red-light) at distances of 0.1 cm – 1 cm in steps of 0.1 cm. One can see the image moving from the Fresnel region into the Fraunhofer region where the Airy pattern is seen.

Circular aperture

The far-field diffraction of a plane wave incident on a circular aperture is often referred to as the Airy Disk. The variation in intensity with angle is given by

$$I(\theta) = I_0 \left(\frac{2J_1(ka\sin\theta)}{ka\sin\theta} \right)^2,$$

where a is the radius of the circular aperture, k is equal to $2\pi/\lambda$ and J_1 is a Bessel function. The smaller the aperture, the larger the spot size at a given distance, and the greater the divergence of the diffracted beams.

General Aperture

The wave that emerges from a point source has amplitude ψ at location r that is given by the solution of the frequency domain wave equation for a point source (The Helmholtz Equation),

$$\nabla^2\psi + k^2\psi = \delta(\mathbf{r})$$

where $\delta(\mathbf{r})$ is the 3-dimensional delta function. The delta function has only radial dependence, so the Laplace operator (aka scalar Laplacian) in the spherical coordinate system simplifies to

$$\nabla^2\psi = \frac{1}{r}\frac{\partial^2}{\partial r^2}(r\psi)$$

By direct substitution, the solution to this equation can be readily shown to be the scalar Green's function, which in the spherical coordinate system (and using the physics time convention $e^{-i\omega t}$) is:

$$\psi(r) = \frac{e^{ikr}}{4\pi r}$$

This solution assumes that the delta function source is located at the origin. If the source is located at an arbitrary source point, denoted by the vector r′ and the field point is located at the point r, then we may represent the scalar Green's function (for arbitrary source location) as:

$$\psi(\mathbf{r} \mid \mathbf{r}') = \frac{e^{ik|\mathbf{r}-\mathbf{r}'|}}{4\pi \mid \mathbf{r} - \mathbf{r}' \mid}$$

Therefore, if an electric field, $E_{inc}(x,y)$ is incident on the aperture, the field produced by this aperture distribution is given by the surface integral:

$$\Psi(r) \propto \iint_{\text{aperture}} E_{inc}(x', y') \frac{e^{ik|\mathbf{r}-\mathbf{r}'|}}{4\pi \mid \mathbf{r} - \mathbf{r}' \mid} dx'dy',$$

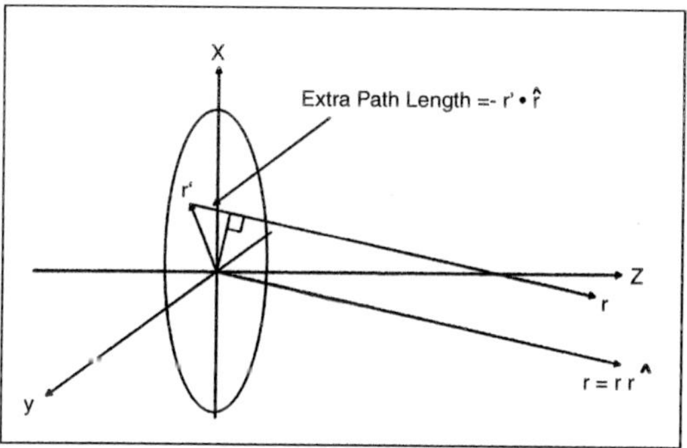

On the calculation of Fraunhofer region fields where the source point in the aperture is given by the vector

$$\mathbf{r}' = x'\hat{\mathbf{x}} + y'\hat{\mathbf{y}}$$

In the far field, wherein the parallel rays approximation can be employed, the Green's function,

$$\psi(\mathbf{r} \mid \mathbf{r}') = \frac{e^{ik|\mathbf{r}-\mathbf{r}'|}}{4\pi \mid \mathbf{r} - \mathbf{r}' \mid}$$

simplifies to

$$\psi(\mathbf{r}\,|\,\mathbf{r}') = \frac{e^{ikr}}{4\pi r} e^{-ik(\mathbf{r}'\cdot\hat{\mathbf{r}})}$$

as can be seen in the figure to the right.

The expression for the far-zone (Fraunhofer region) field becomes

$$\Psi(r) \propto \frac{e^{ikr}}{4\pi r} \iint_{\text{aperture}} E_{inc}(x', y') e^{-ik(\mathbf{r}'\cdot\hat{\mathbf{r}})} dx'dy',$$

Now, since

$$r' = x'\hat{x} + y'\hat{y}$$

and

$$\hat{r} = \sin\theta\cos\phi\hat{x} + \sin\theta\,\sin\phi\hat{y} + \cos\theta\hat{z}$$

the expression for the Fraunhofer region field from a planar aperture now becomes,

$$\Psi(r) \propto \frac{e^{ikr}}{4\pi r} \iint_{aperture} E_{inc}(x', y') e^{-ik\sin\theta(\cos\phi x' + \sin\phi y')} dx'dy'$$

Letting,

$$k_x = k\sin\theta\cos\phi$$

and

$$k_y = k\sin\theta\sin\phi$$

the Fraunhofer region field of the planar aperture assumes the form of a Fourier transform

$$\Psi(r) \propto \frac{e^{ikr}}{4\pi r} \iint_{\text{aperture}} E_{inc}(x', y') e^{-i(k_x x' + k_y y')} dx'dy',$$

In the far-field/Fraunhofer region, this becomes the spatial Fourier transform of the aperture distribution. Huygens' principle when applied to an aperture simply says that the far-field diffraction pattern is the spatial Fourier transform of the aperture shape, and this is a direct by-product of using the parallel-rays approximation, which is identical to doing a plane wave decomposition of the aperture plane fields.

Propagation of a Laser Beam

The way in which the profile of a laser beam changes as it propagates is determined by diffraction. The output mirror of the laser is an aperture, and the subsequent beam shape is determined by that aperture.

Hence, the smaller the output beam, the quicker it diverges.

Paradoxically, it is possible to reduce the divergence of a laser beam by first expanding it with one convex lens, and then collimating it with a second convex lens whose focal point is coincident with that of the first lens. The resulting beam has a larger aperture, and hence a lower divergence.

Diffraction-limited Imaging

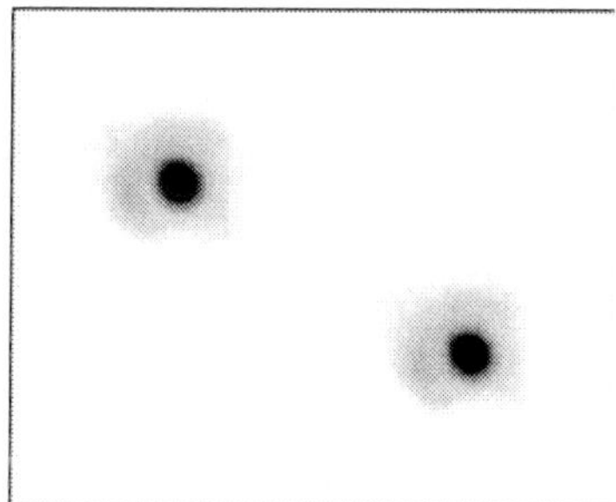

Fig. 5.38 The Airy Disk Around each of the Stars from the 2.56 m Telescope Aperture can be Seen in this *Lucky Image* of the Binary Star Zeta Boötis

The ability of an imaging system to resolve detail is ultimately limited by diffraction.

This is because a plane wave incident on a circular lens or mirror is diffract. The light is not focussed to a point but forms an Airy disk having a central spot in the focal plane with radius to first null of

$$d = 1.22\lambda N,$$

where λ is the wavelength of the light and N is the f-number (focal length divided by diameter) of the imaging optics. In object space, the corresponding angular resolution is

$$\sin\theta = 1.22\frac{\lambda}{D},$$

where D is the diameter of the entrance pupil of the imaging lens (*e.g.*, of a telescope's main mirror).

Two point sources will each produce an Airy pattern—see the photo of a binary star. As the point sources move closer together, the patterns will start to overlap, and ultimately they will merge to form a single pattern, in which case the two point sources cannot be resolved in the image. The Rayleigh criterion specifies that two point sources can be considered to be resolvable if the separation of the two images is at least the radius of the Airy disk, *i.e.* if the first minimum of one coincides with the maximum of the other.

Thus, the larger the aperture of the lens, and the smaller the wavelength, the finer the resolution of an imaging system. This is why telescopes have very large lenses or mirrors, and why optical microscopes are limited in the detail which they can see.

Speckle Patterns

The speckle pattern which is seen when using a laser pointer is another diffraction phenomenon. It is a result of the superpostion of many waves with different phases, which are produced when a laser beam illuminates a rough surface. They add together to give a resultant wave whose amplitude, and therefore intensity varies randomly.

Chapter 6

Solar Neutrinos

INTRODUCTION

Solar neutrinos are produced by the nuclear reactions that power the Sun. The fusion of proton plus proton (pp) to deuterium plus positron plus neutrino is responsible for 98 per cent of the energy production of the sun. Therefore these pp-neutrinos are the most plentiful, and the most reliably estimated. About 60 billion pp-neutrinos pass through a square centimetre at the Earth each second. They are relatively low energy, however, with a continuous spectrum that ends at 420 keV. In addition, there are several rarer reactions which also produce neutrinos. The electron capture on Beryllium-7 produces a sharp line of Beryllium-7 neutrinos at 861 keV. A small fraction of the time, Beryllium-7 captures a proton instead of an electron, to form Boron-8. The beta decay of Boron-8:

$$^{8}B \rightarrow {}^{8}Be + e^{+} + nu\_e$$

produces a continuous spectrum of neutrino energies that extends to 15 MeV. Super-K is sensitive to these rare but high energy Boron-8 neutrinos.

Super-K detects Boron-8 neutrinos when they scatter off of atomic electrons in the water. The recoil electron direction is oriented along the direction of neutrino travel. The electron makes a weak Cherenkov ring in the detector- only 40-50 PMT hits are expected for a 8 MeV electron. At this low energy, there is considerable random background, mostly from radon gas in the water. So we count solar neutrinos by making an angular distribution with respect to the sun's known direction. The sharp peak near cosine equals one is due to solar neutrinos. The area under the peak, after subtracting background, is the measured number of solar neutrinos.

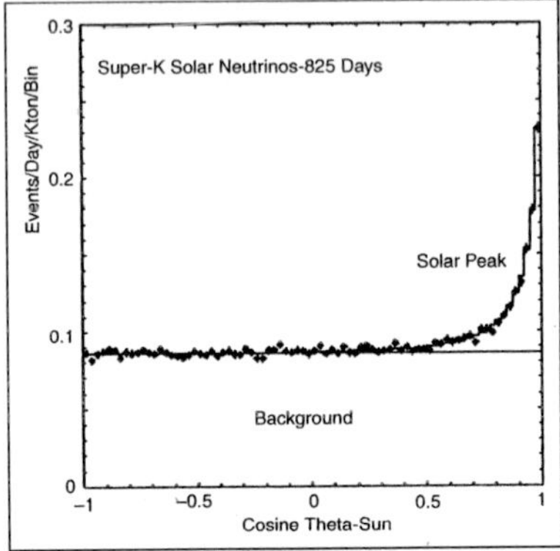

The number of neutrinos can be predicted by the Standard Solar Model. The detected number of electron neutrinos was only 1/3 of the predicted number, and this was known as the solar neutrino problem. It led to the idea of neutrino oscillation and the fact that neutrinos can change flavour. This was confirmed when the total flux of solar neutrinos of all types was measured and it agreed with the earlier predictions of expected electron neutrino flux, as seen by Sudbury Neutrino Observatory, and thus confirmed that neutrinos have mass.

The energy spectrum of solar neutrinos is also predicted by solar models. It is essential to know this energy spectrum because different neutrino detection experiments are sensitive to different neutrino energy ranges. The Homestake Experiment used chlorine and was most sensitive to solar neutrinos produced by the decay of the beryllium isotope ^{7}Be. The Sudbury Neutrino Observatory is most sensitive to solar neutrinos produced by ^{8}B. The detectors that use gallium are most sensitive to the solar neutrinos produced by the proton-proton chain reaction process. In 2012 the collaboration known as Borexino reported detecting low-energy neutrinos for the proton-electron-proton (pep reaction) that produces 1 in 400 deuterium nuclei in the sun. The detector contained 100 metric tons of liquid and saw on average 3 events each day (due to carbon 11 production) from this relatively uncommon thermonuclear reaction.

Neutrinos can trigger nuclear reactions. By looking at ancient ores of various ages that have been exposed to solar neutrinos over geologic time, it may be possible to interrogate the luminosity of the Sun over time, which, according to the Standard Solar Model, has changed with time.

What is Solar Neutrino?

The Sun is the Earth's main foundation of energy. Since the beginning of time, it has been steadily delivering its energy to every inch of the surface of the Earth. The thing that keeps the Sun from using up all of its energy and power is nuclear fusion, where nuclei combine to form much larger nuclei, in the process releasing a tremendous amount of energy. A by-product of nuclear fusion are particles called neutrinos.

Neutrinos from the Sun pass through the Earth and are picked up by neutrino detectors. The influx of these neutrino particles confirms the fact that nuclear fusion really does take place on the Sun. They are also the only known particle that can bring direct data and information from the Sun's interior, as they are the only kind of particle that can escape without interaction from the Sun's core.

The Standard Solar Model can predict or determine the number of neutrinos that pass through the Earth. In the 19602s, John Bahcall developed a formula to predict the neutrino flux, while Raymond Davis tested it. When the results were received, they found that there was a discrepancy between the theoretical prediction of the number of neutrinos and the actual measurements from neutrino detectors. The measurements from the detectors amount to only about 1/3 of the predicted total, much lower than what was anticipated. This became known as the Solar Neutrino Problem.

In recent times however, the Solar Neutrino Problem was eventually solved. The problem existed due to an incomplete knowledge of the inner working of neutrinos and their behaviour during travel from Earth to the Sun. The Standard

Solar Model was eventually modified to include neutrino oscillation.

In 2001, the first strong proof of neutrino oscillation was detected at the Subdury Neutrino Observatory in Canada. Raymond Davis Jr. and Masatoshi Kiba received a Nobel Prize for Physics for their work in determining the correct number of solar neutrinos.

NEUTRINOS AND THE SUN

The neutrino was proposed by Wolfgang Pauli in 1930, but it took 26 more years before the neutrino was actually discovered (detected). Pauli proposed the existence of the neutrino as a solution to a frustrating problem in nuclear beta-decay that was studied in the laboratory, namely that examination of the reaction products always indicated that a variable amount of energy was missing. Pauli concluded that the products must include a third 'almost invisible' particle, one which didn't interact strongly enough for it to be detected. Enrico Fermi called this particle the 'neutrino' (for the 'little neutral one'). In 1956 Reines and Cowan discovered the neutrino interactions in their experiments at a nuclear reactor.

Today, neutrinos are known to be tiny, possibly massless, neutral elementary particles, which interact with matter via the weak nuclear force. The *weakness* of the weak force gives neutrinos the property that matter is almost transparent to them. It is fascinating that the neutrino, which was "invented" to solve a laboratory nuclear physics problem, must also be invoked to explain energy production in our sun and in all other stars. We now know that nuclear fusion and decay processes, which occur within the stellar core, produce copious amounts of neutrinos. The standard solar model predicts that these reactions produce several groups of neutrinos, with differing fluxes and energy spectra. The ranges of detection of existing solar neutrino experiments in different shades of blue, to illustrate that they sample different portions of the solar neutrino energy spectrum.

Since neutrinos rarely interact with matter, they pass through the sun and the earth (and us) virtually unhindered.

Other sources of neutrinos include exploding stars (supernovae), relic neutrinos (from the birth of the universe) and nuclear power plants. For example, the sun produces over two hundred trillion trillion trillion neutrinos every second, and a supernova blast can unleash 1000 times more neutrinos than our sun will produce in its 10-billion year lifetime. About 65-billion neutrinos from the sun stream through every square centimeter on the Earth every second, yet we are oblivious to their passage in our everyday lives.

BNL AND MEASUREMENTS OF SOLAR NEUTRINOS

Radiochemical Neutrino Detectors

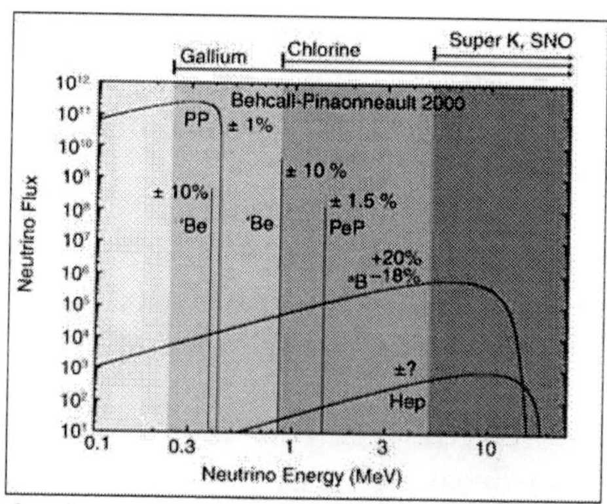

The field of solar neutrino research had its birth in the BNL Chemistry Department, where Raymond Davis and colleagues developed a radiochemical method to separate and detect the few radioactive atoms formed by capture of solar neutrinos in a huge target. This first solar neutrino experiment, in the Homestake Mine in South Dakota, used the isotope, ^{37}Cl, as the target in 680 tons of an organic liquid, perchloroethylene. Neutrino capture on the ^{37}Cl, with an energy threshold of 0.814 MeV, produces radioactive ^{37}Ar, a gas, which is removed from the target, purified, and counted. The results of this experiment revealed a 'solar neutrino problem': The number of measured solar neutrinos was only about one-third of the value predicted from solar theory. Another radiochemical neutrino detector was developed at BNL, using ^{71}Ga as the target. Neutrino capture on the ^{71}Ga produces radioactive ^{71}Ge with an renergy threshold of 0.233 MeV. This ^{71}Ge can be emoved from the liquid target in the form of gaseous $GeCl_4$, chemically purified, and converted to GeH_4 gas for counting. Two gallium detectors based on this scheme were constructed and operated. The BNL Solar Neutrino Group participated in GALLEX at the underground Gran Sasso National Laboratory in Italy, where 30 tons of gallium in the form of a 100-ton aqueous solution of gallium trichloride served as the target; SAGE at the Baksan Neutrino Observatory in Russia instead used 57 tons of liquid gallium metal.

The results from both gallium experiments confirmed the 'deficit' of solar neutrinos, by observing only »60 per cent of the expected neutrino flux. The GALLEX experiment ended in 1998. Subsequently it became the Gallium Neutrino Observatory, GNO, which uses the original GALLEX target. BNL is not a member of GNO.

From these experiments, and the Kamiokande and Super-Kamiokande neutrino detectors in Japan, the consensus has developed in the scientific community that the reason for the observed deficit of solar neutrinos is that the neutrinos 'oscillate'.

In other words, the electron-flavour neutrinos that are produced in beta-decay processes in nuclear reactions in the solar interior can be transformed into the other two known neutrino flavours, those of the muon-neutrino and the tau-neutrino. These neutrinos are not produced in the sun's nuclear reactions. In this scenario, the measured solar neutrino flux is artificially low since these other neutrino flavours are not readily observed by most neutrino detectors, and certainly not at all by the radiochemical neutrino detectors.

Note that for this process to occur requires that at least one of the neutrino types must have non-zero rest mass. Since the current Standard Electroweak Model carries the assumption of massless neutrinos, proof of the existence of neutrino mass would be a major new discovery, leading to major changes in the theory—what has been dubbed 'New Physics'.

'Real-Time' Neutrino Detectors

SNO is a new solar neutrino detector that was constructed in Canada to search for definitive evidence of this postulated new neutrino physics. BNL joined this collaboration in early 1996. The SNO neutrino detector began taking data in October 1999.

SNO was designed to detect neutrino interactions as they occur in real time with energies > 5 MeV. It is situated in a specially constructed underground clean area, at the 6800-foot level of the Creighton mine, which is operated by INCO, the International Nickel Co., near Sudbury, Ontario. The detector contains 1000 tons of ultra-pure heavy water, D_2O, in a 12-meter wide transparent acrylic plastic vessel, surrounded by 7000 tons of ultra-pure light water, H_2O, which acts as shielding. The D_2O, with a value of about $300 million, is being lent by the Canadian Government. In the H_2O, 9600 photomultiplier tubes (PMT's) surround and view the acrylic vessel, detecting the Cerenkov light produced in the D_2O by neutrino interactions and thus measuring the neutrino energy-spectra and fluxes.

Although SNO is not a radiochemical neutrino detector, chemistry still plays a crucially important role in the SNO project. For the detector to function properly, the amounts of radioactive impurities, such as those in the U-238 and Th-232 decay chains, and Rn-222 from the mine air, must be reduced to extraordinarily low levels (*e.g.*, 10^{-15} gram Th per gram D_2O). Other chemical contaminants must also be removed completely, since both the D_2O and H_2O must be optically transparent to allow the Cerenkov light to reach the PMT's.

The deuteron in the D_2O in SNO makes it unique among neutrino detectors, since it can observe all three neutrino flavours. The electron neutrino is the only flavour that can convert the D into 2 protons + a negative electron. This electron provides the signal for the so-called 'charged current' (CC) neutrino reaction. However, all three neutrino flavours are equally effective in breaking apart the D into its constituents, a proton + a neutron. This neutron provides the signal for the 'neutral current' (NC) interaction. If SNO were to measure the NC rate to be greater than the CC rate, this would be definitive proof, a 'smoking gun', for the existence of neutrino oscillations. The cause of the solar neutrino problem would be the transformation of some of the solar electron neutrinos into the other flavours. The physics community is excited by this prospect for new physics. A spin-off of such a result is that massive neutrinos could account for the 'missing mass' that is required for a closed universe.

LENS, the Low-Energy Neutrino Spectrometer

A lot of theoretical scenarios of neutrino oscillations predict strong effects at low energies, in the region of <1 MeV. To date, only the radiochemical detectors have been sensitive to solar neutrinos at such low energies. A major thrust in the solar neutrino field is the development of new real-time detectors that can operate at such low energies. One such detector, Borexino, is being built in Italy with the goal of detecting the main neutrino line from Be-7 line by observing elastic scattering in a liquid scintillator. Note that elastic scattering has contributions from both the charged-current and neutral-current neutrino interactions.

Another concept is LENS, the Low-Energy Neutrino Spectrometer, which has the ambitious goal of doing real-time spectroscopy of the lowest energy, and most intense, solar neutrinos, those from the pp continuum. LENS aims to employ an organometallic LS, with ~10% In, to detect these neutrinos, with the indium serving as the target for neutrino capture. The Q-value = 0.114 MeV in ^{115}In is well below the 0.420-MeV upper cutoff of the pp solar neutrino spectrum. The initial stage of this experiment, called MiniLENS, involves development of a 0.25-T prototype of the In-LS neutrino detector.

SNO Acrylic Vessel

This proposed experiment has the potential to achieve significant new scientific results in the area of double beta-decay. By making use of the existing infrastructure and neutrino-detector components at SNOLab, by filling the existing SNO acrylic vessel with Nd-LS, it has the possibility of overtaking several other planned double beta-decay experiments that are still being planned. SNO+ has received funding from Canadian agencies and is in the process of preparing underground activies including AV rolled-down and liquid purification capacity and production facility. It's expected to start the liquid production in 2012. Yeh is the convener for the design of Nd-LS production and is leading the R&D effort of 2nd phase double-beta experiments with other double-beta isotopes.

ORGANOMETALLIC LIQUID SCINTILLATOR

Metal-loaded liquid scintillators (M-LS) and unloaded liquid scintillators (LS) that are required for successful neutrino and antineutrino detection are being studied at BNL. The work in the development of LS, especially with metal loading, has generated great interest in the fields of particle and nuclear physics. Many interests of exploring the possibility of developing a variety of metal-loaded LS in proposed new experiments, not only for detection of sub-MeV neutrinos, super-nova neutrino and dark matter searches; but also for application of national security and reactor monitoring. There are only a very few groups in the world capable of conducting the type of R&D that applies (nuclear) chemistry to forefront physics experiments.

We have developed and refined recipes for preparing the M-LS, involving organic carboxylates (and/or RP=O organic phosphine oxides) to complex the metal, and scintillating solvents such as PC and LAB. These recipes are being translated into processes that can be applied at the multi-ton chemical scale. This research at BNL focuses on these chemical questions, including determination of the chemical species that constitute the M-LS. Key chemical and nuclear-chemical characteristics (NIM-A) are (*a*) long-term chemical stability; (*b*) high optical transparency; (*c*) high light production by the scintillator; and (*d*) ultra-low impurity content, mainly of natural radioactive contaminants, such as U, Th, and Ra, and of chemical contaminants (NIM-A) that can reduce the light output or light transmission. We also are doing R&D on the determination and reduction of the levels of background impurities, and on the chemical compatibility of the organic LS with transparent plastics, such as acrylics, that will be the material used to construct the detector vessels. Some assay methods will involve using low-level spikes of uranium, thorium, or radium.

Current works focus on the preparations with relatively high concentrations of metals loading in the organic liquid scintillator for nuclear and particle physics. The group has been developing LS-based neutrino detectors for (*a*) 200-ton, 0.1 per cent gadolinium in LS (Gd-LS) to detect antineutrinos and measure the theta-13 mixing angle at Daya Bay; (*b*) 1000-ton, 0.1 per cent neodymium in LS (Nd-LS) to measure neutrino-less double beta decay in 150Nd in the SNO+ experiment in the new SNOLAB in Sudbury (SNO+ is the successor to SNO and will use most of the physical facilities of the SNO experiment); (*c*) 125-t, 8 per cent indium in LS (In-LS) to measure the lowest energy solar neutrinos from the pp, pep, and ^{7}Be solar branches in the Low Energy Neutrino Spectroscopy (LENS) experiment either at the Kimballton Underground Research facility or at Deep Underground Science and Engineering Laboratory (DUSEL), with the prototype Mini-LENS to be built first.

Other metal-loaded LS are also developed for (1) reactor monitoring (Lithium, Gadolinium, and Boron), (2) short half-life calibration source (Yttrium) for liquid scintillation detectors; and (3) other double-beta decay candidates (Zirconium and Tellurium) at SNO+. Yeh is the Daya Bay Level 3 manager for Gd-LS production and leading all M-LS production, (In, Nd and Gd) for LENS and SNO+.

Water-based Liquid Scintillator

A pure many tens of kilotons of liquid scintillator has great sensitivity for sub-MeV neutrinos and dark matter searches and can push the current limit of proton decay lifetime (~10^{33} yrs) by an order of magnitude lower. However due to the cost, ES&H and chemical safety, this large pure LS detector is currently not favoured by funding agencies. The success of water-based liquid scintillator will provide a new generation, cost-effective and environmental benign, detection medium that could make the large PDK$^+$ detector affordable and largely reduce chemical usage and waste. This also has great potential in national security application and reactor monitoring.

The main motivations of developing the water-based liquid scintillator are (1) to optimize the ES&H and chemical safety on DOE missions by the reduction of large quantity (tens of kT) organic liquid scintillator; and (2) to create a significant cost-saving technology for future large-scale physics experiments. A large 50-kT, pure LS-equivalent detector, to reach the predicted sensitivity of proton-decay lifetime (10^{29-35} yrs), in addition to sub-MeV neutrinos, is the main physics interest of this R&D. New applicable detection medium to enhance national security and to replace the current scintillation cocktails motivates the interest. BNL developed a mass-producible recipe for W-LS that has been (1) stable for 1.5 years since synthesis; and (2) capable of producing scintillation light with fast decay time to test the SUSY favoured PDK$^+$ mode.

THE SOLAR NEUTRINO PROBLEM

So What is the Problem?

The Homestake Solar Neutrino Experiment in the Homestake Gold Mine in South Dakota has been attempting to measure neutrino fluxes from space; in particular, this experiment has been gathering information on solar neutrino fluxes. The results of this experiment have been checked against predictions made by standard solar models and it has been discovered that only one-third of the expected solar neutrino flux has been detected. This "Where are the missing neutrinos?" question is known as the Solar Neutrino Problem.

And it is not just the Homestake experiment that is detecting a shortage of neutrinos. Several other experiments, including Kamiokande II, GALLEX, and SAGE, have noticed a definite neutrino shortfall.

Just What is a Neutrino Anyway?

Neutrinos are subatomic particles produced during nuclear fission and fusion processes. Like electrons (and muons and tauons), neutrinos are classified as *leptons*. There are three "flavours" of neutrinos: electron neutrinos, muon neutrinos, and tauon neutrinos. At this time it is unknown whether neutrinos have either mass or magnetic moments but recent observations of Supernova 1987A have set an upper limit on any neutrino magnetic moments at less than about 10^(-13) Bohr magnetons. If neutrinos do have a magnetic moment, then they will either be 'left-handed' or 'right-handed' in orientation.

How Does the Sun Produce Neutrinos?

The Sun produces energy by fusing hydrogen to helium. This may be accomplished in a number of ways but in the Sun, a process known as the *proton-proton chain* is thought to be primarily responsible for energy generation.

H + H $\rightarrow$ D + positron + neutrino
H + H + electron $\rightarrow$ D + neutrino
D + H $\rightarrow$ He_3 + gamma ray
He_3 + He_3 $\rightarrow$ H + H + He4
He_3 + He_4 $\rightarrow$ Be_7 + gamma ray
Be_7 + positron $\rightarrow$ Li_7 + neutrino
Li_7 + H $\rightarrow$ He_4 + He_4
Be_7 + H $\rightarrow$ B_8 + gamma ray
B_8 $\rightarrow$ $Be_8{}^*$ + positron + neutrino
Be8* $\rightarrow$ He_4 + He_4

H is hydrogen, D is deuterium (heavy hydrogen), He is helium, Li is lithium, Be is beryllium, and B is boron. Numbers indicate different isotopes. The Homestake experiment detects only the highest energy neutrinos produced by the Sun, the neutrinos produced by the beryllium/boron reactions.

What is the Solution?

Solutions to the solar neutrino problem are usually classified in one of two categories, astrophysical or physical. Solutions that require a change in the way we think about the

Sun are termed astrophysical solutions while solutions that require a change in the way we think about neutrinos are called physical solutions.

Astrophysical Solutions

One way to solve the solar neutrino problem is to lower the central temperature of the Sun by a few percent. This will mean fewer high-energy nuclear reactions occurring in the solar core and thus, fewer neutrinos being produced and hence detected.

There are a number of ways to lower the central solar temperature. Mixing will cause fresh fuel to be brought into the core, and thus a lower temperature will be needed to maintain equilibrium. Rotation, convection, or other instabilities such as the helium 3 instability could cause mixing in the core. Other more exotic solutions rely changing the metallicity of the core (that is, changing the relative abundances of the heavy elements) and using WIMPs (Weakly Interactive Massive Particles).

Physical Solutions

A current theory in particle physics states that it is possible for neutrinos to transform from one type to another. The *Mikheyev-Smirnov-Wolfenstein (MSW) effect* claims that electron neutrinos may transform or oscillate into either muon or tauon neutrinos.

Other theories state that left-handed neutrinos may precess into right-handed neutrinos, or that neutrinos of one flavour and orientation may transform into neutrinos of another flavour and orientation. If these transformations take place in a vaccum, then they are called *vacuum oscillations*. Transformations taking place in matter are called, reasonably enough, *matter oscillations*. The neutrino experiments currently running on Earth only detect left-handed electron neutrinos. Therefore, if neutrino oscillations are taking place, then some, perhaps two-thirds, of the electron neutrinos produced by the Sun are being transformed into something that we are not detecting.

Neutrinos and Sunspots: Any Correlation?

The Homestake experiment has been running for over two solar activity cycles (1 activity cycle = 11 years approximately) and it has been noticed that *the neutrino fluxes are not constant.* Many researchers have tried to link solar surface activity with neutrino fluxes and, depending upon whether you believe their statistical arguments, have succeeded. It has been claimed that the neutrino flux is correlated to solar radius and solar wind mass flux; and anti-correlated to line-of-sight magnetic flux, p-mode frequencies, and sunspots.

Many of these parameters are (anti-) correlated with each other and are internally consistent. The solar activity cycle is usually defined by sunspot numbers but sunspots are related to magnetic activity in the Sun. Many of these other parameters are also directly affected by magnetism. If these correlations really exist, then it would seem that neutrinos are reacting with the magnetic fields in the heliosphere and magnetosphere. Thus, from this evidence, the solution to the solar neutrino problem is a physical one. Another possibility, rarely discussed, is that the solar neutrino flux is actually constant and it is the cosmic ray background that is varying. Cosmic rays are more likely to get through to the Earth during periods of low solar activity. Therefore, neutrinos generated in the Earth's atmosphere by cosmic rays will increase in number during these times. If this cosmic background flux is not correctly subtracted from the total detections, then it will appear that the solar flux is indeed varying with the solar cycle.

Solving the Mystery of the Missing Neutrinos

The three years 2001 to 2003 were the golden years of solar neutrino research. In this period, scientists solved a mystery with which they had been struggling for four decades. The solution turned out to be important for both physics and for astronomy.

The first two sections summarize the solar neutrino mystery and present the solution that was found in the past three years. The solution means for physics and for astronomy. The solar neutrino research and give my personal view of why it took more than thirty years to solve the mystery of the missing neutrinos.

The Mystery

The Crime Scene

During the first half of the twentieth century, scientists became convinced that the Sun shines by converting, deep in its interior, hydrogen into helium. According to this theory, four hydrogen nuclei called protons (p) are changed in the solar interior into a helium nucleus (^{4}He), two anti-electrons (e^+, positively charged electrons), and two elusive and mysterious particles called neutrinos. This process of nuclear conversion, or nuclear fusion, is believed to be responsible for sunshine and therefore for all life on Earth. The conversion process, which involves many different nuclear reactions, can be written schematically as:

$$4p \rightarrow^4 He + 2e^+ + 2v_e$$

Two neutrinos are produced each time the fusion reaction (1) occurs. Since four protons are heavier than a helium nucleus, two positive electrons and two neutrinos, reaction (1) releases a lot of energy to the Sun that ultimately reaches the Earth as sunlight. The reaction occurs very frequently. Neutrinos escape easily from the Sun and their energy does not appear as solar heat or sunlight. Sometimes neutrinos are produced with relatively low energies and the Sun gets a lot of heat. Sometimes neutrinos are produced with higher energies and the Sun gets less energy.

The neutrinos in equation and the focus of the mystery.

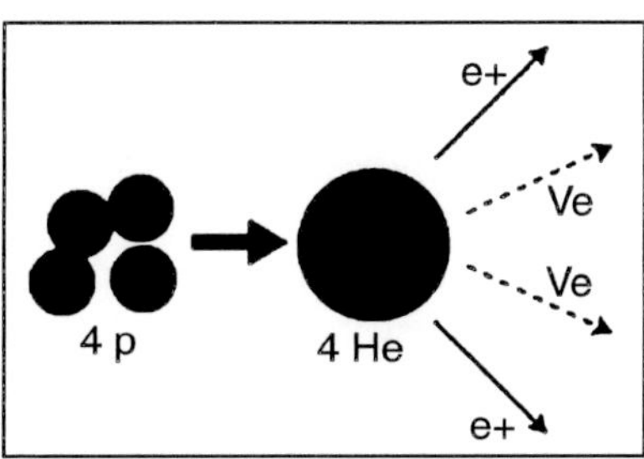

Neutrinos have zero electric charge, interact very rarely with matter, and—according to the textbook version of the standard model of particle physics—are massless. About 100 billion neutrinos from the Sun pass through your thumbnail every second, but you do not feel them because they interact so rarely and so weakly with matter.

Neutrinos are practically indestructible; almost nothing happens to them. For every hundred billion solar neutrinos that pass through the Earth, only about one interacts at all with the stuff of which the Earth is made.

Because they interact so rarely, neutrinos can escape easily from the solar interior where they are created and bring direct information about the solar fusion reactions to us on Earth. There are three known types of neutrinos. Nuclear fusion in the Sun produces only neutrinos that are associated with electrons, the so-called electron neutrinos. The two other types of neutrinos, muon neutrinos and tau neutrinos, are produced, for example, in laboratory accelerators or in exploding stars, together with heavier versions of the electron, the particles muon and tau.

Neutrinos Are Missing

The number of neutrinos of different energies that the Sun produces using a detailed computer model of the Sun and also calculated the number of radioactive argon atoms (^{37}Ar) these solar neutrinos would produce in a large tank of chlorine-based cleaning fluid (C_2Cl_4). Although the idea seemed quixotic to many experts, Ray was sure that he could extract the predicted number of a few atoms of ^{37}Ar per month out of a tank of cleaning fluid that is about the size of a large swimming pool.

The first results of Ray's experiment were announced in 1968. He detected only about one third as many radioactive argon atoms as were predicted. This discrepancy between the number of predicted neutrinos and the number Ray measured soon became known as "The Solar Neutrino Problem" or, in more popular contexts, "The Mystery of the Missing Neutrinos."

Evidence Favours New Physics

In 1989, twenty-one years after the first experimental results were published, a Japanese-American experimental collaboration reported the results of an attempt to 'solve' the solar neutrino problem.

The new experimental group called Kamiokande (led by Masatoshi Koshiba and Yoji Totsuka) used a large detector of pure water to measure the rate at which electrons in the water scattered the highest-energy neutrinos emitted from the Sun. The water detector was very sensitive, but only to high-energy neutrinos that are produced by a rare nuclear reaction (involving the decay of the nucleus ^8B) in the solar energy production cycle. The original Davis experiment with chlorine was primarily, but not exclusively, sensitive to the same high-energy neutrinos.

The Kamiokande experiment confirmed that the number of neutrino events that were observed was less than predicted by the theoretical model of the Sun and by the textbook description of neutrinos. But, the discrepancy in the water detector was somewhat less severe than observed in the chlorine detector of Ray Davis.

In the following decade, three new solar neutrino experiments deepened the mystery of the missing neutrinos. Experiments in Italy and Russia used massive detectors containing gallium to show that lower energy neutrinos were also apparently missing.

These experiments were called GALLEX (led by Till Kirsten of Heidelberg, Germany) and SAGE (led by Vladimir Gavrin of Moscow, Russia). The fact that GALLEX and SAGE were sensitive to lower energy neutrinos was very important since I believed I could calculate more accurately the number of low energy neutrinos than the number of higher energy neutrinos.

In addition, a much larger version of the Japanese water detector, called Super-Kamiokande (led by Totsuka and Yochiro Suzuki), made more precise measurements of the higher energy neutrinos and confirmed the original deficit of higher energy neutrinos found by the chlorine and Kamiokande experiments. So both high and low energy neutrinos were missing, although not in the same proportions.

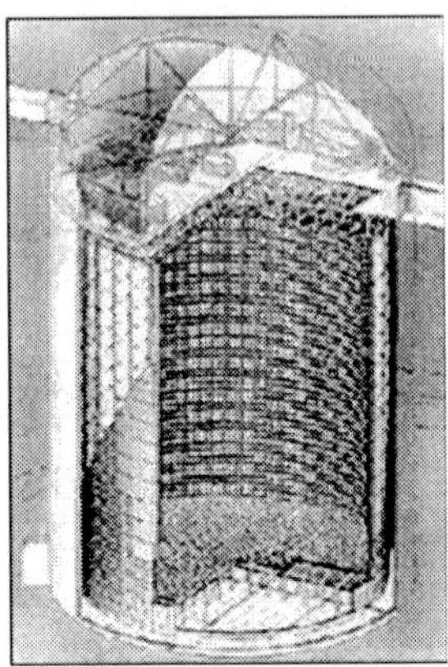

Fig. 6.1 The Super-Kamiokande Detector, University of Tokyo. The Detector Consists of an Inner Volume and an Outer Volume which Contain 32,000 and 18,000 Tons of Pure Water, Respectively. The Outer Volume Shields the Inner Volume in which Neutrino Interactions are Studied. The Inner Volume is Surrounded by 11,000 Photomultiplier Tubes that Detect Pale Blue Cherenkov Light Emitted when Electrons are Struck by Neutrinos

Evidence obtained during this decade indicated that something must happen to the neutrinos on their way to detectors on Earth from the interior of the Sun.

In 1990, Hans Bethe pointed out that new neutrino physics, beyond what was contained in the standard particle physics textbooks, was required to reconcile the results of the Davis chlorine experiment and the Japanese-American water experiment.

His conclusion was based upon an analysis of the relative sensitivity of the chlorine and the water experiments to neutrino number and neutrino energy. The newer solar neutrino experiments in Italy and in Russia increased the difficulty of explaining the neutrino data without invoking new physics.

New evidence also showed that the solar model predictions were reliable. In 1997, precise measurements were made of the sound speed throughout the solar interior using periodic fluctuations observed in ordinary light from the surface of the Sun.

The measured sound speeds agreed to a precision of 0.1 per cent with the sound speeds calculated for our theoretical model of the Sun. These measurements suggested to astronomers that the theoretical model of the Sun was so accurate that the model must also predict correctly the number of solar neutrinos. The last decade of the twentieth century provided strong evidence that a better theory of fundamental physics was required to solve the mystery of the missing neutrinos. But, we still needed to find the smoking gun.

The Solution

On June 18, 2001 at 12:15 PM (eastern daylight time) a collaboration of Canadian, American, and British scientists made a dramatic announcement: they had solved the solar neutrino mystery.

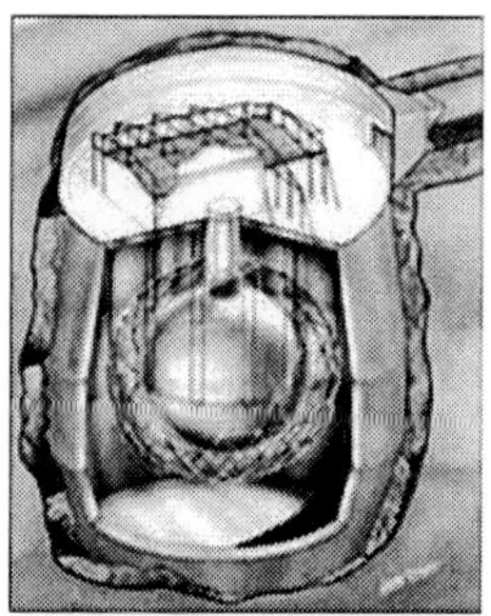

Fig. 6.2 Artist's Drawing Showing Cutaway of the Sudbury Solar Neutrino Observatory, Encased in its Housing and Submerged in a Mine. The Inner Detector Contains 1,000 Tons of Heavy Water and is Surrounded by a Stainless Steel Structure Carrying about 10,000 Photomultiplier Tubes. The Outer, Barrel-shaped Cavity (22 Meters in Diameter and 34 Meters in Height) is Filled with Purified Ordinary Water to Provide Support and to Shield Against Particles other than Neutrinos.

The international collaboration (led by Arthur McDonald of Ontario, Canada) reported the first solar neutrino results obtained with a detector of 1,000 tons of heavy water[2] (D_2O). The new detector, located in a nickel mine in Sudbury, Ontario in Canada, was able to study in a different way the same higher-energy solar neutrinos that had been investigated previously in Japan with the Kamiokande and Super-Kamiokande ordinary-water detectors. The Canadian detector is called SNO for Solar Neutrino Observatory.

The Definitive Experiments

For their first measurements, the SNO collaboration used the heavy-water detector in a mode that is sensitive only to electron neutrinos.

The SNO scientists observed approximately one-third as many electron neutrinos as the standard computer model of the Sun predicted were created in the solar interior. The Super-Kamiokande detector, which is primarily sensitive to electron neutrinos but has some sensitivity to other neutrino types, observed about half as many events as were expected.

If the standard model of particle physics was right, the fraction measured by SNO and the fraction measured by Super-Kamiokande should be the same. All the neutrinos should be electron neutrinos. The fractions were different. The standard textbook model of particle physics was wrong.

Combining the SNO and the Super-Kamiokande measurements, the SNO collaboration determined the total number of solar neutrinos of all types (electron, muon, and tau) as well as the number of just electron neutrinos. The total number of neutrinos of all types agrees with the number predicted by the computer model of the Sun. Electron neutrinos constitute about a third of the total number of neutrinos.

The smoking gun was discovered. The smoking gun is the difference between the total number of neutrinos and the number of only electron neutrinos. The missing neutrinos were actually present, but in the form of the more difficult to detect muon and tau neutrinos.

The epochal results announced in June 2001 were confirmed by subsequent experiments. The SNO collaboration made unique new measurements in which the total number of high energy neutrinos of all types was observed in the heavy water detector. These results from the SNO measurements alone show that most of the neutrinos produced in the interior of the Sun, all of which are electron neutrinos when they are produced, are changed into muon and tau neutrinos by the time they reach the Earth.

The measurement of the total number of neutrinos in the SNO detector provided the fingerprints on the smoking gun. These revolutionary results were verified independently in an extraordinary tour-de-force by a Japanese-American experimental collaboration, Kamland, which studied, instead of solar neutrinos, anti-neutrinos emitted by nuclear power reactors in Japan and in neighbouring countries.

The collaboration (led by Atsuto Suzuki of Sendai, Japan) observed a deficit in the detected number of anti-neutrinos from the nuclear power reactors. A deficit had been predicted for the Kamland experiment based upon the solar model calculations, the solar neutrino measurements, and a theoretical model of neutrino behaviour that explained why the previous calculations and measurements seemed to be in disagreement. The Kamland measurements significantly improved our knowledge of the parameters that characterize neutrinos.

Where Did the Missing Neutrinos Go?

The solution of the mystery of the missing solar neutrinos is that neutrinos are not, in fact, missing. The previously uncounted neutrinos are changed from electron neutrinos into muon and tau neutrinos that are more difficult to detect. The muon and tau neutrinos were not detected by the Davis experiment with chlorine; they were not detected by the gallium experiments in Russia and in Italy; and they were not detected by the first SNO measurement. This lack of sensitivity to muon and tau neutrinos is the reason that these experiments seemed to suggest that most of the expected solar neutrinos were missing. On the other hand, the Kamiokande and Super-Kamiokande water experiments in Japan and the later SNO heavy water experiments had some sensitivity to muon and tau neutrinos in addition to their primary sensitivity to electron neutrinos. These water experiments revealed therefore larger fractions of the predicted solar neutrinos.

SOLAR NEUTRINO SPECTRUM

Solar neutrinos are produced by nuclear reaction chains in the central core of the sun. The solar neutrino flux depends upon the core temperature of the sun, its chemical composition, the cross sections of the nuclear reactions, the opacity of the sun, and so on. The largest fraction of the solar neutrinos are produced by the so called pp-chain; a smaller fraction (1.6 %) is believed to be produced through the CNO cycle.

Chapter 7

Stellar Distances and Magnitudes

Stellar Distances

Measuring distances is one of the most important, and often most difficult, tasks in astronomy. Several methods can be used, but only a few yield the distance in a relatively simple way.

THE PARALLAX METHOD

The most reliable way to determine distances in astronomy: the method of parallax.

Measuring the Parallax Angle

The parallax angle *p* is illustrated in the following figure 7.1.

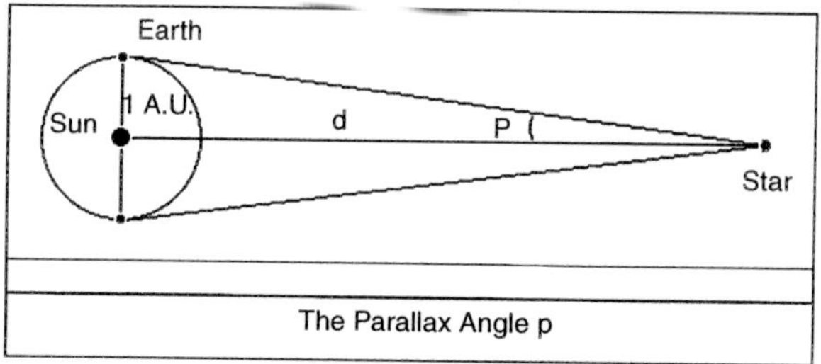

Fig. 7.1 The Parallax Angle *p*

If this angle, which corresponds to a small shift in apparent position on the celestial sphere because of the differing vantage points as the Earth moves around its orbit, can be measured accurately, the distance can then be determined from simple trigonometry.

Limitations on Parallax Measurements

Unfortunately, the parallax angle is very small because of the great distances to stars. Thus, only for the more nearby stars can it be measured reliably. Roughly speaking, ground-based telescopes can only measure parallax reliably for stars that are within a few hundred light years from us. Telescopes above the atmosphere such as the Hubble Telescope can measure smaller parallax shifts and thus larger distance, but even in that case the most distant objects for which distance can be determined by parallax of a few thousand light years away.

Units for Stellar Distances

Because the distances to stars are so large, it is useful to introduce some large units of distance measure. The most common are the light year and the parsec.

The Light Year Distance Unit

In popular discussions, large distances (such as the ones between stars) are often give in units of *light years* (which we shall abbreviate LY). A light year (which is a unit of distance, NOT time!) is the distance that light travels in a single year. Since light is very fast, the light year is a very large distance. From the knowledge that light travels at a speed of 3×10^{10} cm/s in a vacuum, we can determine the length of a light year in centimetres simply by multiplying by the number of seconds in a year (a tropical year has 3.156×10^7 seconds in it). The result is that a light year is equal to 9.46×10^{17} centimetres, or 9.46×10^{12} kilometres.

A light year is often a convenient unit in discussing distances between stars, because the average separation between stars in a galaxy is typically of that order of magnitude. For example, the nearest star to the Sun is Proxima Centauri, which is about 4.4 light years away. Here is a summary of some important distances expressed in light years:

- Light Year: the distance that light travels (through a vacuum) in one year (9.46×10^{17} cm).
- The nearest star (other than the Sun) is 4.4 light years away.
- Our galaxy (the Milky Way) is about 100,000 light years in diametre.
- The distance to the galaxy M87 in the Virgo cluster is 50 million light years.
- The distance to most distant object seen in the universe is about 18 billion light years (18×10^9 light years).

The Parsec Distance Unit

The method of parallax gives rise to a natural distance unit that astronomers call the *parsec* (which we shall abbreviate as pc). The parsec is defined to be the distance at which a star would have a parallax angle p equal to one second of arc.

From basic trigonometry we find that this distance is equal to 206,265 astronomical units (where the astronomical unit is the average separation of the Earth and the Sun) or 3.26 light years.

One also commonly uses the *kiloparsec* (kpc) and the *megaparsec* (Mpc) as a distance unit, which correspond to 1000 and 1,000,000 parsecs, respectively.

Although the light year is often found in popular level discussions, professional astronomers probably use the parsec, kiloparsec, and megaparsec more commonly as units of large distance. It is useful to remember the following average distance scales:

- The average separation between stars in a galaxy like our own is of order parsecs.
- The diametre of a galaxy like our own is typically of order 100 kpc.
- The separation between galaxies in a cluster of galaxies like our own local cluster is typically several Mpc.
- The separation between clusters of galaxies is typically of order 10 Mpc.
- The most distant galaxies observed are thousands of Mpc away from us.

Distances to Stars

Distances are mainly easy to calculate if we use the parsec as our distance unit. In that case, the distance of a star in parsecs is just

$$D = 1/p$$

where D is the distance in pc and p is the parallax angle in seconds of arc. For example, Sirius has a parallax angle of 0.38 seconds of arc and thus its distance from the Earth is $d = 1/0.38 = 2.6$ pc = 8.6 LY. The nearest star (other than the Sun) is the alpha-Centauri system, which has a parallax of 0.76 seconds of arc, corresponding to a distance of 1.315pc = 4.3 LY. Thus, all stars have parallax angles of less than one second of arc.

STELLAR MAGNITUDES

A basic observable quantity for a star is its brightness. Because stars can have a very broad range of brightness, astronomers commonly introduce a logarithmic scale called a *magnitude scale* to classify the brightness.

The Magnitude Scale

The magnitudes m_1 and m_2 for two stars are related to the corresponding brightnesses b_1 and b_2 through the equation

$$m_2 - m_1 = 2.5(\log b_1 - \log b_2) = 2.5\log\left(\frac{b_1}{b_2}\right)$$

where 'log' means the (base-10) logarithm of the corresponding number; that is, the power to which 10 must be raised to give the number. Because this relation is logarithmic, a very large range in brightnesses corresponds to a much smaller range of magnitudes; this is a major utility of the magnitude scale.

Apparent Magnitude

The preceding equation gives us a way to relate the magnitudes and brightnesses of two object, but there are several ways in which we could specify the brightness and this leads to several different magnitudes that astromers define. One important distinction is between whether we are talking about the apparent brightness of an object, or its 'true' brightness. The former is a convolution of the true brightness and the effect of distance on the observed brightness, because the intensity of light from a source decreases as the square of the distance (the inverse square law).

The apparent magnitude of various objects determined using light from the visible part of the spectrum is given in the table 7.1.

Table 7.1 Apparent Visual Magnitudes

Object	*Apparent Visual Magnitude*
Sirius (brightest star)	–1.5
Venus (at brightest)	–4.4
Full Moon	–12.6
The Sun	–26.8
Faintest naked eye stars	6-7
Faintest star visible from Earth telescopes	~25
Faintest star visible from Hubble Space Telescope	~?

The *apparent magnitude* of an object is the "what you see is what you get" magnitude. It is determined using the apparent brightness as observed, with no consideration given to how distance is influencing the observation. Obviously the apparent magnitude is easy to determine because we only need measure the apparent brightness and convert it to a magnitude with no further thought given to the matter. However, the apparent magnitude is not so useful because it mixes up the intrinsic brightness of the star (which is related to its internal energy production) and the effect of distance (which has nothing to do with the intrinsic structure of the star).

Absolute Magnitude

Clearly, a star that is very bright in our sky could be bright primarily because it is very close to us (the Sun, for example), or because it is rather distant but is intrinsically very bright (Betelgeuse, for example). It is the "true" brightness, with the distance dependence factored out, that is of most interest to us as astronomers.

Therefore, it is useful to establish a convention whereby we can compare two stars on the same footing, without variations in brightness due to differing distances complicating the issue. Astronomers define the *absolute magnitude* to be the apparent magnitude that a star would have if it were (in our imagination) placed at a distance of 10 parsecs (which is 32.6 light years) from the Earth.

There is nothing magic about the standard distance of 10 parsecs. We could as well use any other distance as a standard, but 10 parsecs is the distance astronomers have chosen for this standard. A common convention, and one that we will mostly follow, is to use a lower-case 'm' to denote an apparent magnitude and an upper-case 'M' to denote an absolute magnitude. The apparent magnitude m of a star simply by measuring how bright it appears to be, but to determine the absolute magnitude M the distance to the star must also be known. The determining distances to stars is a quite non-trivial matter in the general case.

The Influence of Wavelength

You might think that introducing the apparent and absolute magnitudes would resolve ambiguities about what we mean when we refer to the brightness of a star, but there is a further complication.

The brightness of an object (whether apparent or absolute) depends on the wavelength at which we observe it, as we saw clearly in the discussion of radiation laws.

In general, astronomical observations are made with an instrument that is sensitive to a particular range of wavelengths. For example, if we observe with the naked eye, we are sensitive only to the visible part of the spectrum, with the most sensitivity coming in the yellow-green portion of that. On the other hand, if we use normal photographic film to record our observation, it is more sensitive to blue light than to yellow-green light. Thus, to be precise in discussing brightness or the associated magnitude, we must specify which region of the electromagnetic spectrum our instrument is most sensitive to.

The Brightest Stars

Table 7.2 A List of the 20 Brightest Stars in the Sky

The 20 Brightest Stars in the Sky						
Common Name	Luminosity Solar Units	Distance LY	Spectral Type	Proper Motion arcsec / year	R. A. hours min	Declination deg min
Sirius	40	9	A1V	1.33	06 45.1	-16 43
Canopus	1500	98	F01	0.02	06 24.0	-52 42
Alpha Centauri	2	4	G2V	3.68	14 39.6	-60 50
Arcturus	100	36	K2III	2.28	14 15.7	+19 11
Vega	50	26	A0V	0.34	18 36.9	+38 47
Capella	200	46	G5III	0.44	05 16.7	+46 00
Rigel	80,000	815	B8Ia	0.00	05 12.1	-08 12
Procyon	9	11	F5IV-V	1.25	07 39.3	+05 13
Betelgeuse	100,000	500	M2Iab	0.03	05 55.2	+07 24
Achernar	500	65	B3V	0.10	01 37.7	-57 14
Beta Centauri	9300	300	B1III	0.04	14 03.8	-60 22
Altair	10	17	A7IV-V	0.66	19 50.8	+08 52
Aldeberan	200	20	K5III	0.20	04 35.9	+16 31
Spica	6000	260	B1V	0.05	13 25.2	-11 10
Antares	10,000	390	M1Ib	0.03	16 29.4	-26 26
Pollux	60	39	K0III	0.62	07 45.3	+28 02
Fomalhaut	50	23	A3V	0.37	22 57.6	-29 37
Deneb	80,000	1400	A2Ia	0.00	20 41.4	+45 17
Beta Crucis	10,000	490	B0.5IV	0.05	12 47.7	-59 41
Regulus	150	85	B7V	0.25	10 08.3	+11 58

Source: Fraknoi, Morrison, and Wolff.

COLOUR INDICES AND SURFACE TEMPERATURES

The section on Radiation Laws indicated that there is a relationship between the temperature of a blackbody and the location of the peak in the radiation distribution as a function of wavelength (Wien Law). This allows definition of some continuous quantities called *colour indices* that can be determined directly from observations and that are indirect indicators of temperature for the star.

Astronomical Colour Filters

Optical devices called *filters* may be devised that allow light to pass in a limited range of wavelengths. In astronomy, a variety of filters are used to emphasize light in a particular wavelength region, but the most common are called the U (ultraviolet), B (blue), and photovisual (V) filters. Their transmission of light as a function of wavelength, as well as the response of the average human eye.

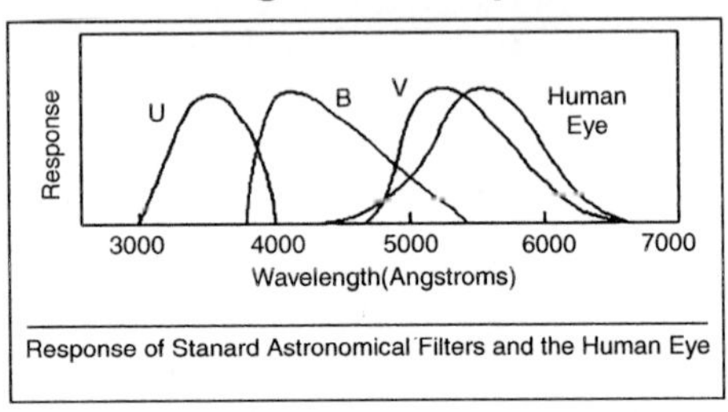

Fig. 7.2 Response of Standard Astronomical Filters and the Human Eye

The names for the filters arise because the peaks for transmission for the U, B, and V filters are in the ultraviolet, blue, and yellow-green region of the spectrum (the human eye is most sensitive to the yellow-green region of the visible-light spectrum). Thus, astronomers can measure the intensity of light from a source like a star in each of these regions of the spectrum by passing the light collected by the telescope through the appropriate filter.

Temperatures and Radiation Distributions

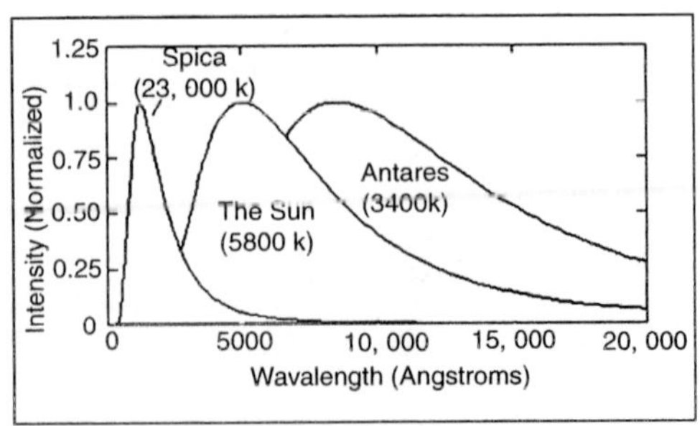

From the Planck Law radiation distributions, for several stars of differing surface temperatures, we see that generally the intensity of light from a star of given temperature will not be the same in the U, B, and V regions.

Colour Indices

A *colour index* is defined by taking the difference in magnitudes (which are related logarithmically to intensity) at two different wavelengths. Using the U, B, and V colour filters, there are three independent possible such differences. For example, the B-V colour index is defined by taking the difference between the magnitudes in the blue and visual regions of the spectrum and the U-B colour index is the analogous difference between the UV and blue regions of the spectrum.

Colour Index Examples

The star Spica has apparent magnitudes U = -0.24, B = 0.7, and V = 0.9 in the UV, blue, and photovisual regions, respectively. The corresponding colour indices are

$$B - V = 0.7 - 0.9 = -0.2$$

$$U - B = -0.24 - 0.7 = -0.94$$

Generally, the negative values of these colour indices are an indication that Spica is a hot star, with most of its radiation coming at shorter wavelengths. On the other hand, for Antares B = 2.7 and V=0.9, and the B – V colour index is

$$B - V = 2.7 - 0.9 = 1.8$$

The positive value of B – V in this case is an indication that Antares is a cool star, with most of its radiation coming at longer wavelengths.

Colour Index and Surface Temperature

The adjacent false colour IR image (Source) shows an emission nebula in the constellation Orion called the Flame Nebula (NGC 2024). The bright star in the lower right is Alnitak, which is the lower left star in the belt of Orion. It is a hot O-B blue supergiant about 15 times larger than the Sun and a little over 800 light years away, with a B-V colour index of -0.21. The negative colour index indicates that this star outputs much of its light in the UV region of the spectrum. The colour and structure of the nearby Flame Nebula is largely because of the ionization of hydrogen by the intense UV flux from Alnitak: light is emitted when electrons knocked from hydrogen by the UV radiation recombine with the hydrogen ions.

PARALLAX METHOD

The parallax method can be used for the nearest stars to about 100 parsec. The parallax method relies on the apparent movement of the stars against the background of further stars as the earth orbits the sun.

The parallax movement are very small and are measured in seconds (3600 seconds = 60 minutes = 1 degree = 1/360 of a full circle).

The apparent movement of the star relative to the background of further stars being measured in seconds of an arc leads to the unit Parsec (or per second).

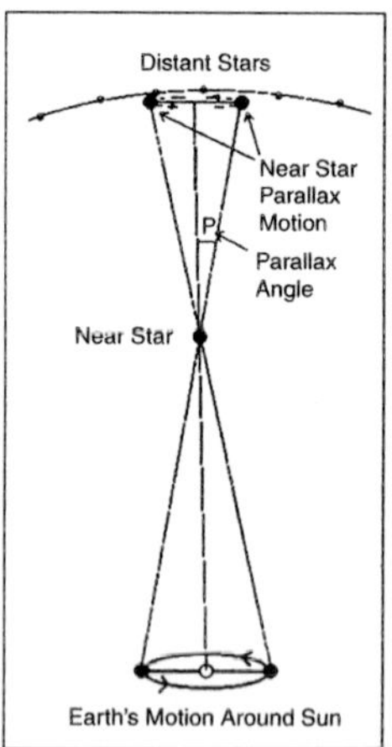

The parallax angle θ is observed and measured as the star position changes over the period of a year. From basic trigonometry and knowing the distance of Earth to the sun, we can work out the distance from the Sun using the following formula:

$$\tan\theta = \frac{Distance\ of\ Earth\ to\ Sun}{Distance\ of\ Star\ to\ Sun}$$

where θ is the parallax angle

As for small angles tanθ = sin θ = θ in radians

Therefore in the case of using parallax to measure stellar distances,

$$\theta \propto \frac{1}{d}$$

where d is distance to the Star

This would mathematical be equivalent to

$$d = \frac{k}{\theta}$$

The constant in the equation can be made equal to one by a careful adoption of an appropriate distance unit so that

$$d = \frac{1}{\theta}$$

Calculations show that this will be the case if d is measured in units equivalent to 3.08×10^{16} m and this defines the distance unit as one parsec (parallax angle of one second).

In other words:

Distance = 1 pc (parsec)

q = 1″

Distance = 2 pc

$$\theta = \frac{1''}{2}$$

Dostamce = 3 pc

$$\theta = \frac{1''}{3}$$

Therefore to measure the distance to the star, observation will be made of the star 'movement' against fixed back of further stars over the period of a year. The movement measurement in seconds of arc can them be applied to the simple formula,

$$d = \frac{1}{\theta}$$

and that produces the distance as measured in parsecs.

Due to the difficulty of measuring small parallax angles, this method is not reliable to stellar distance above 100 parsecs. Parsecs, however, continue to be used for other techniques for measuring greater distances with kpc and Mpc being used for 10^3 and 10^6 parsecs respectively.

Brightness

The apparent magnitude (m) of a star is a measure of its apparent brightness as seen by an observer on Earth. The brighter the object appears, the lower the numerical value of its magnitude. Absolute magnitude is a measure of luminosity, how much light a star radiates into space. Absolute magnitude can be defined as apparent magnitude a star would have 10 pc away from Earth. A star that looks just as bright as one close to us, but being further away has a greater absolute magnitude. The apparent magnitude represents the apparent brightness and the absolute magnitude the absolute luminosity. The absolute magnitude of a star is the apparent magnitude that it would have if it were observed from a distance of 10 parsecs.

The magnitude scale has been used by astronomers for more than 2000 years to classify stars into 6 categories of brightness as it appears to the human naked eye, with magnitude 1 being the brightest and magnitude 6 being the faintest. With the use of telescope and more sensitive instruments, stars beyond magnitude 6 can now be more accurately measured.

The magnitude scale is now defined as magnitude 1 being 100 times brighter than magnitude 6, with the scale being logarithmic. Negative values for stars brighter than magnitude 1 is also allowed. With the difference of magnitude 1 and 6 being defined a 100, this means the each unit decrease of the magnitude scales corresponds to 2.512 times brighter (as $2.512^5=100$).

For example, to compare the power received from the two stars Sirius, with apparent magnitude -1.46, and Betelgeuse, with apparent magnitude 0.5, raise 2.512 to the difference of the apparent magnitude.

Difference in apparent magnitude of the two stars = 0.5 – (-1.46) = 1.96

Therefore power received from Sirius/power received from Betelgeuse = 2.512 × 1.96

While the apparent magnitude is the brightness apparent to an observer on Earth, absolute Magnitude is defined as the apparent magnitude of a star at a fixed distance of 10 parsec. Since the apparent brightness of a star depends on the absolute brightness and distance of the star, the relationship is given by the following formula known as the distance modulus.

$$M = m - 5\log\left(\frac{d}{10}\right)$$

where M is the absolute magnitude and m is the apparent magnitude and d is distance measured in parsec

If the luminosity of a star is known, the inverse square law relating apparent brightness, luminosity and distance can be applied to estimate the distance to the star. The formula being:

$$b = \frac{L}{4\pi d^2}$$

b is apparent brightness (m) L is luminosity (W m^{-2})
d is distance (m)
r is radius of star (m)

Spectroscopic Method

The term *spectroscopic parallax* is a misnomer as it actually has nothing to do with parallax. It is, however, a way to find the distance to stars. Most stars are too far away to have their distance measured directly using trigonometric parallax but by utilising spectroscopy an approximate distance to them can be determined. Let us see how this works.

- If we take a spectrum of a star we can determine its spectral class.
- Knowing either the star's spectral class allows us to place the star on a vertical line or band along a Hertzsprung-Russell Diagram. If we also know its luminosity class we can further constrain its position along this line, that is we can distinguish between a red supergiant, giant or main sequence star for example.
- Once we know its position on the HR diagram we can infer what its absolute magnitude, *M* should be by either reading off across to the vertical scale of the HR diagram or looking it up from a reference table. A main sequence (luminosity class V) star with a colour index of 0.0 has an absolute magnitude of +0.9 for example.
- Now knowing m from measurement and inferring M we can use the distance modulus equation: $m - M = 5 \log(d/10)$ to find the distance to the star, *d*, in parsecs.

The assumption made is that the spectra from distant stars are the same as spectra from nearby stars. The spectra enables us to put the star into a spectral class. If this is the case, the H-R diagram can be used to estimate the luminosity of a star that is far away. In practice this technique is not very precise in determining the distance to an individual star. Uncertainties in the absolute magnitude of stars of specific spectral and luminosity class range from about 0.7 up to 1.25 magnitudes. These then give a factor of 1.4 to 1.8 × variation in the resultant distance. Nonetheless it is still an important methods for estimating distance to stars beyond direct trigonometric parallax measurement.

Example of Spectroscopic Parallax Calculation:

γ Crucis is an M3 III star with a measured value of m_V = 1.63 and a colour index of +1.60. This means that it is a red giant. Plotting its position on the HR we can estimate its absolute magnitude to be about -0.8. In fact if we look up a standard reference table we find the absolute magnitude for a III luminosity class star with a colour index of +1.60 is -0.60.

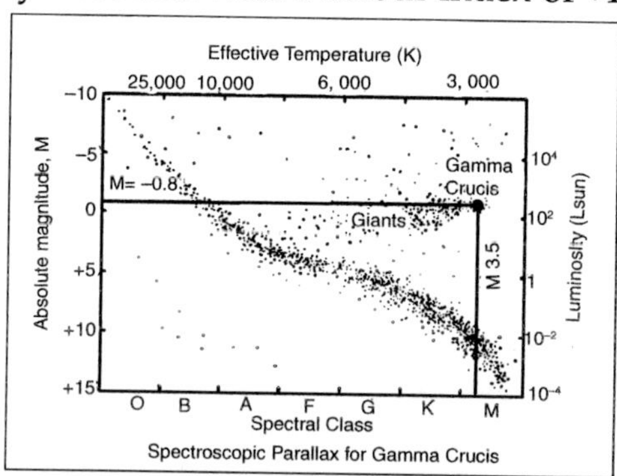

Spectroscopic Parallax for Gamma Crucis

Gamma Crucis is an M3.5 III star, a red giant. Using its spectral and luminosity classes we can place it where the red circle is on the HR diagram. Reading across to the vertical axis this corresponds to an absolute magnitude of about -0.8.

Now if we use the tabulated value of M = -0.60 with the distance modulus equation, we have:

$M = m - 5 \log(d/10)$ so;

$5 \log (d/10) = m - M$

$\log (d/10) = (m - M)/5$

$d/10 = 10^{(m - M)/5}$

$d/10 = 10^{(m - M)/5}$

$d - 10{*}10^{(m - M)/5}$

which can be written as:

$d = 10^{(m - M + 5)/5}$

now substituting in:

$d = 10^{(1.63 - (-0.60) + 5)/5}$

$d = 10^{7.23/5}$

$d = 10^{1.446}$

$d = 27.9$ parsecs

so γ Crucis is about 28 pc distant which is within 1 pc of the published Hipparcos value. If we used the graphically obtained estimate value of M H" -0.8 then:

$d = 10^{(1.63 - (-0.8) + 5)/5}$

$d = 10^{7.43/5}$

$d = 10^{1.486}$

$d = 30.6$ parsecs

so γ Crucis would have a value of about 31 pc distance, about a 15 per cent error.

Although this method is not accurate for individual stars, if carried out for many stars it can yield statistically useful values.

This method involves quite a lot of uncertainty. Matter between the star and the observer (for example, dust) can affect the light that is received. It would absorb some of the light and make the star's apparent brightness less than it should be. In addition, dust can scatter the different frequencies in different ways, making the identification of spectral class harder.

As the stellar distance increases, the uncertainty in the luminosity becomes greater and so the uncertainty in the distance calculation becomes greater. For this reason, spectroscopic parallax is limited to measuring stellar distances up to about 10 Mpc.

Cepheid Variables

Some types of pulsating variable stars such as Cepheids exhibit a definite relationship between their period and their intrinsic luminosity. Such period-luminosity relationships are invaluable to astronomers as they are a vital method in calculating distances within and beyond our galaxy. Cepheid variables are quite rare stars whose outer layers undergo periodic compression and contraction and this produces a periodic variation in its luminosity.

Discovery of the Period-Luminosity Relationship

During the first decade of the 1900s Henrietta Leavitt (1868– 1921), working at the Harvard College Observatory, studying photographic plates of the Large (LMC) and Small (SMC) Magellanic Clouds, compiled a list of 1,777 periodic variables. Eventually she classified 47 of these in the two clouds as Cepheid variables and noticed that those with longer periods were brighter than the shorter-period ones. She correctly inferred that as the stars were in the same distant clouds they were all at much the same relative distance from us. Any difference in apparent magnitude was therefore related to a difference in absolute magnitude. When she plotted her results for the two clouds she noted that they formed distinct relationships between brightness and period.

Her plot showed what is now known as the *period-luminosity relationship*; cepheids with longer periods are intrinsically more luminous than those with shorter periods.

The Danish astronomer, Ejnar Hertzsprung (1873-1967) quickly realised the significance of this discovery. By measuring the period of a Cepheid from its light curve, the distance to that Cepheid could be determined. He used his data on nearby Cepheids to calculate the distance to the Cepheids in the SMC as 37,000 light years away.

Harlow Shapley, an American astronomer using a larger number of Cepheids, recalibrated the absolute magnitude scale for Cepheids and revised the value of the distance to the SMC to 95,000 light years. He also studied Cepheids in 86 globular clusters and found that the few dozen brightest non-variable stars in each cluster was about 10 × brighter than the average Cepheid. From this he could infer the distance to globular cluster too distant to have visible Cepheids and realised that these clusters were all essentially the same size and luminosity. By mapping the distribution and distance of globular clusters he was able to deduce the size of our galaxy, the Milky Way.

In 1924 Edwin Hubble detected Cepheids in the Andromeda nebula, M31 and the Triangulum nebula M33. Using these he determined that their distances were 900,000 and 850,000 light years respectively. He thus established conclusively that these 'spiral nebulae' were in fact other galaxies and not part of our Milky Way. This was a momentous discovery and dramatically expanded the scale of the known Universe. Hubble later went on to observe the redshift of galaxies and propose that this was due to their recession velocity, with more distant galaxies moving away at a higher speed than nearby ones. This relationship is now called

Hubble's Law and is interpreted to mean that the Universe is expanding.

Calculating Distances Using Cepheids

Both types of Cepheids and *RR Lyrae* stars all exhibit distinct period-luminosity relationships.

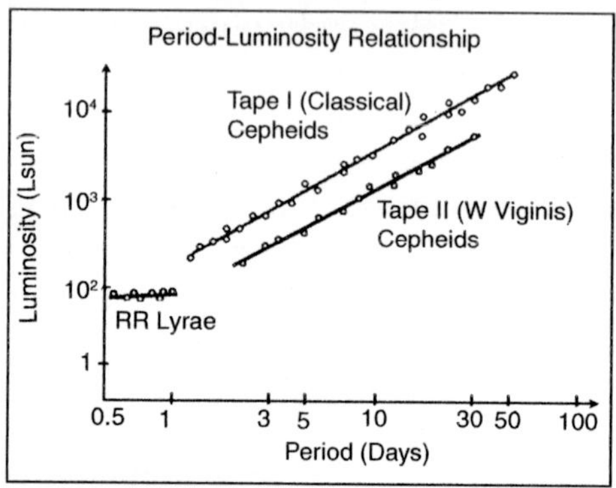

Period-luminosity relationship for Cepheids and RR Lyrae stars.

Let us now observe how this relationship can be used to determine the distance to a Cepheid. For this procedure we will assume that we are dealing with a Type I, Classical Cepheid but the same method applies for *W Virginis* and *RR Lyrae*-type stars.

- Photometric observations, be they naked-eye estimates, photographic plates, or photoelectric CCD images provide the apparent magnitude values for the Cepheid.

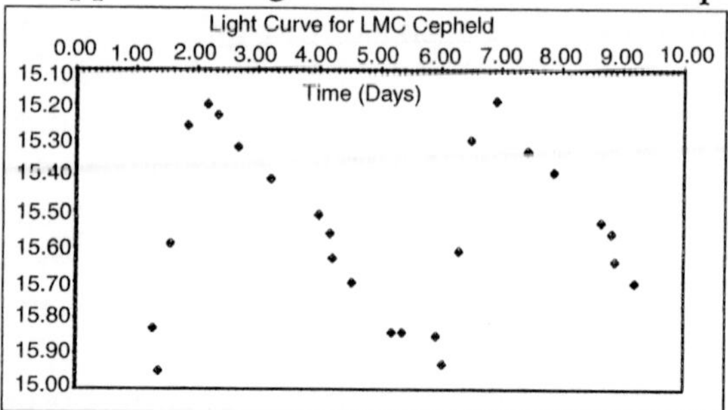

- Plotting apparent magnitude values from observations at different times results in a light curve such as that below for a Cepheid in the LMC.

- From the light curve and the photometric data, two values can be determined; the average apparent magnitude, *m*, of the star and its period in days. In the example above the Cepheid has a mean apparent magnitude of 15.56 and a period of 4.76 days.
- Knowing the period of the Cepheid we can now determine its mean absolute magnitude, *M*, by interpolating on the period-luminosity plot. The vertical axis shows absolute magnitude whilst period is displayed as a log value on the horizontal axes.

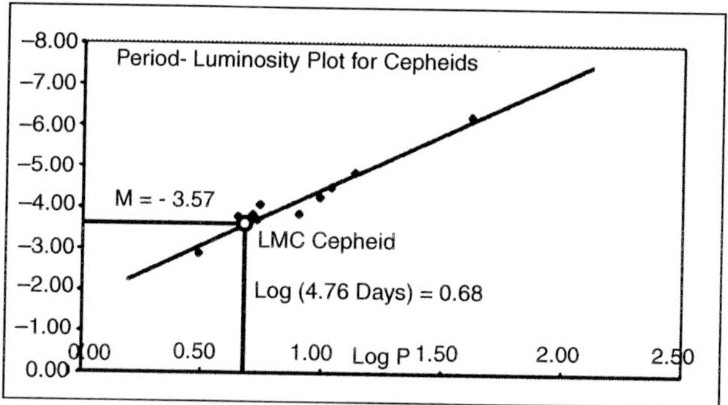

The log of 4.76 days = 0.68. When this is plotted a value of about -3.6 results for absolute magnitude.

- Once both apparent magnitude, *m*, and absolute magnitude, *M* are known we can simply substitute in to the distance-modulus formula and rework it to give a value for *d*, the distance to the Cepheid.

$m - M = 5\log(d/10)$

as you should recall, this can be rewritten as:

$d = 10^{(m - M + 5)/5}$

now substituting in:

$d = 10^{(15.57 - (-3.6) + 5)/5}$

$d = 10^{24.17/5}$

$d = 10^{4.834}$

$d = 68{,}230$ parsecs

This means that the Cepheid in the LMC is about 68.2 kpc (or about 222,000 light years away). More importantly, if we infer that the size of the LMC relative to its distance from us is small we have also found the distance to the LMC within which the Cepheid is located.

- In practice astronomers would try and observe as many Cepheids as possible in another galaxy in order to determine a more accurate distance. As the number of stars observed go up the uncertainties involved in calculations for individual stars can be statistically reduced.

STELLAR MOTION

The sky appears to turn once every 24 hours because of the daily rotation of the Earth (the *diurnal motion*), but the stars appear to be fixed in their relative positions on the celestial sphere. This is an illusion, however, caused by the very large distances to stars. In reality, the stars are in motion with respect to each other and that causes them to slowly change their relative positions. The apparent alter of position of a star on the celestial sphere is called the *proper motion* of the star.

Angular Motion on the Celestial Sphere

Proper motion is usually denoted by the Greek symbol 'mu', and is a velocity that is usually quoted in units of seconds of arc per year. The following image illustrates proper motion.

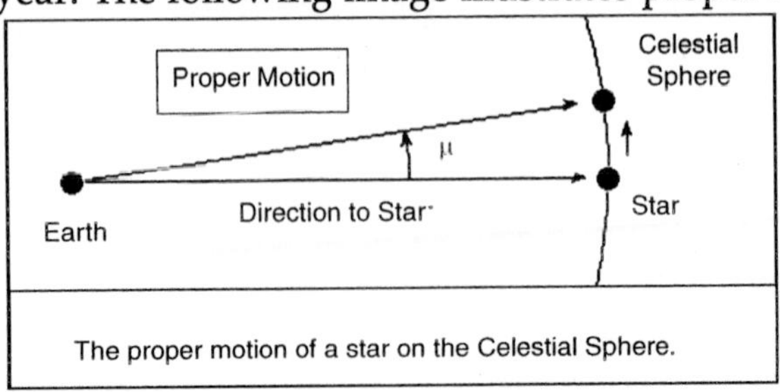

Fig. 7.3 The Proper Motion of a Star on the Celestial Sphere

Barnard's Star

Proper motion is not large. The star with the largest proper motion is called Barnard's Star. It moves 10.3 seconds of arc per year. Since the moon subtends about 1/2 of a degree (which is 1/2 × 60 × 60 = 1800 seconds of arc) on the celestial sphere, it takes Barnard's star about 1800/10.3 ~ 180 years to change its position by the angular diameter of the moon. All other stars have smaller proper motions.

Proper Motion and Parallax

Were it not for the motion of the Earth around the Sun, proper motion would lead to a simple drift of the position of a star on the celestial sphere in a particular direction. However, because of the motion of the Earth on its orbit, there is a parallax effect for stars that are near enough to exhibit significant proper motion that causes the star to execute motion in a small ellipse on the celestial sphere over a period of a year (this ellipse is just a mirror of the actual motion of the Earth on its elliptical orbit). The superposition of these two motions (a straight linear drift from the proper motion and elliptical motion from the parallax effect) then leads to a wavy path of the star on the celestial sphere. The following figure illustrates for Barnard's Star.

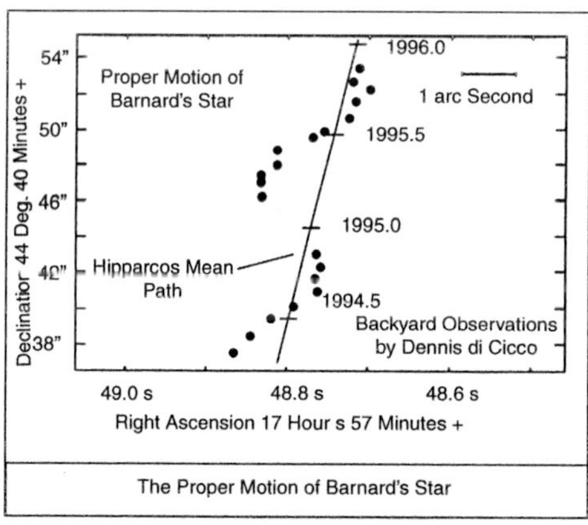

Fig. 7.4 The Proper Motion of Barnard's Star

The wavy motion is the parallax effect for an amateur telescope observation from Earth (notice the periodicity of 1 year). The straight line is the average path as determined by the Hipparcos satellite.

SPACE VELOCITIES

The actual motion of stars involves a path in three space dimensions, so the proper motion is just the projection of this true motion on the celestial sphere.

The Space Velocity and its Components

This true velocity of the star is called the *space velocity.* The space velocity, as the vector v_s.

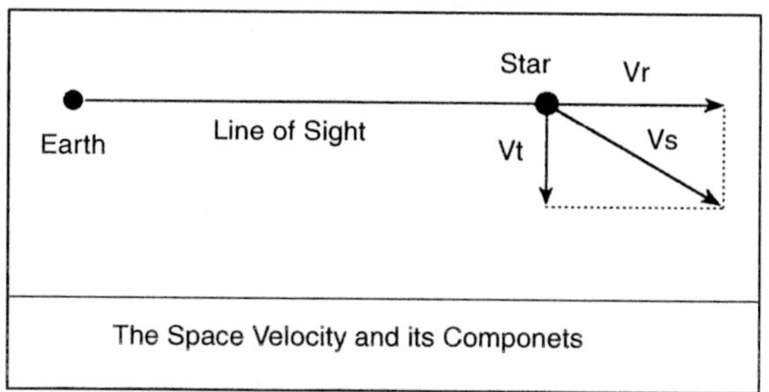

Fig. 7.5 The Space Velocity and its Components

The space velocity may be resolved into a component perpendicular to the line of sight that is called the *tangential velocity,* v_t and a component along the line of sight called the *radial velocity,* v_r.

Measuring the Components of the Space Velocity

It is the tangential velocity that is responsible for the proper motion. If the distance to the star is known, the angular velocity associated with the proper motion can be converted to a tangential velocity using simple trigonometry. On the other hand, the radial component of the velocity is responsible for a Doppler shift of the spectral lines that can be used to determine it directly, even if the distance is unknown.

Typical Space Velocities

The full space velocity of a star follows from Pythagoras' Theorem if both the tangential and radial velocities are known. Notice that this generally requires that we know the distance to the star. Typical values for the space velocities of stars are 20-100 km/s.

Calculations of Star Velocities

A Star Velocity Calculator that allows you to make simple calculations for space velocities in terms of radial velocities, proper motion, and distance to the star.

Gleise 710 is Coming to See You

Presently there is a faint red dwarf star 63 light years away in the constellation Ophiucus that is called Gleise 710. Recently it has been realised that this star is moving towards the Sun at relatively high velocity and will pass within a light year in about a million years. It is now too faint to be seen except with a telescope, but in a million years it will be one of the brighter stars in Earth's sky, with apparent visual magnitude 0.6. Although not a direct threat to the Solar System at that passing distance, it is likely that its gravitational influence will disturb the Oort Cloud of comets and send many more comets than usual into the inner Solar System.

MOTION OF THE SUN

The Sun is in motion, just like any other star.

Motion of the Sun Relative to Local Stars

First, the Sun and the other stars in its vicinity partake of the general rotation of the galaxy (the Milky Way Galaxy rotates once about every 225 million years). This corresponds to an average velocity of about 220 km/s. The space velocities that we measure for other stars then correspond to deviations from this average motion for the stars around the Sun. This happens because the Sun and the stars near it are on somewhat different orbits around the centre of the galaxy, so at any one time the Sun is overtaking some stars and being passed by others.

The Solar Apex and Antapex

This motion of the Sun with respect to the local field of stars is in the direction of an imaginary point in the constellation Hercules, near the bright star Vega. This point is called the *solar apex,* and the Sun is moving towards it (relative to the nearby stars) at a net speed of about 19.7 km/s. The point on the opposite side of the sky from which the Sun appears to be moving away is called the {\em solar antapex}.

Thus, every second we move about 20 km closer to the star Vega. However, there is plenty of time before we get there: Vega is 26.5 light years away! As an exercise, calculate how long it will take the Sun (and therefore the Earth) to travel 26.5 LY at a speed of 20 km/s.

SECULAR AND STATISTICAL PARALLAX

The technique of parallax is the most reliable one for determining distances to stars but it can only be used for more nearby stars. The primary reason is that the parallax shift angle is very small because the stars are so far away. For stars further and further away, the angle finally becomes too small to measure reliably.

The Baseline for Parallax

This limitation on measuring the parallax angle is ultimately set by the length of the 'baseline' that we use to measure the angle. This corresponds to the distance across the Earth's orbit, and is 2 astronomical units (2 AU). We could measure parallax for more distant stars if we had a longer baseline.

The Sun is moving with respect to the local field of stars in the direction of Vega at a speed of about 20 km/s. This means that over a year, the Sun moves a distance of a little over 4 AU.

Thus, this motion of the Sun has the potential to give a longer baseline over which to measure parallax. But, this cannot be used to directly measure the distance to the stars because while the Sun is moving over this distance in a year (taking the Earth with it), all the other stars are in motion too. Thus, the position of any one star changes on the celestial sphere both because of the Sun's motion and because of the motion of the star and we can't disentangle the two without further information.

Measurement of Average Distances using Statistical Arguments

However, this method can still be used to measure the *average distance* to a set of stars, because for a set of stars their motion with respect to the Sun averages approximately to zero. Methods based upon this argument that measure the distance, not to individual stars, but the average distance to a set of stars are called statistical methods. This particular one is called *secular parallax*. Another method relying on somewhat different statistical arguments to determine the average distances to a set of stars is called *statistical parallax*. Although we shall not discuss these statistical methods in detail, they have played an important role in estimating distances to stars that were too large for the standard parallax method.

ATMOSPHERIC EXTINCTION

Atmospheric extinction is the reduction in brightness of stellar objects as their photons pass through our atmosphere. The effects of extinction depend on transparency, elevation of the observer, and the zenith angle, the angle from the zenith to one's line of sight. Therefore, looking vertically, the zenith angle is 0^0, and is 90^0 at the horizon.

It's obvious that as the zenith angle increases, light from stellar objects must pass through more atmosphere, decreasing brightness. Therefore, a star viewed near the zenith appears much brighter than when it nears the horizon. We'll examine a formula, that can quantify this effect.

If we assume that one's air mass at the zenith is unity, the number of air masses X at zenith angle z is

$$X = \frac{1}{\cos z + 0.025e^{-11\cos z}}$$

Where e has the value of 2.71828…

For example, if z = 45^{0},

$$X = \frac{1}{\cos(45) + 0.025x2.71828^{-11\cos(45)}} = 1.4142$$

Therefore, at a zenith angle of 45^0, stellar light passes through about 41.4 per cent more air mass than at the zenith.

Note that the number of air masses at the horizon is 40. That is, stellar light passes through 39x more atmosphere than at the zenith.

There are three factors that can be quantitatively considered to assess the effect of extinction. Molecular absorption, mainly due to atmospheric ozone and water, is a minor one, about 0.02 magnitudes per air mass. More importantly, Rayleigh scattering by air molecules accounts for up to 0.14 magnitude increases per air mass. Finally, aerosol scattering (dust, water and manmade pollutants) adds about 0.12 magnitudes per air mass. The average total effect at sea level is the sum of these factors, in the order of 0.28 magnitudes per air mass at Standard Temperature and Pressure, (STP = 760 mm Hg, 0^0 C). Note that stellar objects are, therefore, 0.28 magnitudes brighter at the top of our atmosphere. At elevations of 0.5 km, 1.0 km, and 2.0 km, the extinction effects are about 0.24, 0.21, and 0.16 magnitudes per air mass, respectively. Therefore, mountain observatories have smaller extinction (and also refraction) effects. Extinction in winter is smaller than in summer due to less atmospheric water. Finally, Rayleigh scattering affects blue light more than red so as zenith angle increases there's a corresponding reddening of a stellar object.

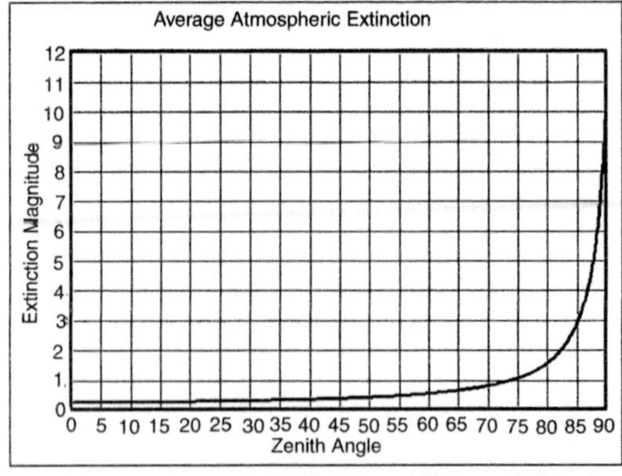

Extinction becomes significant when altitudes are lower than about 45^0. At sea level, zenith extinction is 0.28

magnitudes, and at an altitude of 45^0 it's 0.40 magnitudes, an increase of only 0.12 magnitudes. However, at an altitude of 12.5^0, extinction is 1.28 magnitudes, an increase of 1.00 magnitudes greater than the zenith's. The effect becomes much more dramatic at even lower altitudes. At the horizon, the magnitude effect is 11.2!

The Sun's magnitude at noon is about –26.7, but at the horizon, it would only be in the order of –15.8, a loss of brilliance almost 23,000x from that of noon. In addition, reddening would be very prominent.

Refraction

As planetary light passes through the atmosphere, it is refracted just as through a lens. Blue light is refracted more than red light. Like extinction, the amount of atmospheric refraction depends on the amount of air mass that light has to traverse. There are many formulas and computer programmes available to correct for refraction. Duffett-Smith has several formulas for accurate refraction predictions. A simple approximation that is useful for zenith angles up to 60^0 is

$$r \approx k \tan z$$

where

r is the increased perceived altitude due to refraction

z is the zenith angle (90^0 – altitude)

k depends on the wavelength of the light and the elevation of the observer above sea level.

Note that the actual altitude of a refracted object is (perceived altitude – r). This refraction effect is relatively minor until the zenith angle approaches 90^0.

At STP, k averages about 60.3". However, at an elevation of 2 km, k is about 48.8", a 19 per cent reduction in refraction from sea level. For 400 (blue), 500, 600 and 700 (red) nm wavelengths, the corresponding STP k values are 60.4", 57.8", 57.4", and 57.2", respectively. So as z increases, a tiny spectrum becomes visible in good telescopic seeing, with blue at the top and red at the bottom. For example, at an altitude of 30^0, the size of the spectrum would be about 5.5 arc seconds.

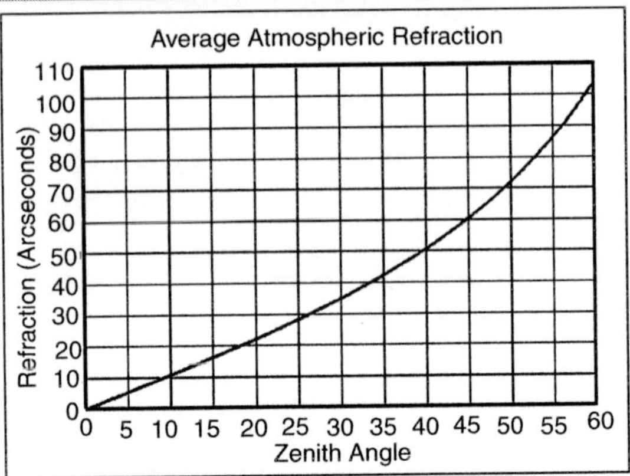

The distortion of a setting Sun or Moon. Recall that these bodies average about 30 arc minutes in size. The following image illustrates the flattening effect. It also includes the effects of atmospheric turbulence.

To make clear this oval shape, we must examine how rapidly atmospheric refraction increases as we near the horizon. At altitudes of 2^0, 1^0 and 0^0 the respective angles of refraction, r, are 18.4′, 24.75′, and 35.35′. The differential refraction of an extended body like the Sun or Moon, where the angle of refraction is greater at the bottom of the body than at its top results in its flattened shape. When the Sun appears to be at the horizon, it has actually set.

Extinction Curves of other Galaxies

The form of the standard extinction curve depends on the composition of the ISM, which varies from galaxy to galaxy. In the Local Group, the best-determined extinction curves are those of the Milky Way, the Small Magellanic Cloud (SMC) and the Large Magellanic Cloud (LMC). In the LMC, there is significant variation in the characteristics of the ultraviolet extinction with a weaker 2175 Å bump and stronger far-UV extinction in the region associated with the LMC2 supershell (near the 30 Doradus starbursting region) than seen elsewhere in the LMC and in the Milky Way.

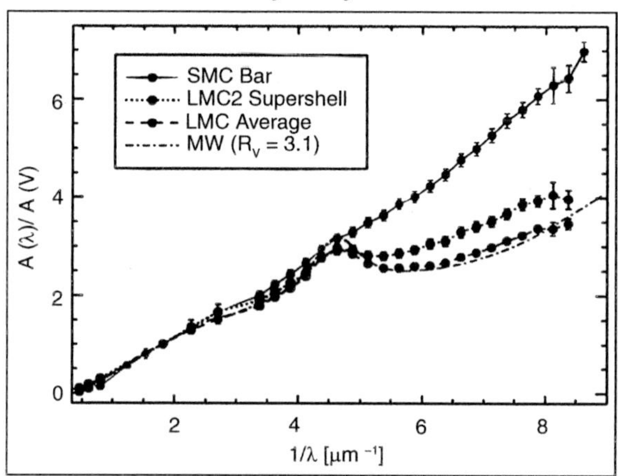

Fig. 7.6 Plot Showing the Average Extinction Curves for the MW, LMC2, LMC, and SMC Bar. The Curves are Plotted versus 1/wavelength to Emphasize the UV.

In the SMC, more extreme variation is seen with no 2175 Å and very strong far-UV extinction in the star forming Bar and fairly normal ultraviolet extinction seen in the more quiescent Wing. This gives clues as to the composition of the ISM in the various galaxies. Previously, the different average extinction curves in the Milky Way, LMC, and SMC were thought to be the result of the different metallicities of the three galaxies: the LMC's metallicity is about 40 per cent of that of the Milky Way, while the SMC's is about 10 per cent.

Finding extinction curves in both the LMC and SMC which are similar to those found in the Milky Way and finding extinction curves in the Milky Way that look more like those found in the LMC2 supershell of the LMC and in the SMC Bar has given rise to a new interpretation. The variations in the curves seen in the Magellanic Clouds and Milky Way may instead be caused by processing of the dust grains by nearby star formation. This interpretation is supported by work in starburst galaxies (which are undergoing intense star formation episodes) that their dust lacks the 2175 Å bump.

Atmospheric Extinction: Location and Altitude

Atmospheric extinction varies with location and altitude. Astronomical observatories generally are able to characterise the local extinction curve very accurately, to allow observations to be corrected for the effect. Nevertheless, the atmosphere is completely opaque to many wavelengths requiring the use of satellites to make observations.

Atmospheric extinction has three main components: Rayleigh scattering by air molecules, scattering by aerosols, and molecular absorption. Molecular absorption is often referred to as 'telluric absorption', as it is caused by the Earth ("telluric" is a synonym of "terrestrial"). The most important sources of telluric absorption are molecular oxygen and ozone, which absorb strongly in the near-ultraviolet, and water, which absorbs strongly in the infrared.

The amount of atmospheric extinction depends on the altitude of an object, being lowest at the zenith and at a maximum near the horizon. It is calculated by multiplying the standard atmospheric extinction curve by the mean airmass calculated over the duration of the observation.

Interstellar Reddening

In astronomy, interstellar reddening is a phenomenon associated with interstellar extinction where the spectrum of electromagnetic radiation from a radiation source changes characteristics from that which the object originally emitted. Reddening occurs due to the light scattering off dust and other matter in the interstellar medium. Interstellar reddening should not be confused with the redshift, which is the proportional frequency shifts of spectra without distortion. Reddening preferentially removes shorter wavelength photons from a radiated spectrum while leaving behind the longer wavelength photons (in the optical, light that is redder), leaving the spectroscopic lines unchanged.

In any photometric system interstellar reddening can be described by colour excess, defined as the difference between an objects observed colour index and its intrinsic colour index (sometimes referred to as its normal colour index). An objects intrinsic colour index is the theoretical colour index which it would have if unaffected by extinction. In the UBV photometric system the colour excess E_{B-V} is related to the B-V colour by:

$$E_{B-V} = (B-V)_{\text{observed}} - (B-V)_{\text{intrinsic}}.$$

Chapter 8

Instrumentation and Space Technology

The payload is all the equipment a satellite needs to do its job—the tools for the task. This can include antennas, cameras, radar and electronics. Each satellite will carry its own unique set of instruments or technology relevant to the mission. The payload for a communications satellite would require large radio antennas to receive and transmit television or telephone signals to Earth. A disaster monitoring satellite might contain cameras to take photographs of the land. The 'bus' is the part of the satellite that carries the payload and all its equipment into space. It holds all the subsystems that propel the spacecraft, coordinate the instruments, provide electrical power and allow the satellite to communicate with Earth.

SPACE TECHNOLOGY

Space technology is technology that is related to entering, and retrieving objects or life forms from space.

'Every day' technologies such as weather forecasting, remote sensing, GPS systems, satellite television, and some long distance communications systems critically rely on space infrastructure. Of sciences astronomy and Earth sciences (via remote sensing) most notably benefit from space technology.

Computers and telemetry were once leading edge technologies that might have been considered 'space technology' because of their criticality to boosters and spacecraft. They existed prior to the Space Race of the Cold

War (between the USSR and the USA.) but their development was vastly accelerated to meet the needs of the two major superpowers' space programmes. While still used today in spacecraft and missiles, the more prosaic applications such as remote monitoring (via telemetry) of patients, water plants, highway conditions, etc. and the widespread use of computers far surpasses their space applications in quantity and variety of application.

Space is such an alien environment that attempting to work in it requires new techniques and knowledge. New technologies originating with or accelerated by space-related endeavours are often subsequently exploited in other economic activities. This has been widely pointed to as beneficial by space advocates and enthusiasts favouring the investment of public funds in space activities and programmes. Political opponents counter that it would be far cheaper to develop specific technologies directly if they are beneficial and scoff at this justification for public expenditures on space-related research.

MULTI-WAVE LENGTH ASTRONOMY

Approximately everything that we know about the Universe comes from studying the light that is emitted or reflected by objects in space. Apart from a few exceptions, such as the collection of moon rocks, astronomers must rely on collecting and analysing the faint light from distant objects in order to study the cosmos. This fact is even more remarkable when you consider the vastness of space. Light may travel for billions of years before reaching our telescopes. Astronomy is primarily a science where we cannot retrieve samples, study objects in a laboratory, or physically enter an environment for detailed study.

Fortunately, light carries a lot of information. By detecting and analysing the light emitted by an object in space astronomers can learn about its distance, motion, temperature, density and chemical composition. Since the light from an object takes time to reach us, it also brings us information about the evolution and history of the Universe. When we receive light from an object in space, we are actually performing a type of archaeology by studying the object's appearance as it was when the light was emitted. For example, when astronomers study a galaxy that is 200 million light-years away, they are examining that galaxy as it looked 200 million years ago. We would have to wait another 200 million years.

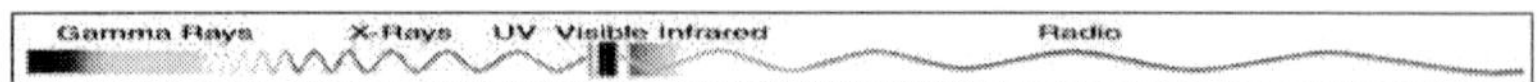

It is natural to think of light as visible light—the light we see with our eyes. However, this is only one type of light. The entire range of light, which includes the rainbow of colours we normally see, is called the electromagnetic spectrum. The electromagnetic spectrum includes gamma rays, X-rays, ultraviolet, visible, infrared, microwaves, and radio waves. The only difference between these different types of radiation is their characteristic wavelength or frequency. Wavelength increases and frequency decreases from gamma rays to radio waves. All of these forms of radiation travel at the speed of light, which is about 186,000 miles per second (or 300 million metres per second).

Each type of radiation (or light) brings us unique information. To get a complete picture of the Universe we need to see it in all of its light, using each part of the electromagnetic spectrum! Technological developments over the past seventy years have led to electronic detectors capable of seeing light that is invisible to human eyes. In addition, we can now place telescopes on satellites and on high-flying airplanes and balloons which operate above the obscuring effects of Earth's atmosphere. This combination has led to a revolution in our understanding of the Universe, and to the discovery of yet more new mysteries.

History of Microwave Astronomy

The Cosmic Microwave Background (CMB) was discovered by chance in 1965 by Penzias and Wilson. A number of ground-based observations have been carried out since, but these are limited by atmospheric disturbance and artificial illumination.

In modern cosmology, CMB measurements are one of the major pillars to test theories about the birth and evolution of the Universe—two Nobel prizes have been awarded in this field.

The first space-based measurements of the CMB were carried out with NASA's Cosmic Background Explorer (COBE) satellite. In 1992, it confirmed for the first time that the temperature of the CMB was not identical all over the sky. The measurements indicated that over angular scales larger than 10°, the CMB temperature varies by about one part in 100, 000 from the average value of 2.73K.

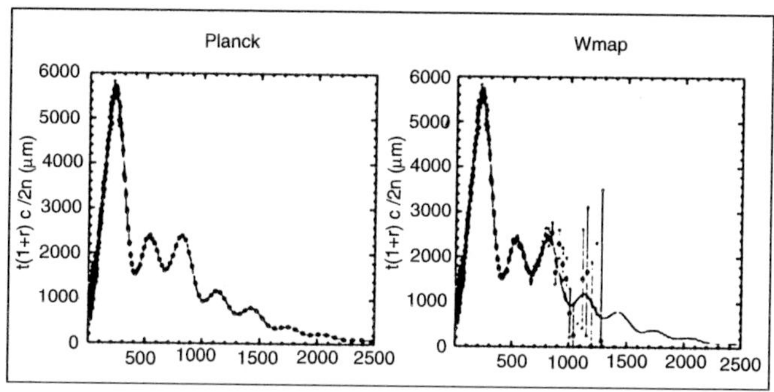

Fig. 8.1 Simulations of Observations of the CMB

Planck has enormously increased capabilities with respect to its predecessors; they will allow it to distinguish details in the structure of the CMB that have been invisible so far, and bring it into sharp focus. In turn, this implies that the conditions of the Universe close to the Big Bang can be probed more accurately than ever before.

Some of the results obtained by Planck will be definitive: no future experiments will be able to improve on them. The reason is that the radiation emitted by the structures of matter created long after the Big Bang creates a background noise that limits the ability to measure variations in the temperature of the CMB. Planck will reach this natural limit, and will extract all the information that the CMB holds.

Planck's measurements will provide the necessary foundation to zero in on more accurate theories and perhaps, surprise us with discoveries that may revolutionise the way we see our Universe.

Astronomical Sources of Microwave Radiation

The closest source of non-terrestrial microwaves is our Sun. Though the specific wavelengths of microwaves that are primarily emitted by our Sun are absorbed by our atmosphere.

Active galaxies (AGN), powered by supermassive black holes at their cores, produce microwave radiation, and are some of the strongest emitters. Additionally, these black hole engines will create massive jets and lobes that glow brightly in the microwave. These lobes can sometimes be larger than the entire galaxy. Similarly, the centre of our own Milky Way Galaxy is a source of microwave radiation. Likely this is linked to the theorized supermassive black hole at our galaxy's core. While ours is not an Active Galaxy, the centre is still quite a dynamic place.

Pulsars (rotating neutron stars) are also strong sources of microwave radiation. These powerful, compact objects are second only to black holes in terms of ultimate density. With powerful magnetic fields and fast rotation rates broad spectrum radiation is produced, with the microwave emission being particularly strong. In fact, most pulsars are usually referred to as 'Radio Pulsars' because of their strong radio emission.

The Cosmic Microwave Background Radiation (CMB)

When a microwave telescope is pointed in nearly all directions a faint microwave glow is apparent. This is known as the Cosmic Microwave Background (CMB).

Effectively the CMB is the afterglow of the big bang, the event that set our Universe in motion. The residual heat from this event was spread out over the entire Universe, but as the Universe expanded the heat density dropped proportionally. Simply, as the Universe evolves and expands the average temperature has continued to drop. Today the CMB represents a temperature of about 2.7 kelvin, which manifests itself as microwave radiation. The CMB is uniform across the entire observable Universe (with error). Discovered in 1964 by radio astronomers Arno Penzias and Robert Wilson, a discovery for which they won the Nobel Prize in 1978, it was the first hard evidence in support of the big bang theory.

Our Solar System

Optical astronomy has provided us with a wealth of information about our solar system. The close up views of the planets and their moons. Through visible light observations we have studied comets and asteroids as well as the surface of the Sun. What more can we learn about our solar system by studying the light from other parts of the spectrum? Multiwavelength studies give us information about the different layers in the atmospheres of planets and some of their moons. The same is true of the Sun—observing the Sun in different parts of the spectrum allows us to study details in different layers of the solar atmosphere. Did you know that comets emit X-rays? Why this happens is still a mystery. Infrared observations have shown us that our solar system is filled with comet dust and that the giant planets Jupiter, Saturn, and Neptune not only reflect heat from the Sun, but create their own heat as well. Ultraviolet observations have led to the discovery of auroras on both Jupiter and Saturn.

Below is what Venus, the second planet from the Sun, looks like when viewed in different parts of the electromagnetic spectrum.

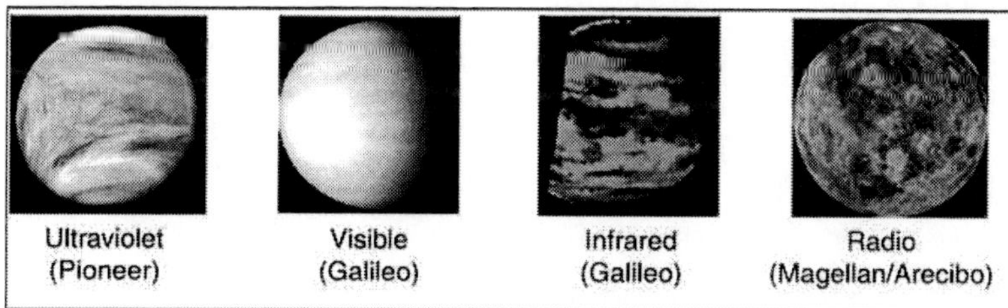

Ultraviolet (Pioneer) | Visible (Galileo) | Infrared (Galileo) | Radio (Magellan/Arecibo)

The ultraviolet view of Venus reveals a thick atmosphere due to a runaway greenhouse effect that causes surface temperatures to reach many hundreds of degrees. The visible light image also shows the thick cloud cover that perpetually enshrouds the surface. The brighter areas are where heat from the lower atmosphere shines through sulfuric acid clouds (dark areas). Longer radio waves can completely penetrate the thick cloud cover, allowing scientists to beam radar waves to map the surface features of Venus.

Let's see what the giant gas planet Saturn and its ring system look like at different wavelengths.

Ultraviolet Trauger JPL/NASA · Visible NASA/JPL/Voyager · Infrared E. Karkoschka UA/HST/NASA · Radio NRAO

Ultraviolet reveals Saturn's auroras which are over 1,000 miles above the clouds. These auroras are caused by solar wind particles interacting with the gases in Saturn's atmosphere. Particles from the Sun are guided to Saturn's polar regions by the planet's magnetic field where they cause emission from atomic and molecular hydrogen in the atmosphere. In visible light we begin to see features in Saturn's atmosphere as well as in its vast ring system. The infrared view shows us more detailed features in the atmosphere with the different colours showing different heights and compositions in the cloud layers. The radio image shows that Saturn actually emits radio waves and that its rings absorb radiation from the planet.

Our Sun is a normal star, but looks very different across the electromagnetic spectrum.

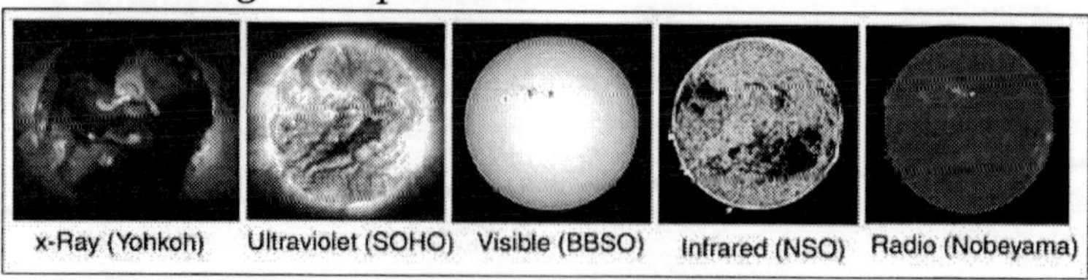

x-Ray (Yohkoh) · Ultraviolet (SOHO) · Visible (BBSO) · Infrared (NSO) · Radio (Nobeyama)

By observing the Sun in different parts of the spectrum, we can get information about the different layers in the Sun's atmosphere. X-ray images show us the structure of the hot corona—the outermost layer of the Sun. The brightest regions in the X-ray image are violent, high-temperature solar flares. The ultraviolet image shows additional regions of activity deeper in the Sun's atmosphere.

In visible light we see sunspots on the Sun's surface. The infrared photo shows large, dark regions of cooler, denser gas where the infrared light is absorbed. The radio image show us the middle layer of the Sun's atmosphere. The composite image to the left shows an ultraviolet view of the Sun (centre) along with a visible light view of the Sun's corona. Combined images like this can show how features and events near the surface of the Sun are connected with the Sun's outer atmosphere.

Radio Astronomy

Optical Astronomy

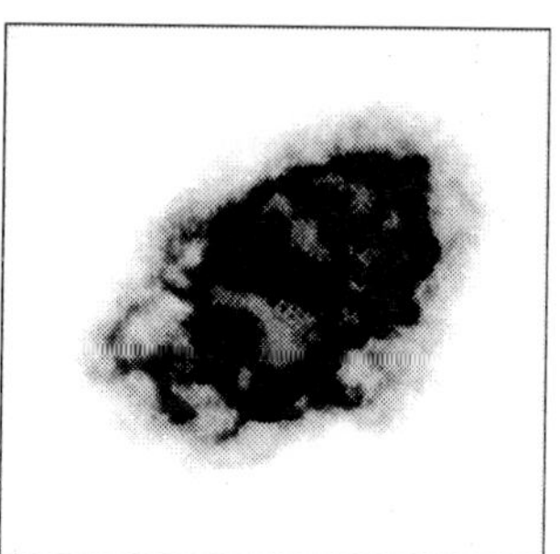

The Crab Nebula in the visible spectrum have two distinct features: a reddish web of filaments at the outer edges of the nebula and a bluish core. The blue core of the nebula is from electrons within the nebula being deflected and accelerated by the magnetic field of the central neutron star. The radiation appears blue because this process emits more light in the shorter (bluer) wavelength portion of the visible spectrum than in the longer (redder) wavelength portion.

The filaments surrounding the edges of the nebula are what is left of the original outer layers of the star. The red colour comes from emission of hydrogen. Blown off the star by the supernova, the filaments are still expanding outward into space, away from the central star. Scientists can measure this expansion by comparing pictures taken several years apart and tracing the motion of these filaments. Extrapolating backward in time shows that the filaments first started expanding away from the centre around 1040-1070 A.D. This agrees well with the 1054 A.D. supernova explosion.

Ultraviolet Astronomy

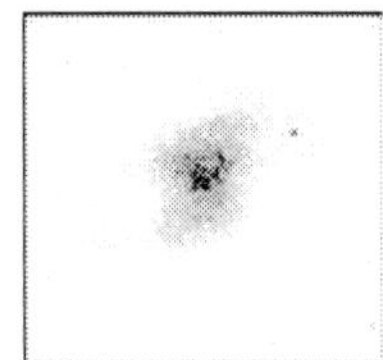

The Crab Nebula in the ultraviolet (or UV) is a nebula that is slightly larger than what is seen in X-rays (photograph from the Ultraviolet Imaging Telescope). This reveals that cooler electrons (responsible for the UV emission) extend out beyond the hot electrons near the central pulsar. This supports the theory that the central pulsar is responsible for energizing the electrons.

X-ray Astronomy

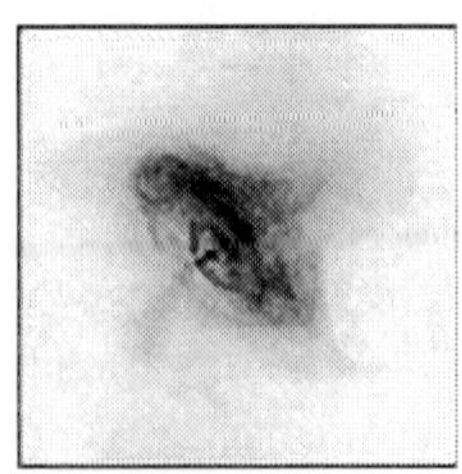

The Crab Nebula in X-rays reveals a condensed core near the central neutron star. The central star is seen to pulse in X-rays, just like it does at radio and optical wavelengths. The Crab Nebula appears smaller and more condensed in X-rays because the electrons that are primarily responsible for the

X-ray emission exist only near the central pulsar. Scientists believe the strong magnetic field near the surface of the neutron star 'heats up' the electrons in it. These 'hot' electrons are responsible for the X-ray emission.

The Multiwavelength Universe

The night sky has always served as a source of wonder and mystery to people. However, it has only been in the past few decades that we have truly begun to 'see' the Universe in all its glory. This is because we have only recently been able to look at the Universe over the entire electromagnetic spectrum. Our Universe contains objects which produce a vast range of radiation with wavelengths either too short or too long for our eyes to see.

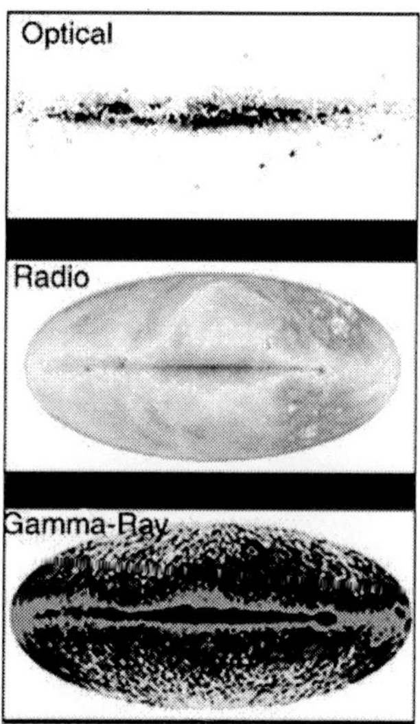

Instruments which examine all parts of the electromagnetic (EM) spectrum have been available to us only in the 20th century, since the rocket age was required to get instruments sensitive to the infrared, ultraviolet, X-rays, and gamma-ray wavelengths above the Earth.

Some astronomical objects emit mostly infrared radiation, others mostly visible light, and still others mostly ultraviolet radiation. What determines the type of electromagnetic radiation emitted by astronomical objects? A solid contains molecules and atoms that are in continuous vibration. Inside a gas are molecules that are flying about freely at high rates, continually bumping into each other and surrounding matter. That energy of motion is called HEAT. The hotter the solid or gas, the more rapid the motion of the molecules. And temperature is just a measure of the average energy of those particles. The optical representation of the cosmos seen on the left (top) is courtesy of the Lund Observatory; the radio image (at 408 MHz; centre) is courtesy of The Max Planck Institute for Radio Astronomy (generated by Glyn Haslam); the gamma-ray image (bottom) is from the EGRET experiment on-board the Compton Gamma-Ray Observatory.

What Kinds of Objects Typically Emit What Kinds of Radiation?

Do you want to understand in more detail the relationship between temperature and electromagnetic radiation (and typical sources that emit both)? Look at the chart below.

Type of Radiation	*Radiated By Objects At This Temperature*	*Typical Sources*
Gamma-rays	more than 10^8 Kelvin (K)	Accretion disks around black holes
X-rays	10^6-10^8 K	Gas in clusters of galaxies; supernova remnants; stellar corona
Ultraviolet	10^4-10^6 K	Supernova remnants; very hot stars
Visible	10^3-10^4 K	Planets, stars, some satellites
Infrared	10-10^3 K	cool clouds of dust and gas; planets
Microwave	1-10 K	Cool clouds of gas, including those around newly formed stars; the cosmic microwave background
Radio	less than 1 K	Radio emission produced by electrons moving in magnetic fields

INFRARED ASTRONOMY

Infrared Astronomy is the detection and study of the infrared radiation (heat energy) emitted from objects in the Universe. Every object that has a temperature radiates in the infrared. So, Infrared Astronomy involves the study of just about everything in the Universe. In the field of astronomy, the infrared region lies within the range of sensitivity of infrared detectors, which is between wavelengths of about 1 and 300 microns (a micron is one millionth of a meter). The human eye detects only 1 per cent of light at 0.69 microns, and 0.01 per cent at 0.75 microns, and so effectively cannot see wavelengths longer than about 0.75 microns unless the light source is extremely bright. The Universe sends us a tremendous amount of information in the form of electromagnetic radiation (or light). Much of this information is in the infrared, which we cannot see with our eyes or with visible light telescopes. Only a small amount of this infrared information reaches the Earth's surface, yet by studying this small range of infrared wavelengths, astronomers have uncovered a wealth of new information. Only since the early 1980's have we been able to send infrared telescopes into orbit around the Earth, above the atmosphere which hides most of the Universe's light from us.

The new discoveries made by these infrared satellite missions has been astounding. The first of these satellites—IRAS (Infrared Astronomical Satellite)—detected about 350,000 infrared sources, increasing the number of catalogued astronomical sources by about 70 per cent.

Exploring the Hidden Universe

In space, there are many regions which are hidden from optical telescopes because they are embedded in dense regions of gas and dust. However, infrared radiation, having wavelengths which are much longer than visible light, can pass through dusty regions of space without being scattered. This means that we can study objects hidden by gas and dust in the infrared, which we cannot see in visible light, such as the centre of our galaxy and regions of newly forming stars.

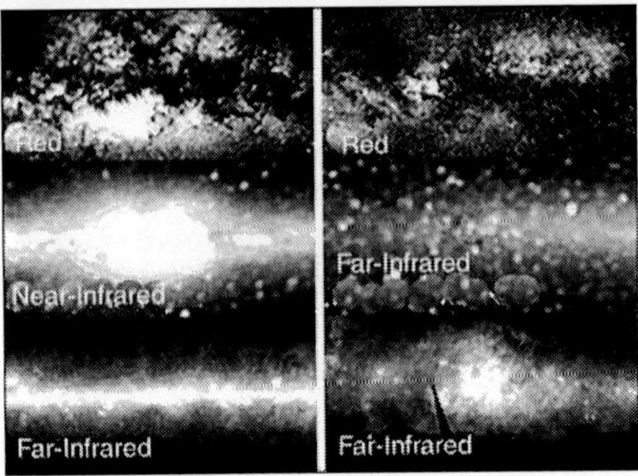

Fig. 8.2 Galactic Centre (Left) and Cygnus Region (Right)

The images to the left, of the central region of our own Milky Way Galaxy and of the Cygnus star-forming region, show how areas which cannot be seen in visible light can show up very brightly in the infrared. The top row shows these regions in visible red light. At this wavelength we are seeing the light from billions of stars, particularly the largest, brightest ones. Note the dark bands where vast clouds of dust block our view of more distant objects. The middle row shows the same regions in the near-infrared (infrared wavelengths closest to visible light). Here the light we see is also generated by stars, but now it better traces the smaller, cooler ones. Notice how the lanes of dust have become partially transparent, allowing us to see things that are hidden in visible light. Our view of the central bulge of stars in our own Milky Way galaxy is particularly striking since it is almost completely obscured at shorter wavelengths! The bottom images show these regions in the far-infrared (infrared wavelengths farther from visible light). At these wavelengths, stars hardly emit any light at all. Instead almost everything we see is generated by the dust clouds themselves. The dust, which is colder than the coldest arctic night on earth, is still warm enough to emit the thermal infrared radiation seen here.

Detecting Cool Objects

Many objects in the universe which are much too cool and faint to be detected in visible light, can be detected in the infrared. These include cool stars, infrared galaxies, clouds of particles around stars, nebulae, interstellar molecules, brown dwarfs and planets. For example, the visible light from a planet is hidden by the brightness of the star that it orbits. In the infrared, where planets have their peak brightness, the brightness of the star is reduced, making it possible to detect a planet in the infrared. Some of the most exciting discoveries in infrared astronomy have been the detection of disks of material and possible planets around other stars. Recently, an infrared survey of the Trapezium star cluster in the Orion Nebula revealed over 100 low mass objects which are brown dwarf candidates.

Exploring the Early Universe

In the infrared, astronomers can gather information about the universe as it was a very long time ago and study the early evolution of galaxies. As a result of the Big Bang (the tremendous explosion which marked the beginning of our

Universe), the Universe is expanding and most of the galaxies within it are moving away from each other. Astronomers have discovered that all distant galaxies are moving away from us and that the farther away they are, the faster they are moving. This recession of galaxies away from us has an interesting effect on the light emitted from these galaxies. When an object is moving away from us, the light that it emits is 'redshifted'. This means that the wavelengths get longer and thereby shifted towards the red part of the spectrum. This effect, called the Doppler effect, is similar to what happens to sound waves emitted from a moving object. For example, if you are standing next to a railroad track and a train passes you while blowing its horn, you will hear the sound change from a higher to a lower frequency as the train passes you by. As a result of this Doppler effect, at large redshifts, all of the ultraviolet and much of the visible light from distant sources is shifted into the infrared part of the spectrum by the time it reaches our telescopes. This means that the only way to study this light is in the infrared. Infrared astronomy will provide a great deal of information on how and when the universe was formed and on what the early universe was like. The image to the left is an infrared view of some of the farthest galaxies ever seen.

Adding to Our Knowledge of Visible Objects

Objects which can be seen in visible light can also be studied in the infrared. Infrared astronomy can not only allow us to discover new objects and view previously unseen areas of the universe, but it can add to what we already know about visible objects. To get a complete picture of any object in the Universe we need to study all of the radiation that it emits. Infrared Astronomy has, and will continue to, add a great deal to our knowledge about the Universe and the origins of our Solar System.

What is Infrared?

Our eyes are detectors which are designed to detect visible light waves (or visible radiation). Visible light is one of the few types of radiation that can penetrate our atmosphere and be detected on the Earth's surface. The discovery of infrared, there are forms of light. Actually we can only see a very small part of the entire range of radiation called the electromagnetic spectrum. The electromagnetic spectrum includes gamma rays, X-rays, ultraviolet, visible, infrared, microwaves, and radio waves. The only difference between these different types of radiation is their wavelength or frequency. Wavelength increases and frequency (as well as energy and temperature) decreases from gamma rays to radio waves. All of these forms of radiation travel at the speed of light (186,000 miles or 300,000,000 metres per second in a vacuum). In addition to visible light, radio, some infrared and a very small amount of ultraviolet radiation also reaches the Earth's surface from space. Fortunately for us, our atmosphere blocks out the rest, much of which is very hazardous, if not deadly, for life on Earth.

Infrared radiation lies between the visible and microwave portions of the electromagnetic spectrum. Infrared waves have wavelengths longer than visible and shorter than microwaves, and have frequencies which are lower than visible and higher than microwaves. Infrared is broken into three categories: near, mid and far-infrared. Near-infrared refers to the part of the infrared spectrum that is closest to visible light and far-infrared refers to the part that is closer to the microwave region. Mid-infrared is the region between these two.

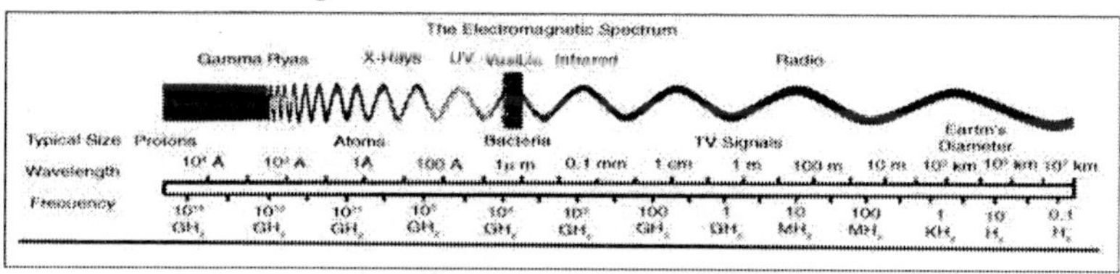

Fig. 8.3 Courtesy of Inframetrics

The primary source of infrared radiation is heat or thermal radiation. This is the radiation produced by the motion of atoms and molecules in an object. The higher the temperature, the more the atoms and molecules move and the more infrared radiation they produce. Any object which has a temperature *i.e.* anything above absolute zero (-459.67 degrees Fahrenheit or -273.15 degrees Celsius or 0 degrees Kelvin), radiates in the infrared. Absolute zero is the temperature at which all atomic and molecular motion ceases.

Even objects that we think of as being very cold, such as an ice cube, emit infrared. When an object is not quite hot enough to radiate visible light, it will emit most of its energy in the infrared. For example, hot charcoal may not give off light but it does emit infrared radiation which we feel as heat. The warmer the object, the more infrared radiation it emits. The infrared image of a landing space shuttle (left) shows the how the tiles underneath the shuttle have been heated during re-entry.

Humans, at normal body temperature, radiate most strongly in the infrared, at a wavelength of about 10 microns (A micron is the term commonly used in astronomy for a micrometer or one millionth of a meter). In the image to the left, the red areas are the warmest, followed by yellow, green and blue (coolest). The image to the right shows a cat in the infrared.

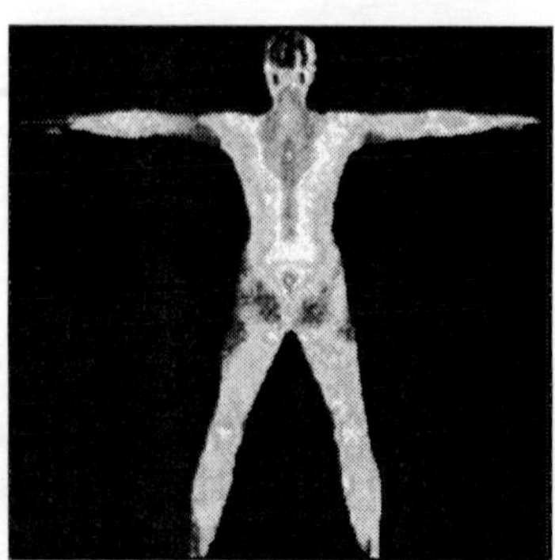

The yellow-white areas are the warmest and the purple areas are the coldest. This image gives us a different view of a familiar animal as well as information that we could not get from a visible light picture. Notice the cold nose and the heat from the cat's eyes, mouth and ears.

Some animals can 'see' in the infrared. For example, snakes in the pit viper family (*e.g.* rattlesnakes) have sensory 'pits,' which are used to detect infrared light. This allows the snake to find warm-blooded animals (even in dark burrows), by detecting the infrared heat that they radiate. Snakes with 2 sensory pits are thought to have some depth perception in the infrared. We experience infrared radiation every day. The heat that we feel from sunlight, a fire, a radiator or a warm sidewalk is infrared. Although our eyes cannot see it, the nerves in our skin can feel it as heat. The temperature-sensitive nerve endings in your skin can detect the difference between your inside body temperature and your outside skin temperature. We also commonly use infrared rays when we operate a television remote.

IR Atmospheric Windows

The Universe sends us light at all wavelengths of the electromagnetic spectrum. However, most of this light does not reach us at ground level here on Earth. Why? Because we have an atmosphere which blocks out many types of radiation while letting other types through. Fortunately for life on Earth, our atmosphere blocks out harmful, high energy radiation like X-rays, gamma rays and most of the ultraviolet rays. It also block out most infrared radiation, as well as very low energy radio waves. On the other hand, our atmosphere lets visible light, most radio waves, and small wavelength ranges of infrared light through, allowing astronomers to view the Universe at these wavelengths. Most of the infrared light coming to us from the Universe is absorbed by water vapour and carbon dioxide in the Earth's atmosphere. Only in a few narrow wavelength ranges, can infrared light make it through (at least partially) to a ground based infrared telescope.

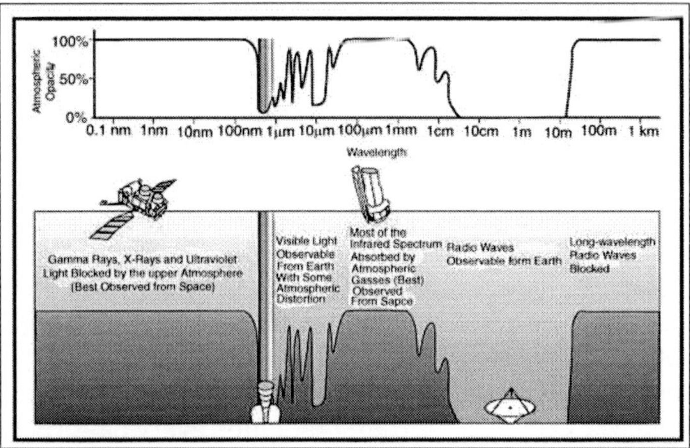

The Earth's atmosphere causes another problem for infrared astronomers. The atmosphere itself radiates strongly in the infrared, often putting out more infrared light than the object in space being observed. This atmospheric infrared emission peaks at a wavelength of about 10 microns (micron is short for a micrometer or one millionth of a metre).

So the best view of the infrared universe, from ground based telescopes, are at infrared wavelengths which can pass through the Earth's atmosphere and at which the atmosphere is dim in the infrared. Ground based infrared observatories are usually placed near the summit of high, dry mountains to get above as much of the atmosphere as possible. Even so, most infrared wavelengths are completely absorbed by the atmosphere and never make it to the ground.

A few of the infrared 'windows' have both high sky transparency and low sky emission. These infrared windows are mainly at infrared wavelengths below 4 microns.

Infrared Windows in the Atmosphere

Wavelength Range	*Band*	*Sky Transparency*	*Sky Brightness*
1.1 – 1.4 microns	J	high	low at night
1.5 – 1.8 microns	H	high	very low
2.0 – 2.4 microns	K	high	very low
3.0 – 4.0 microns	L	3.0 – 3.5 microns: fair	
		3.5 – 4.0 microns: high	low
4.6 – 5.0 microns	M	low	high
7.5 – 14.5 microns	N	8 – 9 microns and	others: low
		10 -12 microns: fair	very high
		other law	
17 – 40 microns	17 – 25 microns: Q		
	28 – 40 microns: Z	very low	very high
330 – 370 microns		very low	low

Basically, everything we have learned about the Universe comes from studying the light or electromagnetic radiation emitted by objects in space. To get a complete picture of the Universe, we need to see it in all of its light, at all wavelengths. This is why it is so important to send observatories into space, to get above our atmosphere which prevents so much of this valuable information from reaching us.

Since most infrared light is blocked by our atmosphere, infrared astronomers have placed instruments onboard, rockets, balloons, aircraft and space telescopes to view regions of the infrared which are not detectable from the ground. As a result, amazing discoveries about our Universe have been made and hundreds of thousands of new astronomical sources have been detected for the first time.

Modern Infrared Astronomy

Infrared radiation with wavelengths just longer than visible light, known as near-infrared, behaves in a very similar way to visible light, and can be detected using similar solid state devices. For this reason, the near infrared region of the spectrum is commonly incorporated as part of the "optical" spectrum, along with the near ultraviolet. Many optical telescopes, such as those at Keck Observatory, operate effectively in the near infrared as well as at visible wavelengths. The far-infrared extends to submillimeter wavelengths, which are observed by telescopes such as the James Clerk Maxwell Telescope at Mauna Kea Observatory.

Like all other forms of electromagnetic radiation, infrared is utilized by astronomers to study the universe. Infrared telescopes, which includes most major optical telescopes as well as a few dedicated infrared telescopes, need to be chilled with liquid nitrogen and shielded from warm objects. The reason for this is that objects with temperatures of a few hundred Kelvin emit most of their thermal energy at infrared wavelengths. If infrared detectors were not kept cooled, the radiation from the detector itself would contribute noise that would dwarf the radiation from any celestial source. This is particularly important in the mid-infrared and far-infrared regions of the spectrum.

To achieve higher angular resolution, some infrared telescopes are combined to form astronomical interferometres. The effective resolution of an interferometer is set by the distance between the telescopes, rather than the size of the individual telescopes. When used together with adaptive optics, infrared interferometres, such as two 10 meter telescopes at Keck Observatory or the four 8.2 metre telescopes that make up the Very Large Telescope Interferometre, can achieve high angular resolution.

The principal limitation on infrared sensitivity from ground-based telescopes is the Earth's atmosphere. Water vapour absorbs a significant amount of infrared radiation, and the atmosphere itself emits at infrared wavelengths. For this reason, most infrared telescopes are built in very dry places at high altitude, so that they are above most of the water vapour in the atmosphere. Suitable locations on Earth include Mauna Kea Observatory at 4205 metres above sea level, the ALMA site at 5000 m in Chile and regions of high altitude ice-desert such as Dome C in Antarctic. Even at high altitudes, the transparency of the Earth's atmosphere is limited except in infrared windows, or wavelengths where the Earth's atmosphere is transparent. The main infrared windows are listed below:

Wavelength range (micrometres)	***Astronomical bands***	***Telescopes***
0.65 to 1.0	R and I bands	All major optical telescopes
1.1 to 1.4	J band	Most major optical telescopes and most dedicated infrared telescopes
1.5 to 1.8	H band	Most major optical telescopes and most dedicated infrared telescopes
2.0 to 2.4	K band	Most major optical telescopes and most dedicated infrared telescopes
3.0 to 4.0	L band	Most dedicated infrared telescopes and some optical telescopes
4.6 to 5.0	M band	Most dedicated infrared telescopes and some optical telescopes
7.5 to 14.5	N band	Most dedicated infrared telescopes and some optical telescopes
17 to 25	Q band	Some dedicated infrared telescopes and some optical telescopes
28 to 40	Z band	Some dedicated infrared telescopes and some optical telescopes
330 to 370		Some dedicated infrared telescopes and some optical telescopes
450	Submillimeter	Submillimeter telescopes

As is the case for visible light telescopes, space is the ideal place for infrared telescopes. In space, images from infrared telescopes can achieve higher resolution, as they do not suffer from blurring caused by the Earth's atmosphere, and are also free from absorption caused by the Earth's atmosphere. Current infrared telescopes in space include the Herschel Space Observatory, the Spitzer Space Telescope, and the Wide-field Infrared Survey Explorer. Since putting telescopes in orbit is expensive, there are also airborne observatories, such as the Stratospheric Observatory for Infrared Astronomy and the Kuiper Airborne Observatory. These observatories place telescopes above most, but not all, of the atmosphere, which means there is absorption of infrared light from space by water vapour in the atmosphere.

Infrared Technology

One of the most ordinary infrared detector arrays used at research telescopes is HgCdTe arrays. These operate well between 0.6 and 5 micrometre wavelengths. For longer wavelength observations or higher sensitivity other detectors may be used, including other narrow gap semiconductor detectors, low temperature bolometer arrays or photon-counting Superconducting Tunnel Junction arrays. Special requirements for infrared astronomy include: very low dark currents to allow long integration times, associated low noise readout circuits and sometimes very high pixel counts.

Low temperature is often achieved by a coolant, which can run out. Space missions have either ended or shifted to "warm" observations when the coolant supply used up. For example, WISE ran out of coolant in October 2010, about ten months after being launched.

ULTRAVIOLET ASTRONOMY

Ultraviolet astronomy, study of the ultraviolet spectra of astronomical objects. Ultraviolet radiation comes from a hotter region of the electromagnetic spectrum than visible light. For example, interstellar gas at temperatures close to 1,000,000 kelvins is quite prominent in the ultraviolet. It has yielded much important information about chemical abundances and processes in the Sun and certain other stellar objects, such as white dwarfs.

Fig. 8.4 Spiral Galaxy M81 (Bottom) and Irregular Galaxy M82 (Top), as Seen in Ultraviolet Light by the Galaxy Evolution Explorer (GALEX) Satellite

Ultraviolet astronomy became feasible with the advent of rockets capable of carrying instruments above Earth's atmosphere, which absorbs most electromagnetic radiation of ultraviolet wavelengths (*i.e.*, roughly 100 to 4,000 angstroms) from celestial sources. Much radiation is lost even at the highest altitudes that balloons can reach. During the 1920s, unsuccessful attempts were made to photograph the Sun's ultraviolet spectrum from balloons; not until 1946 did a rocket-borne camera succeed in doing so.

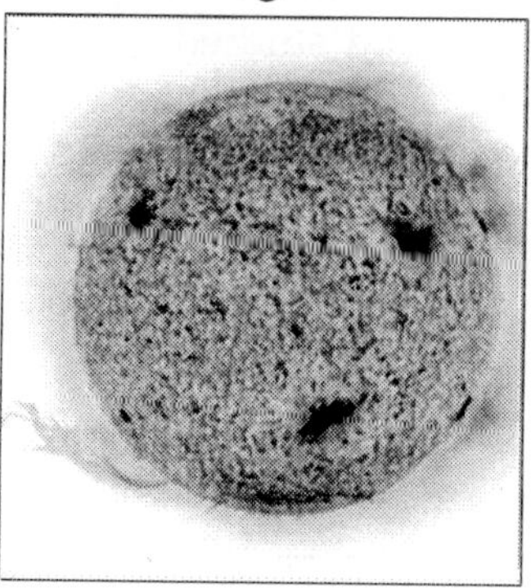

Fig. 8.5 The Sun as Imaged in Extreme Ultraviolet Light by the Earth-orbiting Solar and Heliospheric Observatory (SOHO) Satellite. A Massive Loop-shaped Eruptive Prominence is Visible at the Lower Left. Nearly White Areas are the Hottest; Deeper Reds Indicate Cooler Temperatures

Since the early 1960s the United States and several other countries have placed in Earth orbit unmanned satellite observatories carrying telescopes with optical surfaces specially coated for high ultraviolet reflectivity.

These include eight Orbiting Solar Observatories, launched from 1962 to 1975 by the U.S. National Aeronautics and Space Administration (NASA), which enabled astronomers to obtain thousands of ultraviolet spectra of the Sun's corona. Another series of U.S. satellites, known as Orbiting Astronomical Observatories, in service from 1968 to 1981, permitted the study of the interstellar medium and remote stars in the spectral range of 1,200 to 4,000 angstroms.

A telescope carried aboard the International Ultraviolet Explorer spacecraft (launched in 1978 by the European Space Agency [ESA], NASA, and the United Kingdom) allowed significant ultraviolet observations to be made of objects such as comets and quasars.

The high-resolution Hubble Space Telescope, deployed in 1990, also collected ultraviolet-wavelength data about faint objects such as nebulae and distant star clusters.

NASA's Extreme Ultraviolet Explorer (EUVE) satellite was launched in 1992 and studied stellar evolution and the interstellar medium.

EUVE was succeeded in 1999 by NASA's Far Ultraviolet Spectroscopic Explorer (FUSE), which discovered molecular nitrogen in interstellar space.

Another NASA ultraviolet satellite, the Galaxy Evolution Explorer (GALEX), was launched in 2003 and studied how galaxies change over billions of years. The Solar and Heliospheric Observatory (SOHO), an ESA-NASA satellite launched in 1995, has studied the Sun and its hot corona in ultraviolet light.

Ultraviolet Waves

Ultraviolet (UV) light has shorter wavelengths than visible light. Though these waves are invisible to the human eye, some insects, like bumblebees, can see them!

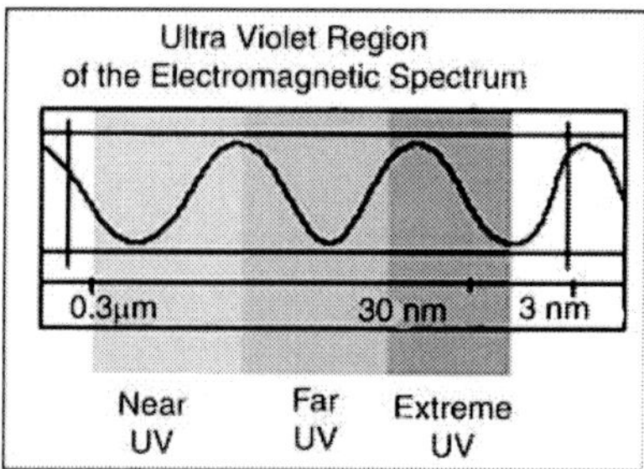

Scientists have divided the ultraviolet part of the spectrum into three regions: the near ultraviolet, the far ultraviolet, and the extreme ultraviolet. The three regions are distinguished by how energetic the ultraviolet radiation is, and by the 'wavelength' of the ultraviolet light, which is related to energy.

The near ultraviolet, abbreviated NUV, is the light closest to optical or visible light. The extreme ultraviolet, abbreviated EUV, is the ultraviolet light closest to X-rays, and is the most energetic of the three types. The far ultraviolet, abbreviated FUV, lies between the near and extreme ultraviolet regions. It is the least explored of the three regions.

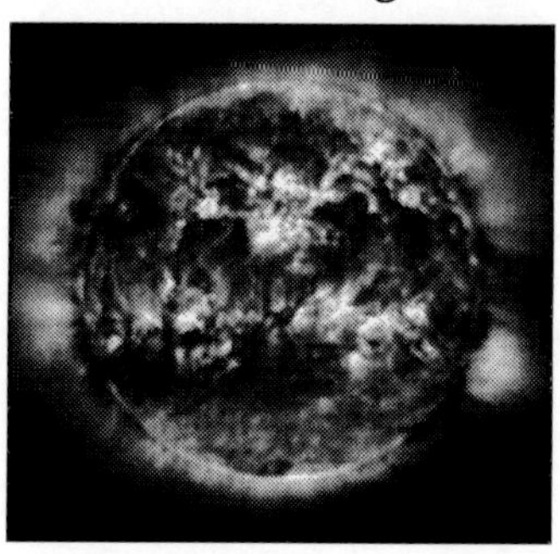

Our Sun emits light at all the different wavelengths in electromagnetic spectrum, but it is ultraviolet waves that are responsible for causing our sunburns. In the last page is an image of the Sun taken at an Extreme Ultraviolet wavelength –171 Angstroms to be exact. (An Angstrom is a unit length equal to 10^{-10} meters.) This image was taken by a satellite named SOHO and it shows what the Sun looked like on April 24, 2000. Though some ultraviolet waves from the Sun penetrate Earth's atmosphere, most of them are blocked from entering by various gases like Ozone. Some days, more ultraviolet waves get through our atmosphere. Scientists have developed a UV index to help people protect themselves from these harmful ultraviolet waves.

How do we 'see' using Ultraviolet Light?

It is good for humans that we are protected from getting too much ultraviolet radiation, but it is bad for scientists! Astronomers have to put ultraviolet telescopes on satellites to measure the ultraviolet light from stars and galaxies—and even closer things like the Sun!

There are many different satellites that help us study ultraviolet astronomy. Many of them only detect a small portion of UV light. For example, the Hubble Space Telescope observes stars and galaxies mostly in near ultraviolet light. NASA's Extreme Ultraviolet Explorer satellite is currently exploring the extreme ultraviolet universe. The International Ultraviolet Explorer (IUE) satellite has observed in the far and near ultraviolet regions for over 17 years.

What does Ultraviolet light show us?

We can study stars and galaxies by studying the UV light they give off - but did you know we can even study the Earth? This false-colour picture shows how the Earth glows in ultraviolet (UV) light.

The Far UV Camera/Spectrograph deployed and left on the Moon by the crew of Apollo 16 took this picture. The part of the Earth facing the Sun reflects much UV light. Even more interesting is the side facing away from the Sun. Here, bands of UV emission are also apparent. These bands are the result of aurora caused by charged particles given off by the Sun. They spiral towards the Earth along Earth's magnetic field lines.

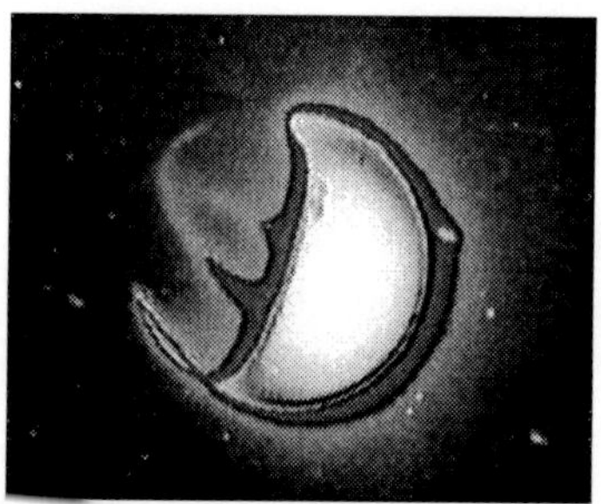

Many scientists are interested in studying the invisible universe of ultraviolet light, since the hottest and the most active objects in the cosmos give off large amounts of ultraviolet energy.

There are three different galaxies taken in visible light and ultraviolet light taken by NASA's Ultraviolet Imaging Telescope (UIT) on the Astro-2 mission.

The difference in how the galaxies appear is due to which type of stars shine brightest in the optical and ultraviolet wavelengths. The mainly clouds of gas containing newly formed stars many times more massive than the sun, which glow strongly in ultraviolet light.

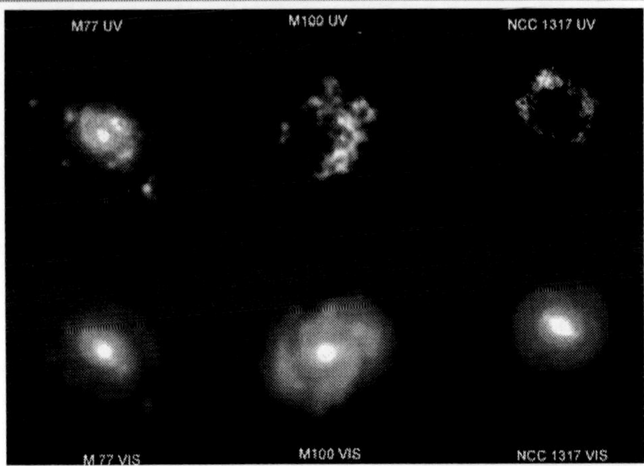

In contrast, visible light pictures of galaxies show mostly the yellow and red light of older stars. By comparing these types of data, astronomers can learn about the structure and evolution of galaxies.

EARTH'S ATMOSPHERIC EFFECTS

The atmosphere is a thin layer of gas which surrounds the Earth.

This picture shows the two most important layers known as the troposphere and the stratosphere. The air gets thinner and thinner the higher you go, 90 per cent of all the molecules in the atmosphere are in the troposphere.

Air is a mixture of various gases, information on the uses of some of these gases can be found here.

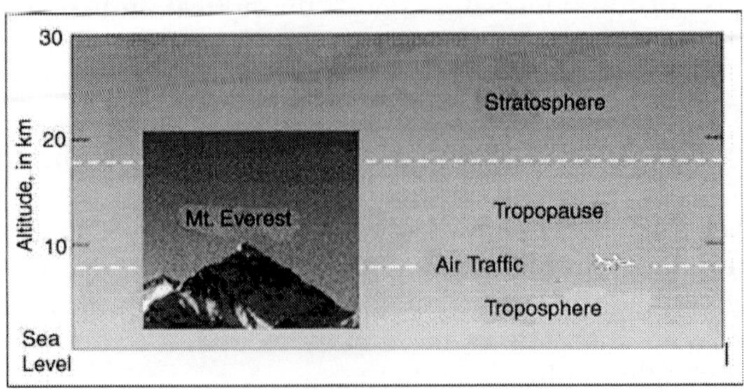

The present composition of the atmosphere is:

21.00%	OXYGEN (O_2)
78.00%	NITROGEN (N_2)
0.04%	CARBON DIOXIDE (CO_2)
~0.09%	ARGON (Ar)

Besides water vapour, several other gases are also present in much smaller amounts:

- Carbon monoxide (formula CO)
- Neon (Ne)
- Oxides of nitrogen
- Methane (CH_4)
- Krypton (Kr).

Concentrations of these gases are measured in parts per million (ppm).

The atmosphere has changed a lot compared to the Earth's early atmosphere, but for the last billion years it has remained pretty constant. We now need to look at 3 very different atmospheric problems:

The Greenhouse Effect

The earth is surrounded by a blanket of gases. This blanket traps energy in the atmosphere, much the same way as glass traps heat inside a greenhouse. This results in an build up of energy, and the overall warming of the atmosphere. The greenhouse effect is a natural process which made life on Earth possible. Without naturally occurring greenhouse gases such as water vapour, carbon dioxide, methane and nitrous oxide, the Earth's surface temperature would be 33°C cooler, a chilly -18°C rather than the tolerable 15°C.

When we talk about the greenhouse effect we mean the ENHANCED effect which is caused by the increase of greenhouse gases from human sources. Since the beginning of industrialization, 200 years ago, concentrations of these gases have increased. It is estimated that the Earth's average temperature has risen by 0.6°C since 1880 because of emissions of greenhouse gases from human activity.

The main sources of these emissions, particularly carbon dioxide, methane and nitrous oxide, are:

- the combustion of large amounts of fossil fuels (producing CO_2)
- deforestation (less trees mean that less CO_2 is being mopped up).

A increase in global temperatures may seem great, you might even think of 'Costa del Blackpool'. Unfortunately global warming will probably result in big swings in weather patterns across the world. Summers will become dryer and hotter, Winters will be wetter and colder. Other things will start to happen:

- Thermal expansion of the water and melting of continental glaciers would cause sea levels to rise, possibly as much as two feet, by the end of next century.
- Rising temperatures could lead to changes in regional wind systems which would influence global rainfall distribution and lead to the redistribution and frequency of floods, droughts and forest fires.
- Increased sea temperatures would cause the destruction of coral reefs around the world.
- Climate change would create favourable conditions for growth in insect populations. This would likely have a bad effect on agriculture and human health and result in a spread of malaria and other tropical diseases.
- Water supplies would become disrupted and droughts would be more common.

There is a lot of controversy surrounding global warming, views range from those who believe that there is nothing to worry about to those who believe that the world is heading for a global catastrophe.

Damage to the Ozone Layer

Ozone is oxygen that contains molecules that have 3 oxygen atoms (O_3). The molecule is triatomic instead of the usual O_2 molecule which is diatomic. There is a layer of ozone high up in the atmosphere which shields the Earth from the sun's harmful UV rays, these rays can lead to an increase in skin cancer. The ozone is present in very small quantities but it is enough to absorb the UV rays preventing them reaching the surface.

Scientists began to investigate the ozone layer in the 1970's, it wasn't until the mid 1980's that alarm bells started to ring. Concentrations of ozone appeared to be dropping in certain areas of the world (the layer was starting to thin-out). The cause of this reduction was thought to be man-made. The Ozone depletion over the Southern Hemisphere 1980-1991:

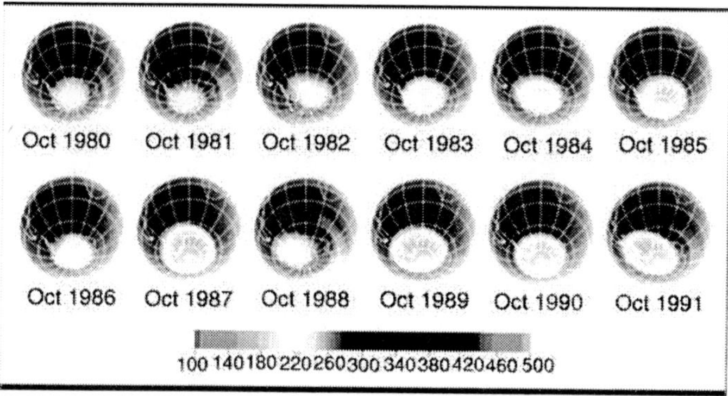

In 1985 over 60 countries pledged to phased out a group of chemicals called CFC's. These very stable chemicals were once widely used in aerosols and refrigerators. It was thought that their release into the atmosphere produced chlorine radicals which reacted with O_3 to produce O_2. The emission of CFC's into the environment is now greatly reduced, unfortunately the damage has already been done and the CFC molecules, thanks to their stability, are still causing ozone depletion.

Acid Rain Water

Rain water is naturally acidic due to carbon dioxide which partially reacts with water to give carbonic acid ($H_2O + CO_2 \rightarrow H_2CO_3$). When we talk about acid rain we mean the ENHANCED effect which is caused by other gases released when fossil fuels are burnt. Two gases are the main culprits:

- Sulphur dioxide—Fossil fuels often contain a lot of sulphur impurities which burn to give sulphur dioxide. The SO_2 reacts with water in the atmosphere to from a weak solution of sulphuric acid.

- Nitrogen oxides—Under normal conditions nitrogen and oxygen don't react together. At very high temperatures (in an engine) a small proportion of oxygen reacts with nitrogen to give nitrogen oxides. These oxides react with water in the atmosphere to from a weak solution of nitric acid.

The dilute acid falls to ground as acid rain which causes the following problems:

- Lakes become acidic and plants and fishes die as a result
- Tree growth is damaged, whole forests can die as a result
- Acid rain attacks metal structures and also buildings made of limestone.

Structure of the Atmosphere

Principal Layers

In universal, air pressure and density decrease in the atmosphere as height increases. However, temperature has a more complicated profile with altitude. Because the general pattern of this profile is constant and recognizable through means such as balloon soundings, temperature provides a useful metric to distinguish between atmospheric layers. In this way, Earth's atmosphere can be divided into five main layers. From highest to lowest, these layers are:

Exosphere

The outermost layer of Earth's atmosphere extends from the exobase upward. It is mainly composed of hydrogen and helium. The particles are so far apart that they can travel hundreds of kilometres without colliding with one another. Since the particles rarely collide, the atmosphere no longer behaves like a fluid. These free-moving particles follow ballistic trajectories and may migrate into and out of the magnetosphere or the solar wind.

Thermosphere

Temperature increases with height in the thermosphere from the mesopause up to the thermopause, then is constant with height. Unlike in the stratosphere, where the inversion is caused by absorption of radiation by ozone, in the thermosphere the inversion is a result of the extremely low density of molecules. The temperature of this layer can rise to 1,500°C (2,700 °F), though the gas molecules are so far apart that temperature in the usual sense is not well defined. The air is so rarefied that an individual molecule (of oxygen, for example) travels an average of 1 kilometre between collisions with other molecules. The International Space Station orbits in this layer, between 320 and 380 km (200 and 240 mi). Because of the relative infrequency of molecular collisions, air above the mesopause is poorly mixed compared to air. While the composition from the troposphere to the mesosphere is fairly constant, above a certain point, air is poorly mixed and becomes compositionally stratified. The point dividing these two regions is known as the turbopause. The homosphere, and the region above is the heterosphere. The top of the thermosphere is the bottom of the exosphere, called the exobase. Its height varies with solar activity and ranges from about 350–800 km (220–500 mi; 1,100,000–2,600,000 ft).

Mesosphere

The mesosphere extends from the stratopause to 80–85 km (50–53 mi; 260,000–280,000 ft). It is the layer where most meteors burn up upon entering the atmosphere. Temperature decreases with height in the mesosphere. The mesopause, the temperature minimum that marks the top of the mesosphere, is the coldest place on Earth and has an average temperature around –85°C (–120°F; 190 K). At the mesopause, temperatures may drop to –100°C (–150°F; 170 K). Due to the cold temperature of the mesosphere, water vapour is frozen, forming ice clouds (or Noctilucent clouds). A type of lightning referred to as either sprites or ELVES, form many miles above thunderclouds in the troposphere.

Stratosphere

The stratosphere extends from the tropopause to about 51 km (32 mi; 170,000 ft). Temperature increases with height due to increased absorption of ultraviolet radiation by the ozone layer, which restricts turbulence and mixing. While the temperature may be –60°C (–76°F; 210 K) at the tropopause, the top of the stratosphere is much warmer, and may be near freezing. The stratopause, which is the boundary between the stratosphere and mesosphere, typically is at 50 to 55 km (31 to 34 mi; 160,000 to 180,000 ft). The pressure here is 1/1000 sea level.

Troposphere

The troposphere begins at the surface and extends to between 9 km (30,000 ft) at the poles and 17 km (56,000 ft) at the equator, with some variation due to weather. The troposphere is mostly heated by transfer of energy from the surface, so on average the lowest part of the troposphere is warmest and temperature decreases with altitude. This promotes vertical mixing.

The troposphere contains roughly 80% of the mass of the atmosphere. The tropopause is the boundary between the troposphere and stratosphere.

Other Layers

Within the five principal layers determined by temperature are several layers determined by other properties:

- The ozone layer is contained within the stratosphere. In this layer ozone concentrations are about 2 to 8 parts per million, which is much higher than in the lower atmosphere but still very small compared to the main components of the atmosphere. It is mainly located in the lower portion of the stratosphere from about 15–35 km (9.3–22 mi; 49,000–110,000 ft), though the thickness varies seasonally and geographically. About 90 per cent of the ozone in our atmosphere is contained in the stratosphere.

- The ionosphere, the part of the atmosphere that is ionized by solar radiation, stretches from 50 to 1,000 km (31 to 620 mi; 160,000 to 3,300,000 ft) and typically overlaps both the exosphere and the thermosphere. It forms the inner edge of the magnetosphere. It has practical importance because it influences, for example, radio propagation on the Earth. It is responsible for auroras.
- The homosphere and heterosphere are defined by whether the atmospheric gases are well mixed. In the homosphere the chemical composition of the atmosphere does not depend on molecular weight because the gases are mixed by turbulence. The homosphere includes the troposphere, stratosphere, and mesosphere. Above the *turbopause* at about 100 km (62 mi; 330,000 ft) (essentially corresponding to the mesopause), the composition varies with altitude. This is because the distance that particles can move without colliding with one another is large compared with the size of motions that cause mixing. This allows the gases to stratify by molecular weight, with the heavier ones such as oxygen and nitrogen present only near the bottom of the heterosphere. The upper part of the heterosphere is composed almost completely of hydrogen, the lightest element.
- The planetary boundary layer is the part of the troposphere that is nearest the Earth's surface and is directly affected by it, mainly through turbulent diffusion. During the day the planetary boundary layer usually is well-mixed, while at night it becomes stably stratified with weak or intermittent mixing. The depth of the planetary boundary layer ranges from as little as about 100 m on clear, calm nights to 3000 m or more during the afternoon in dry regions.

The average temperature of the atmosphere at the surface of Earth is 14°C (57°F; 287 K) or 15°C (59°F; 288 K), depending on the reference.

EVOLUTION OF EARTH'S ATMOSPHERE

Earliest Atmosphere

The outgassings of the Earth were stripped away by solar winds early in the history of the planet until a steady state was established, the first atmosphere. Based on today's volcanic evidence, this atmosphere would have contained 60 per cent hydrogen, 20 per cent oxygen (mostly in the form of water vapour), 10 per cent carbon dioxide, 5 to 7 per cent hydrogen sulfide, and smaller amounts of nitrogen, carbon monoxide, free hydrogen, methane and inert gases. A major rainfall led to the buildup of a vast ocean, enriching the other agents, first carbon dioxide and later nitrogen and inert gases. A major part of carbon dioxide exhalations were soon dissolved in water and built up carbonate sediments.

Second Atmosphere

Water-related sediments have been found dating from as early as 3.8 billion years ago. About 3.4 billion years ago, nitrogen was the major part of the then stable 'second atmosphere'. An influence of life has to be taken into account rather soon in the history of the atmosphere, since hints of early life forms are to be found as early as 3.5 billion years ago. The fact that this is not perfectly in line with the 30 per cent lower solar radiance (compared to today) of the early Sun has been described as the 'faint young Sun paradox'.

The geological record however shows a continually relatively warm surface during the complete early temperature record of the Earth with the exception of one cold glacial phase about 2.4 billion years ago. In the late Archaean eon an oxygen-containing atmosphere began to develop, apparently from photosynthesizing algae which have been found as stromatolite fossils from 2.7 billion years ago. The early basic carbon isotopy (isotope ratio proportions) is very much in line with what is found today, suggesting that the fundamental features of the carbon cycle were established as early as 4 billion years ago.

Third Atmosphere

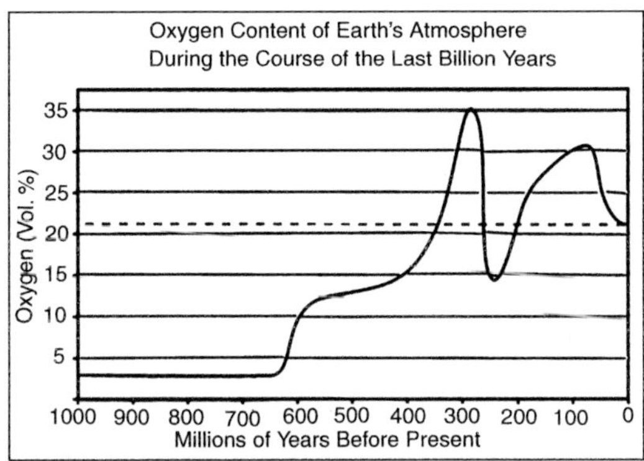

Fig. Oxygen Content of the Atmosphere over the Last Billion Years

The accretion of continents about 3.5 billion years ago added plate tectonics, constantly rearranging the continents and also shaping long-term climate evolution by allowing the transfer of carbon dioxide to large land-based carbonate storages. Free oxygen did not exist until about 1.7 billion years ago and this can be seen with the development of the red beds and the end of the banded iron formations. The Earth had a lot of iron in the beginning, and higher amounts of oxygen was not available in the atmosphere until all the iron had ben oxidized. This signifies a shift from a reducing atmosphere to an oxidising atmosphere. O_2 showed major ups and downs until reaching a steady state of more than 15%. The following time span was the Phanerozoic eon, during which oxygen-breathing metazoan life forms began to appear.

The amount of oxygen in the atmosphere has gone up and down during the last 600 million years. There was a peak 280 million years ago, when the amount of oxygen was about 30 %, much higher than today. The cause of changes in the atmosphere is two main processes: Plants converts carbon dioxide into the bodies of the plants, which emits oxygen into the atmosphere, and break down of pyrite rocks cause sulphur to be added to the oceans. Volcanos cause this sulphur to be oxidized, reducing the amount of oxygen in the atmosphere. But volcanos also emit carbon dioxide, so that plants can convert this to oxygen. The exact cause of the variation of oxygen in the atmosphere is not known. Periods with much oxygen in the atmosphere are believed to cause rapid development of animals. Even if the atmosphere today has only 21 per cent oxygen, today is still regarded as a period with rapid development of animals because of a high amount of oxygen in the atmosphere. Currently, anthropogenic greenhouse gases are increasing in the atmosphere. According to the Intergovernmental Panel on Climate Change, this increase is the main cause of global warming.

Air Pollution

Air pollution is the introduction of chemicals, particulate matter, or biological materials that cause harm or discomfort to organisms into the atmosphere. Stratospheric ozone depletion is believed to be caused by air pollution (chiefly from chlorofluorocarbons).

THE GREENHOUSE EFFECT

The Goldilocks Principle can be summed up neatly as "Venus is too hot, Mars is too cold, and Earth is just right." The fact that Earth has an average surface temperature comfortably between the boiling point and freezing point of water, and thus is suitable for our sort of life, cannot be explained by simply suggesting that our planet orbits at just the right distance from the sun to absorb just the right amount of solar radiation.

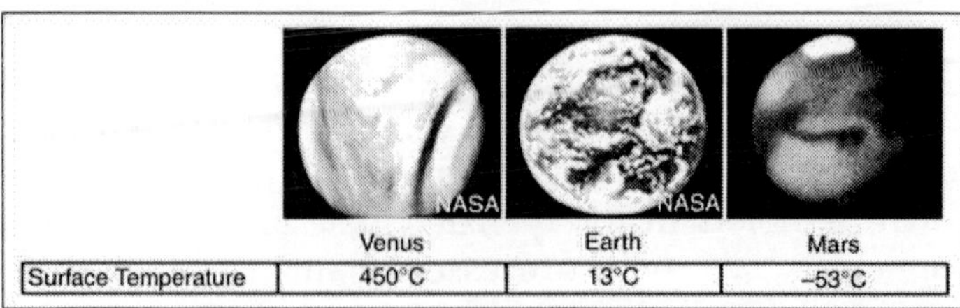

Our moderate temperatures are also the result of having just the right kind of atmosphere. A Venus-type atmosphere would produce hellish, Venus-like conditions on our planet; a Mars atmosphere would leave us shivering in a Martian-type deep freeze. Instead, parts of our atmosphere act as an insulating blanket of just the right thickness, trapping sufficient solar energy to keep the global average temperature in a pleasant range. The Martian blanket is too thin, and the Venusian blanket is way too thick! The 'blanket' here is a collection of atmospheric gases called 'greenhouse gases' based on the idea that the gases also 'trap' heat like the glass walls of a greenhouse do.

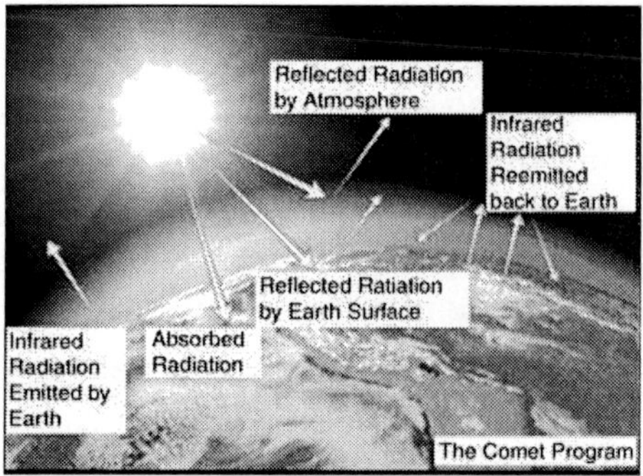

These gases, mainly water vapour (H_2O), carbon dioxide (CO_2), methane (CH_4), and nitrous oxide (N_2O), all act as effective global insulators. To understand why, it's important to understand a few basic facts about solar radiation and the structure of atmospheric gases.

Solar Radiation

The sun radiates vast quantities of energy into space, across a wide spectrum of wavelengths.

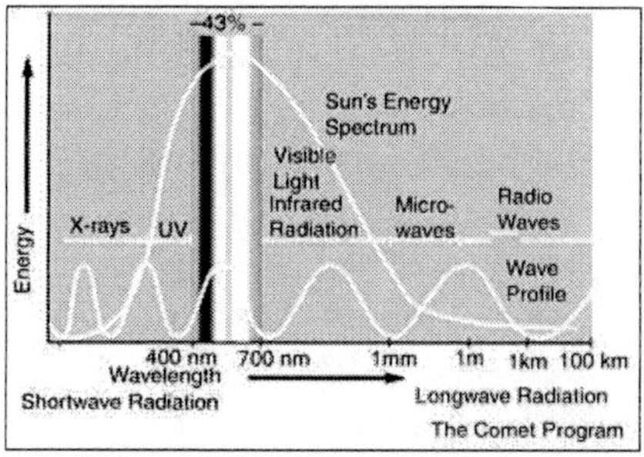

Most of the radiant energy from the sun is concentrated in the visible and near-visible parts of the spectrum. The narrow band of visible light, between 400 and 700 nm, represents 43 per cent of the total radiant energy emitted. Wavelengths shorter than the visible account for 7 to 8 per cent of the total, but are extremely important because of their high energy per photon. The shorter the wavelength of light, the more energy it contains. Thus, ultraviolet light is very energetic (capable of breaking apart stable biological molecules and causing sunburn and skin cancers). The remaining 49–50 per cent of the radiant energy is spread over the wavelengths longer than those of visible light. These lie in the near infrared range from 700 to 1000 nm; the thermal infrared, between 5 and 20 microns; and the far infrared regions. Various components of earth's atmosphere absorb ultraviolet and infrared solar radiation before it penetrates to the surface, but the atmosphere is quite transparent to visible light.

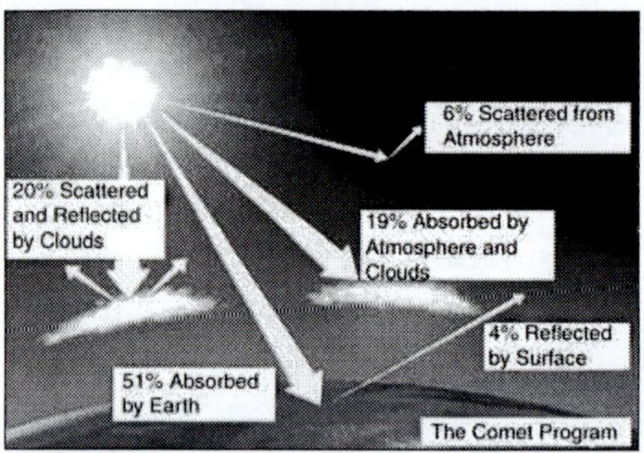

Absorbed by land, oceans, and vegetation at the surface, the visible light is transformed into heat and re-radiates in the form of invisible infrared radiation. If that was all there was to the story, then during the day earth would heat up, but at night, all the accumulated energy would radiate back into space and the planet's surface temperature. The reason this doesn't happen is that earth's atmosphere contains molecules that absorb the heat and re-radiate the heat in all directions. This reduces the heat radiated out to space. Called 'greenhouse gases' because they serve to hold heat in like the glass walls of a greenhouse, these molecules are responsible for the fact that the earth enjoys temperatures suitable for our active and complex biosphere.

The Greenhouse Gases

Carbon dioxide (CO_2) is one of the greenhouse gases. It consists of one carbon atom with an oxygen atom bonded to each side. When its atoms are bonded tightly together, the carbon dioxide molecule can absorb infrared radiation and the molecule starts to vibrate. Eventually, the vibrating molecule will emit the radiation again, and it will likely be absorbed by yet another greenhouse gas molecule. This absorption-emission-absorption cycle serves to keep the heat near the surface, effectively insulating the surface from the cold of space.

The Comet Program

Carbon dioxide, water vapour (H_2O), methane (CH_4), nitorus oxide (N_2O), and a few other gases are greenhouse gases. They all are molecules composed of more than two component atoms, bound loosely enough together to be able to vibrate with the absorption of heat. The major components of the atmosphere (N_2 and O_2) are two-atom molecules too tightly bound together to vibrate and thus they do not absorb heat and contribute to the greenhouse effect.

Greenhouse Effect

Atmospheric scientists first second-hand the term 'greenhouse effect' in the early 1800s. At that time, it was used to describe the naturally occurring functions of trace gases in the atmosphere and did not have any negative connotations. It was not until the mid-1950s that the term greenhouse effect was coupled with concern over climate change. And in recent decades, we often hear about the greenhouse effect in somewhat negative terms. The negative concerns are related to the possible impacts of an enhanced greenhouse effect. It is important to remember that without the greenhouse effect, life on earth as we know it would not be possible.

While the earth's temperature is dependent upon the greenhouse-like action of the atmosphere, the amount of heating and cooling are strongly influenced by several factors just as greenhouses are affected by various factors.

In the atmospheric greenhouse effect, the type of surface that sunlight first encounters is the most important factor. Forests, grasslands, ocean surfaces, ice caps, deserts, and cities all absorb, reflect, and radiate radiation differently. Sunlight falling on a white glacier surface strongly reflects back into space, resulting in minimal heating of the surface and lower atmosphere.

Sunlight falling on a dark desert soil is strongly absorbed, on the other hand, and contributes to significant heating of the surface and lower atmosphere. Cloud cover also affects greenhouse warming by both reducing the amount of solar radiation reaching the earth's surface and by reducing the amount of radiation energy emitted into space.

Scientists use the term albedo to define the percentage of solar energy reflected back by a surface. Understanding local, regional, and global albedo effects is critical to predicting global climate change.

ATMOSPHERIC EFFECTS ON INCOMING SOLAR RADIATION

Three atmospheric processes modify the solar radiation passing through our atmosphere destined to the Earth's surface.

These processes act on the radiation when it interacts with gases and suspended particles found in the atmosphere. The process of scattering occurs when small particles and gas molecules diffuse part of the incoming solar radiation in random directions without any alteration to the wavelength of the electromagnetic energy.

Scattering does, however, reduce the amount of incoming radiation reaching the Earth's surface. A significant proportion of scattered shortwave solar radiation is redirected back to space. The amount of scattering that takes place is dependent on two factors: wavelength of the incoming radiation and the size of the scattering particle or gas molecule.

In the Earth's atmosphere, the presence of a large number of particles with a size of about 0.5 microns results in shorter wavelengths being preferentially scattered. This factor also causes our sky to look blue because this colour corresponds to those wavelengths that are best diffused. If scattering did not occur in our atmosphere the daylight sky would be black.

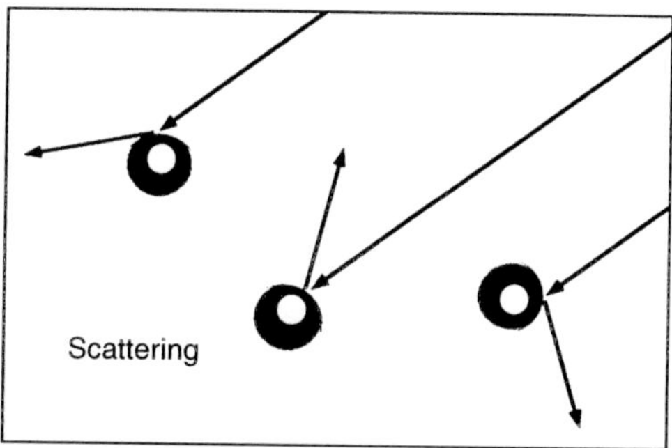

Fig. 8.7 The Process of Atmospheric Scattering Causes Rays of Sunlight to be Redirected to a New Direction After Hitting a Particle in the Atmosphere. In this Illustration, Three Particles Send Light Rays Off Into Three Different Directions. Scattering does not Change the Striking Light Ray's Wavelength or Intensity

If intercepted, some gases and particles in the atmosphere have the ability to absorb incoming insolation. Absorption is defined as a process in which solar radiation is retained by a substance and converted into heat energy. The creation of heat energy also causes the substance to emit its own radiation. In general, the absorption of solar radiation by substances in the Earth's atmosphere results in temperatures that get no higher than 1800° Celsius.

According to Wien's Law, bodies with temperatures at this level or lower would emit their radiation in the longwave band. Further, this emission of radiation is in all directions so a sizable proportion of this energy is lost to space.

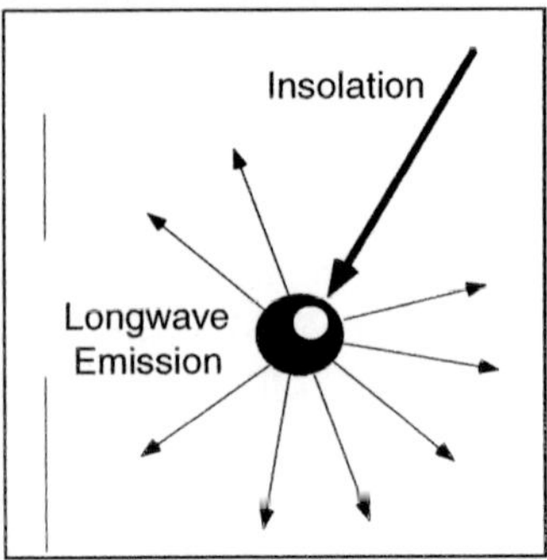

Fig. 8.8 Atmospheric Absorption. In this Process, Sunlight is Absorbed by an Atmospheric Particle, Transferred Into Heat Energy, and then Converted into Longwave Radiation Emissions that Come from the Particle

The final process in the atmosphere that modifies incoming solar radiation is reflection. Reflection is a process where sunlight is redirect by 180° after it strikes an atmospheric particle. This redirection causes a 100 per cent loss of the insolation. Most of the reflection in our atmosphere occurs in clouds when light is intercepted by particles of liquid and frozen water. The reflectivity of a cloud can range from 40 to 90 per cent.

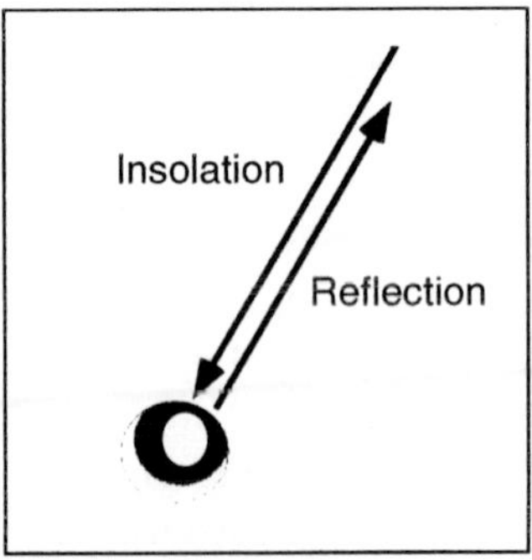

Fig 8.9 Atmospheric Reflection. In this Process, the Solar Radiation Striking an Atmospheric Particle is Redirected Back to Space Unchanged.

Sunlight reaching the Earth's surface unmodified by any of the above atmospheric processes is termed direct solar radiation. Solar radiation that reaches the Earth's surface after it was altered by the process of scattering is called diffused solar radiation. Not all of the direct and diffused radiation available at the Earth's surface is used to do *work* (photosynthesis, creation of sensible heat, evaporation, etc.). As in the atmosphere, some of the radiation received at the Earth's surface is redirected back to space by reflection. The following image describes the spatial pattern of surface reflectivity as measured for the year 1987.

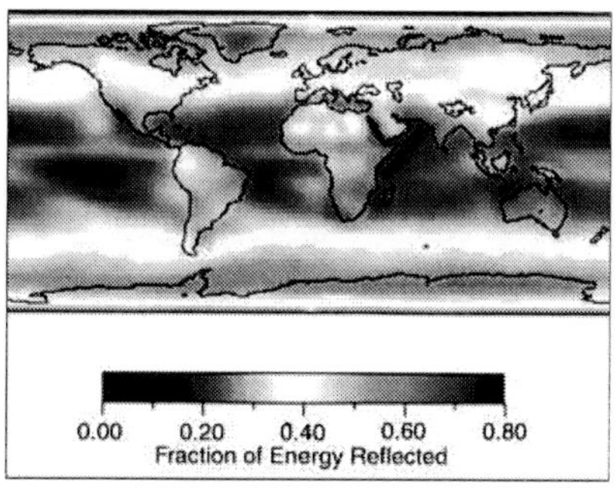

Fig. 8.10 Annual (1987) Reflectivity of the Earth's Surface

The reflectivity or albedo of the Earth's surface varies with the type of material that covers it. For example, fresh snow can reflect up to 95 per cent of the insolation that reaches it surface. Some other surface type reflectivities are:

- Dry sand 35 to 45 per cent
- Broadleaf deciduous forest 5 to 10 per cent
- Needleleaf confierous forest 10 to 20 per cent
- Grass type vegetation 15 to 25 per cent.

Reflectivity of the surface is often described by the term *surface* albedo. The Earth's average *albedo*, reflectance from both the atmosphere and the surface, is about 30 per cent.

The modification of solar radiation by atmospheric and surface processes for the whole Earth over a period of one year. Of all the sunlight that passes through the atmosphere annually, only 51 per cent is available at the Earth's surface to do work. This energy is used to heat the Earth's surface and lower atmosphere, *melt* and evaporate water, and run photosynthesis in plants. Of the other 49 per cent, 4 per cent is reflected back to space by the Earth's surface, 26 per cent is scattered or reflected to space by clouds and atmospheric particles, and 19 per cent is absorbed by atmospheric gases, particles, and clouds.

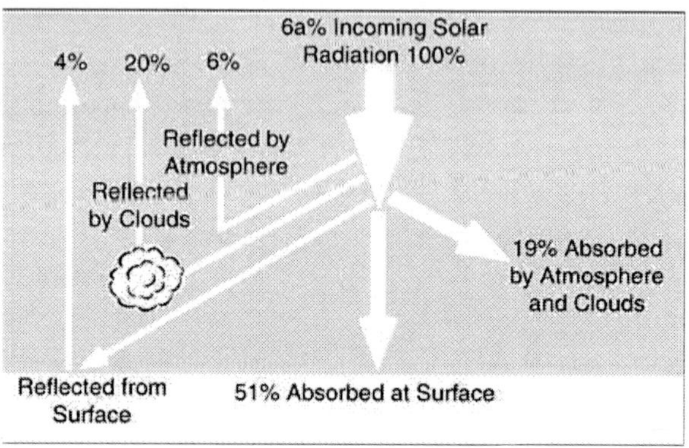

Fig. 8.11 Global Modification of Incoming Solar Radiation by Atmospheric and Surface Processes.

Atmospheric Effects on Planetary Surface Temperatures

Clouds Reflect the Heat of the Sun Away From the Planet

If a planet has no atmosphere, all of the sunlight which strikes it reaches the surface, and usually, 90 per cent or more of that is absorbed, and 10 per cent or less is reflected back into space. However, if the planet has an atmosphere, particularly a thick, cloud-filled atmosphere, part of the sunlight will be reflected into space before even reaching the surface. The percentage of light reflected by a planet is referred to as its *albedo*, and subtracting that from 100 per cent tells us how much energy is absorbed by, and heats up, the planet.

As an example of how this works, the Earth and Moon are the same distance from the Sun, within 1/4 per cent accuracy, and have the same amount of sunlight falling on them, but the Moon reflects only about 10 per cent of the sunlight that it receives, and absorbs about 90 per cent of it, while the Earth, because of its extensive cloud cover, reflects about 30 per cent of the sunlight that it receives, and absorbs only about 70 per cent. The values for the Moon vary because the highlands are lighter, and reflect more light, and the maria are darker, and reflect less light, and the values for the Earth vary according to the local weather topography, but these average values are adequate for a general comparison. As a result of the difference in absorption, the Earth only receives about 2/3 as much sunlight during the day as the Moon does, and the Moon becomes much hotter, reaching temperatures in excess of 250°F, which is over 150F° hotter than normal Earth temperatures.

However, you should note that clouds are not the only factor that determines a planet's temperature, as you can tell by considering the case of Venus, which has an albedo of 65%, meaning that it only absorbs 35 per cent of the sunlight which falls on it, which is only half as much as the Earth absorbs. If all other factors could be ignored, this difference in heat absorption would completely make up for the fact that Venus is only 70 per cent as far from the Sun as we are, and the Earth and Venus would have similar surface temperatures, and in fact, until the early 1970's, it was presumed that Venus had temperatures that weren't all that much higher than those of the Earth. In that era, and earlier, it was generally thought that surface conditions on Venus were similar to those in the Sahara (hot and dry), or the Amazon basin (hot and wet). As it turns out, as discussed under Greenhouse Gases, Venus is over 800° warmer than the Earth, so looking only at the albedo doesn't tell you the whole story. It is, however, the first piece of the puzzle, and is, for most planets, a very significant factor in determining their temperature.

Winds Circulate Heat From Hot Places to Cool Place

The winds in our atmosphere represent a gigantic heat engine driven by the heat from the Sun. They carry heat from the Equator towards the Poles, and from the day side of the planet to the night side (of course, our rotation also helps with this), and help moderate the differences in heat between the Equator and the Pole, and between the day and night sides of the planet.

The efficiency of these winds in circulating heat depends upon how thick the atmosphere is. On the Moon, with no air, there is, of course, no such effect, and temperatures range from very high values on the day side, to very low values on the night side, with no way to moderate them. On Mars, with a thin atmosphere, the difference in temperature between hotter and cooler places creates pressure differences which drive relatively fast winds. If the atmosphere were thicker, it might be able to substantially moderate the temperature, but because the air there is only about 1 per cent as thick as ours, it isn't able to do a very good job of evening out the temperature differences, and they remain quite large, although not as large as on the Moon. On the Earth, with a thicker atmosphere, temperature differences are considerably reduced. This reduces pressure differences, which on Mars can be in excess of 50 per cent, but on Earth, are rarely in excess of 5 per cent, so wind velocities on the Earth are generally slower than on Mars, but because the atmosphere is so much thicker, it is quite capable of producing substantial reductions in temperature extremes.

Venus is, again, an example of a relatively extreme version of this effect. Since its atmosphere is 100 times thicker than ours, it does a very good job of transporting heat from one place to another, even at relatively low wind velocities, so that, despite its relatively long night (about two Earth months long), and the very high temperatures (which mean that even a small percentage difference in temperature could be a large difference in the actual number of degrees), it has a surprisingly small temperature range. In fact, from Equator to Pole, and from day to night, temperature variations are rarely more than 50F° at the surface of the planet. The small temperature difference causes relatively low wind velocities (close to zero at the surface), but the thickness of the atmosphere allows even those low velocities to be quite adequate to produce a remarkably even temperature.

Since the Jovian planets have even thicker atmospheres, we can expect that they should have relatively even temperatures, an relatively slow wind velocities, as well. However, there is, as it turns out, huge amounts of heat radiating from the interior of the planet, in fact, over twice as much heat as the planet receives from the Sun, and wind velocities and temperature differences aren't as small as on Venus. In fact, the rapid rotation of these planets drive such strong Coriolis effects that wind velocities in the belts and zones (circulation patterns parallel to the Equator) of Jupiter are several hundred miles per hour, and at the boundaries between a belt and a zone, where the wind velocities are in opposite directions, wind shear velocities are in excess of a thousand miles an hour.

'Greenhouse' Gases Hold in the Heat of the Planet

During the day sunlight pours down onto the surface of a planet, heating it up. As the surface gets warmer, it radiates infrared heat back into space. Once the heat radiated by the surface is equal to the sunlight being absorbed by it, the surface stops heating up, and temperatures remain relatively stable. However, once the Sun goes down, there is no sunlight striking the surface, and the surface of the planet cools, as it radiates heat into space.

On the Moon, the temperature rises very quickly in the morning, because, very little sunlight is reflected away, and temperatures reach 250°F within a few hours. When the Sun goes down, however, about two weeks later, temperatures drop just as quickly, reaching sub-zero temperatures within a very few hours (in fact, this can even happen during a lunar eclipse, when the Moon passes through the Earth's shadow, and cuts off the sunlight).

As the temperature drops, heat is radiated away more slowly, so it takes more than a day to reach temperatures of 200°F below zero, and a week or so to get to -250°F. If the night continued for several months, as it does on Mercury, temperatures would slowly drop still further (on Mercury, the temperature reaches -350°F before sunrise), and if it lasted for years, temperatures could eventually drop to just a few degrees above absolute zero (over -450°F). On Pluto, where the winter lasts for half of the nearly 250-year orbital period, temperatures undoubtedly do drop to such low values.

On the Earth, however, and other planets with an atmosphere, so-called *greenhouse gases* can trap part of the heat radiated by the surface, keeping the surface warmer. There is nothing particularly special about greenhouse gases. All gases can, to a certain extent, block the infrared radiation from the surface of a planet.

It is just that some gases, particularly those made of polyatomic, or multi-atom molecules, are better at blocking such radiation than other gases, such as the diatomic molecules of nitrogen and oxygen which make up the bulk of our atmosphere. Since the bulk of the gases in our atmosphere aren't particularly good at blocking infrared radiation, the rarer gases which are good at it seem special, but they are actually quite common. In fact, water vapour and carbon dioxide, which are the primary greenhouse gases on the Earth, Mars and Venus, are among the most common molecules in the Universe.

The Earth doesn't have much carbon dioxide in its atmosphere (only about 1/30 of 1 per cent), so although carbon dioxide does contribute to the greenhouse effect, our most important greenhouse gas is water vapour.

If you live near the ocean, or in a humid climate, it cools off less at night than if you live in a dry area, such as a desert. In particular, in winter, if temperatures are expected to get especially cold, you will hear about farmers worrying about radiation cooling if the night is going to be clear (so that heat can be radiated into space), but you will not hear about that if the night is going to be cloudy (so that heat is blocked by the water vapour in the clouds, keeping things warmer).

This, of course, has the unfortunate effect that during winter, the clearest nights, when you would like to look at the stars, are generally colder than the cloudier nights, when you can't do so. (Traditionally, astronomers were expected to bundle up, and endure the cold, rather than worrying about it. At Yerkes Observatory, near Green Bay, Wisconsin, observations would continue on even the coldest nights, if it was clear, until temperatures dropped so low that the grease used to lubricate the telescope mounting began to freeze.

Long before then, observers were pretty well frozen, as well. Nowadays, however, with computerized telescope controls, you can sit in a nice, toasty warm room, on one side of the Earth, while controlling a telescope operating in sub-zero temperatures on some distant mountaintop, and only the support staff which has to make sure the telescope keeps working has to worry about freezing.)

Now, although water vapour is our most important greenhouse gas, the fact that there are others means that wavelengths of infrared light which are not blocked by water vapour could be blocked by the other greenhouse gases, keeping temperatures warmer than when you have only one kind of greenhouse gas.

As an example, Mars has a considerable amount of carbon dioxide in its atmosphere. Even though the planet's atmosphere is only about 1% as thick as ours, it is almost entirely carbon dioxide, so there is about 30 times as much carbon dioxide as in the Earth's atmosphere.

However, although this carbon dioxide does a good job of blocking the wavelengths that it can block, it cannot block all infrared wavelengths, and there just isn't much in the way of other greenhouse gases on Mars. Water vapour, in particular, is relatively rare, amounting to only a millionth of an inch or so of liquid, even in places where the relative humidity is close to 100%, because the low temperature and low density of the atmosphere doesn't allow it to contain very much water vapour.

If there were any significant amount, it would crystallize as snowflakes, and float to the ground. As a result, although the temperatures on Mars don't drop as fast as those on the Moon, they do drop substantially, and nighttime temperatures average about 100°F less than daytime temperatures.

Once again, we come to Venus, and once again, we encounter extraordinary effects due to its thick atmosphere. With 100 times more air than the Earth, and almost all of it carbon dioxide, Venus has three hundred thousand times as much carbon dioxide as the Earth, and the clouds, although composed primarily of fuming sulfuric acid, have enough water vapour to help block the heat of the planet, as well. As a result, even though it is hard for sunlight to reach the surface of the planet (2/3 of it being reflected away by the clouds), it is even harder for the infrared heat of the surface to escape into space.

This causes the planet to heat up until the extra radiation caused by its extra heat is able to balance the extra blockage of heat by its greenhouse gases, and what escapes is what would have escaped if there were no atmosphere to block it. The blockage of heat by the greenhouse gases in Venus' atmosphere is so effective that only about 1 per cent of the heat radiated by the planet is able to escape.

This is more than 20 times less than the percentage of sunlight which reaches the surface and is absorbed, and the planet has to heat up to almost three times the temperature that we would expect, or more than 900°F, or more than 1400F° above absolute zero, which is hotter than Mercury ever gets, even when Mercury is at perihelion, and receives nearly five times as much sunlight per square foot as falls onto the Venusian atmosphere.

Could We Have a Runaway Greenhouse Effect on Earth?

Because the greenhouse effect on Venus is so extreme, it is referred to as a *runaway greenhouse effect*. Needless to say, environmentalists worry about whether such a thing could happen on the Earth.

If we could somehow increase the amount of greenhouse gases in our atmosphere, could we reach a point at which the temperature of the Earth would drastically increase, boiling away our oceans and ending all life on Earth? In a word, yes. However, to do this, we would have to work very, very hard to undo something which happened many billions of years ago, when the Earth was relatively young, and its atmosphere was very different from now.

At that time, the atmosphere of the Earth was very much like that of Venus—more than a hundred times thicker than our current atmosphere, and made almost entirely of carbon dioxide—and temperatures on the Earth were a few hundred degrees above zero Fahrenheit. However, we did not have as extreme temperatures as Venus currently does, for two reasons. (1) We are further from the Sun, so temperatures would be a little cooler, even with an identical atmosphere. (2) When we had a Venusian atmosphere, the Sun was a little fainter than it is now. And because the Earth was not as hot as Venus, something happened which is quite different from what happened to Venus.

On Venus, the extreme temperatures caused its oceans to boil away into the atmosphere (or prevented water vapour from condensing to form oceans, in the first place). All Venus' water was in its atmosphere, exposed to ultraviolet radiation from the Sun which was continually dissociating it into hydrogen and oxygen.

The oxygen combined with the surface rocks, while the hydrogen escaped into space. Over a period of time, all of the hydrogen compounds in the atmosphere were lost, and since all of its water was in the atmosphere, hardly any remains, save for traces tied up in the sulfurous clouds which obscure its surface.

Since the Earth was further from the Sun and cooler than Venus, although it must have been hotter than the *current* boiling temperature of water (212 degrees Fahrenheit), *it would not have been hotter than the (much higher) boiling temperature of water, under the high pressure conditions which then existed at the surface of the Earth.* As a result, the Earth developed and still retains oceans of liquid water.

These oceans gradually dissolved the carbon dioxide, turning it into carbonic acid (a mild acid present in all soda waters, flavoured or otherwise), and chemical reactions between the carbonic acid and metal oxides removed from the continents by weathering and erosion converted the atmospheric carbon dioxide into insoluble carbonate rocks, such as limestone (calcium carbonate), siderite (iron carbonate), and dolomite (magnesium carbonate).

There are mountain ranges made of these carbonate rocks, and the amount of carbon dioxide trapped in them is equivalent to the carbon dioxide in the atmosphere of Venus. If we were to heat these rocks to about a thousand degrees (or 'roast' them), we could restore the carbon dioxide to its gaseous form, recreating the earlier atmosphere of the Earth, and cause a return to extremely hot conditions. In fact, since the Sun is now a little brighter, we might even boil away the oceans, preventing the carbon dioxide from being removed again. Fortunately, the time, effort, and expense involved in doing such a thing would make it completely impractical, but it is at least theoretically possible.

And What of the Future?

Projecting the future is even less certain than assessing the past, because we can't be sure of a number of factors. How much more carbon dioxide will we pump into the atmosphere? Certainly a lot more than we should, but the exact amount, and its effect, depends upon economic conditions (when times are good, people create more carbon dioxide than when times are bad), population increases (more people doing the same thing means more carbon dioxide), changes in technology (more efficient automobiles, lighting, and air conditioning might reduce fossil fuel use, or simply slow its rate of increase), and changes in cultural behaviour.

None of these can be predicted with certainty, so estimates of the amount of carbon dioxide that will be dumped into the atmosphere over the next century vary by as much as a factor of five. It is also hard to determine what will happen to that carbon dioxide, once it is put into the atmosphere.

Some will be absorbed by plants, helping them grow, some will be absorbed by the soil and organisms in the soil, and some will be absorbed by the oceans.

Estimates can be made of how these various factors work, but calculations of expected carbon dioxide 'uptake' can vary from observations by as much as a factor of two. And even if we knew exactly how much carbon dioxide will be present in the atmosphere in the future, predicting exactly how it will affect the Earth's temperature is very difficult.

Changes in temperature are different at different latitudes, being more extreme near the Poles, and less extreme near the Equator, and changes in weather patterns are more variable yet, causing warmer, drier weather in some areas, and cooler, wetter weather in other areas, even at the same latitude. So all we can be certain of is that there will be change, and given our tendency to think of current conditions as 'normal', that much of that change will feel unnatural, and unpleasant.

How unpleasant depends upon the power and privilege of those affected. In Bangladesh and similar poverty-stricken coastal areas, the next century is going to be very unpleasant. As sea level rises by perhaps one to three feet, upwards of fifty million people will see their homes and livelihoods disappear.

In the Arctic, creatures such as polar bears, which rely on sea ice for their existence, may become extinct as that sea ice disappears. But on the beaches at Malibu, changes in sea level are more likely to lead to resistance to the effects of those changes, than to any retreat to landward areas, or any abandonment of the lifestyles that help cause the rise in sea level.

It might be noted that the change in sea level is small compared to what would happen if temperatures continued to increase for many centuries.

That might well cause a return to 'average' conditions for the past few hundred million years—ending the Ice Era which has gripped the Earth for the past couple of million years—and a two hundred foot rise in sea level, which would cause the displacement of billions of people, and perhaps end civilization as we know it.

But again, the importance of these effects depends upon your perspective. From our viewpoint, such changes would be catastrophic; but for life in general, a return to paleohistoric conditions would probably result in a fecund diversity similar to that which occurred in the more tropical conditions of the Age of Dinosaurs.

And although our descendants might mourn the loss of their significance, those creatures which replace Man would probably feel that little was lost by the change.

What, Me Worry?

So, what should we make of what we hear in the news, and what should we do about it? We are now certain that carbon dioxide concentrations in the Earth's atmosphere have increased, and will continue to increase, barring inconceivable changes in our lifestyles. As a result, there will be temperature increases of uncertain amount, and changes in the weather of uncertain nature and extent. Life as we know it will change to a greater or lesser extent, depending upon where we live, but will be more like now than not, for a few decades; and less like now than not, in the following centuries. Continental and sea ice will retreat and disappear, and sea levels will rise throughout our lifetimes, and the lifetimes of our descendants. And there is nothing that we can do, to prevent this. The only question is, what can we do to reduce these effects, and in some distant future, reverse them?

The 'greenhouse effect' is real, and of considerable concern to many people. It is not, perhaps, quite as immediately worrisome as the threat of global warfare and nuclear or biological annihilation. But if you are concerned about the 'fate of the Earth', or the future faced by your children and grandchildren, then perhaps it would be better to do what you can to use less energy, and to convince your representatives to vote for measures which would make it easier for you to use less energy, than to seek ways to burn more and more fossil fuels at a faster and faster rate. Or, if it seems too painful to do anything, you could do nothing. For many lifeforms, such as mosquitoes and millipedes, crocodiles and cockroaches, molds and mildews, a warmer, wetter Earth would be marvellous. It just depends upon whom or what you want to inherit the Earth.

Bibliography

Abhyankar, K.D. : *Astrophysics : Stars and Galaxies*, Universities Press, Delhi, 2001.

Arnett, D.: *Supernovae and Nucleosynthesis*, Princeton University, Princeton, 1996.

Arthur Schuster: *An Introduction to the Theory of Optics*, London: Edward Arnold, 1904.

Bacon, Dennis Henry, and Percy Seymour: *A Mechanical History of the Universe.* London: Philip Wilson Publishing, Ltd., 2003.

Bahcall, J. N.: *Neutrino Astrophysics*, Cambridge University, Cambridge, 1989.

Barnes, C. A.: *Essays in Nuclear Astrophysics: Presented to William A. Fowler, on the Occasion of His Seventieth Birthday*, Cambridge University Press, Cambridge, 1982.

Basu, S K : *Encyclopaedic Dictionary of Astrophysics*, Global Vision Pub, Delhi, 2007.

Clayton, D. D.: *Principles of Stellar Evolution and Nucleosynthesis*, University of Chicago Press, Chicago, 1983.

Cline, D., Peccei, R.: *Trends in AstroParticle Physics*, World Scientific, Singapore, 1992.

Fowler, William A.: *Nuclear Astrophysics*, American Philosophical Society, Philadelphia, 1967.

Gorres, J., Mathews, G., Shore, S., and Wiescher, M. : *Nuclei in the Cosmos, Proceedings Fourth International Symposium on Nuclei in the Cosmos*, North Holland, Amsterdam, 1997.

Green, S.F. & Jones, M.H.: *An Introduction to the Sun and Stars*, Cambridge University Press, London, 2006.

Hugh D. Young: *University Physics*. Addison-Wesley, 1992.

John E.Prussing, Bruce A.Conway: *Orbital Mechanics,* Oxford University Press, London, 1993.

Jones, M.H. & Lambourne, R.J.A.: *An Introduction to Galaxies & Cosmology,* Cambridge University Press, London, 2000.

Kamp, P. van de : *Elements of Astromechanics,* San Francisco: W. H. Freeman, 1964.

Kaufmann, William J. : *Discovering the Universe.* New York: W. H. Freeman, 1990.

Kolb, E. W., and Turner, M. S.: *The Early Universe,* New York: Addison-Wesley, 1990.

Kutner, M.L.: *Astronomy: A Physical Perspective,* Cambridge University Press, London, 2003.

Landau, L. D. and E. M. Lifshitz: *Mechanics,* Oxford: Pergamon Press, 1960.

Morison, I.: *Introduction to Astronomy and Cosmology,* Wiley, NY, 2002.

Moulton, F. R. : *An Introduction to Celestial Mechanics,* New York: MacMillan, 1914.

Pagel, B. E. J.: *Nucleosynthesis and Chemical Evolution of Galaxies,* Cambridge University Press, Cambridge, 1997.

Pasachoff, Jay M. :*Contemporary Astronomy.* Philadelphia: Saunders College Publishing, 1989.

Ridpath, I. : *Norton's 2000.0 Star Atlas and Reference Handbook,* New York: John Wiley & Sons, 1989.

Rolfs, C., and Rodney, W. S.: *Cauldrons in the Cosmos,* Chicago: University of Chicago, 1988.

Russell M. Kulsrud: *Plasma Physics For Astrophysics,* New Age International, Delhi, 2010.

Ryabov, Y. : *An Elementary Survey of Celestial Mechanics,* New York: Dover, 1961.

Schramm, David N.: *The Big Bang and Other Explosions in Nuclear and Particle Astrophysics,* World Scientific, 1996.

Seidelmann, P. K. : *Explanatory Supplement to the Astronomical Almanac,* Mill Valley, CA: University Science Books, 1992.

Weinberg, S.: *Gravitation and Cosmology,* New York: John Wiley & Sons, 1972.

Index

A

Astronomical Calendars, 106.
Astronomical Time Keeping, 94.
Atmospheric Extinction, 277, 282.

B

Bayer Naming System, 89.

C

Celestial Coordinate Systems, 78.
Celestial Measurements, 129.
Celestial Mechanics, 29, 30, 33, 36, 41, 53, 65, 68, 72.
Cepheid Variables, 268.
Chaotic Orbits, 65, 69.
Compound Microscope, 214.
Coordinate System, 44, 45, 60, 61, 78, 85, 91, 92, 226.

D

Diffraction, 185, 186, 187, 188, 219, 220, 221, 222, 224, 225, 226, 228, 229, 230.

E

Earth Oceans, 125.
Electromagnetic Spectrum, 28, 181, 182, 183, 184, 191, 192, 194, 195, 197, 258, 286, 290, 293, 299, 301, 306, 310.

F

Formation of Stars, 140.

G

Geometrical Optics, 197.
Greenhouse Effect, 289, 313, 325, 326, 334, 336, 340.
Gregorian Calendar, 105, 109, 112, 113, 137.

H

Hemisphere Seasons, 115.

I

Infrared Astronomy, 295, 298, 303, 306.
Inverse Square Law, 188, 189, 257, 265.

J

Julian Calendar, 104, 105, 107, 108, 110, 111, 113.

L

Light System, 201.

Lunar Eclipses, 121, 128.
Lunar Tides, 125.

M

Massive Stars, 20, 145, 146, 164, 165, 178.
Microwave Astronomy, 286.
Microwave Radiation, 190, 193, 288.
Moon Appears, 119.
Motion of Stars, 134.

N

Neutrinos, 16, 17, 28, 152, 160, 183, 231, 232, 233, 234, 235, 236, 238, 239, 240, 241, 242, 243, 244, 245, 246, 247, 248, 249, 250, 251, 252.

O

Optical Telescopes, 181, 183, 216, 217, 295, 304, 305.
Organometallic Liquid Scintillator, 239.

P

Parallax Method, 253, 262.
Perceptible Motion, 80.
Planetary Motion, 30, 31, 33, 40, 60, 82.
Planetary Surface Temperatures, 330.
Ptolemaic Universe, 83, 84.

R

Radio Astronomy, 21, 24, 182, 183.
Roman Lunar Calendar, 107.

S

Solar Eclipses, 9, 121, 123, 125, 128.
Solar Mass Stars, 146.
Solar Neutrino Spectrum, 252.
Solar Neutrinos, 17, 231, 232, 233, 234, 235, 236, 238, 240, 246, 249, 250, 251, 252, 253.
Solar Radiation, 57, 319, 322, 323, 324, 326, 327, 328, 329, 330.
Space Technology, 284.
Space Velocities, 274, 275.
Spectroscopy, 3, 4, 6, 9, 25, 28, 190, 238, 240, 266.
Stellar Distances, 253, 254.
Stellar Magnitudes, 256.
Stellar Motion, 272.
Surface Temperatures, 13, 163, 260, 289, 331.

T

Telescopes, 6, 10, 12, 180, 181, 182, 183, 216, 217, 218, 230, 254, 257, 285, 286, 295, 298, 302, 303, 304, 305, 306, 308, 310.
Tidal Development, 71.
Time Zones, 106.

U

Ultraviolet Astronomy, 292, 306, 307, 310.
Ultraviolet Waves, 308, 310.
Universal Time, 95, 96, 97, 98, 99, 100, 106.